University of Cambridge Oriental Publications No. 28

Mori Ōgai and the modernization of Japanese culture

University of Cambridge Oriental Publications
published for the
Faculty of Oriental Studies
See page 297
for the complete list

Mori Ōgai in 1911, aged forty-nine

Mori Ōgai
and the modernization of
Japanese culture

RICHARD JOHN BOWRING
Lecturer in Japanese, Monash University

CAMBRIDGE UNIVERSITY PRESS
CAMBRIDGE
LONDON · NEW YORK · MELBOURNE

Published by the Syndics of the Cambridge University Press
The Pitt Building, Trumpington Street, Cambridge CB2 1RP
Bentley House, 200 Euston Road, London NW1 2DB
32 East 57th Street, New York, NY 10022, USA
296 Beaconsfield Parade, Middle Park, Melbourne 3206, Australia

First published 1979

Printed in Great Britain at the
University Press Cambridge

Library of Congress Cataloguing in Publication Data
Bowring, Richard John, 1947 −
Mori Ōgai and the modernization of Japanese culture.

(University of Cambridge oriental publications; no. 28)
Bibliography: p.
Includes index.
1. Mori, Ōgai, 1862-1922. I. Title. II. Series: Cambridge.
University. Oriental publications; no. 28.
PL811.07Z58 895.6'3'4 [B] 76-11074
ISBN O 521 21319 3

CONTENTS

ILLUSTRATIONS

PREFACE

It is a well-known fact that most Japanese if asked to name the two greatest writers of the Meiji and Taishō periods would reply with little hesitation, Natsume Sōseki and Mori Ōgai. The reputation of the former is relatively secure, if tempered a little when one measures him against a James or a Proust, but Ōgai presents somewhat more of a problem. The usual reaction is to resort to some inexplicable idolatry on the part of Japanese scholars. To the extent that Ōgai is at all familiar to students of modern Japanese literature, the image that most people have is of an austere figure, an army doctor writing in his spare time, and a member and supporter of that convenient scapegoat 'the establishment'. Like all superficial views this does contain a certain amount of truth. Ōgai was perhaps the only writer of the age to maintain substantial links with the bureaucracy, and he could not have been a very comfortable person to live with. But there is a tendency to gloss over elements of conflict and disappointment in his life, and to lose sight of his intense involvement with the process and results of modernization in Japan with all the suffering that it entailed.

Part of the problem of Ōgai's low reputation in the West is that he cannot with much justification be called a novelist. It is true that he wrote three novels, *Gan* (The Wild Goose), *Seinen* (Youth) and *Kaijin* (Ashes), but the first is mediocre, the second a failure, and the third unfinished. None of these works even approaches the best of Sōseki or Shimazaki Tōson. However, to call Ōgai a novelist and then dismiss him as a bad novelist is an easy, but not very edifying, business. The truth is that Ōgai was far more at home with the novella and the short story. But the novel form has achieved such dominance in the West that it threatens to obliterate all other forms of prose narrative. The distinction between novel and short story tends to imply a judgement not so much of genre as of value, and this acts as a hidden obstacle to appreciation. It should also be mentioned from the outset that Ōgai is known and admired in Japan as a stylist of rare quality. This is something that the reader who has no knowledge of Japanese must take on trust, but it is of the greatest importance. Style is at once a vital (some might say the vital) ingredient of any literary art, and the most difficult aspect to present in objective critical terms. Suffice it to say that the problem of explaining the effect of Ōgai's style is somewhat akin to the difficulty of explaining the stature of Goethe's poetry to those who know no German, or of explaining to the Japanese why Jane Austen is accorded the admiration and affection she is.

This book, however, is not an attempt to prove that Ōgai was a first-class literary artist; his faults are too obvious for that. But it is written in the belief that much of value has been overlooked. While I have not hesitated to discard views and opinions that smacked of prejudice and have judged many of his works with a harshness that will surprise and pain some Japanese friends, I have endeavoured to show exactly why Ōgai is worth the attention of anyone interested in the cultural and spiritual history of modern Japan.

Ōgai's reputation during his lifetime was as a translator and a critic of formidable intellect. His reputation as an author in his own right is, I would suggest, largely a posthumous affair; a consequence not of popular acclaim or even hagiographic writing by a collection of 'disciples', but of conscious work by critics of literary and cultural history who have found in their study of Ōgai much of value. It is undeniable that by virtue of the fascination that his life and character hold for the Japanese the works themselves are given a vicarious lustre which easily tarnishes if one approaches them entirely on their own merits. But Ōgai is a touchstone against which many Japanese intellectuals can measure themselves, and this acts as a strong if often subconscious attraction.

In the sense that a reading of his works together with an intimate knowledge of his life illustrates many of the tensions that are still inherently part of the modern Japanese intellectual's birthright, he takes on almost symbolic meaning. As a youth he seized the opportunity that travel abroad gave him and forcibly carved for himself a not inconsiderable role in the modernization of Japan in the 1890s. He had an insatiable desire to master the secrets of European civilization, but his sojourn in Germany has the additional attraction of romance; he was human enough to make at least one mistake with a German girl who subsequently took the extraordinarily bold step of following him to Japan. Here we have all the elements of what has become a myth of great potency in the modern Japanese imagination.

Once back in Japan, Ōgai's sense of mission drove him to extreme lengths of belligerent journalism in his impatient desire to put all he had learnt into practice as quickly as possible. In addition to making a significant contribution to the spread of modern medical practices, outside the framework of his official life, he was one of the major sources of information about European literature in the late Meiji period. Then came disappointment in his own life coupled with the painful realization that reforging Japan would take many more years than he had at first fondly hoped. There was a definite change of pace, but beneath lay the same obsessive concern with the fate of his country's culture. He experienced a feeling of being left behind by the frightening speed of change that was shared by all his contemporaries, especially when it became clear that the only answer that the country's leaders had to social discontent was blanket repression.

In the light, then, of the number of Japanese writers who either came to grief or fell into an uneasy silence as a result of the conflict between the intoxicating effect of an individualism learned abroad and the appealing comfort of authoritarianism sanctioned by tradition, Ōgai's balance and his never-ending effort to live within the system and yet maintain intellectual honesty and integrity, is a vitally important subject for study. It is no accident that one of the best books on Ōgai, Ikimatsu Keizō's *Mori Ōgai,* was written as part of a series entitled 'Modern Japanese Thinkers'. Behind the vast and ever growing number of works on the life and writings of this man lies a deeply rooted desire to understand the mechanism that enabled him to maintain a fragile but effective synthesis not only of East and West but also of science and art. He represents in many ways a microcosm of the great mental upheaval that came in the wake of the modernization; and through a study of his life and work the modern Japanese can shed light on his own predicament, which is not in essence so very different from that which Ōgai faced. This is where the sympathetic reaction lies.

The form this book takes is chronological, largely because the process of change in Ōgai's writings and his ideas is one of the most important and interesting facets of the man. The reader used to Western biographies might legitimately complain of the paucity of detailed, truly personal material. This is a shortcoming which must be faced up to. Although Ōgai was only too willing to express his ideas and opinions, he was particularly reticent about revealing his own feelings either in conversation or in print. One doubts whether anyone ever really got to know him except for his best friend, Kako Tsurudo. What is more, there is comparatively little information available about him from other sources which is not either trivial or suspect. It seems at times as if he were disembodied; the man *is* his ideas and his works, and it may be that in the conscious attempt to avoid using his many semi-autobiographical works as a source for biographical detail I have been too severe. It is to be hoped however that I have succeeded in illustrating not only his importance but also in passing on some of the fascination he exerts on many of his countrymen, much of which has rubbed off on to me.

I wish to record my overwhelming debt of gratitude to Dr Douglas Mills of the University of Cambridge for the unfailing patience and kindness he showed and the amount of time he devoted to the supervision of the thesis on which this book is largely based. I would also like to express thanks to Professor Donald Keene of Columbia University for taking the trouble to read the penultimate manuscript; his carefully considered advice was of great value. Financial support for two years' work in Japan was generously given by the Leverhulme Trust Fund of London, without whom I would not have been able to write this book in such a short time. Thanks also go to the journal, *Monumenta Nipponica,* for permission to use one of my own articles and two short passages of translation from 'Fumizukai' and 'Doitsu nikki' by Professor Karen Brazell. Lastly, much more than mere thanks are due to my wife who has been a constant source of encouragement throughout the five years that have passed since I first made the acquaintance of Mori Ōgai.

The reference numbers which appear in the text refer to the latest Complete Works, *Ōgai Zenshū,* ed. Kinoshita Mokutarō *et al.* (Iwanami Shoten, 1971-5), 38 vols. All translations, except when otherwise noted, are my own. There may, of course, be places where previous translators will recognize themselves, but these, I hope, will be taken as a gesture not of plagiarism but of admiration for the right phrase.

Nezu, 1975

The young Mori Ōgai, Germany c. 1884

To Arthur and Mabel
'All sky'

PART I

1862–1894

A SENSE OF MISSION

The early years

The castle town of Tsuwano in the province of Iwami — present-day Shimane ken — deep in the heart of western Japan, surrounded by hills and somewhat inaccessible in the days before the Restoration, had been the centre of a small fief of 43,000 *koku*[1] belonging to the Kamei daimyos since 1617. In 1862, the year of Mori Ōgai's birth, the then daimyo was Kamei Koremi. The Mori family had been doctors in the town for many generations and although they were at the lower end of the samurai class with a stipend of about fifty *koku*, the special role of doctor probably gave them higher status than this might at first suggest.

Ōgai was the fourteenth in line in a family which had not been very successful in producing male heirs and had been forced to arrange a number of judicious male adoptions for the last few generations. Ōgai's grandfather, who had studied medicine at Nagasaki and Edo, had been adopted when already in his forties, and his wife, who joined the Mori family in 1845 at the age of twenty-seven, was the daughter of a Chōshū samurai. This couple had two children, a son who died at the age of three, and a daughter, Mine. Ōgai's father Shizuo, who was also from neighbouring Chōshū and had studied medicine at Nagasaki, was adopted as her husband in 1861 when he was twenty-six and Mine sixteen. Ōgai's birth on 17 February 1862 was thus a particularly auspicious one for the family. His grandfather had died suddenly two months previously in the province of Ōmi while accompanying the daimyo on the return from an alternate period of residence in Edo, and in the words of Ōgai's younger sister, Kimiko, 'Our grandfather, who had just passed away, had written in his travel diary a number of times how happy he would be to see the face of his first grandchild. The family's grief was somewhat lessened by the thought that here after all was a life in exchange for his.'[2] It is worth stressing at this early stage that Ōgai's position as a precious eldest son with its mixture of special care and concern on the part of the parents, and the early realization of the burden of future responsibilities, contrasts strongly with the miserable childhood of his famous contemporary, the novelist, Natsume Sōseki, who was later to articulate a personal anguish and despair not to be found in the works of Ōgai.

From the few writings we have on the subject it is clear that Ogai's mother was the driving force in the family. His father, having been adopted, was in a traditionally difficult position, but in any case he seems to have been by nature a quiet, unassuming man devoted to his work and his patients, showing little interest in literature, and finding relaxation rather in such pursuits as bonsai and the tea ceremony.[3]

Where his mother did take particular care was in Ōgai's education. He began by studying the Confucian Analects in 1867 at the age of five and in the following year was guided in his reading of Mencius by a relative of the family, Yonehara Tsunae.[4] His mother, who had not been able to read before his birth, went to great pains to learn from her mother and was able to help Ōgai in his very early studies. His younger brother, Junzaburō, later recorded the concern that was lavished on the eldest son: 'It was just under a mile from the house to Yonehara Sensei's and he left to arrive at seven in the morning. He was scared of the dogs and also of being teased by other children on the way there, so our grandmother would take him. On the way back he would be accompanied by a retainer of the Yoneharas.'[5]

In 1869 he started to attend the fief school, the Yōrōkan, where he continued with a typical Confucian education, showing his intelligence and fascination with books at an early age, winning the top prizes in each year and revealing that seriousness of purpose that was to characterize his whole life. The ability to live within himself and be emotionally self-contained which a lifetime of continuous hard study demanded was clearly fostered during these early years, as he became aware of the solitude that is so often the fate of an unusually gifted child. Looking back on his childhood, he once wrote:

> They say I have loved books ever since I was a child. I was born at a time when there were no magazines for children to read or any of Iwaya Sazanami's fairy stories, and so I had to rely on books like the *Hundred Poems*, which my grandmother was said to have brought with her as a bride, the texts of puppet plays which remained as a reminder of the time my grandfather had practised reciting, and picture books which explained the plots of Nō plays. I never flew kites and I never played with tops. Nor did I ever make any deep friendship with any of the boys in the

neighbourhood. So it was that I gradually became absorbed in reading books, and the names of various things stuck in my memory, just like bits of dust settle on a household object. (XXVI, 459).

The fief school had been founded in 1786 and had first been in the hands of a disciple of the famous scholar, Yamazaki Ansai. Orthodox Confucianism of the Chu Hsi school had been taught there from the beginning and had continued until 1849, at which time the daimyo, Kamei Koremi, who had sympathy for scholarship of a more indigenous nature (*kokugaku*), introduced a number of changes. By the time Ōgai attended, there was a broad scope of studies including military arts, mathematics, Chinese and Dutch medicine, and Japanese studies of the Hirata school. As most fiefs had such institutions and as it was usual for intelligent boys to start their studies early, Ōgai had a comparable education to scores of other similarly placed children in the Bakumatsu period, although there was perhaps slightly more emphasis on 'national learning' than in many other schools. The first article of the school code enjoined the pupils to work for Emperor and the Shinto deities and it is of interest that Kamei's first position in the new Meiji government was with the Department for Religious Affairs.[6] About this time Ōgai's father started to teach him the rudiments of Dutch grammar, and he also received instruction in that language from a qualified teacher in 1871.

His father had already been approached about sending the boy to Tokyo to study under the auspices of Nishi Amane, who was Shizuo's cousin through adoption, and who was already an intellectual figure of some prominence. It is also possible that Nishi himself returned from Tokyo to persuade the father, but the offer was refused, even though the suggestion may first have come from Kamei who had heard of the boy's prowess. Kamei had seen early on that the times were changing and that the country would need the best brains it could muster, so he had already set up a system of scholarships that enabled young men from the fief to travel and study in the capital.

In the summer of 1871 came the dissolution of the fiefs and on 4 August of that year Kamei left to take up permanent residence in Tokyo. The school closed in the November and from then on Ōgai was left without any real possibilities for further education, as Tsuwano, having lost its position as a castle town, quickly became a backwater. The family was growing and there were possible financial problems in store if they remained, so the decision was made to move to the capital. Ōgai and his father set out on 26 June 1872, leaving the rest of the family to stay for the time being with the Yoneharas and to follow on a year later. On their arrival in Tokyo they stayed at first in a house in the grounds of Kamei's second mansion at Mukōjima, and three years later they bought a house of their own in the vicinity. Shizuo continued in his role as Kamei's private physician, but also took in outside work to supplement the family's income.

Not long after they were thus settled, in October 1872, Ōgai entered a small school in Hongō where, among other subjects, he started to study German, which had supplanted Dutch as the language for the instruction of medicine. Hongō was a long way from Mukōjima, and so Ōgai stayed with the Nishi family in Kanda, going home only at weekends. Although in 1898 he was later to write Nishi's biography, there is very little clue as to the nature of their relationship. Perhaps the very lack of comment speaks for itself. What is certain, however, is that relations between them seriously worsened before Nishi died.

In January 1874 Ōgai managed to gain admittance to the preparatory course for the most important medical school in Tokyo at the time, by pretending to be two years older than he really was. When, in November 1876, the school moved from Kanda to Hongō, Ōgai left the Nishis' house and entered the school dormitory, which he was later to describe in the autobiographical *Vita Sexualis*. He was admitted into the main school in May 1877, one month after it had become the medical department of the University of Tokyo.

For the next four years he studied medicine under the German lecturers who were responsible for much of the instruction. From the glimpses that we can gain from *Vita Sexualis*, it would not appear that he found much difficulty in absorbing what was taught, despite the fact that all the lectures and books were in German. He even found time to apply himself to the study of Japanese poetry, and classical Chinese under the tutelage of the well-known writer, Yoda Gakkai. His reading at first centred on the kind of Tokugawa fiction provided by the lending libraries, but later, under the influence of Yoda Gakkai, he turned to more serious Chinese fiction and poetry.[7]

About 1880, in his third year at the university, Ōgai moved into new lodgings, the 'Kamijō' in Hongō that forms the background to his later story *Gan* (The Wild Goose). His family were concerned about his health and so the grandmother was sent to look after him and cook his meals. As it happened their fears were not ungrounded; in the spring of 1881, just before his final exams, he contracted mild pleurisy. A further difficulty was the fire at his lodgings in March when he lost all his valuable notes. Despite this, however, he successfully graduated that summer. He was, by virtue of deceit, the youngest to do so, but his position, eighth out of twenty-eight, was a great disappointment to him. Considering his illness and the fire, it was perhaps only to be expected, but, as Ōgai realized, it would have far-reaching effects on his future career.

Ōgai's father had moved to Senju, north of Tokyo, in June 1879 and in the August had set up a practice of his own. Immediately after graduating, Ōgai moved to Senju to help his father with his patients. Not much information is available for these few months, but we do know that Ōgai tried his hand at translating the *Asagao Nikki* and some poems from the *Genji Monogatari* into Chinese. He also undertook the translation from German into Chinese of Wilhelm Hauff's 'Die Geschichte von der abgehauenen Hand', which was later published in January 1885.

There can be little doubt that Ōgai's overriding wish was to travel abroad as soon as possible. Having been on a government scholarship at the university, he had hoped for further financial aid from the Ministry of Education, which would have allowed him to study for a number of years in Germany and then return to an almost certain post at the university. But his relatively low position in the final exams meant that this was a forlorn hope. Many of his fellow graduates, such as Koike Masanao and Kako Tsurudo, had stipendiaries from the army, but Ōgai had not gone to university with that aim in mind. His parents, on the other hand, felt that in view of his position, the army was a very suitable career which offered a secure post with room for promotion and possible fame.

His youth and the fact that he had not previously shown any strong desire to join the army did not bode well for him, but the family had connections. Nishi Amane's adopted son, Shinrokurō, was the younger brother of Hayashi Tsuna, who had succeeded his uncle, Matsumoto Ryojun, as Chief of the Army Medical Staff in 1879. Ōgai's father had also studied medicine under Matsumoto. Hayashi wrote to Nishi on 16 September 1881 informing him that Ōgai was certain of a post, so it is clear that the matter was almost settled by that date, at least in the eyes of his parents.[8] In addition, a letter written by Koike Masanao to Hayashi's deputy, Ishiguro Tadanori, dated 7 April 1881, shows that some of his friends had been urging Ōgai to join the army for a long time. The letter is worth quoting in entirety, for it shows well the impression that Ōgai had made at the university.

Sir. I have a personal request on behalf of a friend of mine.

I have always been given to understand that in matters concerning the country it is disloyal for a subject to keep silent
when he knows something of advantage, and it is a misfortune
for the ruler if a subject finds himself misplaced.

I have a friend whose name is Mori Rintarō.[9] He is twenty-
one years old. We have studied together for ten years and have
just successfully graduated. Mori is by nature clever and enjoys
studying. He is widely read and has an excellent memory.
Exceptionally talented, he has no time for fools and is most
concerned at the present confused state of medicine in Japan.
He once said to me: 'The West is so remote. The climate and
customs are different from ours, and so is the clothing, the
food, and the way they make use of different implements.
Should we just blindly accept the whole of Western medicine
with so little discrimination? In view of the fact that they
founded this branch of science in the West long ago, and seeing
that their experience is so great, I think we should learn from
them for a while and then use that learning as material for the
foundation of our own studies some day.'

This shows the breadth of his ambition and how different he
is from the other students who are so intoxicated with the West.
What is more, in his spare time, when he was not studying hard
for the main course, he was mastering the art of writing Japanese
and Chinese poetry. He even searched out books on Chinese
medicine leaving no stone unturned, wishing to put this knowledge to public use at a later stage.

Although he is as talented and able as I have just described,
his recent examination results seem to prove very much the
opposite. There generally is a lot of luck involved in exams, not
to mention the clash of characters between Mori and Dr Schultze.
Dr Schultze is stern, narrow-minded and bigoted. If anyone
disagrees with him in the slightest way he flares up in anger. He
simply refuses to discuss things further if there is ever a difference of opinion. Mori did not wish to give in to him or solicit
his goodwill in the slightest, but preferred to put things to the
test, and time and time again did not hesitate to say that Japanese
medicines should also be tested. Inevitably this meant that he
clashed with Dr Schultze, and this was probably the reason for
his poor results.

Within the school, however, there was a natural consensus of
opinion that his irregular marks were ultimately insignificant and
did not reflect his real capabilities. However, if this is not
realized and people make the mistake of judging him by these
marks, it would not only be a misfortune for him but for the
whole country.

Leaders of men and people of genius are rare and precious. At the present time students of the West can be counted by the cartload and although they may understand Western culture — that screeching of shrikes and crabwise scrawl — they are muddled and vague about their own culture. They are not true to themselves. As soon as a Westerner says anything, they all immediately conform and make no distinction between good and bad. Everything is put into practice quite indiscriminately with no thought as to whether it will be of benefit or should be introduced more gradually. It goes without saying how undesirable this is. Mori, however, towers above the rest of them, quite untainted by this corruption. He is a general among men, a man in a thousand. He is exceptionally able and if his talents are well used he will regenerate Japanese medicine, put order into chaos, and be of great benefit to the country. I submit the matter to your superior judgement and merely await your pleasure.

I have dared to submit this recommendation, because I found myself unable to stifle my own humble desire that, through your wisdom, Mori might gain his proper place and realize his genius.[10]

This valuable portrait of Ōgai as a university student testifies to his strength of character which tended to manifest itself in an intransigent attitude towards his superiors if he believed that they were in the wrong — a tendency that should perhaps have sounded a warning to his future peers in the army.

While his parents and relatives were independently arranging matters so that by September of that year his acceptance by the army was a foregone conclusion, Ōgai himself was still trying to get abroad by other means. There fortunately remains a revealing letter that he wrote to his closest friend, Kako Tsurudo, on 20 November 1881 which shows he was giving in somewhat against his will:

When I remember your visit yesterday, your kind advice on a certain question, and your recent letter, it makes me realize how sincere a friend you are. As regards the matter in hand, I went to visit Miyake Hiizu this morning to discuss it with him, but according to him the question of travel abroad is not yet decided. He told me that there will probably be not more than three people going, and one of those will be someone who graduated last year. As the method of selection lays stress on the examination results, it will never come to my turn and so I'd better resign myself to the fact. All I can really do is give up hoping and join the army as my parents wish.

If the army authorities come to hear of my various enquiries

about travelling abroad, there's no telling whether those meticulous men in the Ministry might feel I was naturally indecisive.
I would rather let the whole matter drop. Do not show this
letter to anyone else I beg of you. We can talk of this when we
meet again. (XXXVI, 1)[11]

As his first hope of travelling abroad under the auspices of the
Ministry of Education was stillborn, one can only imagine that he in
fact accepted the offer of a place in the army with good grace, because,
although travel to the West was by no means certain, it probably
offered him the best chance. When he was officially accepted as second-
lieutenant·in the Medical Corps on 16 December 1881, the event was
greeted with great relief by his parents who were justifiably proud of
his success. The seeds of conflict were, however, already sown.

Information about Ōgai's activity during the period from December
1881 to August 1884, when he left for Germany, is scarce. At first he
worked in the military hospital in Tokyo where his superior was
another Tsuwano man. In May 1882 he was moved to the Medical
Affairs Bureau at the Ministry of War where he was ordered to carry
out research into the system of army hygiene in Prussia. The end result
of this work was a twelve-volume manuscript which he submitted in
February 1883; a difficult undertaking which probably influenced his
choice of speciality — hygiene and the administration of medical
affairs.[12]

Confined to such desk work, these must have been frustrating years
for a youth still bent on travelling abroad at the first opportunity.
The extent of his impatience can be judged from the fact that sometime before February 1884 he visited the head of the military hospital,
Hashimoto Tsunatsune, who was to be sent abroad as part of an observation party, and begged to be allowed to accompany him. He waited
for Hashimoto for ten hours — a measure of his desperation — but the
request was turned down. The Medical Bureau had, however, already
applied to send someone to Germany to study hygiene in June 1883,
and Ōgai was finally informed he had been chosen on 7 May 1884.

Ōgai's diary for his journey to Europe, the 'Kōsei nikki', is short
and to the point. It gives us only a brief glimpse of his emotional
reaction to what was a great adventure and the fulfilment of a dream.
But one can tell from the opening entry that he was overjoyed to be
going.

> 23 August 1884. Left Tokyo by train at 6 p.m. and arrived in
> Yokohama. Stayed the night at the Hayashis.
>   On 17 June I received my orders to travel to Germany, study
> hygiene and investigate the administration of medical affairs in

the army. On 28 July I proceeded to the Palace, had audience with the Emperor, and then took leave of my ancestors. On 20 August I collected my passport from the Ministry of War.

I have wanted to travel to the West from the moment I graduated. Modern medicine stems from the West. I have always felt that even if you can read and speak their language, unless you become familiar with the country itself, you are in danger of putting your own interpretation on what they write.

In 1881 I had the fortune to graduate, and on that occasion I composed a Chinese poem:

How laughable! Such fame and yet so feeble:
The same old attitude — raising proud shoulders
And watching the garlands bring a little joy.
But who really praises the youngest on graduation?

Sympathize with Su Ch'in ashamed in defeat:
So futile to make Tsu T'i look to his laurels!
Yet my desire for fame is still unbroken:
I dream to undertake some great enterprise!'[13]

Perhaps my spirit was already winging its way to the river Elbe.

Not long after, I became an army doctor connected with Medical Headquarters. I marked time and was kept busy submerged in registers and documents for three long years. Now I am setting out on this journey. It is impossible not to feel great joy. (XXXV, 75).

The diary records details of the hospital in Hong Kong, the botanical gardens in ports such as Saigon, Singapore, Colombo and Aden, together with observations on the flora, fauna, and housing conditions. There is little overt enthusiasm in what is a very subdued and terse account of the voyage; the only lyrical moments being the occasional Chinese poem that records impressions of natural beauty. One poem, however, shows him sleeping on deck, apparently unconcerned and yet with a strong awareness of the future:

By himself sits Mori at peace with the world,
Snoring like thunder, but no one dares complain.
On his return from European travels
I wonder if there will be any change? (XXXV, 76)

Germany

Arriving in Marseilles on 7 October 1884, Ōgai took the train for Paris, where he spent the evening at the theatre in the company of a friend who was returning to Japan. He arrived in Berlin on 11 October.

From this point on, the main source of information is his own

'Doitsu nikki' (a German diary), which was almost certainly rewritten many years later and probably heavily self-censored. Although it gives us little impression of his emotional life and is certainly not the kind of diary one would associate with a prospective writer, it does reveal much about his activities in Germany and the variety and importance of these years for his later development.[14]

Ōgai's initial stay in Berlin was only for ten days while the Legation finalized his itinerary. His first impressions of the city must have been very similar to those of the central figure in the story 'Maihime' (The dancing girl), which he was to write on his return to Japan:

> But suddenly here I was, standing in the middle of this most modern of European capitals. My eyes were dazzled by its brilliance, my mind was dazed by the riot of colour. To translate Unter den Linden as 'under the Bodhi tree' would suggest a quiet secluded spot. But just come and see the groups of men and women sauntering along the pavements that line each side of that great thoroughfare as it runs, straight as a die, through the city. It was still in the days when Wilhelm I would come to his window and gaze down upon his capital. The tall, broad-shouldered officers in their colourful dress uniform, and the attractive girls, their hair made up in the Parisian style, were everywhere a delight to the eye. Carriages ran silently on asphalt roads. Just visible in the clear sky between the towering buildings were fountains cascading with the sound of heavy rain. Looking into the distance, one could see the statue of the goddess on the victory column. She seemed to be floating half-way to heaven from the midst of the green trees on the other side of the Brandenburg Gate. All these myriad sights were gathered so close at hand that it was quite bewildering for the newcomer. (I, 426–7).

The day after his arrival he visited Hashimoto Tsunatsune who was on the study tour that Ōgai had wanted to join some ten months previously. Hashimoto told him to concentrate on his studies of hygiene, but also to be sure to follow German customs. Aoki Shūzō, the Minister for Japan, put it more explicitly:

> The Minister said that it was good I was studying hygiene, but he was afraid that when I returned to Japan I would find it difficult to put what I had learnt into practice immediately. 'Discussions about hygiene are meaningless to people who go about with geta thongs between their toes,' he said. 'Learning isn't limited to reading books. If you carefully observe how Europeans think, how they live, and what their manners are, your trip abroad will have been warranted.' (XXXV, 87–8)[15]

When Ōgai returned to Japan he was to try and prove that Aoki's supposition was false and that the Japanese were in no way intellectually inferior to Europeans merely because their customs differed. Later he was even to write an article in which he specifically argued in favour of the hygienic nature of Japanese footwear.

Arriving in Leipzig, where he was to stay from 22 October 1884 to 11 October 1885, he was soon ensconced in a rented room where bed and breakfast were provided but where he had to eat out at a different boarding house. He began work at the university under Franz Hoffmann, whose speciality was the study of human metabolism. During this period, he spent two days in the May of 1885 at Dresden watching training manoeuvres for the evacuation of battle wounded at the invitation of Major General Wilhelm Roth, commander of the Saxony Army Medical Corps, who later became a very close friend. He travelled back to Berlin again from 26 to 30 May in order to discuss his course of study and to request that the Legation arrange for him to attend the regular autumn training manoeuvres of the 12th Saxony Army Corps, for which permission was subsequently granted.

The overall impression from reading the entries for this Leipzig period is that Ōgai was enjoying a full social life. The New Year brought a number of dances and masked balls. The visit to Dresden and the account of the autumn manoeuvres, which took place from 27 August to 12 September and which provided much of the material for the story 'Fumizukai' (The courier), are treated mainly from the social angle, and there are not a few entries appreciative of the beauty and vivacity of German women.

This, however, tells only part of the story. There were signs very early on that he was to devote many evenings to reading literature. On 24 October 1884 he wrote: 'When I return from school, my English tutor Ferdinand Ilgner is waiting for me in my room. Since most of the language teachers are poor, they come to your room rather than make you go to theirs. I have decided that at night I will read extensively in the German poets' (XXXV, 89-90).

On 12 November he received a letter from a friend in Heidelberg together with his Chinese translation of Hauff's *märchen,* which had been corrected and commented on by Inoue Tetsujirō. Inoue was already a highly respected figure in Japan, and his approval of Ōgai's work must have been gratifying.[16] The extent of his reading and interest in European literature can be seen from a further entry for 13 August 1885:

Since Iijima left, I have been in his old room. I have already amassed over 170 Western books on my bookshelf. The University has been on holiday recently and so I have had some spare time to take them down and read them. It goes without saying how convenient this is. Among the books that I find most moving are plays of the Greek masters such as Sophocles, Euripides and Aeschylus, and I find the love stories by the French writers Ohnet, Halévy and Gréville the best written. Dante's *Divine Comedy* is truly profound and inspiring, and the Collected Works of Goethe so vast and imposing. My pleasure in these books is obvious to everyone who comes to see me. (XXXV, 102).

Ōgai was fortunate in that in Germany at that time foreign works were being translated in great numbers; a knowledge of German was in this respect more valuable than a knowledge of English. As he was in the habit of recording the date he finished a particular work, one can follow his reading in Leipzig from the marginal notes in his personal library. It is of interest that from April to September 1885 he was concentrating on the twenty-four volume collection of German *novellen* entitled *Deutscher Novellenschatz* compiled by Paul Heyse and Hermann Kurz — the introduction of this novella form by Ōgai was to be one of his major contributions to modern Japanese literature.[17]

As far as Ōgai's medical studies were concerned, the main product of the year spent at Leipzig was a study of the diet of Japanese soldiers which, from entries in the diary, seems to have been completed between February and October 1885. It was written in German and was published in October 1886.[18] This study did not represent Ōgai's own research on the problem, but had been planned before he left Japan and was based on previously published work. The question whether Japan should aim for a complete changeover to a Western diet was an important point of controversy at the time, and it had special reference to the armed forces where a desperate attempt was being made to cut down the incidence of beri-beri. The navy had successfully done this by changing to a completely Western diet, which meant not only more meat but the substitution of barley, or wheat, for rice. Ōgai himself was far from convinced that diet was the cause of the illness, and the paper was a defence of the traditional Japanese rice diet. To back up his argument he pointed out that even German scholars were at variance as to the relative efficiency of rice and barley, some citing the small stature of the Japanese as a whole, and some praising their physical strength and energy.

Ōgai's argument was that although barley might have a higher protein content, rice was far more efficiently digested. The clue to a better diet was not a one to one exchange, but merely a certain amount of adaptation. From a common-sense point of view, he argued that:

> I am driven to point out at this juncture that the Japanese are
> trying their utmost to make best use of European science as soon
> as is humanly possible. As a result, proposals to change old estab-
> lished customs are made with such abandon all over the land that
> a proper examination of the proposed changes often comes too
> late. We must never forget that customs and habits that have
> been accepted and maintained for centuries must have a solid
> core, otherwise they would never have lasted so long! (XXVIII,
> 572)

Ōgai's second point was that a European diet would, in any case,
be almost impossible to introduce into the army for purely economic
reasons. Being already concerned at the way Europe tended to see
Japan merely as a market for manufactured goods — a new area for
exploitation — he argued strongly against any change that would
involve large importation of foodstuffs. This would lead to a dangerous
dependence on foreign countries for Japan's very livelihood; something that 'no Japanese patriot would ever desire!' (XXVIII, 566).
There is here an exemplification of Koike Masanao's earlier description of Ōgai as a man who was far from convinced of the superiority
of everything Western. Ōgai's own opinions on the policies to be
adopted in the process of modernization were always based on the
premise that objective scientific results must take precedence over any
vague idealistic theories.

Ōgai moved to Dresden on 11 October 1885. This stay, which
lasted until 7 March, 1886, was not originally planned, but on the
instigation of Wilhelm Roth he had requested the Legation in Berlin
to arrange his attendance at the medical lectures at Dresden during
the winter. This was the period when he was most at ease with his
fellow German officers and was introduced to the highest social ranks
in Saxony, due no doubt to his close friendship with Roth. Ōgai had
already been introduced to King Albert at the manoeuvres on 6 September 1885, but over the New Year in Dresden he attended the
Palace and was invited to a number of soirées and dances. His facility
with German allowed him to move confidently among this class,
and his success must have been rare for a Japanese abroad. Here again
the comparison with Sōseki's, admittedly much later, dog's life among
English gentlemen is inescapable. It is worth stressing the uniqueness
of this experience and Ōgai's contact with the upper levels of German
society that reached its peak in Dresden. His years in Germany were
gradually to assume the nature of an idyllic dream when he returned
to Japan. There is also some indication that his social success was not

looked upon with too much favour by his superiors, to whom it may have seemed that he was enjoying himself too much. Ishiguro Tadanori must have heard something of his life at Leipzig, for on 3 January 1886 a letter arrived which warned him not to spend too much time on 'military affairs' and to concentrate more on his studies of hygiene.

At Dresden, Ōgai continued to read from Heyse and Kurz's collection of *novellen,* attended other lectures besides those on the course, and started learning a little Spanish from another German friend, George Wilke. Having dealt with the subject of the Japanese diet, he then turned to the question of Japanese housing and produced a paper which was eventually published in Berlin in 1888.[19] This work was a detailed discussion of Japanese houses, their construction, materials, size, the movement of air, heating, lighting and sewerage, and behind it lay the basic criticism that Japan was following Western practice with little or no real discrimination. Japanese houses, he argued, were suited to the Japanese climate by virtue of their superior ventilation and the excellent absorbing properties of wood. No one had yet tried to find out whether Western housing really was intrinsically better than Japanese, and it was this lack of a rational basis to the modernization movement that Ōgai was to continue to criticize.

Ōgai left Dresden on 7 March 1886 and arrived in Munich the next day. The strength of his attachment for Roth can be seen from the following simple entry in his diary:

> At noon met Captain Hayakawa at Schumanns. Three in the afternoon went to a farewell party which Roth was giving for me. The Head of the Military Hospital Klien and his wife were there and a vast number of other guests. During the party Roth read out a poem he had written for me. Half-way through he could not stop himself from crying. I too found myself in tears. (XXXV, 133–4)

The entries for the diary which deal with his stay in Munich give a very different impression from either Leipzig or Dresden where he had spent most of his time with German officers. Munich is marked by his close friendship with other Japanese students abroad, notably Iwasa Shin, Katō Terumaro and the artist, Harada Naojirō. At times they seem an inseparable group, and after two years abroad, a little of his countrymen's company may not have come amiss. Something of the atmosphere of this period can be felt from the following entry for 15 August 1886, in which he records that Harada was having an affair with a local waitress:

> Harada Naojirō has set up his mistress in a house on Landwehr-strasse. She's called Marie Huber and was formerly a waitress

at the Cafe Minerva. No real beauty — pale and rather thin, and not very bright either. They stick together like glue. When Harada was studying at the Academy of Fine Arts there was a beautiful girl called Caecilia Pfaff, daughter of a university lecturer at Erlangen. Jet black hair and skin as white as snow. Piercing eyes and a proud nose. Her English and French were good and she could write better than most — they said she wrote over half her father's work. I never got to know her well, but when I saw a picture of her at Harada's I could just see she was talented. I knew without asking that she was quite a woman. She got to know Harada because she was also studying art at the Academy. They gradually got closer and she has wanted to marry him for some time now, but Harada seems moved not the slightest. Now here he is setting up house for a waitress. I just can't understand it.

I suppose he thought that as Caecilia was the daughter of a good family, if he got engaged to her it would be for life. Marie is just a waitress and probably satisfies him for the moment. But which is more desirable — to become engaged to a talented girl like Caecilia, or to consort with a dull, plain waitress like Marie? What is more, Caecilia is well off! She proposed that they should go off together for a study trip to Paris on her money. Marie's parents are terribly poor; I wouldn't be surprised if he has a lot of problems in the future. His behaviour really is quite a mystery. He is usually so open and uncomplicated. I like him a lot and that's why I feel sorry when he goes and does something like this. (XXXV, 145–6)

Here in this frank record of a relationship that he was later to incorporate into the romantic tale 'Utakata no ki' (This transient world) we are given an insight into his reaction to a situation that was not uncommon among Japanese students studying abroad.

In quieter moments, Ōgai continued with his reading, starting Heyse's *Neuer Deutscher Novellenschatz,* and keeping up with his study of Goethe, Schiller and Heine. Among the plays he saw were some by Calderon and Lessing, and a performance of the *Mikado* by an English group, at which he was somewhat surprised to note that the costumes and props seemed to be authentically Japanese. Much of his spare time, however, was spent in taking trips to the lakes around Munich either alone or with friends. It was while he was staying at Munich that King Ludwig II drowned in the Starnbergersee — an event which clearly captured Ōgai's imagination. He described it in his diary on 13 June 1886:

Went to a bar on Maximilianstrasse with Katō and Iwasa in the evening. We had some wine and then went home when we felt tired. As I heard the next day, the King of Bavaria had drowned in the Wurmsee; Ludwig II it was. He had been suffering from a mental illness for some time. He hated the daytime, when he would lie on his bed surrounded by flowers at all four corners of his darkened room with stars and the moon painted on the ceiling. He much preferred the night, when he would get up and wander in the garden. He had recently started a lot of public works and was near to emptying the national coffers, so his illness was announced and he was forced to retire.

On the evening of the twelfth he had moved from the castle at Hohenschwangau to Schloss Berg by the Starnbergersee, in the company of his physician Gudden who was a specialist in mental disorders. The lake is also called the Wurmsee.

On the evening of the thirteenth they went out for a walk by the lake and never came back. Both their bodies have been found. Probably the King rushed into the water and Gudden followed, trying to save him — they died together. The report on the bodies says that Gudden had tried to save the King by grasping his collar. His fingers were bruised and his nails ripped. The King was so strong however that his cloak had come off in the physician's hands and he had plunged on. Gudden rushed after him, reached him, and tried to prevent the King from drowning. The scars left by the King's nails were on Gudden's face. A terrible tragedy. (XXXV, 141–2)

The mystery of the King's death was to provide Ōgai with ideal background material for 'Utakata no ki'.

Studying at the university under the guidance of the founder of experimental hygiene, Max von Pettenkofer, Ōgai was able to start his first scientific experiments in collaboration with one of the assistants, K. B. Lehmann. The results of this research into the dietary effects of beer and the poisons in rotting corn were published in one of the most important medical journals of the time.[20] Perhaps the most interesting articles he wrote at Munich, however, were concerned with what has become known as the Naumann Debate, which reveals many of his own fears and prejudices as a Japanese abroad. Edmund Naumann was a geologist who had been teaching in Japan, with one short break, from 1875 to 1885. His contract was not renewed because of the Japanese policy of replacing foreign professors with native scholars as soon as possible, not least because of financial considerations. Ōgai first encountered Naumann on 6 March 1886, the night before he left Dresden, when he heard him give a lecture on Japan. On that occasion he wrote in his diary:

The lecturer was an Edmund Naumann. He had lived for some

time in Japan, and had returned to Germany decorated with the Order of the Rising Sun, but for some reason he seemed extremely discontent. He lectured on Japan's geography, customs, politics and arts in front of about three hundred men and women. Much of what he said disturbed me. He said for instance: 'Ladies and Gentlemen. When you see the advanced state of Japan's modernization, do not think that the Japanese themselves realized that their civilization was inferior to that of Europe or revealed this spirit of progress through their own initiative. This state of affairs came about willy nilly because they were put under pressure by foreigners.' And then at the end, he said: 'I have now finished my outline of the situation in Japan, but I would like to end with a humorous story. The Japanese once bought a steam ship. As they had just newly learned the art of navigation, they boarded it in triumph and sailed out to sea. A few months later, approaching their own shores again, they found that unfortunately although the engineer knew how to operate the machine, he did not know how to stop it. They had to wait in the offing until it stopped of its own accord. Many Japanese techniques are still at this stage. But I have hopes that one day they will transcend such mistakes.'

I was extremely upset when I heard this, but I could not really attack his thesis at the formal lecture that evening. Roth saw my face and came up to me. 'You look annoyed,' he said. 'Why? As far as I can see, Naumann has great hopes that Japan will develop in the future. I think it was a very reasonable lecture.' I replied that Roth knew nothing of the state of civilization in Japan, and so he had thought Naumann's speech was good. If Roth with his intelligence thought that, what would everyone else think! I became more and more ill at ease and could not taste the food or drink. (XXXV, 132)

The idea that germinated here, to produce a counter argument to what he saw as Naumann's belittling of Japan, took some time to come to fruition. Eventually the opportunity came when a long article by Naumann appeared in the *Allgemeine Zeitung* on 26 and 29 June 1886. On 30 June in the same paper there was a report of a lecture given by Naumann to the Munich Anthropological Society, which was apparently very similar, if not identical, to the one Ōgai had heard in Dresden.

Naumann's article was an evocative description of the beauty of Japan's natural scenery in the form of a travelogue, and was interspersed with a number of interesting observations on Japanese customs, religion, history and the present state of affairs. Ōgai was moved to compose a reply which was printed in the same newspaper on 29

December 1886 under the title 'Die Wahrheit über Nipon' (The truth about Japan). Pettenkofer himself undoubtedly helped to get the article accepted by such a distinguished newspaper. The long gap is difficult to explain, but it suggests how deeply Naumann's speech had rankled. Ōgai's reaction was very strong:

> I was astounded when I read that article. It is quite incomprehensible how a scholar who has lived in Japan for so long could commit such errors and draw such false conclusions in his description. I decided then that I would counter Naumann's statements with factual arguments of my own, but I have not had the opportunity to do so until now. While I now take this opportunity to speak out against Dr Naumann, I wish to make it clear that it is not based on any personal motives. I have written it only in the interest of my country and my compatriots, especially those who are living in Germany. (XXXVI, 619)

As Naumann pointed out in a reply, half the problem was that Ōgai picked on statements found in the résumé of his speech that had not been written by Naumann, but by a reporter. It therefore contained a number of changes of emphasis that were not the fault of the speaker. There can be little doubt that Ōgai read into Naumann's account a sarcasm that was not intended; and the violence of his reaction showed that his sense of humour did not coincide with Naumann's. The tendency to criticize one's own nation freely and yet defend it with an irrational tenacity when criticized by an outsider is hardly a peculiarly Japanese trait, but matters were probably exacerbated because Ōgai himself was only too aware of Japan's weakness in the eyes of the West. A humorous anecdote easily became interpreted as a grave slight, and it was not the first or the last time that Japanese abroad were to feel over-sensitive about matters which touched the raw nerves of national pride.

Many of Ōgai's complaints were trivial and he maintained a rather offensive tone throughout; but some important points were touched on. Ōgai was particularly incensed by the report that the Japanese went around 'almost naked'. Naumann declared — and there is no reason to doubt him — that he had often seen Japanese wearing nothing but loincloths, despite the new ruling that clothes had to cover the leg above the knee. Ōgai was of course desperately anxious lest such a statement might suggest to the European readers that the Japanese were savages.

Naumann's main thesis was that the modernization had been forced from outside and that the treaties would have never been signed if it had not been for strong external pressure. Ōgai agreed with this but not with the implications: he pictured the Japanese as having been the victims of foreign pressure throughout their history, and he saw the Japanese state before the Restoration as an economic Utopia, economically self-sufficient and so having no real motivation for external trade.[21] The real crux of the problem, however, was whether the modernization underway was being handled in the right manner. Naumann felt that the wholesale importation of Western culture and customs was dangerous and, if carried to extremes, might destroy the country. He himself appreciated the value of traditional Japanese culture and had raised the example of the steam boat more as a warning than a piece of ridicule. Ōgai's reaction to this was understandably equivocal. He was essentially in agreement with Naumann's charge of superficiality, and yet found himself bound to defend the importation of Western culture and knowledge, for it was almost his own raison d'être. He was to be plagued all his life by this contradiction. At this early stage, however, he was more concerned with his own sense of mission and so wrote:

> Naumann goes on to say that 'the undiluted adoption of European culture might weaken instead of strengthen the Japanese, and bring about the collapse of the race'. What kind of 'European culture' is it which, if adopted, brings with it the danger of destruction? Does true European culture not lie in the recognition of freedom and beauty in the purest sense of those words? Is this recognition capable of bringing about destruction? (XXVI, 611)

It was only somewhat later that he was to realize the partial truth of what Naumann had said. The adoption of an alien culture was to set up stresses and threaten to leave a spiritual vacuum that became one of Ōgai's major preoccupations in later life. He was already fully convinced that, as he wrote in some unpublished notes in Berlin, 'Civilization is based on *historical* foundations'. (XXVIII, 88). The problem was to be, to what extent could the importation of Western culture and thought continue before it caused a fatal break with the past.

Ōgai returned to Berlin on 16 April 1887. In contrast to his life in the other three cities, his 'Berlin period' was somewhat dull, an ominous prelude to his return to Japan and official life within the army. The entries in the diary are uninteresting in the main and reflect this change of mood. He found himself forced to spend time with Japanese who were poles apart from his Munich friends. These men, not being interested in learning much about the country they were living in, kept very much to themselves. On 2 January 1888 Ōgai gave a speech at the Japanese club which he castigated as existing for no other purpose than to drink with compatriots instead of performing some useful function, such as representing Japan correctly in Berlin. That his strictures had no effect can be seen from a second speech, made on his departure, in which he apologized rather sarcastically for having been mistaken in his hopes for the society.

Ōgai's work under Robert Koch at the Hygienisches Institut of Berlin University, which had only opened in 1885, started promisingly. He attended the lectures, took part in research and practicals, and in May was given a research project of his own. This work was interrupted by the rather unwelcome arrival in Berlin of his superior, Ishiguro Tadanori, with whom Ōgai was forced to spend much time in attendance as translator, and not until October could he return to his own work.[22] Ishiguro's arrival in Germany forced Ōgai back into the position of subordinate after the freedom he had enjoyed for the last three years. It was a reluctant and uncomfortable return to the fold.

From 16 September to 6 October Ōgai accompanied Ishiguro to the fourth International Red Cross Congress at Karlsruhe, where, although officially he only acted as interpreter, he figures in the records as the main Japanese delegate. Here he had a chance meeting with Pompe van Meerdevoort, the Dutch doctor who had been in Japan from 1857 to 1862 and who had done so much to help the introduction of Western medicine. The party then moved on to Vienna to attend a meeting of the International Society for the Study of Hygiene. On 10 March 1888 he left for a short spell with the Prussian Imperial Guard, work of a tedious nature that he would, no doubt, have preferred to have refused if it had been possible, and he finally left Berlin for the return to Japan on 5 July 1888.

Ōgai's period in Berlin is of interest because it forms the background to his most famous story, 'Maihime', but much is left undocumented. There can be little doubt that expunged from the diary is the account of his relationship with a German girl, known to us as 'Elis', who was to follow him to Japan, but the details of this important affair will never be fully clear.[23] Whether as a result of this personal entanglement, his disappointment with his own countrymen in Berlin, or as a natural reaction to the loss of undreamed-of freedom, we know that Ōgai turned to the study of European philosophy while in Berlin. The dating, notes and underlining show that he read in particular two outlines of the history of Western philosophy which gave him the grounding in philosophical ideas, especially German Idealism, that was to play such a great part in his early literary criticism.[24]

The contrast between the voyage to Europe and his return is marked. The diary for the trip home, the 'Kantō nichijō', is short and contains little of interest apart from a few poems in Chinese. He passed through London where he met Ozaki Yukio, who had been barred from entering Tokyo as a result of the Peace Preservation Law in 1887, and when he reached Paris he wrote the following poem of condolence:

Does a snake show anger if it is not touched?
The best policy is to wait and see, and hold your tongue.
I remember that night at the quiet restaurant across the sea
Where we two outcasts talked together of our absurd anxieties.
(XXXV, 222)

Whether Ōgai saw himself as an outcast out of mere fellow feeling for Ozaki or because he too felt a certain sense of alienation from the Japan to which he was returning is not clear, but a sense of tension and foreboding was certainly in the air. Passing through the straits at the end of the Red Sea, he wrote:

How dull I was in those three years of study!
Coming home, how can I repay the Emperor's favour?
Not only the remorse of lost love weighs on my mind tonight
As the ship returns through the Gate of Tears. (XXXV, 223)

While it is of course possible that the poem was composed merely as an exercise to incorporate the name 'Bab el Mandeb' (Gate of Tears), the theme would also seem to fit in with the depressing nature of the voyage home. Perhaps he was only now feeling the full significance of his original decision to enter the army, his dream of travelling to Europe having been fulfilled. Perhaps the reference to lost love is more important. The only other clue we have to his emotional state on his return is the semi-autobiographical 'Mōsō' (Day-dreams), which he wrote in 1911. While it must always be kept in mind that 'Mōsō' is a peculiarly Japanese mixture of reminiscence, fact and speculation, and that its melancholy tone is far more typical of Ōgai in 1911 than in 1888, the following passage is of interest:

Glancing back to that country where the atmosphere was so conducive to the growth of Natural Sciences, I set out for the native land of my dreams. I had to leave of course, but I did not leave out of a feeling of duty. The balance of my desires, with a land of so many conveniences in one scale and my homeland in the other, definitely inclined towards the latter, despite the fact that a gentle white hand was softly pulling on the cord from which the former was suspended.

As the Siberian railway was not yet completed, I returned across the Indian Ocean. The way back always seems shorter than the way there, even if the trip takes only a day, and I had the same impression although my journey took forty or fifty days. In contrast to the past when I had set out full of hope to an unknown world, the voyage back seemed not only short but lonely. Reclining in my wicker deck-chair I thought about the presents I had in my trunk.

In my branch of the Natural Sciences I was not bringing back merely the results of my work. It was my intention to return with seeds which could be developed in the future. But the climate to nourish those seeds did not exist at home; at least not yet. I was worried lest these seeds might wither away to nothing, and was overcome with fatalism and a dark sense of depression . . .

In Ceylon I was sold a beautiful bird with blue wings by a man with a red checked cloth around his head and loins. When I came back to the ship carrying the cage, one of the French sailors made a strange gesture. 'Il ne vivra pas!' he said. That beautiful blue bird did indeed die before the ship reached Yokohama. It too was an ephemeral souvenir. (VIII, 206–7)

As Ōgai returned home, he must have been prey to a number of conflicting emotions. On the personal level he was leaving a land where he had, largely through his own efforts, experienced a rich and rewarding three years. He had gained a solid grounding in rigorous modern methods of scientific research under some of the most famous men in his field. He had gained too an unrivalled knowledge of European literature and thought, and had been accepted as an equal in the highest ranks of society. He was returning to a Japan where he had no such privileged position, where he would be subject to the whims of his superiors, and where family responsibilities would be reimposed. There was a natural sense of anticlimax, for there was little hope that his life in Japan would ever approach his European experience in variety or novelty.

On the broader scale he knew the distance that Japan had to travel to reach the goal of equality with the West, especially in the field of scientific research. It was the lack of a rational basis that was leading Japan into so many unnecessary and ill-considered steps, where a slight modification of the traditional way of doing things would have made more sense. He was a conservative only to the extent that he realized the value of much of Japanese culture at a time when most Japanese were in favour of radical Westernization. He had already experienced the unsettling contradiction between the need to import knowledge and his instinctive dislike of such a necessity as a patriotic Japanese. But he was, perhaps, one of the first Japanese to realize that modernization and Westernization were not synonymous concepts, however linked they might have seemed at the time. For Ōgai, the essential element in the former process was the rational, analytical mode of thought, and it was this seed that he knew would be the most difficult to transplant. Although he was fully aware of the danger if history and tradition were totally discarded, he drew hope and inspiration from the discovery that Germany had once been in a somewhat similar position, of having to rely on a foreign land for new knowledge and cultural guidance. His Berlin notes reveal how interested he was that modern European medicine had its source in Arabic medicine, and that until the advent of Lessing, Goethe and Schiller, Germany had looked entirely to France as its cultural mentor.[25]

The best comment on Ōgai's attitude while abroad is probably his own commentary. Talking of the dangers of excessive Japanese self-confidence in 1902, he said of his three years of study in Germany:

> Those of my companions who went to study abroad and kept to their own viewpoint from the very beginning produced very little in the way of results on their return. But those who first cleared their minds, listened to what they were taught, and only fixed their opinions after some considerable time, produced great results.
>
> Needless to say, when men like myself first went to Europe we felt just like rustics arriving in a big city. But I do not regret this in the slightest even now. And so I would say every time: if you want to get the best results from your travel abroad, discard the mental apperception you have before you go and rebuild this faculty anew once you reach that foreign land. It is no use taking your trunk with you on your back hoping to store what you learn in its drawers. You must build a trunk when you get there. (XXXIV, 225)

A rational basis for modernization

The five years between Ōgai's return to Japan in September 1888 and his departure for Korea and the Sino-Japanese War in November 1894 were marked by intense activity in both medical and literary journalism, as he tried to put to the best possible use his experience and knowledge of Europe. Through a succession of polemics carried out in his own and other journals, he made his voice heard on most of the important questions of the day. At times these debates were conducted with such ferocity that it seems as if he were trying to sublimate his frustration with his own personal and official problems. His efforts during these years were to earn him notoriety as an angry young man, and his belligerence and intransigence were to cause much trouble later on in his career.[26]

His first pronouncement on arriving home was quite remarkable.

Standing in front of his colleagues who were all agog to hear an absorbing account of his trip, he said:

> Today I should be speaking to you about what I saw abroad, but there are various reasons why I cannot take it upon myself to do so. In European armies, where rules are especially strict, it is generally the case that when young officers make statements in connection with army matters, they first report the gist to their superiors. Once they have obtained permission they can then make a speech in public. In this way regulations are maintained. Personally I am envious of this system. I am not saying that I would want this to be generally applicable in the Japanese army as well, but as far as I myself am concerned, although I do have things to tell you some day, I would rather have them checked by a superior first. This is why I do not wish to ramble on freely about it today. (XXVIII, 50)

It is almost impossible to take this at face value, although whether Ōgai was complaining that he had not received permission or had actually had his speech heavily censored is not clear. He was not to remain muzzled for long, however.

Ōgai's interests in the field of medicine can be divided into two broad categories, practical and pure — that is public hygiene and scientific research. The first question to demand his attention was practical and concerned the Japanese diet. In view of his interest in the problem in Germany it was only natural that he should pursue it, and he reiterated his opinion that rice was a perfectly adequate basis for the diet.[27] In a very strong speech, given a few months after his return, we have an early example of his method and his forthright opinions: the outright rejection of traditional learning, the stress on the increasing role that medicine had to play in the modern world, and the desire that the Japanese should be made aware of what was meant by public health. Talking of the increasing trend towards the popularization of more advanced medical ideas, he said:

> This change is not confined to the public sphere. It is even more noticeable among doctors themselves. That group of shaven-headed priests who used to crawl and grovel around testing pulses and examining tongues have already disappeared from the face of the earth. Today's men of medicine are directly concerned in the business of government. They are part of the machinery of the courts when they deal with legal medicine, and when they debate matters to do with the Red Cross they are dealing in international affairs. They are now in fact assuming a large role — that of hygiene — in internal administration. It is hardly surprising that men like the Austrian Röhner and the

German Virchow have become pioneers in the process of civilization and appear in the forefront of society. (XXVIII, 78-9)

There is here an implicit conflict with authority in the statement
that it was the duty of men of medicine to busy themselves with
matters which impinged on the administration of the whole state. The
tension between a conservative administrative body and a progressive
doctor can clearly be seen in the case of the German, Rudolf Virchow
(1821-1902), one of the outstanding names in modern medicine.
Virchow's work with disease went hand in hand with his activities as
a social reformer, and he was continually in trouble for his liberalism.
With this example staring Ōgai in the face it is not surprising that problems with the authorities were soon to emerge.

Another area in which Ōgai showed interest was housing and city
planning. Reminiscing about his early activities, he wrote in 'Mōsō'
(1911):

> In Tokyo the debate about the reconstruction of the city was
> at its height, and the smart set wanted to build houses in the
> style the Germans call *Wolkenkratzer,* skyscrapers, which the
> Americans number in blocks. I argued that when too many
> people live in a confined space the death rate is high, in particular
> for children. Rather than piling houses on top of each other —
> houses which had been arranged horizontally up to now — it
> would make more sense to reconstruct the water supply and the
> sewerage.
>
> Then there was a committee formed which wanted to impose
> restrictions on architecture, saying that we should try to achieve
> the beauty of an ordered exterior by standardizing the height of
> roofs in Tokyo. I argued that houses lined up like so many
> soldiers on parade were not at all attractive. If we really wanted
> the Western style, we should, on the contrary, forget about the
> height and let each particular form of architecture have its own
> roof. It would be better to build the fine spectacle of a random
> mixture as they had in Venice. (VIII, 208)

Ōgai had already touched on the question of housing in Germany.
He knew very well that Tokyo had a chance to avoid many of the pit-
falls of growth that were so evident in European cities. That chance
was not to be lost. He was insistent on the formation of building
regulations as soon as possible, primarily from the point of view of
public health. He believed, using the opinions of foreigners who had
visited Japan as extra proof, that the traditional Japanese house was
superior to the European in most respects, especially when the climate
was taken into consideration. Two major drawbacks were the danger
of fire and the problem of heating in winter, but from the point of

view of ventilation and the amount of light per floor space they were ideal. It is of interest that he did not refer at all to their aesthetic qualities, for to him the matter was primarily one of hygiene.

As a result of his undoubted knowledge of European cities, Ōgai was asked by the Committee for the Renovation of Tokyo in October 1888 to undertake part-time investigation into building regulations. Mainly in reply to this request, but also to stress his own views, he wrote a number of articles on the subject.[28] He was concerned that public hygiene was not being given priority in the reconstruction plans. One important part of the decision process was the correct use of statistics to compute population growth balanced against the concept of an ideal size for the city. His proposals, based on German guidelines, were for the modern concept of a garden city, but it is clear that his grasp of the theories involved, and his demand that all the resources of modern science should be brought to bear on the problem, were far more advanced than anything that could be attempted in Japan in 1890.

Ōgai was also interested in the provision of housing for the poorer working class, the 'proletariat'. The suggestion of one critic, that only by chasing out the poor and destroying their tenements could a hygienic, modern city be created, was, he felt, not only impractical but pernicious:

> If this idea is proposed and accepted, then the reconstruction of the city will be for the benefit of the rich and to the detriment of the poor. Public health will be the health of the rich.
>
> This view of hygiene is quite widely held throughout Japan and we should not put the blame all on this one writer. But I cannot but be amazed at this interpretation of the word 'public'. What it amounts to is that the poor are a menace to themselves and others. What is the best way to remedy such a situation? If we were to follow the writer's suggestion, chase out the dangerous poor and drive them outside the city boundaries, this would mean we were throwing public health out of the window with the poor. Whatever you say, the rich who live within the city boundaries are just a small part of the public and by no means the whole. Without the public, what happens to public health? (XXVIII, 136)

This striking defence of the concept of public health and the duties of those concerned in its administration is typical of Ōgai. He had been brought up with the Confucian concept of cultural responsibility and all his life was to feel the drive to educate and fight stupidity. The traditional moral demands on the ruler with respect to the ruled were not far removed from the relationship between government and people that modern public health was based on. When most of the talk in Japan was of externals, Ōgai was concerned with essentials. Moderniza-tion had to be based on a rational appraisal rather than on an emotional reaction. It was thus that he found himself defending geta on grounds of hygiene, 'Kutsu? Geta?' (Shoes or geta?) in May 1889, and deciding in January 1890 that, faced with the possibility of unchecked growth of venereal disease, a system of licensed areas was the lesser of two evils, 'Kōshōhai-go no saku ikan' (On the best policy after public prostitution has been abolished).

In keeping with his self-appointed role as public educator, journalism played a large part in his early attempts to popularize knowledge: a journalism modelled on the German counterpart which had so impressed him.[29] The foundation of a modern system of public health would prove easier if everyone knew the reasons for certain measures, and this meant that the people must stop looking on the government as something remote which occasionally ordered troublesome measures for no apparent reason. The aim must therefore be to educate the people to think rationally for themselves, for only by so doing could the correct balance be maintained in the reciprocal relationship of ruler and ruled. Ōgai was convinced that this ideal was possible:

> Hygiene is essential. If hygiene is disregarded, health cannot be maintained. When health is lost the basis of all work crumbles. Once people at least realize this, why can they not then pro-gress by themselves, grasp authority over hygiene, discard their sense of dependence on officials for their health, and so take the first step towards escaping from oppression by putting hygienic methods into practice on their own! . . . .
>
> We are not saying, however, that the authorities have nothing to do with hygiene. On the contrary, public health is one import-ant aim of government. The people have the right to turn to the government and demand 'Make us healthy!', and the government has the responsibility to turn to the people and say 'Make your-selves healthy!' All we want to do is to define that part which belongs to government and that part which should be carried out by the people, and we hope that they will not interfere with one another . . .
>
> Japanese today have come of age and do not need to suck at their mother's breast, of course. But if the mother still wants to suckle the child and the child makes no protest and accepts it, then where are we to put the blame? (XXIX, 5–6)

What is being said here is reasonable, but the expression of it is certainly unusual for a member of the army. Underlying the argument is the implicit suggestion that the correct education of the people must presuppose their intellectual liberation. Exactly what 'oppression' the people must rid themselves of is not clear, but these liberal sentiments contain elements of a conflict that was to be a key theme of his writings.

Part of the modernization of Japanese medicine entailed the gradual demise of old methods based on traditional Chinese medicine, known as *kampō*. Not only Ōgai but also his predecessors saw this as a necessary step, but the practical problems were enormous. Doctors could not be trained overnight, and there were very few who had knowledge of modern techniques. When Ōgai graduated in 1881 there were 63 graduates from the medical course compared with 37,000 *kampō* practitioners; the imbalance was still overwhelming in 1889.[30] Ōgai was convinced that traditional medicine was a mere cipher,[31] and so new Japanese medicine could never be anything but a pure import. His insistence that *kampō* was little more than charlatanism appears very soon after his return from Germany and became a recurrent theme. What he was unwilling to accept was that, given the ratio at that time, the traditional doctors had to be accepted for the time being as a stopgap. He wanted to change things too fast.

> We now know that you cannot build a generation of medicine from one man's experience. We also know that when one compares the stagnant classics of Japanese and Chinese medicine with modern medical learning they have no real value and are merely of historical interest. In the world of today there is only one medicine: modern medicine. Anything which does not have this foundation is on a par with the acupuncture of the priests, the old cure for ringworm, and herbalists. That the government is letting them have their last breath is merely a policy of expediency. (XXIX, 458)

Despite his vigorous campaign against traditional medicine, Ōgai knew its canon fairly well, and, according to Koike's letter of recommendation, had been interested in it from his student days. The outright rejection of tradition in this case is understandable if one takes into account his desire that medicine and indeed all science should be put on a rational foundation. It should not be forgotten, however, that Ōgai was to return to the subject of these practitioners and study them in greater detail near the end of his life.

The importance of Ōgai's work in journalism was that it not only dealt with army hygiene but spanned the whole area of public health. With the example of Virchow before him, Ōgai found himself proclaiming on a variety of social problems in a liberal and enlightened manner. As an army doctor he was to find that circumstances were to curtail this direct involvement in social questions, but at this stage he threw himself into every argument with enthusiasm. Underlining all his actions was the belief that the discussion of hygiene was *not* meaningless to 'people who go about with geta thongs between their toes'. His sense of mission, which expressed itself through the desire to educate, was never to leave him, although the peak of activity was during these first few years after his return.

Reminiscing in 1911, in 'Mōsō', Ōgai wrote:

> I was received with disappointment by my friends in Japan, and not without reason. To return as I did was unprecedented. Those before me had come back bright with hope, taking out the things they had brought in their cases and showing off some new trick or other. I did exactly the opposite . . . So whenever people tried to reform things, I advocated that they should be kept as they were, and was thus driven into the company of conservatives. Later, for different motives, it became popular to return to Japan as a conservative, but I was probably the first to do so.
>
> (VIII, 208–9)

There is, as we have seen, more than a grain of truth here. A glance at Ōgai's official life would also suggest such a conclusion. During the five years between his return and his departure for Korea much of his time was taken up with lecturing. He was lecturer at the Military Academy and the Military Staff College, and also taught anatomy at the Tokyo Academy of Fine Arts from June 1889 and at Keiō University from September 1892. In 1891 he was honoured with the degree of Doctor of Medicine, a distinction held by only thirty other men in Japan at the time. In 1893 he was appointed Head of the Military Academy with the rank of Surgeon Lieutenant-Colonel, and from that time on found that administration took up more and more of his time.

To characterize the young Ōgai as a conservative, however, would be grossly misleading, since he favoured tradition in certain fields as a result of rational thought rather than any preconceived pattern. Apart from the introduction of practical medicine, Ōgai was most concerned that the scientific method itself should be imported as soon as possible. Only by transplanting the very roots of Western medicine could Japan hope to achieve equality in the intellectual sphere. If merely the fruits of knowledge were imported, Japan would be for ever dependent on foreign inventiveness, and would never be able to contribute to the advance of science in the world. This was not merely a matter of the trappings of research, but demanded a radical change in traditional attitudes – a mental revolution. It was in the effort to spur on the development of such a change that Ōgai was at his most belligerent, and it was here that he met his heaviest opposition.

Undoubtedly, one of the reasons why Ōgai felt so strongly that the introduction of the modern scientific method was imperative was that European medicine itself had only recently been transformed from an art into a science. Ōgai and his fellow students at the university had studied under men whose contemporaries, such as Pettenkofer, Virchow and Koch, had revolutionized medicine, and while in Germany he had had the great fortune to work under these men; it is hardly surprising that he should have been intensely aware of the spirit that informed them. Ōgai's insistence on the independence of learning and the inevitable clash with the deeply rooted system of seniority in Japan made him few friends in the army hierarchy. His first argument was with Koike Masanao over whether reports of Japanese research should be published in German as well as Japanese. Ōgai was not so naïve as to think that Japanese science could achieve recognition without the use of a more international language. Science was not a tool to be used by nationalists, but the common property of all nations.

A more serious debate, however, was one over the correct translation and the real meaning of the word 'statistics', which started in February 1889 and lasted until November, becoming more personal and vituperative as it progressed. This process by which he came into direct and bitter confrontation with his superiors was given further impetus by his uncompromising attitude to the first Japan Medical Congress.[32] As a result of an article which sharply criticized its aims and in which some of the most important figures in the Japanese medical world were presented as a clique of villains, Ōgai incurred much displeasure, and it was in reaction to this that he wrote in December 1889:

> At the moment in the medical world I am indeed the general of a defeated army, alone and independent, like a horse without a cart or a dog without a master . . . I returned to Japan in the September of 1888, and from January this year I founded a debate column in the *Tōkyō Iji Shinshi*, which lasted until last month (November). It was somewhat arbitrary and rambling, but the arguments were hard hitting and time and time again caused me unlooked-for problems. There were a number of elements who wanted to obstruct my activities. They planned in secret, spread their net in secret, and with their superior weight brought down my beloved column. Yes, my column has been destroyed. Those swarming ants broke down the barricades. Some people may have thought that the reactionaries would have jumped at this chance and risen in a flood to bury me for ever. That proves they do not know me very well! As I have promised in the past —

though my honour be besmirched and my future activities blocked, my spirit is invincible! My spirit will never be crushed!

(XXIX, 333–4)

Ōgai continued with the conflict when the Congress actually took place in the April of 1890. We know from a letter dated 3 April that at the last moment he cancelled a speech he was to have given on hygiene. He was almost alone in his extraordinary boycott. It is not difficult to see why Ōgai's superiors, and in particular Ishiguro, were galled at such behaviour. Ōgai's enthusiasm for hastening the process of education had brought him into conflict with the most revered men in his field; and for an army doctor teaching at the Academy such fire and belligerence must have been unparalleled. From this time on, Ōgai's career in the army was almost to assume the guise of a succession of personal feuds.

One might be forgiven for supposing that Ōgai had done enough damage. But the worst was yet to come. There was an interlude of three years between this attack on the first Congress and the next outburst. In the meantime, Ōgai had been given the degree of Doctor of Medicine in 1891 and had devoted himself mainly to literary controversies. The whole complaint against the older generation welled up again, however, in the April of 1893 when the second Congress was held.

It was in the articles that he wrote on this occasion, articles which continued for over a year until he left for Korea, that all the radical elements in Ōgai's approach so far became sharply defined. It was in the pages of his own *Eisei Ryōbyōshi* that his all-out attack on the medical establishment took place. For Ōgai it was rather a lonely battle, as one can surmise from the name of the special column he devoted to the subject, the 'Bōkan kikan' or 'Spectator's medium'. He used the word 'bōkan' in a very different sense from that of a resigned bystander — an attitude which is representative of his middle age only, and which has become a cliché of Ōgai criticism. These 'comments from the sideline' were the very essence of passionate commitment. In the first of these articles, entitled 'The reactionaries and the spectator', he described his superiors as a collection of 'old schemers' using younger 'hypocrite scholars' as a front for their reactionary activities. The second Congress, which he disdainfully referred to as the 'Festival of the Reactionaries', was ostensibly under the control of the younger men, but Ōgai knew and regretted that the old guard were behind them.

Two major points can be extracted from this bitter and lengthy argument. When criticized for saying that research results would have to be written in a more international language, he did not spare his ridicule. He likened such a narrow view of nationalism, *falsche*

Patriotismus, to the attitude of Hideyoshi demanding that the Chinese
should speak Japanese. Ōgai was very well aware, if no one else was, of
Japan's true position in the world of learning. There was also his continued insistence on the freedom of thought. It was for this reason,
he considered, that authority over learning should be in the hands of
the bona fide academics and kept out of the grasp of the medical
establishment. He classed the 'old schemers' as politicians (*seikaku*),
and even equated conservatism in the medical world with that in the
political world. 'Reactionary attitudes seem to be symbolic of the
whole state of Japan today. If I was a reporter of an ordinary newspaper and debated matters of politics, I have no doubt that I would
be complaining of reactionary attitudes in government circles' (XXX,
572).

The belief in progress, the ambition for himself and Japan, and the
impatience with the older generation were all part of youth. But his
persistence and intransigence were highly unusual and are a measure
of his self-confidence in the face of traditional modes of thought. The
battle for the independence of learning was in contrast to the spirit of
the Imperial Rescript on Education which stressed the importance of
purely national goals, and his internationalism was far too advanced for
a state that was only just beginning to flex its muscles.

There is, however, another side to this radicalism. As a man of outstanding intellect and a born educator, he was not arguing for the
destruction of authority, merely for its transference. There can be
little doubt that much of the bitterness revealed in this debate was
personal. It came as the culmination of much frustration which had
built up over the years since he had been manoeuvred into the army
on leaving university. He himself felt instinctively that he was a member
of an intellectual elite, the *Geistesaristokratie* as he called it (XXX,
480), although in reality he was to stand alone all his life.

2

FIRST STEPS TOWARDS A NEW LITERATURE

Background

The transference of Western literary concepts into Meiji Japan was a long and difficult task, demanding a far deeper understanding of Western culture than was necessary for the industrial, military or institutional modernization. The initial reaction was one of indifference; once Japan became a powerful nation, what need would it have for Western literature? The first writings of the 'enlighteners' such as Nishi Amane and Fukuzawa Yukichi were inspired by a desire to popularize practical knowledge of the West. Facts, techniques and the spirit of scientific enquiry were essential if Japan was to withstand the European onslaught, but literature and more subtle aspects were hardly considered necessary and inevitably took second place. As a result, the imaginative writing of the first decades of the Meiji era showed no appreciable change from that of the late Tokugawa.

Literature in Japan, however, had fallen to a very low ebb. The robust realism of earlier Tokugawa writers such as Saikaku had long been lost. There remained the mere light-hearted and trivial work of the so-called *gesakusha,* among them men like Mantei Ōga (1818–90), Kanagaki Robun (1829–94), and Takabatake Ransen (1838–85). The upheavals Japan was experiencing, the radical changes which left hardly anyone untouched, went by almost unnoticed in their works. There was the occasional satire which ridiculed the Western fads that were sweeping the country, of which *Aguranabe* (The Beefeater, 1871) by Robun is perhaps the best known. But in general the subject matter still centred on the pleasure quarters and the lives of the courtesans — the old themes. They were 'books of formless, almost meaningless gossip'[1] with a liberal spicing of libidinous fantasy. The writers themselves were treated as unworthy hacks. Despite the occasional attempt to correct this situation, they and their profession were despised and ignored by the intellectuals, and no serious scholar ever considered demeaning himself by writing fiction.

There was, however, material for the more seriously minded reader. There were reprints of works in the style of the allegorical, historical romances of which Takizawa Bakin (1767–1848) had been the prime exponent. The traditional Confucian attitude towards literature was that it had to be morally edifying to be justifiable, the watchword being *kanzen chōaku* (the castigation of vice and the encouragement of virtue). The style of these interminable romances was heavily influenced by Chinese, the characters stereotyped, and the plot manipulated to point a moral. Realism in such a context was unnecessary, indeed unthinkable.

Gradually writers began to notice that the status of literature in the West was somewhat higher than in Japan. Work began in earnest in the 1880s to introduce European literature through translation, although the results were often of dubious quality, managing in many cases to transpose little more than the plot. The selection was at first understandably indiscriminate, but the political novels of Disraeli and Bulwer-Lytton soon became established as favourites.

From here it was only a short step to 'political' novels by the Japanese themselves, such as Yano Fumio's *Keikoku Bidan* (A Noble Tale of Statesmanship, 1883), and Shiba Shirō's *Kajin no Kigū* (Strange Encounters with Elegant Females, 1885), but these thinly disguised romances, political theory gift-wrapped in a florid style for easy consumption, are now no more than literary curiosities. Their popularity was closely connected to the rise of the newspapers and the activities of·the People's Rights Movement, and their decline was in turn related to the waning of interest in politics among the young that became apparent after the granting of the Constitution in 1889.

The political novel was followed by the works of Ozaki Kōyō (1867–1903) and Kōda Rohan (1867–1947), who, although very different writers, became famous at almost the same time, 1890. In 1885 Kōyō had founded a loosely knit group of writers known as the Ken'yūsha who produced a literary journal called *Garakuta Bunko* for the next four years. The group attempted to revive the realistic elements of Tokugawa writing, and Kōyō, who studied the style of Saikaku in great detail, made considerable strides in this direction. Their undoubted success was due in part to the resurgence of interest in traditional culture that followed the excesses of the *Rokumeikan* era, when Western fads reached their height, but in retrospect the reputation of many of these stories has suffered. Despite the attempt to introduce a certain realism, the majority still portray stereotyped characters, and the atmosphere is more akin to Edo than to modern Tokyo. Although Kōda Rohan was later to show an interest in realism, he concentrated at this early stage on such themes as artistic inspiration and obsession, and his view of literature as essentially 'poetic' had, as we shall see, similarities with Ōgai's position.

It was then to be many years before anything like a modern realistic novel was accepted as the norm. The literary history of the years from 1880 to 1900 concerns the struggle by those writers who were convinced that this was the form of literature most capable of expressing the spirit of the age; a struggle against the continuing popularity of less realistically conceived works; a struggle to educate the intelligent reading public to accept their theories. Against the background of the novels of Kōyō and Rohan, we must picture a different kind of writing, more isolated from the public at first, intent on creating a revolution in literature, but not clear as to the direction it should take. The movement towards modern realism entailed an internal struggle and argument among these writers as to the nature of the new literature they envisaged. It was a period of polemic and overstatement. Like all other innovators in the Meiji period, they were faced with not one but a multitude of theories from which to choose, and underlying all their work was the impossibility of the total rejection of their own cultural heritage.

The year 1885 can be conveniently taken as marking the real beginning of the introduction of European concepts of literature into Japan, especially in the field of the novel. It was in that year that Tsubouchi Shōyō published the first part of his long essay on the novel, *Shōsetsu Shinzui* (The Essence of the Novel). From his studies of English literature Shōyō was convinced that the novel, rather than poetry or drama, was the best instrument for the modern writer. As he stated in the preface, the Japanese novel as it stood, however, was inadequate:

> It has long been the custom in Japan to consider the novel as an instrument of education, and it has frequently been proclaimed that the novel's chief function is the castigation of vice and the encouragement of virtue. In actual practice, however, only stories of bloodthirsty cruelty or else of pornography are welcomed, and very few readers indeed even cast so much as a glance on works of a more serious nature. Moreover, since popular writers have no choice but to be devoid of self-respect and in all things slaves to public fancy and the lackeys of fashion, each one attempts to go to greater lengths than the last in pandering to the tastes of the time.[2]

The popular fiction of the *gesakusha* and similar writers had to be discarded and the reading public re-educated. This did not mean a return to the didactic novels of Bakin however, for, although serious and therefore worthy of attention, they were written with a specific moral purpose in mind and did not demand the kind of realistic portrayal of human emotions that Shōyō saw as central to the English novel. Although he tried to distinguish between two types of novel, the didactic and the artistic, he in effect nullified the distinction by the claim that the latter could also teach by portraying truths. What he was in fact propounding was a Victorian view of the novel as an art form that could appeal to the moral sense of the reader through the artistically pleasing portrayal of the truth of reality. By stressing the element of realism, the element that was most noticeably lacking in traditional stories, Shōyō did not want to underplay either the artistic or moral considerations. His prime intention was to prove the seriousness of the novel and of literature in general. His contemporaries, however, took the essay as an attack on didacticism and a manifesto for pure realism. It took Ōgai to see that Shōyō was not rejecting the moral element totally, and this was partly because Ōgai was to take a far more definite stand on the clear separation of art, truth and morality.[3]

Shōyō was, it turned out, a better critic than a writer, and it was left to his friend, Futabatei Shimei, to write what has been called Japan's first modern novel, *Ukigumo* (Drifting Clouds, 1887-9), which stands out as a remarkable tour de force and was not to be equalled for many years.

This, in outline, was the state of literature when Ōgai returned in September 1888, and within a few months he had thrown himself wholeheartedly into the debate. His return was of great significance, for he was the first of the young writers to have experienced Western culture at first hand. He was, of course, chiefly responsible for the introduction of German literature and literary forms, through translations, but he also felt urged to produce some original work based on his experiences in Germany.

Translations

One year after his return from Germany, in August 1889, the collection of translated poems entitled *Omokage* (Visions) was published in the magazine *Kokumin no Tomo. Omokage* was the result of collaboration between Ōgai, Ochiai Naobumi (1861-1903), then a lecturer at the Imperial Institute for the Study of Classical Japanese Literature, Inoue

Michiyasu (1866–1941), a student of medicine at Tokyo University, Ichimura Sanjirō (1864–1947), lecturer at the Gakushūin, and Ōgai's sister, Kimiko, who had married Koganei Yoshikiyo in the April of that year. The group called themselves the Shinseisha, or the S.S.S., and it was the payment for this collection of poems that made possible the founding of the journal, *Shigarami-zōshi,* in October 1889. From the later recollections of Ichimura it is clear that the driving force behind the group was Ōgai himself:

> My long standing friendship with Mori began with the Shinseisha . . . So we were not schoolboy friends. It came about because Mori and Kako Tsurudo knew each other well and the circle grew from there; Kako knew Inoue Michiyasu, Inoue knew me and I knew Ochiai Naobumi. It was, of course, the result of a gradual process of introduction, but it was all due to Mori's initiative that the group was formed. It's true that from the very moment he returned from Germany he had great ambitions to play an active part in literary circles. It was entirely due to this desire that he gathered us all together and undertook the work of the Shinseisha.
>
> Our actual activity began with the production of *Omokage* in the summer supplement to *Kokumin no Tomo,* August 1889. It was made up of seventeen translations under the pen-name, S.S.S., our collective title. We planned to create a great sensation in the literary world at the time . . .
>
> Sometime before this, when we received the request from *Kokumin no Tomo,* we met at Mori's house, which was then in Hanazono-chō, Ueno. We sat up late into the night congratulating ourselves on our future prospects and making outlandish plans. As I remember, that was when the title *Omokage* was decided on . . . It was so called after a discussion between Mori and Ochiai.[4]

In 1905, Ōgai himself wrote a short introduction to a reprint of the collection recalling that night:

> We chose the poems with no special plans in mind and collected them in no special order. Everyone in the group sat late into the night at my house which overlooked the Shinobazu pond. When I recall that time we compiled this volume, every poem, every pause, every phrase and every word conjures up deep emotions. In particular I remember Ochiai Naobumi who translated the poem about the trumpeter on Capri — he was so soon to be numbered among the dead. (XIX, 618)

The collection was prefaced by two poems which were chosen to symbolize the intention of the authors. The first was from the third book of the *Manyōshū:*

Michinoku no   Far off as the reed-plain of Mano
Mano no kayahara   Lies in 'Road's End',
Tōkedomo   Yet in vision, they say,
Omokage ni shite   It can be seen.[5]
Miyu to u mono o

The operative word here is vision (*omokage*), and the use of it as the title suggests that the translations were to be seen as a vision of far-off Europe.

The second poem was an extract from lines by the Sung poet, Su Tung-p'o (1063-1101):

Binga wa ten no ippō ni
Ungetsu wa waga katawara ni ari

The mountains of Min and Wo Mei tower to the heavens
But the clouds and moon are here by my side.

thus perhaps implying that the task of bringing far-away places into focus lies with the translator. The poems were to be an attempt to transmit some of the feeling and essence of the West to the reader.

The seventeen translations, mostly based on German originals, are treated in four different ways, thus providing an excellent example of how the problem presented by Western rhyme and metre was faced, and, to some extent, overcome.[6] The largest group, of eight, was intended merely to transmit the meaning of the original and so traditional Japanese and Chinese forms were used; one *tanka* (5, 7, 5, 7, 7 syllable metre), one *imayō* (four lines with a 7, 5 metre for each line), three 'extended *imayō*' (same 7, 5 pattern but an unspecified number of lines), and three Chinese *ku-shih* (ancient verse).

Far more interesting from the point of view of technique are the three other groups where something more than the mere meaning of the original is considered. Three of the poems, translated into the 'extended *imayō*' form mentioned above, attempt, in addition, to reproduce the rhyming pattern of the original. A particularly successful example was the translation of Ophelia's song from *Hamlet*:

Ophelia no uta

Wie erkenn' ich dein Treulieb	Izure o kimi ga koibito to	A
Vor den andern nun	Wakite shirubeki sube ya aru	B
An dem Muschelhut und Stab	Kai no kammuri to tsukuzue to	A
Und den Sandalschuhn.	Hakeru kutsu to zo shirushi naru	B
Er ist lange tot und hin	Kare wa shinikeri waga hime yo	C

Tot und hin, Fräulein!	Kare wa yomiji e tachinikeri	D
Ihm zu Häupten ein Rasen grün,	Kashira no kata no koke o miyo	C
Ihm zu Fuss ein Stein.	Ashi no kata ni wa ishi tateri	D
Sein Leichenhemd weiss wie Schnee zu sehn	Hitsugi o ōu kinu no iro wa	E
Geziert mit Blumensegen	Takane no yuki to mimagainu	F
Das unbetränt zum Grab musst' gehn	Namida yadoseru hana no wa wa	E
Von Liebesregen.	Nuretaru mama ni hōmurinu	F

It is noticeable in this excellent rendition that the rhyme has actually been made much stricter than the German, and there are certain differences between the Japanese and the German which might be difficult to account for. Kobori Keiichirō, in his study of the collection, has proved conclusively that the poem was in fact translated from Shakespeare's original English, while the German, by Schlegel and Tieck, was only used as extra reference.[7] The last verse in particular shows much more in common with the English:

> White his shroud as the mountain snow,
> Larded all with sweet flowers;
> Which bewept to the grave did go,
> With true-love showers.

The mountain snow of the English has only 'white as snow' as a counterpart in the German, whereas 'takane no yuki' preserves the sense of 'mountain'; and, more importantly, the German has the negative 'unbetränt' where both the English and the Japanese have the positive 'bewept'.

That there were dangers in this attempt to reproduce the rhyme in Japanese, however, is clear from another poem in this group, 'Fue no ne':

Fue no ne (from J. V. Scheffel's *Der Trompeter von Säkkingen*)

Als ich zum erstenmal dich sah	Kimi o hajimete miteshi toki	—
Verstummten meine Worte	Sono ureshisa ya ika narishi	A
Er löste all mein Denken sich	Musubu omoi mo tokesomete	—
In schwellende Akkorde	Fue no ne to wa narinikeri	A
Drum steh' ich arm Trompeterlein	Omoi omoi no areba koso	—
Musizierend auf dem Rasen,	Yosugara kaku wa fukisusabe	B
Kann dir nicht sagen, was ich will,	Aware to kimi mo kikinekashi	—
Kann mein Lieb' nur blasen.	Kokoro kometaru fue no ne	B

This hardly deserves to be called an attempt at rhyming at all, although the poem itself improves, if anything, on the original. Ōgai himself noted that they had had problems with this poem:

> There is one poem in *Omokage* called 'Fue no ne', by the German Scheffel. I read it and then suggested to Ochiai that we should try and make the translation rhyme. He did so with enthusiasm. But because everything had been done in such a rush there were some mistakes. I asked him whether we could revise it before publication, but he was not too concerned, he said, and so we left it as it was. (XXVI, 37)

The question of whether the rhyme should be based on the last vowel or the last syllable was not fully resolved, and, in any case, the attempt to reproduce the rhyme in Japanese fails to have much effect due to the nature of the language.

If the attempt to incorporate rhyme as a significant element in Japanese poetry was not too successful, the third group of four poems, which experimented with new metres based to varying degrees on the syllable count of the originals, had great influence on later translations. Goethe's 'Mignon' was translated as follows:

> Kennst du das Land, wo die Zitronen blühn,
> Im dunkeln Laub die Gold-Orangen glühn,
> Ein sanfter Wind vom blauen Himmel weht,
> Die Myrte still und hoch der Lorbeer steht,
> Kennst du es wohl?
>   Dahin! Dahin!
> Möcht ich mit dir, o mein Geliebter, ziehn.[9]

> 'Remon' no ki wa hana saki kuraki hayashi no naka ni
> Kogane iro shitaru kōji wa e mo tawawa ni minori
> Aoku hareshi sora yori shizuyaka ni kaze fuki
> 'Mirute' no ki wa shizuka ni 'raureru' no ki wa tataku
> Kumo ni sobiete tateru kuni o shiru ya kanata e
> Kimi to tomo ni yukamashi

In this, the first of three verses, no attempt has been made to reproduce the rhyme of the original, but the metre within the Japanese lines 20, 21, 19, 20, 20 and 10 — syllables — would seem to be roughly based on a doubling of the predominantly 10-syllable lines of the original. This new metre of a 20-syllable line with a caesura at the 10th syllable was an interesting innovation, especially when the sense demanded that the caesura be run over in certain places, thus producing a kind of counterpoint. Ten syllables was, however, to prove too large a unit to handle and has never been very popular.

A somewhat different adaptation was tried in 'Ashi no kyoku' which was based on a poem by the German, Lenau. The first of three verses begins:

Drüben geht die Sonne scheiden,	Hi wa katabukikeri anata no kishi ni
Und der müde Tag entschlief.	Hine mo sutsukareshi hiru mo nemurinu
Niederhangen hier die Weiden	Kono ike no tsura ni midori no iro no
In den Teich, so still, so tief.[10]	Fukaku mo utsureru aoyagi no ito

Rather than a doubling of syllables here, the 8, 7, 8, 7 metre of the original has been adapted to form four 8/7-syllable lines in the Japanese. This method of inventing a new metrical foot was repeated in the poem 'Aru toki' which had an 8/6-syllable line corresponding to the 8, 6 metre of the original. The fourth poem in this group, part of Byron's *Manfred,* had a similar 10/10 count to 'Mignon no uta', although the German translation by Heine that they worked on had an irregular blank verse line.

The 8/7 and 8/6 metre line had already been used for Christian prayers and songs and was to prove to be a more valid contribution than either the rather unwieldy 10/10 line, which did not seem to fit well with the 'specific gravity'[11] of the poetic language, or the experiments with rhyme, which were doomed to failure owing to the paucity of Japanese vowel sounds.

The fourth and last group of poems in this collection comprises only two examples, but is in many ways the most interesting of them all. With a translation of another of Lenau's poems, 'Das Mondlicht', and a song from Byron's *Manfred,* or rather Heine's version of Byron, an attempt was made to transmit not only the meaning and rhyme, but also the rhythm within the line. As this could not be done in Japanese, the translations were into classical Chinese, in which both rhyme and rhythm could be simulated. Using one character for each syllable in the original, the Chinese tone pattern of 'level' and 'deflected' was ingeniously made to correspond with the 'long' and 'short' syllables of the German, and care was taken to ensure that the rhyme, possible in Chinese, was also correctly transposed. This attempt was, of course, a purely academic exercise, because the German poem would not have been read out in accordance with the strict trochaic pattern but counterpointed with the natural stress of the language, and, more important perhaps, when the Chinese poem was read out in the Japanese, it would lose all the effect of the carefully chosen tones. So, although a technical success of considerable complexity, it is not surprising that this method of translation never met with much favour. The question of precedent is a difficult one. It seems that a Dutch poem was translated by Ōtsuki Gentaku in 1816 using a somewhat similar method, but this is the only example found to date and it is doubtful whether Ōgai ever came across that earlier poem.[12] While it is possible that translations of this type had been attempted in China before this date, it is reasonable to attribute Ōgai's to his ingenuity alone.

Ōgai had shown his concern with the problem of translating poetry even before *Omokage* was produced, when in March 1889 he wrote in an article entitled 'Shugyō ga shitai': 'Of course when translating Western poetry into Chinese one could force matters somewhat, making the trochees and iambics correspond to the level and deflected tones, and producing hexameters and pentameters. But what are we going to do about this rhythm if we try to transpose it, as Ningetsu has done, into Japanese?' (XXXVIII, 453)[13]

In another article, written in the April but later rewritten in 1896 for inclusion in the collection of critical and other essays entitled *Tsukikusa,* he remarked:

> In today's 'new style poetry' we do have rhyme, but as I see it, it stands to reason that the Japanese language will not really allow rhyme. The present writers of this poetry just press on without realizing this. Needless to say, they write badly and have nothing to teach us. With the exception of one or two famous poems, Japanese poetry uses on the whole a metrical foot based on a syllable count. The words which correspond to Western prepositions are all gathered at the end of phrases. Japanese is quite different from Western languages where phrases end in uninflected verbs. We have a repetition of suffixes such as 'te', 'ni', 'keri' and 'ran'. It is hardly surprising that we find rhyme difficult. (XXII, 5)

It is of interest that despite his views he was to experiment with rhyme some four months later, although it may have been on the insistence of Ochiai Naobumi that the attempt was made. Ōgai discussed criticism of the collection itself soon after it was published:

> The idea of poetry does not change because its form changes. Whether one expresses it in old or modern words, Chinese characters or Western script, it all comes to the same thing . . . It is better of course if you can transmit both feeling and form when translating poetry. You could say that to transmit the feeling alone is to import the literary tastes of that country, whereas to transmit just the form is to import a foreign structure. They are both effective in their own way. German tastes,

for instance, were imported into Russia, and the Alexandrine structure was imported into Northern Europe.

In the *Omokage* translations we were mainly concerned to transmit the taste, but we were loath to reject the phrasing, metre and rhyme. We knew very well how dubious it was to try and pick up both root and bud, but we tried a little transplantation . . .

Yoda Gakkai criticized *Omokage* as follows: 'Prose is mainly concerned with the quality of the content, and style is of secondary importance. Poetry is naturally mainly concerned with style and rhythm. This is where one should distinguish between competence and the lack of it; it has nothing whatever to do with content. Prose can be translated, whereas poetry cannot. Even if a translated poem does have beauty, it is the beauty of the translated poem, not of the original. The beauty of the original is bound to be lost. It is a pointless exercise.' Harsh words!

At first glance this theory is reasonable. But sound is also important in prose. Han Yu said: 'The length of words and the level of the tones should all be correct', and the beauty of Gutzkow's prose is based on metre and constructed like verse. The importance of content in poetry needs no special pleading. Imaginative creativity and technical skill should be evaluated similarly in either type of writing.

Prose is obviously easier to translate into Japanese than poetry, but whether the beauty of the original work is lost or not is entirely up to the skill of the translator; it does not relate to the difference between prose and poetry. If the translations in *Omokage* are a pointless exercise, I have not much future ahead of me in the literary world. Perhaps I should think of becoming a critic. Yes, harsh words indeed! (XIX, 67-8)[14]

Omokage reveals a willingness to experiment with new metres and rhyme, but the prime object was to transmit the 'essence' of poetry by all available means. For this reason, traditional metres were as acceptable as new ones. Ōgai's main criticism of the only other compilation of translations before *Omokage*, *Shintaishi-shō*, was that many of the subjects treated were not poetic — he was in no way dogmatic about whether one should use a new vocabulary or a new structure. As he wrote in a letter to a friend in October 1889: 'The "new style poetry" of Yatabe and Toyama is just not poetry. There is nothing wrong with using the Japanese *uta,* and Chinese poetry is by no means inferior to Western poetry, from Greece right down to the present' (XXXVI, 11).

The main influence of *Omokage* itself was through its subject matter, for as a collection of Romantic lyrics it greatly impressed younger writers such as Tōson and Tōkoku, who were to rise to prominence with their magazine, *Bungakkai*, in 1893. The question of direct influence is, of course, always a vexed one, but Tōson described the moving effect of reading 'Ophelia no uta' on him and his friends in his autobiographical novel, *Haru* (Spring), and it is also generally accepted that Tōkoku's interest in English Romanticism was given initial impetus by the Byron translations.

It may seem extravagant to claim too much for such a short collection of lyrics, but *Omokage* occupies an important position in the development of modern poetry in Japan. It showed for the first time that successful poems could be written in old and new metres, in addition to introducing some of the major themes and subjects of European Romantic poetry. Although perhaps not as adventurous as *Shintaishi-shō* in abandoning the artificial restrictions of a hallowed poetic vocabulary, it illustrated that experiment in new and unusual techniques of translation did not preclude the reaffirmation of the vitality of the classical language as a vehicle for modern poetic expression.

As Ōgai was fully aware that the introduction of Western literature through reliable translations was of paramount importance if Japan was truly to understand the nature of the European mind, the years from 1889 to 1892 saw a steady stream of twenty-two translations of European prose and drama. These were published for the most part in his own literary journal, *Shigarami-zōshi,* which he had founded in October 1889.[15]

Among the translations, French literature was represented by three poignant vignettes by Daudet, 'Kadour et Katel', 'Le Cabecilla' and 'Un teneur de livres', and a fragment from Rousseau's *Confessions.* From American literature he chose two short stories; Washington Irving's 'Rip van Winkle' and Bret Harte's 'High Water Mark', a tale of the miraculous escape of a woman and her child from a flood on the Dedlow marshes on the coast of California, interesting for its local colour and the vivid description of the power of natural forces. The four Russian works were: 'Lucerne' by Leo Tolstoy, a story of the inhumanity of a group of rich English tourists towards a poor ballad singer in Lucerne – a passionate account of a personal experience that burns with moral indignation; two very short pieces by Turgenev, and the chapter entitled 'Taman' from 'Pechorin's Journal' in Lermontov's *Geroi nashego vremeni* (A Hero of Our Times).

The rest of the translations were all from German originals and represent a strange mixture of *novellen.* Hoffmann's 'Das Fräulein von Scudery' is a forerunner of the detective story and has as its central theme the obsession of a master jeweller for the products of his own genius, and the crimes he commits to retrieve his jewels from the nobles who commission them. Hackländer's 'Zwei Nächte' and 'Fünfter Windstoss' in *Geschichten einer Wetterfahne* are two very inconsequential and second-rate stories: the former being an account of how an officer in the Hungarian army meets and falls in love with the daughter of the host at a post-station in Italy, only to find four years later when he revisits the area that she has married a brutal man who was subsequently shot as a spy by the Hungarians; the latter is a reconciliation scene between man and wife built around a newspaper advertisement.

In 'Das Erdbeben in Chili' Kleist explores the innate cruelty of religious fanaticism, and in 'Die Verlobung in St. Domingo' the hero, who is escaping from a native uprising, makes a tragic mistake, kills the girl who was trying to save him, and shoots himself on finding out the truth. Ossip Schubin's lengthy 'Die Geschichte eines Genies' traces the rise and miserable failure of a musician who is convinced that he is a composer of genius; and 'Die Flut des Lebens', by the literary historian, A. Stern, is a tale set in the forests of Eastern Europe where a young man finds that fulfilment of his dream to be caught up in important events leads to his death.

Futabatei Shimei, in 1888, had pioneered new standards of accuracy with his translations from Turgenev, and Ōgai was soon to achieve a similar reputation as a translator of distinction. He by no means slavishly followed the original text, however, retaining a certain amount of freedom which was a natural outcome of his interest in essence rather than pure form. At times the freedom amounts to almost adaptation, odd phrases being omitted here and there so that the overall effect is to emphasize plot at the expense of some of the richness and texture of the originals. On two occasions he drastically altered the structure. A long section in the Hoffmann story which explains the founding of the 'Chambre Ardente', a court set up to combat violence in the streets of Paris, and which provides much interesting and detailed background material, was relegated to an explanatory appendix in the Japanese; and a large part of the beginning of Hackländer's 'Fünfter Windstoss' was cut to a few lines. Ōgai no doubt felt that the stories were thereby improved.

One of the most vexing problems that beset early translators was the amount of foreign words which had to be made intelligible in translation. Ōgai sometimes used the nearest Chinese equivalent and added a kana gloss, but more often he preferred to leave the original word in the text in katakana and add an explanation in Japanese where necessary, so that not only his translations but also many of his own stories are well known for the liberal use of foreign words. In 'Die Geschichte eines Genies', for instance, words such as 'spinnet' 'violin' 'piano', 'melody', 'opera', 'orchestra' and 'organ' appear in katakana with little or no explanation, and phrases such as 'A' mon cher ami', 'comme c'est tsigane' and 'pauvre petit chat' are treated in the same way, giving a very distinctive foreign flavour to the text and making little concession to the reader.

The argument over whether or not the colloquial style of Futabatei and Yamada Bimyō was feasible was raging at about the time Ōgai was making these translations and the fact that he experimented with both classical and colloquial styles mirrors this uncertainty. He was not to write an original work in the more modern style, 'Hannichi' (Half a day), until the comparatively late date of 1909, and his own contribution to the language debate, 'Gembunron' (April 1890), shows how uncommitted he was at this stage. He recognized that an effort had to be made to bring the written style more in line with contemporary speech, and he had praise for Yamada's attempts. Neither had he any objection to the use of new words or dialect, but saw no particular reason why this should entail a complete rejection of traditional written grammar. Like Futabatei and many other writers, Ōgai felt that the central problem was how the colloquial language could be given a dignity of expression and richness of allusion compatible with the demands of a work of art, and he emphasized the pointlessness of rejecting the resources of Chinese and classical Japanese, for to do so would be to cripple the writer by restricting the tools of his trade. The challenge of the rehabilitation of Japanese prose lay not so much in the invention of a new style as in the transmission of the essence and seriousness of Western literature, a task to which all the resources of the language would have to be brought to bear.

Perhaps the central question posed by these translations concerns the selection of the originals which, given Ōgai's knowledge of the European classics, is to say the least surprising. Ōgai himself gives us very few clues as to his own attitude to these works, except for a number of rather insubstantial comments made in 1905 in the introduction to a revised version of the collection of his translations entitled *Minawashū*. It is tempting to claim that his translations were chosen for the specific purpose of 'educating' the Japanese reader and introducing some representative European literature, but his choice would not seem to bear this out. It is clear that in choosing stories, Ōgai took what appealed to him rather than any recognized classics. Most of the stories are, as we shall see, informed by a similar approach to art as that expressed in both his literary theories and his own early novellas. They would hardly spring to mind as representative of the best in the wide range of European literature that was open to him, and he was indeed to look back on them with a certain amount of misgiving.

Three early novellas

The influence of Ōgai's reading in Germany, and in particular the large number of German *novellen* of the late Romantic period that he devoured, can be clearly seen in the three stories with which he began his career as a writer: 'Maihime' (January 1890), 'Utakata no ki' (August 1890) and 'Fumizukai' (January 1891).

Although it would seem that 'Maihime' was in fact the second of these stories to be written, it is convenient to treat it as his maiden work. Not only was it the first to be published, but it is by far the most important. Perhaps no other single work by Ōgai has received so much attention from Japanese critics, and the reasons for its fame are not hard to find.

The story concerns a young Japanese, Ōta Toyotarō, who is sent to Berlin by the Japanese government to study there for five years. A tendency to assert his own views in his official despatches combined with an unfavourable report by a fellow Japanese that he is living a somewhat loose life brings about his dismissal. His mother dies in Japan, leaving him with no ties at home, and so he decides to stay on and at least complete his studies in Germany. His relationship with a German dancing girl, Elis, whom he meets quite by accident, starts innocently enough, but then becomes a full-blown love affair. When a friend, Aizawa Kenkichi, arrives from Japan as part of the suite of a Count Amakata, and tells Ōta that he might have a chance of returning to Japan and restoring his fortunes, he is driven to decide between Elis and Japan. Eventually amid much self-recrimination for his innate weakness, he finds himself choosing in favour of Japan. Elis, who is by this time pregnant, becomes incurably insane on hearing how Ōta has deceived her, and it is in that condition that he leaves her and sails for home.

Even from the outline given above, it is clear that a good deal of the story relies for its background on Ōgai's own experiences in Germany, but this is by no means all. When Ōgai returned to Japan in the September of 1888, he found himself in the embarrassing position of having to warn his parents of the distinct possibility that he might be followed by a German girl. The consternation that this

The first page of the 'Maihime' manuscript in Ōgai's own hand, late 1889.
(Original in possession of Ueno Junichi, Asahi Shimbunsha, Tokyo)

news caused can well be imagined. As all reference to this girl was expunged from the 'Doitsu nikki', which Ōgai rewrote around 1899 while living in 'exile' in Kokura, the only solid information we have about the affair is the recollections of his younger sister, Koganei Kimiko. They are therefore worth quoting in detail. The first passage comes from an article entitled 'Tsugi no ani' which appeared in the magazine *Tōhaku* in 1937 and which was later included in her book *Ōgai no Keizoku*.

Kimiko tells how her mother had announced that she might want to discuss something of importance with her son-in-law, Koganei Yoshikiyo, in the near future:

> The days flew by. Then early on the morning of 24 September Mother came over from Senju and told me that my brother had been followed to Japan by a girl with whom he had been on intimate terms in Germany, and that she was now staying at the Seiyōken in Tsukiji. I was absolutely amazed.
>
> 'I've been wanting to come and talk it over with you for some days, but we've had so many visitors, and anyway I thought it might blow over without my having to mention it. Toku[16] has gone to the university this morning to tell your husband. We must talk it over with him and so we are asking him to come to Senju this evening. Don't worry if he's late,' she said, and rushed back home in a hurry.
>
> It appeared that my brother had immediately mentioned the possibility to Father the evening he returned — the eighth. It had been the usual kind of affair, but he wasn't very skilful at handling that type of person, and just for the fun of it some of the many Japanese students there had spread the rumour that he came from a rich family. Being a simple girl at heart, she believed them and told him that she would come to Japan. She could dance, but was also good with her hands, and so she assumed she would be able to support herself without putting him to any inconvenience. He had told her that he doubted if she could get by with nothing but nimble fingers, but she would think of something, she said, and on that they had parted.
>
> When they heard this, Mother and Father, who knew nothing about European matters, had wanted to come and discuss it with us. But they had been eighty per cent certain that she would not come. If she had not in fact done so, there would have been no need to mention the matter.
>
> As was arranged that evening at Senju, my husband went next day to the Seiyōken and talked to the girl in question for the first time; her name was Elis. I was worried and so immediately he returned I asked him what kind of girl she was.

'Small and attractive. She doesn't seem to be in the least put out, because she is absolutely convinced that he is the son of a rich family. What low tricks people will play!' That was all he would say.

After that, in order to win her round and explain the situation here in Japan in detail, my husband went every day to the Seiyōken whenever he could spare the time. She would look forward to seeing him because she wanted someone to talk to. My brother was very busy with his official duties and his uniform was conspicuous, so he kept away. My husband had a more flexible timetable at the university and so went frequently. Whenever he could, Tokujirō too took her out and showed her round. His German wasn't very good, but he was easygoing and must have soon got on good terms with her. I asked him what she was like, but he laughed nonchalantly: 'I just go for my daily language lesson!' he said. How provoking that he seemed so unaware of other people's worries.

My husband would go off to Senju to report, and he would stay late into the night talking the matter over. There was always some little present for me in the cab which they were kind enough to send him home in. I was touched to think that Mother was thinking of me, what with all her anxiety.

In the midst of all the comings and goings, it seemed that Elis gradually came to understand the situation more clearly every day, and then all of a sudden she resigned herself to going back to Germany. A day was arranged for my brother to go and see her. He discussed various matters with her and they decided which ship she would go on. My husband was busy for a couple of days after that, but when he went to see her at the Seiyōken again she was in the best of spirits and told him she had been out shopping with Tokujirō to buy some things. He told me how she had got out a lot of little presents and showed them to him delightedly. As she was interested in handicrafts, Japanese bags and wallets had caught her eye and she had bought quite a few.

He commented on her artlessness: 'Elis is really a nice girl; almost too naïve. I wonder how he got to know someone like her?'

'Perhaps he just thought of her as a flower by the wayside,' I suggested.

When she decided to return home, I heaved a sigh of relief. The fare and the tickets were all prepared and my husband took them to her. On the afternoon of 16 October, he went to Tsukiji, met up with my brother and Elis, and then all three went to Yokohama. Tokujirō had gone there earlier to arrange everything and was there to meet them. After supper they all went out for a walk along Bashamichi, Ōtamachi and Bentendōri. Next morning they got up early, boarded a lighter at seven and went to see her off on the French ship.

What must my brother have felt as he stood there in the crowd? Anyone would have felt sorry for this young girl who had come so far and was now returning with her hopes dashed. And yet, as they commented in the train on the way back, it was very strange how she had shown no sign of sadness as she waved farewell with her handkerchief from the side of the ship.

So Elis went home without complaint. We thought a lot about the future of the poor girl, for she hadn't had even the common sense to distinguish between truth and falsehood. Neither Father nor Mother tried to discuss the matter with Kako, and Tokujirō was young, so they discussed it all with my husband, although they did not know him very well. Of course, it was through this affair that my husband got to know Kako.

Everyone in the family was so pleased that our beloved brother had come through unscathed. I was deeply grateful to my husband for the trouble he had taken . . .[17]

The second relevant passage written by Kimiko appeared in the journal *Bungaku* (April 1936), in an article entitled 'Mori Otto ni', and it contains an interesting account of the writing of 'Maihime':

When it was all over, he [Ōgai] came to thank us. 'I feel so sorry for her,' I said. 'I heard there was something about her being pregnant.'

'That was probably a pretext for following me,' he replied. 'There was some talk of a miscarriage, but I don't think that was very likely. She told me that before she left she had arranged to work in the design section of a hat manufacturers on her return. Tell Koganei I'm sorry to have given him so much trouble.'

That was all that was said . . .

Then he wrote 'Maihime'. All his colleagues were so full of the affair that he probably intended to make a clean breast of it himself . . . Near the end of the year I had gone over to the house at Senju when your uncle hurried over himself from the house at Ueno.[18] Seeing me there, he burst out:

'You here? That's lucky!'

'Why? Has anything happened?' I asked.

'No!' He laughed at my worried expression. 'Our brother has just written a story about that dancing girl. He sent me so that you could all be the first to hear it. Father's out on a consultation? Well, I can read it to him later. Come on, get everyone rounded up and I'll read it out to you like Benkei reading the subscription list.' He was always doing things in a theatrical manner.

He started to read in a normal voice:

'They have finished loading the coal and the tables here in the second-class saloon stand in silence. Even the bright glare from the electric lights seems wasted . . .'

Everyone listened intently. As he progressed, he became more emotional and you could hear tears in his voice. Each of us listening to him had our own thoughts, but the remembrance was so fresh and the prose so evocative that we all blew our noses frequently. He came to the end.

'Friends like Aizawa Kenkichi are rare indeed, and yet to this very day there remains a part of me that curses him.'

Everyone took a deep breath. There was silence for a while, and then I burst out:

'How well he writes!'

Your grandmother nodded.

'What will Kako-san say about it?' she asked.

'He turned up yesterday evening and so we read it to him,' said Tokujirō. 'He was immensely pleased at the representation of his role as friend and adviser, and happy that a direct attack was being made on those who have been spreading idle and malicious gossip. He suggested a drink to celebrate and we carried on late into the night.'

It was published that spring in *Kokumin no Tomo* and had good reviews. We were delighted that what had been weighing on his mind for some time now had been exorcized.[19]

There is clearly much in 'Maihime' that corresponds to Ōgai's own experiences in Germany, but the degree to which he incorporated reality into the story is a source of perennial discussion. At least a tentative connection between Count Amakata and the politician, Yamagata Aritomo, is admissible, and depending on how close the individual reader believes this connection to be, the name is often read as 'Amagata'. The meeting between Ōta and the Count in the story takes place in the winter of 1888, which coincided with the period Yamagata was actually abroad, November 1888 to October 1889. As Kako Tsurudo was with Yamagata on this trip, he can be seen as providing, at least in part, a prototype for Aizawa Kenkichi.

It is also highly likely that Ōgai had in mind the unfortunate case of a fellow army student, Takeshima Tsutomu, whom he had known since 1882. Takeshima came from the village of Ōta in Chichibu and it would not be beyond the bounds of possibility for this to be more than just coincidence. He had gone to Germany on his own funds, but fell into financial difficulties and was ordered to return to Japan by Captain Fukushima Yasumasa who was attached to the Legation in

Berlin and had specific charge over the army students. This order was endorsed by Surgeon Major-General Ishiguro Tadanori when he arrived in Berlin in July 1887. But Takeshima decided to stay on and continue his studies in medicine, and so was dismissed from the army. He died in Dresden in May 1890 from illness brought on by poverty. There are a number of entries in 'Doitsu nikki' which record this affair, although not of course Takeshima's death, which occurred after Ōgai had returned to Japan. There was a suggestion that another army student, Taniguchi Ken, an old enemy of Ōgai who was later to be unsympathetically treated as Waniguchi in *Vita Sexualis,* had been spreading malicious tales about Takeshima. Ōgai felt unable to broach the matter with Ishiguro when the latter arrived, but from a number of subsequent entries in the diary it is clear that he kept in contact with Takeshima at least until the end of the year.[20]

The real point of interest, however, is Elis, if indeed that was her real name. Both Ishiguro's and Koganei Yoshikiyo's diaries omit any reference to her name[21] and it is possible that Kimiko, writing so many years after the event, was guilty of a little embellishment, but this cannot be proved. It is not difficult to see why 'Maihime' has been incessantly mined by critics searching for Ōgai's attitude to what really happened, when total silence surrounds the events themselves. The temptation to treat 'Maihime' as a biographical document is just too strong. A favourite approach is to see it as a story of the compromise and defeat of a newly liberated youth by the oppressive forces of a 'feudal' tradition: a chronicle of the birth and premature stifling of the modern sense of individualism and self-awareness of the Meiji intellectual — in this case Ōgai. There is no question that Ōgai's criticism of his superiors, and in particular Ishiguro, which was beginning to be overtly shown about the time 'Maihime' was written, shows through in the first part of the story, but this factor should not be exaggerated.

One of the most intriguing questions about 'Maihime' is the reason for its composition. Was it written to silence harmful rumours as Kimiko's record would seem to suggest? There are two theories here which must be mentioned if only to be rejected.

Shibukawa Gyō has suggested that the choice of Yamagata Aritomo as a model was crucial.[22] By using such an eminent figure the story would have been given an air of authenticity, and malicious tales that Ōgai had been followed to Japan by a German girl would be quashed. This view is given weight by the fact that in the first of several versions of the story, the following passage can be found after the third paragraph. It was deleted in all subsequent versions.

> Foreign policy in Japan at the moment is in a somewhat con-
> fused state, and the head of our party, Count Amakata, is
> extremely concerned about matters at home. He is worried
> enough for it to show in his expression. Perhaps as a member
> of his suite I too am so anxious that I cannot put pen to paper.
> While we were abroad I was for some strange reason deep in the
> Count's confidence, but I am not a brilliant scholar nor especially
> talented. Could I be too worried about my own future to be
> able to write? No, there is another reason. (XXXVIII, 467)

The deletion of this passage, however, was probably not because
it had served its purpose and so was no longer needed, but for more
artistic reasons. Its omission served to withhold, until much later
in the story, knowledge of one of the main reasons for Ōta's return
to Japan. But in any case the whole idea of Ōgai being somehow on
the defensive and worried about rumours at this time is difficult to
accept. A full year had elapsed since the episode had occurred and
he had already launched into an attack on his superiors by criticizing
their plans for the first Japan Medical Congress. Far from being an
attempt at silencing any rumours, the publication of such a story can
almost be seen as a piece of deliberate provocation. Ishiguro had been
privy to the Elis affair and could hardly have been pleased that it
was being resurrected. To write such a story would have been a strange
way of scotching rumours.

The second theory is that the composition of 'Maihime' was connected with relationships within the Mori family.[23] Soon after the
Elis affair Ōgai was somewhat unwillingly forced by his parents to
marry Toshiko, the daughter of Akamatsu Noriyoshi, a Vice-Admiral
and personal friend of Nishi Amane. The marriage was a failure, however, partly because Ōgai was made to feel rather like an adopted son.
Within eighteen months he had walked out on her — a drastic step when
one considers how much was at stake. Was 'Maihime' written to spite
Toshiko, or as a protest against a family system which had driven him
to send Elis back to Germany against his will?

This view presupposes that Ōgai was deeply involved with Elis and
resented the family pressure; and is certainly attractive to those who
see 'Maihime' as a parable of independence trampled underfoot by
tradition. But the impression left by the entries in Koganei Yoshikiyo's
diary is that Ōgai and his family decided very early on to send the girl
home. We also have Kimiko's reminiscences which, although possibly
biased, are our most reliable source; she insists that nothing suggested
that Ōgai was ever deeply in love with Elis or that he had thought of

their relationship in Germany as anything more than the 'usual kind of affair'. The whole matter was a distasteful mistake and he was grateful to the family for managing the problem so tactfully.

Barring the discovery of any additional diaries, the details of the real Elis affair are likely to remain obscure. While it is important to understand that the existence of a real Elis has added to its fascination, 'Maihime' was a very typical mixture of fact and fiction, and Ōgai's motives for publishing it were primarily literary. He himself showed little inclination to confuse author with hero. Indeed, the majority of his readers would have been unaware of the real facts.

In a subsequent discussion of the story with the young critic Ishibashi Ningetsu, Ōgai wrote, '"Maihime" is a variation of the diary form; what Hartmann calls a *Tagebuch Lyrik*' (XXII, 167); further, '"Maihime" stems from the diary form and is a kind of *Ich Roman,* and so the hero is identified as "I"' (XXII, 168). Ōgai is not stating here that 'Maihime' was a confessional *watakushi-shōsetsu,* a concept and a term that came in much later, but merely that it was a bona fide example of first-person fiction. That there was no one-to-one relationship in his mind between author and hero is clear from the following conversation that Ōgai had with the critic, Gotō Chūgai, in 1897:

> . . . in 'Maihime' I wanted to describe an event taking place in Berlin, the capital of northern Germany. I wanted to concentrate more or less on the customs and the locality. There are many poor students who go there from Japan and make their living as newspaper correspondents and the like . . . And then there are those dancers who work in the little theatres, and many types of high-class mistresses − the demi-monde, as they call them in Paris. The word *maihime* is a translation of balletteuse, a girl who dances ballet. There is an English translation called *My Dance of Lady* [*sic*] [24] in some magazine or other. It would appear that the translator mistook the meaning . . .
>
> 'Maihime' is not based on the truth, although there has been a lot of that kind of talk. There is a story by a man called Bodenstadt in which a young German goes to Paris and lives with a poor girl. The plot is similar to mine. I didn't plagiarize it, of course, but it's about a foreigner's life in Paris, and so the circumstances resemble those in my story, don't they? I think in the end the girl dies by throwing herself on to the pavement from a second or third-floor window. There are quite a few other works in a similar vein. (XXXVIII, 154–5)

'Utakata no ki', published in Ōgai's journal *Shigarami-zōshi* in August 1890, provides critics with fewer problems than 'Maihime', if only because it is less overtly autobiographical and most of the material used can be easily traced. The bare bones of the story are quickly told. A Japanese artist, Kose, arrives in Munich to finish a painting of a flower girl whom he helped on a previous visit and whom he cannot forget. Introduced by a German friend, Exter, to the students at the Academy of Fine Arts, he meets one of the models, Marie, who eventually turns out to be his flower girl. They go to the Starn-bergersee, south of Munich, one evening, and while rowing on the lake they see the mad King Ludwig on the shore. Ludwig mistakes Marie for her mother, with whom he used to be in love, and rushes into the lake towards them. The King, together with his physician Gudden, drowns in the lake. Marie loses her balance in the boat, strikes her chest on a hidden pile in the water and she too is destined to die. In the days that follow, the whole of Munich is in uproar and nobody thinks of Kose and the girl, or comes near to guessing the real cause of the King's death.

As we have already seen from the record of Ōgai's stay in Munich, the King's death by drowning and most of the background material is verifiable. Using this factual basis Ōgai constructed a slightly altered version of the real life love affair between his friend, Harada Naojirō, and the waitress, which is also recorded in the diary. It is best to see the Marie in the story as a composite of the waitress and Caecilia Pfaff. When Ōgai talked of the story to Gotō Chūgai, he said:

> The King's death described in the story is a historical fact. There was this mad King whose name was Ludwig. He was famous for his proposal that an Emperor for all Germany should be elected, and for his relationship with Wagner. He was the latter's patron and planned to build a large theatre in Munich, but the people would not permit it. As a result he severed his ties with society and went into retreat. It was he who built the opera house at Bayreuth, and it seems that he was acting rather strangely even then.
>
> He was already a recluse when I went to Bavaria and he drowned in a lake while I was there; the Starnbergersee it was called. It's only about one or two hours by train from Munich, and we were always going there and staying overnight. I stayed there on a short holiday in the summer as well, but I was not there when the King died.
>
> The physician, Gudden, mentioned in the story, was a real person too and he died in the lake with the King at the same spot. Exter, the artist, is still alive. We had a good time with him as a student, but now he's an important figure on the German artistic scene; very progressive – left wing I think. He's well

known now, but at the time I didn't think he would be so famous and so I used his real name, Julius Exter. His friend, the Japanese artist (Kose), is Harada Naojirō, but I would rather you didn't ask about the love affair . . .

While I was in Germany someone wrote a play about the King's death. It was put out by Reclam, the publishers who print very cheap editions of everything from the classics to present-day authors. If the play had been good I would not have wanted to use exactly the same material, but it was so bad that I felt no compunction. From what I have seen in the papers recently, it seems that someone else has written a story about this same affair, but I haven't read that as yet.

That's all I know about the King's death. The girl who became the model is not based on anyone. (XXXVIII, 152)

Harada had in fact left a wife and child in Japan when he went to Munich in February 1884. He chose Munich for his studies because his elder brother Toyokichi, who had returned from Munich in 1883 to succeed Edmund Naumann at Tokyo University, had made great friends with Gabriel Max who was a member of the Bavarian Academy at the time. Max was a well-known painter in Europe and Harada no doubt took advantage of this connection. When Ōgai met Harada in Munich they struck up a friendship that lasted until the latter's death in December 1899.[25]

If 'Maihime' expresses the dark atmosphere of Ōgai's Berlin days, 'Utakata no ki' is full of the light and gaiety of the time spent at Munich. The beauty of the Bavarian landscape and the carefree life of the art students is captured with vividness and economy. Elements of the story can, of course, be traced to much of Ōgai's reading, works such as *Faust* and Andersen's *Improvisatoren,* but the game of chasing sources is of limited value. More important is the expression of the Romantic view of artistic creation based on inspiration that is evident in the story, and which fully accords with his theories at this early stage. The attitudes he had towards literature and art are embodied more fully here than in 'Maihime'. There is much serious talk of madness, the evils of imitation, and the whole tale itself relies much on the effect of the miraculous, bearing a strong resemblance to a *märchen* or fairy tale, where the real and the unreal are expertly mingled. A somewhat similar tendency was to emerge in some of his later historical works.

The third story in this group, 'Fumizukai', is slighter than the other two, having neither the exceptional personal interest of 'Maihime' nor the lyricism of 'Utakata no ki'. It is set in Saxony and deals in particular with the period from August to September 1885, when Ōgai was invited to see some training manoeuvres by Roth. The story concerns the daughter of a Count Bulow, who wishes to avoid an arranged marriage. To this end she sends a secret note by a Japanese officer to her aunt at the Court in Dresden, begging to be invited to serve there. She knows that once a formal invitation comes from the Court her father will not be able to refuse, and she will be able to escape from her unwanted suitor.

Much of the background has been traced to passages in the 'Doitsu nikki', and the exact relationship between the two has been fully researched in both English and Japanese. The plot itself is an addition of Ōgai's. As he said himself:

> 'Utakata no ki' is set in southern Germany, 'Maihime' in northern Germany, and 'Fumizukai' in central Germany (Dresden). Dresden was the only place where I frequented the royal palace and associated with the highest classes of society. In 'Fumizukai' I wrote about the palace. The manoeuvres and other events are taken from my actual experiences, but the characters in the story don't really resemble the actual people. Such things as the audience with the King and the festivities at the royal palace are based on my observations – I did not make up any of that. (XXXVIII, 155)[26]

The main point of the story is the girl's escape from a miserable future with a man she does not love; and it can hardly be a coincidence that Ōgai walked out on his first wife in October 1890, two months before the story was published.

After the affair with Elis, Ōgai's parents had thought it prudent to find him a suitable Japanese wife as soon as possible, and they must have been overjoyed when Nishi Amane came forward with a very advantageous proposition, Akamatsu Toshiko. Toshiko's aunt was the wife of Enomoto Takeaki, an influential Meiji statesman, and such connections would have assured Ōgai of success in the army and elsewhere. The arrangements were soon completed and the couple moved into a small house near Ueno in the second week of March 1889. At the end of May they moved to a house in the grounds of the Akamatsu mansion, which they shared with Ōgai's two brothers and two of Toshiko's sisters. The marriage was a failure. A combination of Toshiko's ill health and Ōgai's irritation at having been pressed into marrying finally led him to walk out on her soon after she had given birth to their son, Otto, in September 1890. The arrangements for the separation were made on 27 November; but Ōgai had already left at the beginning of the October. There is even some doubt as to whether this step could legitimately be called a divorce, as it is not clear whether the marriage had been properly registered at the time. Some hint of the atmosphere that reigned in the house while they were living together can be gathered from the following reminiscence of Ōgai's younger brother, Junzaburō:

> One evening my elder brother returned and saw that I only had a miserable portion of vegetables on my plate. He gave me the grilled sea bream that was on his plate. Asking the maid about it, he was told that it was his wife's orders. 'Jun is my brother!' he shouted at her. 'He must have the same food as I from now on!' I was treated a little better after that.[27]

Ōgai's decision to leave Toshiko not only caused Nishi Amane acute embarrassment, but also represented resistance to his parents' wishes. His stay in Europe had strengthened his self-confidence, but the sense of liberty he had gained abroad made life much more difficult on his return. Later, in 1900, while he was in Kokura, he heard from Kako Tsurudo that Toshiko, who had married another of his acquaintances, Miyazaki Michisaburō, had died of tuberculosis. He wrote in his diary: 'Ah! She was my wife, Otto's mother, Akamatsu Toshiko. She was neither pretty nor attractive, but tall and pale. She could read both Japanese and Chinese, especially the latter which she could absorb fluently at one glance. We lived together for two years and then parted for some reason or other' (XXXV, 314).[28] The whole tradition of arranged marriages comes under fire in 'Fumizukai', and it is reasonable to suppose that Ōgai was venting his own feelings when he makes the German girl say to the Japanese officer:

> Recently I've been reading a couple of books about Japanese customs in which European authors note with scorn that in your country marriages are arranged by the parents, and that consequently many couples don't know what real love is. Such scorn is ironical for the same thing happens in Europe. Long friendships before an engagement are supposed to enable a couple to get to know each other before they decide whether to marry or not, but among the nobility marriages are arranged by one's superiors, and even though the couple may not be suited to each other, there is no getting out of it. After you have met so often that you can't stand the sight of one another, then you are married. That shows what a reasonable world this is. (II, 45)[29]

When one turns to the structure of these stories there can be little doubt that all three owe much to German models. The importance of form and technique in 'Maihime' was pointed out in one of the very first articles of criticism on the story, 'Maihime saihyō', which appeared in Ōgai's own journal, *Shigarami-zōshi*, in the same month as the story was carried in *Kokumin no Tomo*. The critic was a university friend of Ōgai, Yamaguchi Toratarō.

> 'Maihime' is a novella. It uses psychological observation, but
> does not impair the beauty of Idea. Broadly speaking, it is both
> emotional and psychological (*sentimental: psychologisch*).
> Would it be correct to suppose that Ōgai is interested in German
> literature and is used to borrowing from Goethe? The con-
> struction of the work, which resembles that of *Werther, Wilhelm
> Meister*, and the play *Clavigo*, agrees with Heyse's definition that
> a novella must treat one main event from one single aspect.
>
> Autobiography, however, is not basically a legitimate form of
> the Epic. One can see its dangers in many *Ich Roman*, but a story
> is essentially a living thing and in the hands of a great craftsman a
> balance can always be achieved. At the end of the last century, in
> the gloomy universe of pre-Kantian philosophy, the ultimate
> method was to seek the essence through a study of the self.
> Hundreds of autobiographies followed Rousseau's *Confessions*.
> This method does not accord with purely philosophical standards,
> but when it is used to good effect in a story it can have
> marvellous results.[30]

While this account already shows a tendency to blur the distinction
between first-person fiction and autobiography, it is difficult to believe
that it was written without Ōgai's advice. Not only is it couched in
characteristic German vocabulary favoured by Ōgai, but the mention of
Heyse is particularly significant. Paul Heyse, a Nobel prize winner who
has now faded into obscurity, was a member of the late-Romantic
group of writers who were based in Munich, and he was a bitter opponent of the Naturalists. As he was one of the foremost theoreticians of
the *novelle* form, Ōgai could hardly have failed to be aware of the
particular formal demands of the genre, the emphasis on techniques and
the importance of style.

All three stories use many of the techniques common to German
novellen. We have seen the effect of the use of the first person as a
conscious literary artifice and the presentation of the contents as
remembered history in 'Maihime', a form known as *Erinnerungs-
novelle* which was very popular in Germany. 'Utakata no ki' has a
somewhat complex structure in comparison. Perspective is provided
not by a simple form of recollection, but by the use of two internal
frames, Kose's story of his last visit to Munich and Marie's own life
story, which both interrupt the chronological progression and yet
are organic to the central plot. The second frame connects with the
first one at the point where Marie and Kose first meet, and it also
serves as an excellent prelude to later events by referring to the lake
and the mad King Ludwig. All the signs are that this story was care-

fully planned, if not contrived, to build up to a climax which is a confirmation of the reader's expectations rather than any sudden surprise. This too was very characteristic of the *novelle* form.

The last of the stories, 'Fumizukai', is similar to 'Utakata no ki' in that it has two internal frames, an explanation of the girl's outburst while playing the piano, and her own confession. But it had the addition of an outer frame, a form of presentation, called a *Rahmennovelle,* much favoured by Heyse himself. The care with form and the conscious attempt to vary the time sequence clearly shows the influence of Ōgai's reading in Germany, and it marks the beginning of such concerns in the modern Japanese story.

If the stories are European in structure, however, the same can hardly be said of the style, which is the antithesis of modernity. It is notable that eight out of Ōgai's first eleven translations were in the colloquial style and in the first year after his return from Germany he was regarded as being part of the modernization movement begun two years previously by writers such as Yamada Bimyō and Futabatei Shimei. But Ōgai's experiments in this line were limited to the realm of translation until the very late date of 1909. It has been suggested that he may have been influenced in this respect by his early friendship with classical scholars such as Ochiai Naobumi and Inoue Michiyasu,[31] but in fact the vast majority of his critical articles were written in a heavily sinicized style. The new experiments might have been acceptable for translations, but when it came to original work, Ōgai went out of his way to produce a classical elegance that was highly idiosyncratic. It was, of course, an experiment in its own way, but firmly based on classical lines.

It is interesting to note that Ōgai wrote no more original work until 1909, a gap of eighteen years. There may have been many reasons for this long silence, but one of them must have been related to a discontent with either his early theory or his early works. Ōgai's stories were firmly rooted in the European Romantic tradition despite the fact that the movement was in its death throes when he was in Germany and had already died in France as a result of the challenge of the modern realistic novel. They are not Romantic merely because they deal with tragic love or because they explore the various facets of the susceptibility of youth to the charms of unusual women. The matter is far deeper. They are based on a concept of the autonomy of art, the belief in the primacy of the Beautiful, and a self-centred vision of the world.[32] They deal with private rather than public values. There is little concern for the outside world, however much critics look for a critique of authoritarianism in 'Maihime'.

Although there was a brief attempt in Japanese literature to treat serious social problems with objective realism after 1900, it soon gave way to a seemingly irresistible urge to discover, examine and lay bare the self. Thus it was that the so-called Japanese Naturalists wrote mainly about themselves. A degree of objectivity was attained, but the vision was turned inwards rather than outwards.

This self-centredness was to be central to Ōgai's own work until 1912, although as early as 1896 he was abandoning his early Romanticism. Indeed, the work produced immediately after the period of silence, in the years 1909 to 1912, shows more allegiance to the True than the Beautiful. This would suggest that, like most writers, he was coming to feel that a self-centred vision of the world could and should be married to a commitment to realism. For a short time, writing became nothing more than a private conversation, a piece of public self-examination, providing excellent, if dangerous, material for biographers, but usually not good art. Fortunately for Japanese literature he was to abandon such uncomfortable soul-searching in 1912.

In European Romanticism self-revelation, or at least, a self-centred vision of the world, was closely tied to poetic expression. The switch of allegiance to the factual seems to be a basic underlying trend in Japanese literature of this period. It could be argued that this came about because the self experienced a kind of willing release into a free sphere of artistic expression in Europe, whereas in Meiji Japan the self was rudely uprooted from its foundations and experienced an insecurity that made it search desperately for solid fact and reality. Anything unreal or fictitious might have increased rather than soothed the anxiety. It was also easier to write about oneself, and so one finds a reluctance to trust the imagination.

Ōgai's silence can be seen as a period of readjustment during which this metamorphosis took place. The three novellas reflect his European experience, but his later work, written from 1909 to 1912, reflects the man after these early ideas had been adjusted according to the requirements of the Japanese experience.

3

THEORY FOR A NEW LITERATURE

Early literary criticism

A major factor in the process by which literature became once again
worthy of the attention of intellectuals was the fostering of the serious
discussion of literary theory. Ōgai was not slow in realizing that a
journal devoted to this purpose was essential, and it was with this aim
in mind that he founded *Shigarami-zōshi* in October 1889. In the
manifesto which prefaced the first issue he wrote:

When Western learning first advanced eastward, the substance was
imparted but not the spirit. Everyone knew that the Westerners
were people of resourcefulness in the study of natural science and
in the technqiues of medicine and war, but they were not aware
they were people with a sense of ethics, let alone taste. So those
who believed in Western learning did so for purely utilitarian
reasons, and when something was of no use it was discarded. . .

Now the tendency has changed and both the graceful literature
and the profound philosophy of the West have come to our
shores. Their literature includes the Lyric, the Epic, and Drama,
but the most important is the novel, popular of late throughout
Europe. Although not in fact limited to any particular genre, it is
treated as part of the Epic. Yes, the world of Meiji has become
the world of the novel! The phrase 'novel fever' is a good parallel
to the 'Dichteritis'[1] of modern Westerners.

We already have, however, many elements in our literature that
have come from outside. In the past, Buddhism was transmitted
by means of translations via the Chinese and so Indian literature
did not accompany it. But Chinese literature, coming as it did
together with Chinese methods of government, habits and teachings, greatly changed the tastes of our nation. Indeed, we now
have among our men of letters those who compose Japanese
poetry and those who compose Chinese; men who excel in writing
Japanese and those who excel in writing Chinese; those who are
good at the classical style and those who specialize in the collo-

quial. All the various elements of Japanese, Chinese and Western aesthetics lie scattered among them. This state of confusion cannot possibly last for long. We know the time for purification is at hand; only criticism can bring this about.[2]

Ōgai had in fact already started to propound his own views on literature in a number of articles, the dominant theme of which was a virulent criticism of Zola's Naturalist theories. In this and many other respects he was governed by his reading of German literature and in particular the kind of literary criticism he had come across while abroad.

Zola, as a theorist, was guided by a desire to modernize literature, and especially the novel, by making it relevant to the new world in a way that the Romantic imagination found impossible. He advanced further than anyone before him in an attempt to apply scientific methods to art, and as part of this impractical task he called to his aid the ideas of the medical researcher, Claude Bernard, who was the founder of the modern method of testing hypotheses by controlled observation and experiment. Zola tried to claim that the new novel had to be based on a similar method of scientific analysis and that the novelist as social scientist had a responsibility to be purely objective.

> The imagination no longer has a function; intrigue is of little importance to the novelist. . . We begin with the idea that nature is all we need; it is necessary to accept her as she is, without modifying her or diminishing her in any respect; she is sufficiently beautiful and great to provide a beginning, a middle and an end. Instead of imagining an adventure, complicating it, and arranging a series of theatrical effects to lead to a final conclusion, we simply take from life the story of a being or group of beings whose acts we faithfully set down. The work becomes an official record, nothing more; its only merit is that of exact observation, of the more or less profound penetration of analysis, of the logical concatenation of facts.[3]

It hardly needs saying that in the attempt to come closer to a depiction of real life and carry on a continual search for truth unclouded by the author's subjectivity, there were many elements which militated against the successful realization of this theory. The search for truth led to a portrayal of the average man in the street and this process tended to lead the writer to concentrate on the lower strata of society. Ideally, nothing could be recorded that the writer had not experienced, and the attempt to escape all forms of self-censorship led to a tendency to delineate sexual habits with great frankness; truth came to mean unpleasant truth. The flaw in Zola's argument was of course that realism, as a literary term, only describes a certain degree of approximation of art to reality, and the contrast between theory and practice is perhaps nowhere so marked as in the case of Zola himself: his works only really succeed to the extent that artistic concerns become paramount and theory is forgotten.

Although German Naturalism, more successful in the field of drama than in the novel, cannot be said to have started until 1889 when the Freie Bühne gave its inaugural performance of Ibsen's *Ghosts*, the works and the theories of Zola had been under constant discussion ever since 1875. The early reception of Zola in Germany was almost universally hostile and diatribes against him from such critics as T. Zolling, Rudolf von Gottschall, and Paul Lindau were common in the 1880s.[4] He was attacked by them all as being not only immoral but also unaesthetic. The uniformity of such denunciations has been explained as 'due partly to the fact that Zola's radical theory was colliding with a clearly defined, homogeneous, and fully organised body of aesthetic theory with which all the critics were in thorough agreement'.[5]

It was not until Karl Bleibtreu's *Revolution der Literatur* of 1885 and M. G. Conrad's founding of the journal *Die Gesellschaft* in the same year that a sympathetic voice began to be heard. The period from 1885-90 was known as the period of the *Zola Krieg*, and the polemics of this period tended to be between the younger critics who were in favour of Zola, and the older men who stood by their former denunciations.

It is thus of no surprise that Ōgai should show interest in Zola's theories, as he was in Germany from 1884-8 and could hardly have failed to have been aware of the conflict over Naturalism. Neither is it surprising that he should take particular interest in Zola's central thesis — that of the identity of science and art — as he was both doctor and prospective writer himself and saw the introduction of the scientific method as part of his mission on his return to Japan.

The essay 'Shōsetsuron' (On the novel) which deals with this subject, appeared in the *Yomiuri Shimbun* on 3 January 1889, about three months after his return from Germany. In it Ōgai immediately set out to deny any such connection between medicine and literature:

> Writing this essay as a doctor, I will not base it on such a super-ficial idea as this. But it must be borne in mind that the kind of novel that pervades the whole of Europe today does in fact originate from the study of medicine. My readers will no doubt have already heard the name, Emile Zola. Zola is a Frenchman from Provence. The novels of today's Naturalists are his work, and the name 'experimental novel' (*le roman expérimental*), as he himself called them, is well known throughout the civilized

world.

Zola adopted the phrase 'experimental novel', making it the title of the first part of his essay on the novel, from the *Introduction a l'étude de la medicine expérimentale* by the eminent French physiologist, Claude Bernard.

Claude Bernard says that modern science has two fundamentals; observation and experimentation. The scholar who comes across those things in the universe that no man has the power to alter, observes them. The scholar who comes across those things he can change, experiments with them. If a doctor wishes to discover the real truth about the processes of the living human body, he should use the merits of observation supplemented by the results of experimentation. If you do not confront that fetid and palpitating world (*fétide ou palpitant*) in the hospitals, the lecture-halls and the laboratories, you cannot hope to make genuine medical discoveries. It is just like having to pass through the kitchens before entering a large mansion lit with silver candlesticks. (XXXVIII, 451)

The subtitle of this essay reads: 'Cfr. Rudolf von Gottschall, Studien' and refers to the second half of a book by Gottschall, *Literarische Todtenklänge und Lebensfragen* (Literary sounds from the Past and Questions from the Present) which Ōgai possessed. Ōgai's essay is, as Kobori Keiichirō has demonstrated in detail,[6] a paraphrase of the first chapter in this *Studien*. Having explained Bernard's thesis, Ōgai then starts to criticize Zola, still following arguments used by Gottschall:

Zola quotes these words, applying them directly to the construction of the novel. Everything in his novels has undergone his analysis and dissection. In analysing human emotions he makes no effort to make them palatable; in dissecting the state of society he never questions the sharpness of his knife. The results, then, of this progression from analysis to dissection are his so-called *études,* his so-called novels.

Having put forward this theory of practical application, he ably applies it. Look for instance at that long work *Les Rougon-Macquart* which is planned in about twenty volumes. From the first book entitled *La Fortune des Rougon* to the latest entitled *La Terre,* when it doesn't read like the weekly report from a department of anatomy, it reads like the diary from a chemist's laboratory. People would hold their noses and shun both laboratory and department, but with Zola's works they approach eyes peeled. Why is this? It is because the vital, pent-up, living flesh of the naked prostitute, Nana, posing in a myriad ways in front of her mirror cannot be seen in the same light as the corpse of a criminal at an autopsy with its pallid, cold skin. (XXXVIII, 451–2)

This criticism, the accusation of obscenity, and the specific example of Nana are all borrowed directly from Gottschall, who spends some twelve pages discussing the plot of *Nana* and the reasons for its success. Gottschall was, of course, a member of that group of critics who denounced Zola in the 1880s and has been described as 'Zola's most bitter adversary'.[7] It is difficult to believe that Ōgai would have been quite so condemnatory had he read Zola's novels himself, and, although this may be possible, his essay should be seen primarily as a distillation of Gottschall's opinions.

In the next passage, Ōgai brings the argument nearer home:

> It is of course quite legitimate to use analysis and dissection when constructing a novel. But to treat, as Zola does, the results of analysis and dissection as a novel is something that no one could regard as appropriate. *Ultimately the results of experiment are real facts.* We doctors may be satisfied with the search for real facts, but should novelists ever be thus satisfied? If we saw Zola's 'brutal works and terrifying pictures' as true history, we would certainly have no such dislike. Accounts of the punishment of burning in oil at the stake in China or the cruelties of the Auto da Fé in Spain should be read because they are true history. The same is true of those ugly stinking affairs reported in the daily newspapers. But only because they are real facts.
>
> Can novelists ultimately be satisfied to wander around within the confines of this kind of reality? If so, then where in the world will they display the subtle thoughts of their imaginative life? The results of analysis and dissection are good material for the writer, but the actual method of adapting and using them *can only be through his intuition.*
>
> How true this is! When Disraeli in England and Daudet in France use the results of experiment they transform it and bring it to life. They are of course quite unlike Zola in this respect. You can say that there is in their writings at times an insubstantial, dreamlike echo, a fusion of form and content. The Saxon scholar, Gottschall, calls this the 'photographische Roman'.
>
> I am a doctor. The scalpel is never out of my grasp for long and my test tubes are always at hand. But this desire to seek real facts has never hindered dreams of visiting the Infinite. (XXXVIII, 452)

Although much of the phrasing here can be traced to Gottschall, the particular distinction drawn between the novel and history and the juxtaposition of historical record and scientific results as having similar appeals is stressed by Ōgai. This is interesting and should be kept in mind in view of the move he himself was to make towards the study of history in later life.

We already have in this essay an awareness of the supposedly different demands of science and art, the one being concerned with unadulterated facts, and the other relying to some extent on intuition and imagination. This dichotomy was to develop within the man himself and the essay is in this sense the discussion of a personal problem. One might have expected him to have been, on the contrary, attracted to a theory that offered the best chance of synthesizing the two disciplines, but the repudiation of any connection between the scientific and artistic process is central to much of his early criticism. His adoption of Gottschall's views, as distinct from those of the younger generation of German critics, is mirrored by his predilection for Romantic literature.

We have little reliable information about his choice of books as a student, but it seems likely that he was well versed in Tokugawa literature and Chinese romances. Apart from the odd clue that can be gathered from both *Gan* and *Vita Sexualis,* which give a good idea of the reading habits of students at the time Ōgai was studying in Tokyo, there is a more explicit statement in the much later work 'Saiki Kōi', in which he recalled:

> When I was young I devoured the books of a lending library man. At that time they used to walk around with books piled on their backs in a sort of pannier. These books were mainly of three kinds: tales, copy books, and popular love stories. The tales were mainly by Kyōden and Bakin, the love stories by Shunsui and Kinsui, and the copy books were what we now call scripts for storytellers. When I had finished all these I asked the man if he had anything I hadn't read. He recommended I should read some miscellaneous essays. If you can read these, and even get through books like the antiquarian writings of Ise Teijō, you deserve to graduate in lending library literature, which I duly did.
>
> I first became addicted to Bakin, but then came to enjoy reading Kyōden more; and I always preferred Shunsui to Kinsui. I developed a similar partiality later on when I read German literature, always having a greater taste for Hauptmann than Sudermann. (XVIII, 67)

In addition to this, Ōgai was also well versed in Chinese romances, as the list of the books in his library testifies.[8] In his early period, then, Ōgai saw in fiction a release and change from work. His rejection of Zola's theories was motivated by an instinctive realization that, in his own case, science and art pulled in two different directions. 'Shōsetsuron' was to be the first of many warnings he was to issue on the dangers of adhering to a purely Naturalistic view of literature, but it was primarily a private discussion, as the matters it treated were, to all intents and purposes unknown in Japan in 1889.

The major part of the next essay of any importance, ' "Bungaku to shizen" o yomu' (On reading 'Literature and nature', May 1889), was based on very similar material: the first chapter of Gottschall's *Poetik* entitled 'Das Schöne und die Kunst' (The beautiful and art), where Ōgai found an extension of the theory of the nature of art on which the German critic based his rejection of Zola.[9] The argument is couched in the terminology of German aesthetics and revolves around a discussion of the three central elements, the True, the Good and the Beautiful. Ōgai explained the role of the Beautiful in belles lettres as follows:

> Now let us take a natural phenomenon. This phenomenon arises from some cause and thus is itself an effect. But because it can again give rise to another phenomenon, it is also a cause. It is cause and effect. It follows that, no matter how far we go back or forward in time, we will never finally know where the ultimate lies. When someone perceives this phenomenon, however, having first broken this endless chain and transcended the bounds of cause and effect, there arises the Idea. The Idea is the perceiving of the unbounded principle behind the finite matter.
>
> The scientist, who believes in truth, thinks no more of matter once he is in possession of Idea, but the artist, who believes in beauty, creates matter from Idea and Idea from matter... The Idea in matter and the matter from Idea we call the Beautiful. This is the definition of the eternally unchanging Beautiful. (XXXVIII, 459)

One hesitates to speculate on how much of this was understood by Japanese of the time. Metaphysical speculation was not of course foreign to men schooled in Neo-Confucianism, but this passage is an elliptic rendering of the German original, which is itself highly eclectic. Gott-schall believed in a blend of the Hegelian concept of the Idea as manifested in Art with the view of art as providing a means of escape from the tyranny of the Will, which stems from Schopenhauer. He was firmly rooted in the tradition of German Idealism and worked from the premise that beauty — the essential ingredient without which art cannot be called art — is the direct expression of the metaphysical world that lies behind phenomenal reality. Ōgai continued his attempt to define the nature of art by stressing the special nature of the Beautiful:

> Because the Beautiful is Idea, it has no cause, no effect and no end; but the reason why it differs from the True and the Good is that it must be manifest in the individual phenomenon. Truth seeks a law outside phenomena. Once the fish is caught, why

worry about the trap? Scientists, who believe in truth, treat
phenomena as their fish trap. Goodness too seeks perfection outside phenomena. Perfection is something that the Beautiful has
already achieved, but which the Good is still trying to achieve.
Truth seeks to attain the fusion of individual phenomena into
itself; goodness seeks to make the individual phenomena its
victim; only beauty allows the individual phenomena to stand
independent and free. . . Because a combination of the learning of
India, which extols truth, and the philosophy of China, which
extols goodness, was the material for our country's civilization,
we have been unable to let the individual phenomenon have
sufficient freedom. A mind that despises form is ignorant of the
fact that after the form has been burned in the fires of the Idea,
the dross is destroyed and the Beautiful remains. To throw away
the baby with the bath water − that is the fate of the Orientals.
(XXXVIII, 460)

Once the difference between the True, the Good and the Beautiful has
been firmly established, Ōgai is in a position to refute any idea that
tries to burden art either with a moral purpose or with the imitation of
nature 'as it is'.

The whole essay finishes with a postscript, which is a restatement of
the theory that art is a matter of creation rather than imitation, and
that nature, as the artist's material, must first pass through his imagination before being incorporated in the work of art:

Conscious Idea is Mind; unconscious Idea is Nature. Beauty is
dormant in Nature and awake in Mind. The Imagination proclaims
this beauty within Mind. When the Imagination achieves beauty,
it does so through Nature, but it does not depict Nature merely as
it is within Mind; it creates beauty by burning most of the dirt
that surrounds Nature in the fires of the Idea. The Beautiful
already exists within the Imagination and cries out to be united
with the outer form. That which gives it form is art. Art is thus
the creation of beauty with one's own hands, the animation of
dead objects; it is one and the same thing from the sculptor's
chisel to the artist's colours and the writer's brush.

Thus art is creation. The difference between beauty and Nature
is precisely this matter of creation. It is called Transubstantiation.
It is unknown to those who merely imitate Nature. (XXXVIII,
463)

This essay hardly provided a very clear exposition of Hegelian
aesthetics, but the main concepts do stand out: art must be judged on
its own terms, is of a transcendental quality, and as a result the mere
imitation of nature is totally inadequate.

Perhaps the most interesting problem posed by Ōgai's reaction to

Zola and the principle of the autonomy of art, with beauty as its only standard, was his approach to a definition of obscenity and pornography. The question became more important to him personally many years later when his own *Vita Sexualis* was banned on the grounds of being harmful to public morals. But this question clearly occupied his thoughts even at this early stage. How, one might ask, could he square a principle of the freedom of art from any standard except the Beautiful with a condemnation of Zola on grounds of obscenity? To claim that the erotic was not beautiful and therefore not art was begging the question.

There can be little doubt that Ōgai's profession made him view sex as a medical phenomenon. It is amusing to note that the salacious Chinese stories that he read as a student have the German translations for many of the sexual perversions described written in the margin, almost as if he had used the chance to improve his German medical vocabulary.[10] As will be seen later, he had a personal disinclination to treat sex as a very important part of his emotional life, and his later attack on the Japanese Naturalists was based very much on a dislike of their obsession with sex.

Ōgai was, however, also concerned over the danger of good works of art being banned merely because they dealt with love, and it was in an attempt to get to grips with this problem that he wrote an article in September 1889 entitled 'Jōshi no genkai o ronjite waisetsu no teigi ni oyobu' (Towards a definition of pornography through a discussion of the limits of the love story). Having discussed the various methods of portrayal, he writes:

> As you see there are many ways of portraying love. So where does obscenity lie? I would say, not here. One is not committing the offence of pornography when one excites people's emotions with the power of the Beautiful, since literature and art are not then giving in to the end in itself. It arises only when a crafty author deliberately probes people's nerves and fans their desires. Pornography avoids the imaginary and tends towards the realistic, and is thus similar to the imitation of nature . . .
>
> I venture to give this warning to Japanese critics. When you criticize a man's work and call it obscene, you must first investigate the meaning of that concept and hand down your judgement only after having prepared a standard for belles lettres. You must not label everything which deals vaguely with love between man and woman pornography. Educationalists treat as pornographic all novels that contain material that they do not want young girls and boys to read. Everything that reveals the true state of society, with not even a fig leaf in front of the mouth [sic] as they say in

the West, is pornographic to theologians. But the world of the artistic novel should on no account be restricted to the world of children, and there is no point in preventing the truth about society being portrayed. I would call pornography that which probes people's nerves and fans their desires, and I would have this banned. Why? Because this kind of literature stands outside the aim of art in itself, and therefore has not the slightest aesthetic value. (XXII, 517–18)

The definition was, of course, not forthcoming. To claim that if the author's intention is to fan illicit desires in the reader, then the work automatically falls outside the realm of art, and is therefore obscene, is somewhat suspect. It is of great interest to find Ōgai basing a definition of pornography on the seriousness and sincerity of the author, at a time when he was also trying to argue for the complete autonomy of art and a clear distinction between the Good and the Beautiful. Only later was he to realize the impracticality of such a sharp division. There is a sign here of that moralist approach to art which was always with him, although he denounced it at this early stage. Always the teacher, he was to find the divorce of morality from beauty was not really possible.[11]

It is interesting to note here that another attempt to introduce theories which were based on German Idealist Aesthetics was made by Futabatei Shimei in his 'Shōsetsu sōron' of 1886. Futabatei based his essay on the writings of the Russian Belinsky who in turn was a champion of Hegel for at least part of his career as a critic. According to Futabatei it was the duty of the novelist to portray reality in such a way as to reveal the Idea that lay behind external phenomena directly to the reader. He rejected the didactic novel in much stronger terms than did Shōyō. There was no discussion of the nature of the Beautiful, however, and Futabatei used the essentially idealist aesthetics to provide a rationale for realism.[12]

Ōgai, working from Gottschall and yet ultimately from the same base, stressed the autonomy of the Beautiful not only in relation to the Good but also the True. Emphasizing the role of the Imagination and damning imitation, he argued for a more romantic concept of literature. Ōgai was not limiting his view to the novel, but the point is still valid. Futabatei saw the writer's skill as a matter of selection and technique in the representation of reality. Ōgai saw the artistic process as one of creation and transformation of reality. It provides an interesting example of the extent to which opposing views can be traced to a common source.

There can be no doubt that '"Bungaku to shizen" o yomu' represents undigested knowledge, in that the greater part is paraphrased from Gottschall. The latter, moreover, was merely writing an introduction to a book of which the primary concern was the technique of poetry. It was a synthesis of widely disparate elements and an unfortunate choice for Ōgai to use as a first guide. He was soon to realize the need for a more integrated, systematic theory of aesthetics.

Despite an over-reliance on Gottschall, who himself had no real grasp of the nature or potential of the novel, Ōgai's early critical articles brought a seriousness and depth to literary debate that augured well for the future. He went much further than Shōyō in the attempt to divorce art from standards other than the Beautiful, and was beginning to find in German aesthetics that solid base for criticism that he had demanded in the manifesto to *Shigarami-zōshi*, although whether it was to prove long lasting or fully apposite was a different question. His condemnation of Zola and his warnings about the tenets of Naturalism in Europe were somewhat premature in Japan. Nevertheless, the excessive concern with real fact and truth, together with a concentration on the more sordid aspects of life that characterized the later Japanese Naturalists, gives his articles a prophetic ring. Although far removed from Zola, their lack of concern with form suggests that Ōgai's obsession with the dangers of treating the True rather than the Beautiful as the standard for literature was not unwarranted.

Aesthetics

The system of aesthetics to which Ōgai turned in an attempt to find a more satisfactory basis for his understanding of the nature of art was that of Karl Robert Eduard von Hartmann (1842-1906) who had refined and adapted Hegelian aesthetics to his own philosophical beliefs. These ideas are relatively unfamiliar, and in order to understand the kind of concepts with which Ōgai was dealing a short résumé may be helpful.

In the first volume of his two-volume work on aesthetics — the historical section entitled *Die Deutsche Aesthetik seit Kant* (German Aesthetics since Kant), Hartmann laid great emphasis on the distinction between what he called abstract or pure idealism, where the role of the work of art itself was ignored, and concrete idealism, where the physical work of art was all-important. Hegel had been the first to grasp the essential truth, that beauty was inevitably tied to physical matter, and Hartmann accepted Hegel's definition of beauty in art as the 'sensuous semblance of the Idea'.

In the second volume, *Philosophie des Schönen* (Philosophy of the Beautiful), Hartmann set out his own system. He identified six stages of formal beauty in which the Beautiful, representative of the Idea that lies behind all reality, becomes more and more concrete, until it reaches absolute concreteness in the individual work of art. These 'planes of consciousness' *(Konkretionsstufen)* were as follows: unconscious formal beauty, or the sensuously pleasant; the mathematically pleasant; the dynamically pleasant; the passively teleological, that is the beauty of the unconscious purposiveness of a particular natural mechanism; the living, that is the beauty of life in nature; and lastly the beauty of the type or genus of any given species, that which gives distinctiveness to a particular genre *(Gattungsmässige)*. It is at this point that beauty enters the realm of art; in Hegelian terms, Idea becomes Ideal.

Art which reveals this last kind of beauty, however, is limited, derivative and prone to the dangers of mere imitation of types. Hartmann goes one stage further and posits a last plane where the Idea becomes totally concrete, not in a type or genre, but in an individual work of art. The Idea shines through the matter and gives the object its own individuality.

If we accept that the presence of the Idea is that which gives art beauty, what is its mode of existence and how does the receptive process work? Is beauty subjective, in the eye of the beholder; objective, a physical quality of the object beheld; or does it exist in some other sphere? Ōgai explained the theory as follows:

> Once we say that beauty is not reality, we must consider the proposition that it is subjective. When a poet produces a poem from his imagination (the inner work of art) he must put it into words and move it from the subjective to the objective (the outer work of art). If we say that beauty is subjective, we will never understand how it becomes an outer work of art in this way. Now if we go a stage further and ask why the outer work of art excites a subjective feeling in the reader, this theory that beauty is subjective becomes even more untenable. While a writer produces a poem over a long period of time, doesn't everyone who reads or recites it have a common subjective reaction on the instant? The reason why it is difficult to compose and easy to read can not be found in the theory that beauty is subjective. (XXIII, 53)[13]

The answer to the problem is that beauty is neither subjective nor objective but is a process by which the Idea in the matter, where it lies by virtue of the creator, becomes detached from objective reality and merges with the subjective consciousness of the observer. It is therefore transcendental but dependent on the real.

The production of subjective beauty is limited to the writer. The reader receives the objectively real form or sound wave through his own senses. At this moment the objective beauty of the poem invades the reader through the medium of the objectively real form or sound wave. The outer work of art is objectively real and thus not of itself beautiful, but the beauty engendered from the subjectivity of the writer has been transferred into the outer work of art, and thus the latter becomes the cause destined to produce a beautiful imaginative reaction in the reader. Beauty is not real, but except through the medium of reality it cannot enter subjectivity. This entrance of beauty through the real into the subjective while yet being divorced from the real is called the semblance of beauty. This is the theory of transcendental realism. (XXIII, 53)

Correct perception of beauty should be untrammelled by conscious thought. Thus the self too must be absorbed unconsciously into the semblance. The postulation of this semblance helps to explain the fact that aesthetic emotion is or should be different from real emotion. The reaction to a beautiful woman and a picture of a beautiful woman are thus of a different nature. This is the outline of the rather complex aesthetic theory that Ōgai tried to introduce into his discussions of art and literature.

Ōgai first mentioned Hartmann in an article dated April 1890, but the ideas were first used in two articles in which he criticized Toyama Masakazu's opinions on the future of Japanese art and painting.[14] This discussion, like many of his early polemical writings, was not so much a debate as a one-sided statement of theory. Form, he claimed, must not be forgotten. Content was, of course, important, but the theory of painting should be more concerned with technique and the way the artist used his material. In response to Toyama's call for intellectual art (*shisōga*), he stressed the independence of art from any social or moral interference, and argued for the ideal of the inspired genius. Ōgai's articles on painting were usually more abstract than practical and show considerable knowledge of modern developments in European art. A supporter of Harada's romanticism against those advocates of French impressionism, the influence of his friendship with Harada and Gabriel Max was strong. He did show interest in the technical aspects, however, as is evidenced from his *Yōga Tebiki Sō* (Handbook of Western Painting) which he produced in collaboration with Ōmura Seigai in 1898. This work was a manual for artists and was based on K. Raupp's *Katechismus der Malerei* (1894).

A similar use of Hartmann's theories can be seen in a short debate conducted with Ishibashi Ningetsu over the latter's criticism of 'Utakata no ki' in November 1890. Ōgai reiterated the importance of form and style in the work of art, and discussed the term *yūgen,* using it as a synonym for Hartmann's Unconscious.

The fullest use of Hartmann, however, was in the long series of articles exchanged with Tsubouchi Shōyō which began as a discussion of the nature of literary criticism and became known as the *Botsurisō Ronsō* or debate over 'submerged ideas'. At the start, Ōgai recorded that:

> When I was engaged in the founding of the Shinseisha I relied on the *Poetik* of Gottschall and discussed the critical methods of my contemporaries by dividing them into the two schools of Idealism and Realism. But that is now in the past. After a while I became interested in Hartmann's philosophy, and when I came to his work on aesthetics I at last felt as if I knew where I had gone wrong. (XXIII, 5)

It is not known for certain when Ōgai first came into contact with Hartmann's work. For a long time it was assumed that a passage in the story 'Mōsō' (1911) which refers to him buying a copy of Hartmann's *Philosophie des Unbewussten* (Philosophy of the Unconscious) one morning in Berlin was factually correct, but Kanda Takao has shown that Ōgai's copy of this book is dated 1889, after he had returned to Japan.[15] There was an excellent outline of Hartmann's philosophy, but not his aesthetics, in the books on the history of philosophy by Schwegler and Borelius that he read in Germany, and this was probably where he first 'became interested in Hartmann's philosophy'.

There can be little doubt, however, that his major interest was in the aesthetics, and he was later to argue that Hartmann's ideas on art could easily be accepted without having recourse to his pessimistic philosophy.[16] The passage in 'Mōsō' is thus more a reflection of his outlook at forty-nine than a faithful account of his attitudes at twenty-six.

The *Botsurisō* controversy began when Ōgai criticized Shōyō for his system of classification of prose and poetry, and attempted to put forward his own system by borrowing concepts and terms taken from Hartmann. His study of literary theory up to this point had convinced him that there were certain *a priori* aesthetic standards that had to be applied in literary criticism, whereas Shōyō took a far less theoretical view. On the question of the distinction between Idealism and Realism, for instance, Ōgai began by quoting from Gottschall:

> Gottschall calls that which stems from the imitation of nature and the portrayal of reality Realism, and that which stems from the world of Ideas, the sphere of the mind, Idealism (*Poetik*

I, 99). This would relate to Shōyō's Realists, devoted to nature, and his Lyricists, devoted to ideas. Gottschall goes on to say that those who tend towards Realism will produce works of art that centre on nature without mind, and those who tend towards Idealism will produce works of art that centre on mind without nature. (XXIII, 12)

This, however, is rejected in favour of Hartmann's theory:

Hartmann does not recognize the difference between Idealist and Realist. He rejects the abstract and accepts the concrete; he despises the Idea of Genre but values the Idea of Individuality. He once discussed the revolution in Art and said that the revolutionaries believed in what they called realism and naturalism, but it was just a mask. In nature there is the Individual but no Genre. Therefore, although to treat Art as imitation is of course a mistake, while under that misapprehension it is better to imitate nature rather than the abstract form of Genre. There is no reality in Genre, but there is in the Individual, and so to treat the Ideal as unnecessary and to take reality as material for Art is to move away from the Idea of Genre and to approach closer to the Idea of Individuality. The source of the strength of the revolutionaries lies in the Microcosmic Idea. The Ideal they are rejecting as unnecessary is actually the Ideal of Genre. They do not realize that there exists an Ideal of Individuality as distinct from an Ideal of Genre.

Since Beauty is a semblance divorced from reality, there is no way that the Real can be part of Art. When we create an aspect of the Idea, the fact that it may resemble reality is entirely accidental. The reason why the beauty of the Individual is more beautiful than that of Genre is not because it is closer to reality. The reason why the beauty of reality is greater than a work of Genre-beauty is that it approximates more to the real concrete Individual (*Aesthetik* II, 188–9).

It would not be a very satisfactory theory if we tried to equate Idealism exclusively with Lyric poetry and Realism with Epic poetry. Both the baneful effects of concentrating on the idealistic Idea of Genre and the profit to be gained from a concentration on the realistic Idea of Individuality can be seen throughout the three groups, Lyric, Epic and Drama. Similarly one has the profit to be gained from the vivid idealism of the poetic semblance, which deals with only a few important matters, and the baneful effects of realism, which bores the reader with too many trifling details. (XXIII, 12–13)

Whether Shōyō really understood what was being said here behind such esoteric terminology is doubtful, but he continued the debate with two further articles in which he repeated his position, using the slogan 'reporting facts' *(kijitsu)* in contrast to what he called Ōgai's 'discussion of ideas' *(danri)*. Shōyō felt that criticism of a writer like Shakespeare was difficult because:

> Shakespeare's works are like a totally impartial mirror. In them everyone's countenance is reflected. To put it more clearly, the reflection of any reader's ideas *(risō)* can be discovered in his work . . . In admiring Shakespeare we can of course praise his technique in bringing human nature alive, and we can praise the miracle of his metaphor, his imagination and his conception as something unprecedented and unique. But it is difficult to accept praise of his ideas as being as great as those of a great philosopher. We should rather value his work for its submerged ideas *(Botsurisō)*.[17]

Shōyō was saying that a great work of art was a perfect mirror, an amoral objective picture of reality. The critic's business was to describe the work to the reader who could then supply his own ideas which corresponded to the infinite variety of ideas that lay submerged within.

Ōgai's reaction to this was characteristic. In a second article entitled '*Waseda Bungaku* no botsurisō', he moved away from a discussion of inductive and deductive criticism, and concentrated on giving a fuller picture of what he meant by the term Idea. He made no concessions concerning the use of the word *risō*. Because he used the word to translate the German *Idee* the articles diverged from the very beginning. The argument degenerated to the point where Ōgai was merely quoting Shōyō in order to expound at even greater length on Hartmann's aesthetics, and one is tempted to think that his misinterpretation of Shōyō was deliberate and entirely for his own benefit. Not only did he interpret Shōyō's *risō* as the equivalent of *Idee* rather than the English 'ideas' in a very general sense, but he also treated the word 'submerged' as if it meant 'non-existent'. He thus made it seem that Shōyō was denying the existence of Idea, whereas he was arguing on a totally different plane. What started promisingly as a debate over inductive and deductive literary criticism became a one-sided explanation of the system of concrete idealist aesthetics at Shōyō's expense.

Somewhat unwisely Shōyō allowed himself to be drawn into further dispute and the misdirected polemics continued. One searches in vain for any clues as to how these ideas might relate to Ōgai's own work. Hartmann's aesthetic in fact did very little to change his former convictions. The most one can see is a slight retreat from the bitter attack on Realism and Naturalism, in that Ōgai came to realize that the theory and not the practice of Zola was the culprit.[18]

That the debate was a semantic wrangle is indisputable, and Ōgai was later to confess that it was Shōyō's insistence on inductive criticism that had really started the whole affair:

> At the time Tsubouchi was advocating *kijitsu* and had decided not to apportion praise or censure. However, he did not contradict the fact that in the 'reporting of facts' he was unwittingly praising and criticizing. This was because, no matter how impartial his judgement, he was not a god. Seeing this I got very upset and the so-called *Botsurisō* debate started. (XXVI, 431)

Viewed from the declared aim of Ōgai to establish an aesthetic foundation for literary criticism, the debate must be judged an almost complete failure, but it was of prime importance in the history of literary criticism. It was the first such debate to deal with complex philosophical questions in relation to literature and criticism, and can be seen as having an important role in the advancement of the serious study of literature in Meiji Japan.

Science and art

We have already seen how from the very beginning Ōgai held to a sharp distinction between science and art, and he was continually stressing the fundamental difference between both their methods and their demands. He believed firmly at this stage that in his own experience they were irreconcilable opposites. The division between the Beautiful and the True went hand in hand with a clear division between his official life in the army and the more private life within literature. As he wrote in June 1889:

> Belles lettres, poetry, on the one hand, and medicine, as a branch of science, on the other, are essentially and absolutely independent, and have had not the slightest connection since the very beginning.
>
> I believe that there is in man a vein which is called the poetic vein. Dissection will never reveal its shape or construction, and no physiologist will ever know how it functions. (XXIX, 157)

Possibly this was the only way that Ōgai could continue to work. Science and art were combined in the one man by paradoxically keeping them in different watertight compartments. His espousal of the tenets of German Idealism and his close reading of much of German Romantic literature meant that he saw literature as something divorced from the hard reality of the world as he knew it. The depth of his belief in the total validity of the poetic world is also revealed in the long and difficult translation of Hans Christian Andersen's *Improvisatoren* (1835)[19] on which he spent so much of his spare time, and which took nearly nine years to complete — from November 1892 to January 1901. Although it takes us out of his early period, it raises many questions which are crucial to an understanding of his early work.

This story, told in the first person, is the record of the life of an Italian improvisor and musician who, after many tribulations, eventually succeeds as an artist and finds fulfilment in his love for a beautiful Venetian. Thus as 'Die Geschichte eines Genies' by Ossip Schubin ends in despair, this story ends in romantic bliss. The novel was Andersen's first great success, both in Denmark and the rest of Europe, and the majority of the background seems to have been taken from his own experiences during his travels through Italy as a young man. The novel comes very close to being a mere travelogue at times.

The youthful protagonist is the typical romantic figure, a child of poetic inspiration, whose one guiding light is 'love' and adoration for the ideal woman that he seeks and eventually finds. The story recounts, often in a tone of insufferable egotism, a catalogue of important love affairs, each woman embodying a different facet of the ideal love he seeks. The whole journey towards the attainment of his dreams is set against the idyllic background of an Italian landscape. In many passages the novel can charm and delight by its descriptions of natural grandeur, but the plot is so contrived and unconvincing and the characters so lifeless and stereotyped that it can only be seen as a second-rate novel which perhaps deserves its present-day obscurity.

Nine years spent on a painstaking translation suggests more than the usual degree of love for the work in hand, and demands an explanation.

The nearest we have to an apologia can be found in an article written in May 1893.[20] Ōgai had already started on *Improvisatoren,* or *Sokkyō Shijin* as it is known in Japanese, but was concentrating at the time on medical matters. The article tries to explain the role of the journal in answer to criticism that it was losing some of its former sharpness and relevance:

> What has *Shigarami-zōshi* introduced in the way of stories? Here let us mention just a few of the main ones. From French there are the works of Daudet; from German, the recent work of Ossip Schubin; from Danish, Andersen's *Improvisatoren*; and from Russian, a work of Lermontov's. Do they not all stand apart from the trends of any particular period? Are they not an excellent collection? Especially *Improvisatoren*. I may not be that partial to the Romantics, but when I picked this up and read it through to see what it was like, at a time when the so-called Realists are getting more and more obscene and bestial, it seemed as though I had emerged from the grime of the city factories into quite another world of natural beauty.

What is realism? One could define it as that which is based on psychological study and which uses shock tactics such as brutality or obscenity. However, if one thereby loses beauty, what value does it have as art? I am not disputing that a novel should contain psychological actuality, but it should be clear from the aesthetics of Hartmann, which I have recently touched upon, that this actuality is Idea, not reality.

There are realists who go to extremes and say that reality is the world devoid of Idea, and that it is not possible to enter the realm of art without relating to nature alone. The works of writers who fall into this error merely imitate nature to no purpose. They become mere records of someone's life history. Just as in the past there was a professor of Chinese who became excited that pleasure was to be found even in the classics, I set out to translate a work like *Improvisatoren* with the intention of showing how the actualities of this world can be depicted in a novel without rejecting beauty. (XXIII, 210–11)

Ōgai then turns to the general question of translation and its merits over the writing of mere synopses of foreign works, a form of introducing Western literature favoured at the time by the journal, *Waseda Bungaku:*

It is necessary to investigate English and German literature through translations. Schopenhauer disliked the translation of Greek and Latin works into German, comparing it to boiling chicory root instead of proper coffee. But in the past poets rich in creative ability have produced many translations and introduced the work of other men – take for instance Schiller's translation of *Macbeth.* Although some may have felt that they did not want to be idle at a time when their creativity failed them, the majority have sincerely wanted to try and introduce poetic works they loved to their countrymen.

Moreover, as the example of Schlegel and Tieck's introduction of Shakespeare into Germany testifies, translation, as necessary work, can be enough in itself to transform a writer into a true master. Thus people prize translations because the recipient of the poetry, in other words the reader, can to a certain extent create in his own imagination something that approximates to what the poet created in his. (XXXIII, 212)

The translation of *Improvisatoren,* then, was undertaken to illustrate Ōgai's belief that beauty and the depiction of 'reality' were not incompatible. In the process, however, he ignored the distinction between mere realistic description of the setting on the one hand, and fidelity to psychological reality – the provision of believable characters and a feasible plot – on the other. The latter was quite absent from

Andersen's novel, which was more of a romance. It was in fact precisely that kind of 'idealism' that Ōgai had warned against in the much earlier article, 'Gendai shoka no shōsetsuron o yomu' (On reading essays on the novel by contemporary critics) when he had written:

> However, the idealism that stands in contrast to this realism also had its bad points. Just look at the novels of the German romantics or the recent *yomihon* of Japan. They almost all go counter to the real world. Thus the reader may meet men of genius and women of beauty in the stories, but they are all stereotyped figures each personifying an ideal. They are not individually minded characters of outstanding presence who can only be portrayed by means of psychological observation . . . Therefore I say: when idealism is taken to extremes it ends up by merely copying old patterns. (XXII, 72)

Perhaps the most remarkable thing about *Sokkyō Shijin* is its popularity in Japan. Both this translation and 'Umoregi', the work by Ossip Schubin, were widely read, and formed the background to the romanticism of the *Bungakkai* group in much the same way as *Omokage*. Even men like the critic, Masamune Hakuchō, were to look back on these works and recall their delight:

> As a novel that describes young love and combines emotion with external nature, there has been nothing to surpass *Sokkyō Shijin* since the Meiji era. I read this story three times . . . Of the translations I read in my twenties, the ones which left really unforgettable impressions were this *Sokkyō Shijin* and Kimiko's story of a young girl, *Yokusenki*. A few years ago, reminiscing on the past, I bought the newer edition and tried to review it a third time, but I did find that my sympathies were alienated from the characters in the story.[21]

At the time its failure as a novel mattered far less than the lyrical approach to life, the idealization of love, and the pure exoticism of the descriptions of the Italian countryside which clearly caught the imagination of young Japanese. Even today there are some Japanese who make a point of visiting many of the places mentioned in the story as a sentimental pilgrimage.

The main reason for its continued fame, however, is probably its style, in which Ōgai aimed for 'a harmonization of Japanese and Chinese, and a fusion of elegant and common phrasing' (II, 213). The question of its influence is a difficult one. It doubtless made a deep impression on the minds of young writers, but led to very few, if any, works of a similar vein.

As was the case with his other translations at this stage, the choice was guided more by his personal tastes than by any desire to 'educate' or 'enlighten' the reading public, although this element cannot, of course, be totally discounted. A consideration of *Sokkyō Shijin*, however, leads us into the years after 1894, his so-called 'silent years', during which he produced no original fiction. The translation of this long work was to occupy the major part of those years and Ōgai hinted at the effort involved in the introduction to the first printing of the complete book:

> This translation was begun on 10 September 1892 and finished on 15 January 1901. It took almost nine years. However, I had my army duties and wrote usually at night, on holidays, Sundays, and whenever I happened to be at home with no visitors. I regret that through the years my tastes have often changed, and I have found it difficult to produce a uniform style. Moreover I repeatedly stopped writing and found it impossible to put pen to paper again with any enthusiasm. Some people have said that I neglected my duties and selfishly indulged myself in writing. This is a gross misrepresentation. (II, 213)

It would appear that Ōgai's attitude towards literature changed during the period he was engaged in writing *Sokkyō Shijin*, and that the work proved difficult to finish. Part of the reason he persevered may be sought in his comment that writers and poets who undertook translations 'may have felt that they did not want to be idle at a time when their creativity failed them'. *Sokkyō Shijin*, especially the later part, is in some ways more transformation than translation, and it can be seen as an attempt to satisfy a creative urge while his imagination proved unproductive. It was also a form of relaxation from the down to earth duties of an army surgeon; a form of escape.

The fervour with which he had espoused the theory of the primacy of the Beautiful and the Imagination as a justification for the delight in the discovery of European literature was to wane as he found increasingly that he could not apply the theory to fit his own capabilities. When literature becomes a form of escape, its seriousness and relevance is brought into question. The feeling of disappointment when having to face up to his own limitations can be sensed in the introduction just quoted above, and it must have been all the stronger because that very work was to appear more and more immature to a man who was slowly undergoing the drastic change of allegiance from the Beautiful to the True that has already been hinted at.

There comes a time when it is legitimate to ask how far two supposedly opposite drives, in this case the scientific and the artistic, can be accommodated in one mind and remain mutually unaffected. Was it possible to live two lives, one internal and the other external, one poetic and ideal and the other prosaic and real? It is in this context that his interest in Hartmann is revealing.

Helped by the concept of an all-pervading Idea, Hartmann aimed to synthesize the apparent opposites of science and art. In the introduction to his book, *Philosophie des Unbewussten,* he saw the problem as:

> to combine the speculative (mystically gained) principles with the highest results hitherto attained of inductive science according to inductive method, in order to bridge over the gulf between the two, and to elevate what hitherto have been merely subjective convictions to the rank of objective truths. It was in reference to this great and seasonable problem that I chose the motto 'Speculative results according to inductive scientific method'.[22]

The change, however slight, in Ōgai's attitude towards realism which accompanied his move from the theories of Gottschall to those of Hartmann is indicative of a softening of the rigid divisions that he started out with. The strict line between the Beautiful and the True that is such a marked feature of his early articles is combined with a striking lack of any discussion of the relationship between literature and nature, apart from the rather muddled article, '"Bungaku to shizen" o yomu'. If no connection was allowed, then this is partly understandable, but could literature in fact be cut off from reality in this way?

That the theory of the autonomy of beauty, truth and morality was practically untenable is clear from his own stories which contain a very great deal of 'nature', and from his discussion of pornography where the line between beauty and morality became of necessity blurred. It is perhaps symbolic that during these early years Ōgai taught anatomy at the Tokyo Academy of Fine Arts. What in fact was to happen in the years to come was the gradual breakdown of these artificial barriers and the eventual abandonment by Ōgai of any attempt to classify literature into a mould.

When one looks below the surface of this distinction, it becomes clear that even at the very beginning Ōgai's attitude towards literary criticism and aesthetics was scientific. Discarding relativism he was continually looking for objective and secure standards for literature, and was for ever dissecting and analysing. Hartmann's detailed theory of the stages of the Beautiful was nothing if not ordered and clear cut. There was a fundamental contradiction between the method and the idealism that lay behind the theories. Ōgai was applying logic, that tool that was so essential to the rational scientific method, to the sphere of literature where it was inappropriate. The resultant breakdown was inevitable.

One area where the use of logic could help, however, was in that of language. It is doubtful whether Japanese had ever been used to bear such a rational train of thought before. Ōgai's unending analysis of meaning and nuance was one of the mainstays of his debating method, and it proved too strong for most opponents. This continual concern with rational thought and the rigorous search for the correct means of expression which was second nature to Ōgai is perhaps his greatest hidden gift to the development of the modern Japanese language.

After the *Botsurisō* debate with Shōyō, Ōgai felt that further and more systematic explanation of Hartmann's aesthetic was necessary, for he began to translate the whole of the *Philosophie des Schönen* and publish it from October 1892 in *Shigarami-zōshi*. The task was to prove too time-consuming, however, and he gave the project up after finishing only the first fifty pages. The Sino-Japanese War of 1894-5 proved to be more than a mere physical break and it marks a change in his attitude towards his own work. The move away from a dependence on Hartmann is revealed in a preface to a collection of his earlier articles, 'Tsukikusa jo', which appeared in 1896. After a short review of recent European art and literary criticism, he moves on to talk about himself:

> When I tried my hand at criticism of the arts in Japan, I chose the aesthetics of Hartmann, who had perfected answers to this type of aesthetical problem, and I based myself on him. Some people's reaction to this was to say that if I took his aesthetics as a base I must believe in his whole philosophical system. But while I agreed that his Unconscious should be studied to a certain extent, it was my intention neither to go into a cosy retreat behind the wall of his whole system, nor to take up his aesthetical metaphysics *en bloc* and peddle it piecemeal . . .
>
> Even my opponents cannot deny that since I took Hartmann's normative aesthetics as a basis for my criticism, I have influenced to some extent both the standing of aesthetics as a subject for study and the authority of Hartmann as a scholar in Japan. It was in 1883 that the Ministry of Education published a translation of the anti-metaphysical, or rather unscientific aesthetics of Véron, which they had commissioned from Nakae Chōmin. But it had hardly any effect at all on our country's literature or art. The reason why more emphasis has been placed on aesthetics, lectures have been inaugurated in the universities and some of the schools, and why there are even those who now call themselves specialists in aesthetics can be said without exaggeration to be at least in part due to the fact that I encouraged it in the somewhat

naive articles which appeared in *Shigarami-zōshi,* the journal that I and a few friends of like mind issued between 1889 and 1894.

At the same time some people's attention was drawn, either directly or indirectly, to Hartmann's philosophy, and the very ideas of the metaphysical school, which had until then been utterly crushed by the experimentalists, came to be widely studied here and there in Japan. Even today, when there are those who arrogantly maintain that people like Hartmann should be locked away in a high tower, my name still comes up whenever aesthetics is mentioned, and as soon as my name is brought up it is followed by that of Hartmann. Not only do people ridicule me as a critic who swears by him, but they have even begun to attack Hartmann himself on the principle that to shoot down the rider one must first shoot down his horse. I find it annoying, but so must Hartmann. Do I in fact swear by him? Are his aesthetics my hobby horse, and would I fall if the horse were shot down? The facts give ample evidence to the contrary . . .

Where will future developments in aesthetics come from? In a nutshell, I think that the actual details of the history of the arts will be accumulated and stimulate a scientific interpretation; in other words, empiricism. If the old abstract idealist aesthetics cannot embrace art stemming from nineteenth-century Naturalism, and if concrete idealist aesthetics cannot embrace art thereafter, I will glady expand my present view of the arts in the empirical direction, and even go so far as to change my standpoint fundamentally. In this sense I look forward to future developments. (XXIII, 298–301)

Despite this clear sign of a move towards relativism, Ōgai continued to work at translating and summarizing books on German aesthetics until the beginning of 1902. The most important of these were *Shimbi Shinsetsu,* a summary of Johannes Volkelt's *Aesthetische Zeitfragen* (Contemporary Problems in Aesthetics, 1895), from 1898 to 1899; a similar long summary of the whole of Hartmann's *Philosophie des Schönen* in collaboration with the art historian Ōmura Seigai, which was published in book form in 1899; and a translation of Otto Liebmann's *Zur Analyse der Wirklichkeit* (Towards an Analysis of Reality, 1900) in 1901. His strong desire to keep up with the latest developments is obvious when one compares the date of their first publication in Germany and the date of Ōgai's translations. The sombre truth is, however, that by this stage Ōgai's work in this field attracted very little attention. The summary of Volkelt was noticed by the *Tetsugaku Zasshi* and that of Liebmann by the *Teikoku Bungaku,* but this was only in passing. His summary of Hartmann did cause some temporary stir in academic circles when it was attacked by Takayama Chogyū and defended by Ōgai in August and September 1899, but the interest soon faded.

It should also perhaps be noted that his work in aesthetics had little effect on his ideas about literature, and in particular the novel. Hartmann was still working within the old framework of Epic, Lyric and Drama that had characterized Gottschall. It was well nigh impossible to classify the novel in this manner, and the attempt to place it somewhere between the Epic and the Lyric was only half-hearted. Ōgai was at last beginning to realize that theory must follow practice in the arts, and that the idea of the supremacy of the Imagination made this inevitable. The abandonment of aesthetics and indeed theorizing of any kind with regards to the arts was somehow symbolized in his last translation, the two page introduction to Heinrich von Stein's book, *Vorlesungen über Aesthetik* (Lectures on Aesthetics). The title 'Is aesthetics as a science possible?' may well be a pointer to the fact that Ōgai was seriously beginning to doubt the possibility himself.

PART II

1894 – 1912

4

TWO WARS

The Sino-Japanese War

The Sino-Japanese War of 1894–5 is a convenient point to place the end of Ōgai's early period. Not only is it a natural historical break, but a distinct change in his work can be seen after his return from the front. War with China was declared on 1 August 1894, but hostilities had already begun, with the result that by 16 August the Japanese First Army under Yamagata was in Pyongyang. Ōgai himself was ordered to take up the post of Chief Medical Officer for the Central Lines of Communication, and he left Ujina (Hiroshima) for Pusan on 2 September.

He was to stay in Pusan for only a month. The official reports, sent to Ishiguro Tadanori, who was in charge of hygiene in the field, are, as one might expect, dry and to the point. The eighteen reports sent back from Pusan deal with the state of the roads, rivers, hospitals, disease, and the problem of a safe water supply in which he took particular interest. On 3 October Ōgai was ordered to join the Second Army under General Ōyama which was to occupy the Liaotung Peninsula and then in the new year cross south to Shantung and capture Weihaiwei in February 1895. After a few days back in Japan, Ōgai arrived in Liaotung at Hwa Yuan K'ou on 24 October 1894, moving to Liu Shu Tun on 13 November. Following the army to Shantung he saw the battle for Weihaiwei from a vantage point behind the lines and stayed there until 28 February. March, April and early May were spent back in Liu Shu Tun, where he also received a visit from Masaoka Shiki on 10 May. He was then ordered to travel to the newly acquired island of Taiwan, where he dealt with general matters of hygiene from 29 May to 22 September. Eventually he arrived back in Tokyo on 4 October 1895. Forty official reports were sent to Ishiguro while with the Second Army and eight from Taiwan.

One might expect to glean clues to his reaction to his first experience of war from the diary, the 'Sosei nikki', which covers the period from 25 August 1894 to 4 October 1895, but, as Donald Keene has noted, it reveals very little.[1] His post kept him for the most part behind the lines and although he saw the wounded every day, he saw the enemy seldom. The only times he was in any personal danger were on 21 November 1894, when there was a possibility that the Chinese retreating from the defeat at Kinchow might attack the clearing hospital at Liu Shu Tun, and in the first days of June 1895 when he landed at San Tiao Chueh in northern Taiwan. The diary records these moments with little passion.

The only interesting parts of Ōgai's diary have nothing to do with the war or the fighting. There are details of the instruments and dances at a Korean party on 23 September, notes on a Chinese play he saw in Lu Shun on 18 December, a delighted description of the house where he was staying in Hwa Yuan K'ou, and a poem on some socks that his sister had sent him. The only moment of light relief is the following entry for 1 December: 'Stores in the Mine Section had a number of cans of mock turtle soup. They couldn't read English and so mistook it for medicine and sent it to us. We enjoyed it' (XXXV, 242). The diary is in fact notable for the distinct lack of patriotic sentiment and the total absence of enthusiasm, which is in great contrast to the reactions of the majority of Japanese literary figures at the time.

The only other work of Ōgai's which has any connection with this war is his biography of Prince Kitashirakawa Yoshihisa, which was written at the request of Genéral Kitamura and published in June 1908. The movements of the Prince, as Head of the Imperial Guard Division in Manchuria and then in Taiwan, where he died of malaria on 28 October 1895, are recorded in great detail.

The lack of enthusiasm in the diary tells its own story. An army doctor is always in an unwelcome position in wartime, and it is difficult to be thrilled about victories when one is seeing to the results of carnage. There is only one poem of note where this unsettling contradiction comes to the fore. On 2 December 1894 he wrote:

> *As if to my wife*
> While the north wind invades the battle tent
> And cold pierces through my tattered nightshirt
> We talk of the battle at sea;
> Suddenly I long for home.

Leaning on my pillow, the candle flickering,
Comes the sound of voices through the open flaps.
At parting the frosted leaves fall,
Snow petals thick on the path ahead.

Two tears on my travelling clothes,
Measureless sorrow in the lanterns.
But emotions cannot be the deciding factor,
Reason alone must prevail.

Banner and drum – the army stands prepared
While the doctor applies his cures.
I want the ability to raise the dead,
Not a return to the middle ages! (XXXV, 242–3)

When Ōgai returned to Japan he was reappointed to his old posts
as Head of the Staff College and lecturer at the Military Academy.
The next two years saw the publication of the large handbook on
hygiene, entitled *Eisei Shimpen,* which represents the culmination
of much of his earlier work in the medical field. This book, the first
half of which was published in December 1896 and the second in June
1897, went through five editions in all (1897, 1899, 1904, 1908 and
1914), additional material increasing its extent from 942 to 1830
pages. It was published in two different issues, one for use within the
army and one for a more general use as a textbook in the universities.

Recent research has revealed that *Eisei Shimpen* started as the translation of Max Rubner's *Lehrbuch der Hygiene* (1890) by Ōgai and
Nakahama Tōichirō, with certain additions by Koike Masanao. Much
of the material had already been published over the years from November 1889 to July 1894 in Ōgai's own medical journals.[2] Although the
book grew a little with each edition, the last change added some eight
hundred pages. It was at this point that Ōgai added a number of independent studies, many of which had also previously been published.
These articles were based on a combination of later revised versions of
Rubner's book plus a number of other books and papers that Ōgai
was always receiving from Germany. Chief among these studies was a
treatment of sexuality, originally entitled 'Seiyoku zassetsu' (Various
theories concerning the sexual drive, November 1902) which, although
clearly based on secondary sources, discussed European studies of sex

ranging from Krafft-Ebing to the earliest work of Freud.[3] It was something of a pioneering essay in Japan.

The final edition of *Eisei Shimpen* thus represented a much augmented and revised version of one of the best German books on the subject at the time and was an important landmark, a reliable and comprehensive textbook. Although in the early stages it was envisaged as a joint venture, the major part of the initial work and all the revisions were Ōgai's. We know from a letter he wrote to Kako Tsurudo dated 18 October 1904 that he had much trouble persuading Koike that revision was necessary and that he was eventually forced to carry it out himself.

In the January of 1897 Ōgai founded the medical journal *Kōshū Iji* to replace the *Eisei Ryōbyōshi* which had terminated with the war. The latter journal carried a number of his articles, some of which, as we have seen, were incorporated later into the revised *Eisei Shimpen.* As Ōgai was determined to carry on his popularization of public health and hygiene, *Kōshū Iji* was informed by the same journalistic spirit as his earlier products. He was also working about this time on a book of anatomy for artists, which was eventually published in collaboration with Kume Keiichirō as *Geiyō Kaibōgaku* (1903). But if one area is to be singled out as a central concern during these years, it is his old bugbear of the army diet and the question of beri-beri. In September 1900 he made a vigorous defence of his views in response to general criticism by reporters who had followed the Japanese expedition to Peking at the time of the Boxer Rebellion. Reiterating his claim that rice was more digestible than bread and far easier to prepare and carry while on the march, he pointed out that the dry 'biscuit' that the Western soldiers had to eat may have looked handy, but was in the long run ruinous to the stomach lining and in any case far from appetising.[4]

If this journalistic activity cannot be compared with that of his extraordinary early period, one must remember that there were now younger men to bring in new information, and that Ōgai was in an administrative position where he had to resign himself to a more passive role. However, if his writings were less prolific, his deep concern with the process of modernization and the real rather than imaginary advance of Japanese science remained. It was, if anything, strengthened as he saw that his early dreams would take much longer to come true than he had first anticipated. Even before the war in an interview he gave in September 1891 he said:

> I returned to Japan about three years ago. At that time I hoped
> to give myself wholly to scientific research and produce some

new results, as I had done in Germany. I still have such hopes today. But when you look at the matter in perspective, Japan at the moment has not advanced to the point where students who return from studies abroad can be allowed to produce new work and nothing else. For such scientific work one needs space, materials, equipment for experiments and the necessary scientific reference books. Wherever you look these are all still lacking. There are those of my contemporaries who put up with such deficiencies and struggle on, but most of them are poor and what with life as it is in Japan today they cannot afford the luxury of research . . . (XXX, 196)

His appointment as Head of the Staff College in 1893, meant that he was to move further and further away from the chance of carrying out such study on his own. In a lecture he gave in 1903, entitled 'Eiseidan' (Thoughts on the study of hygiene), he mentioned his work and that of his friends in Germany:

I too studied with a will and dreamed of making some great discovery in the laboratory.

On returning, I worked for a while in the laboratory of the Military Medical College researching into food stuffs, but thanks to the system we in army circles call 'the conveyor belt', whereby new students push up from underneath, I was ejected from the laboratory before I knew where I was, and I was put in charge of a department. Thereafter I dealt with assigning personnel and compiling statistics, so that my studies were limited to reading the most recent Western journals . . .

This experience of ours is very strange, isn't it? I must apologize for talking about myself all the time, but I am convinced that this kind of experience is not restricted to Nagamatsu or myself. I believe that ours is a good example of what those who wish to study in Japan today have to face. (XXXIV, 246)

At the same time he talked of the fear that the Japanese might be racially incapable of producing original scientific research and results, only once again to reject this pessimistic approach. And yet the same troubled outlook can be seen in another lecture entitled 'Yōgaku no seisui o ronzu' (On the rise and fall of Western studies) which he had given in June 1902, a few months previously. While proclaiming much hope for the future of Japanese science, he warned at the same time of complacency and false national pride. The lecture was partly based on a speech made by Ōgai's old teacher Erwin Baelz in November 1901 on the occasion of his twenty-fifth anniversary as a lecturer at the University of Tokyo. Baelz sent Ōgai a copy of this lecture and it is clear that Ōgai felt the points made were valid and worth passing on.

The trend by this time was against replacing foreign professors as they left and to look upon travel to the West as already outmoded. Ōgai took pains to point out the dire consequences of such facile assumptions. If Japan was to achieve the status of an internationally recognized source of original work, young scholars had to do more than learn facts; they had to absorb the atmosphere of independent enquiry which was such a distinguishing feature of European culture. This was not to be achieved, however, by sending all the foreign professors back to Europe as soon as possible, or by deciding prematurely that Japan had little more to learn. Such superficial patriotism was mere arrogance.

While acutely aware of the gap in scientific learning and worried that the inner spirit was being overlooked, he was hopeful — using Baelz's metaphor — that the seeds would take root eventually and make it possible for the Japanese to produce their own fruit instead of merely importing it. In 'Mōsō' he invested a description of his return to Japan with attitudes held later:

> I longed for home. I longed for home as I had imagined it; a beautiful familiar land of dreams. But it was a pity that I would be returning to a land that was not yet equipped for either the serious scientific research that I had to undertake or the opening up of new fields within that science. I venture to say 'not yet'. A German who has been in Japan for a long time and who is said to know the country inside out has warned that not only are conditions for such study lacking at the moment, but that they might never arise in the Orient. He claims that the atmosphere to nourish the Natural Sciences does not exist here in the Far East. If this is in fact the case, then we can never expect the Imperial University or the Research Institute for Infectious Diseases to be anything more than places where scientific results from Europe are passed on. This same kind of judgement appears in the play *Taifun*[5] which is so popular in Europe in the wake of our war with Russia. But I venture to say 'not yet' because I do not think the Japanese are such a hopelessly incompetent race. I have always felt that the time will come when the fruits of scientific research carried out in Japan will be exported to Europe. (VIII, 206)

Ōgai had always tried to maintain a balanced view between national pride and the need to learn from the West, but the immense effort entailed in this attempt must have contributed to his sense of anxiety. The same problem is alluded to in the short story 'Fushigi na kagami'

(1912). Ōgai's wife is complaining that he is spending too much money on books:

'. . . Most of them are Western books, as usual.'
'I know, but I can't help that. I'm borrowing from the West because I haven't enough brains of my own. I know I can't hope to match original thinkers with all the borrowing I do, but without it I'd be in a mess.'
'But you're borrowing so much. When will you give it back?'
'That won't be possible in my lifetime. I'm not too sure about the next two generations either, but the time will come in the end.' (X, 125)

Here the personal problem is seen as a national one and nothing is more indicative of the intensity of Ōgai's historical awareness.

On the literary side, the journal *Mezamashigusa,* which replaced *Shigarami-zōshi,* carried his critical articles and translations such as *Sokkyō Shijin.* The period from 1896 to 1898 was devoted to criticism of contemporary writing in collaboration with Kōda Rohan, Saitō Ryokuu, Aeba Kōson, Morita Shiken, and Ozaki Kōyō.[6] The one story that Ōgai wrote himself at this time, 'Somechigae' (Separate dyes, 1897), was an experiment in the Edo-flavoured style of some of these men. In 1898, however, *Mezamashigusa* ceased its role as a journal of criticism and was used to carry his many translations of recent works on aesthetics until its demise in February 1902.

Fashions were quick to change in Meiji Japan and younger writers were beginning to draw attention away from men like Ōgai and Shōyō. Following the *Botsuriso* debate Ōgai had been concentrating on his medical journal and had then been involved in the war. Kitamura Tōkoku had made his brief and tragic appearance on the literary scene, and the period after the war belonged to the 'Romantics' such as Shimazaki Tōson and Kunikida Doppo who explored the freedom of expression to be found in European Romantic poetry, introduced seven years earlier by Ōgai in *Omokage.* At thirty-four Ōgai found himself counted as one of the older generation. It was as if he had somehow spent his youth, with all its enthusiasm and energy, and felt obliged to sit back and review his situation. The memories of four years abroad were becoming dimmed after seven years at home, and although the men with whom he now collaborated might seem strange company for one who had argued in favour of Western literary concepts with such vigour, he was redressing an imbalance in his own outlook, reminding himself of the more traditional aspects of Japanese literature in an effort to discover roots that were in danger of being lost. Kōda Rohan, whose life-long passion was Bashō, had in fact known Ōgai since the *Shigarami-zōshi* days, and some of his work had been published in that journal. Their views on literature were, at this point, quite similar.

It was inevitable that the frenzied activity of the early years should give way to a period of reflection during which the slow process of assimilation took place. This was the time when he moved away from a reliance on Hartmann and towards a more open view of aesthetics. The eventual abandonment of this theorizing in 1901–2 was because he realized that theory tended to cramp artistic expression and could easily lead to a fight to preserve obsolescent norms. By 1909 his ideas were totally at variance with his earlier views.

Kokura

The years immediately following Ōgai's return to Japan after the war are of little literary importance, with one exception. In 1897 Nishi Amane died and, partly perhaps from a desire to atone for the acute embarrassment he had caused the Nishi family by leaving his first wife, Toshiko, Ōgai obtained permission to write his biography. This was published the following year and in many ways repaid his debt to the great man.[7]

It was in the June of 1899 that the blow fell which was to bring him close to resigning his commission and which was to cause so much suffering and soul-searching. He was appointed to the post of Chief Medical Officer for the Twelfth Division which was stationed at Kokura in northern Kyushu. This demotion, as it was in fact if not in name, can be traced to his earlier violent attacks on his superiors in the 'Bōkan kikan' debate, but the immediate cause was the jealousy of Koike Masanao. Koike was eight years older than Ōgai and had been instrumental in obtaining the latter's commission; yet he was forced to sit by while Ōgai travelled to Germany before him, became Doctor of Medicine in 1891 at the age of twenty-nine, and achieved fame in both literary and medical journalism. Despite such humiliation, however, both men worked together on experiments and medical textbooks until 1897. Relationships had shown signs of strain as early as 1889 when they argued over the question of German translations of the results of Japanese research. In 1899, however, Koike rose to the position of Surgeon General and, once in power, he did not hesitate to work against Ōgai and engineer his demotion.

The new posting was a cruel setback for Ōgai's hopes of promotion and he was only just dissuaded from resigning by Kako Tsurudo, who argued correctly that to do so would only be playing into the enemy's hands. There is no mistaking the bitterness of his reaction. The third entry in his 'Kokura nikki' (A Kokura diary) for 18 June 1899 reads: 'Privately I feel that I'd rather be puppet station master than Chief Medical Officer for this Division' (XXXV, 285) and in a letter to his mother dated 27 June he wrote:

> I know that one problem at the meeting of the General Staff in Tokyo, which will take place from the end of this month, will be Bureau Director Koike's complaints, but I have no idea what the outcome will be. From one point of view the Kikuchi-Eguchi affair rebounds on me; goodness knows what I shall be blamed for. It really is a time of crisis. All I can do is sit still and work hard at my duties, but it is not a very easy time to be going through. Will Koike buckle under and get on to the right path again? Will he stop attacking me? These two questions will be probably decided in the not too distant future. (XXXVI, 40–1)

The Kikuchi-Eguchi affair referred to here concerned the question of whether army staff should be allowed to work in civilian hospitals; both men had been working extramurally and Koike was insistent that they should keep to army duties. As half of Ōgai's work was in a sense extramural, the problem concerned him too. In another letter to his friend Takeya Suijō, dated 2 August 1899, we are given a glimpse of deep resentment:

> Since arriving in the provinces I have said nothing about the frequency of attacks on me in a number of Tokyo journals. I see no need to explain away criticisms of my incompetence and the like, which are, of course, elaborated on by Koike and the rest of them. But when they start accusing me of neglecting my official duties, mistaking my ineptitude for unwillingness, I am not a little annoyed. They even go so far as to say that my criteria for choosing men for posts are unsound because I enjoy reading German books, and also that I try to promote and demote men by seeing whether they can read Schiller or not. This is absolute rubbish. As foreign languages are particularly encouraged by the Ministry, I feel that if an army doctor really can read Schiller it should redound to the credit of the Medical Department.
>
> This may sound as if I am doing nothing but complaining, but public opinion is something greatly to be feared. As you are at the centre of things, I would be most grateful if you could help me a little by asking Koike and the rest not to misunderstand me, whenever the occasion might arise. If there is any misunderstanding then please do your best to disabuse them. Please also bear in mind that although there are rumours that I am agitating for a

return to Tokyo, I have never said or written anything to that
effect. I suspect that this misunderstanding has arisen because
one or two of my friends want me to return. (XXXVI, 43–4)

Such appeals for reason were to no effect. Even Ishiguro was watching from the wings as we can see from a diary entry dated 30 August
1899: 'Had a letter from Ishiguro Tadanori today. He was afraid
I might be going to Akamagaseki too often. I replied that since arriving
at this frontier post I have taken great pains to concentrate. Even when
on official business I travel to such places in the morning and return
the same evening' (XXXV, 292). The strain of such constant and
unwelcome interference must have been considerable, especially for a
man of such independence of mind as Ōgai. The demotion, however,
meant far more than a mere setback to his career prospects; it was of
great significance for his position in the literary world.

The importance of Tokyo as the centre of cultural change and
innovation during this period cannot be exaggerated, and Ōgai's
removal to a somewhat remote backwater must have accentuated his
feeling of no longer being at the centre of things. The resentment at
his premature withdrawal lies behind an important article that Ōgai
wrote for the *Fukuoka Nichinichi Shimbun* on 1 January 1900 entitled
'Ōgai gyoshi wa tare zo' (Who is this man Ōgai?). The young man who
used to sign himself 'Ōgai Gyoshi' and who burst onto the literary
scene in 1889 is now dead and gone:

I have not signed myself Ōgai Gyoshi for some time now. When
I hear it, it is almost like hearing another man's name. What is
more, that man seems to belong to quite another world from
my own. For a short time during the Meiji period in the field of
literature it was said that the writers were Rohan, Kōyō, Shimei,
Kōson, Ryokuu and Bimyō, and that the critics were Shōyō and
Ōgai. This was asserted among writers themselves and as a result
the general public mistakenly came to count me as one of these
men of talent. All of these men I have just mentioned made
writing their profession; the only exceptions being Shimei who
became a bureaucrat and Shōyō who became a college teacher.
I alone am a doctor, and an army doctor at that. As my false
reputation spread, people started calling me a writer. Those who
know nothing of literature are vague even about the distinction
between writing and criticism.

Why do they call me a writer? There are only about four of
my works that could be called stories and they are all extremely
short, ranging from only a couple to twenty pages. I probably
spent a week on them all told. If I am a writer, there are an
awful lot of them around in Japan. And so it came about that

the literary world of the time forced me to accept inappropriate fame and misplaced luck — assuming that fame does bring luck, that is. At the same time, however, my associates in medicine claimed that I was not competent to discuss medicine because I was a writer, and my associates in office claimed that I could not be entrusted with important matters for the same reason. Who knows to what extent they have secretly obstructed my advancement and ruined my success. To enjoy inappropriate fame is the opposite of good fortune. I now study with a modicum of sincerity and work hard at my official duties. Whenever I see others affording me no recognition of my true abilities, however, be it with good or bad intention, I cannot help feeling sorry for myself. As a result I have made a gradual effort to shun fame, and this is why I have not signed myself Ōgai Gyoshi for so long and why I felt such a shock when the reporter for the *Fukuoka Nichinichi Shimbun* dragged it up. (XXV, 122-3)

Ōgai then turns to a discussion of the literary world of 1900:

What is the literary world? It is made up of those writers who are currently active in Japan. However sympathetic I may feel towards Kyushu, it certainly is a remote Western province. It is only by reading two or three Kyoto and Osaka newspapers that I can get to know whose writing is admired and praised in the heart of Japan. It is like seeing a beautiful woman through a rattan blind.

According to what they say in the papers, the *Taiyō* [Sun] of the Hakubunkan dominates the heavens and Chogyū holds sway over Japanese literature. It seems that the literati are continually praising him to the skies for setting them new problems. Chogyu too has pride in himself and claims that his theories are original in the field of aesthetics.

Those ranged around him like bright stars are so far off that I cannot see them clearly, but I can make out the heads of Chūgai of Shunyōdō's *Shinshōsetsu* and Hōgetsu of Nichijukusha's *Yomiuri Shimbun*. Both are men of outstanding character and are just sitting back biding their time. They have the courage to challenge even the empire of the Hakubunkan and so Chogyū too must keep on his toes.

Apart from them, there is the *Teikoku Bungaku* where countless young and fearless warriors borrow the lustrous glory of Tokyo Imperial University. They come and go acting out their parts on the literary stage.

This then is the literary world. Between these men and myself there are at times no points of contact, and at other times just a few. But even then it is just a matter of passing each other by on the road, glancing back for an instant, and then immediately

> forgetting each other. I seek nothing from them and they seek
> nothing from me. (XXV, 123–4)

Looking back to the height of his early fame, he traces the process by
which he fell from grace:

> It was at the height of the *Shigarami-zōshi* period that the name
> Ōgai was tossed about in a whirlwind of criticism and praise.
> I was given that inappropriate, false good fortune and lost the
> confidence of the academic and the official world alike.
>
> At that time Rohan said to me: 'You enjoy debating with
> others and have won nearly every time. But a good swimmer
> will drown and a good rider will fall from his horse. Sooner or
> later a great debater will emerge and you will suffer defeat.' In
> a sense these words were true, no they were too true. That
> period saw not one great debater emerge, but countless numbers.
> They were the new men of letters.
>
> If you try looking at the first ten or so issues of *Teikoku
> Bungaku* and the various journals which appeared at that time
> such as Hakubunkan's *Taiyō*, or even various Tokyo newspapers,
> you will probably find how many arrows pierced the name Ōgai.
> The name Ōgai ceased to be heard during the course of those
> skirmishes. It was at that point that Ōgai Gyoshi died.
> (XXV, 125)

There is a strong, almost unpleasant, sense of self-pity and rejection
here, which is unusual in such a resilient character and shows how deep
this crisis must have been. Like most public figures Ōgai needed
audience response and for the first time in his life this response was
lacking; it was never really to be regained. The time had now come for
Ōgai to readjust to the new situation and seek a new identity, and this
search was to take the next ten years. But during his stay at Kokura,
from June 1899 to March 1902, Ōgai was very far from being inactive;
it was a period of intense study and introspection. Continuing with
Sokkyō Shijin, he helped his brother Tokujirō to found the journal
Kabuki in 1900, lectured on and translated Clausewitz's *Vom Kriege*
(On War), continued with his work on aesthetics, studied the ethics of
Paulsen and the political thought of Machiavelli, and even found time
to write his first play, *Tamakushige Futari Urashima* (The Jewelled
Casket and the Two Urashimas) which was published in *Kabuki* in
1902. He described a typical day in a letter to his brother Junzaburō
dated 19 December 1899:

> Recently I have been going to work at nine in the morning and
> coming home at three in the afternoon. Immediately I get
> changed and go to my French teacher. The lesson finishes at
> six. I go back home, wash, have supper, and then go for a stroll

and a cigar. The cigar lasts exactly one hour by which time I can walk right round Kokura; it leaves me feeling excellent. That takes to about nine. Then I write up my French notebook and study a little Sanscrit which takes me to half past ten or eleven, when I go to bed. (XXXVI, 61)

Ōgai's work on Clausewitz has particular significance for a proper understanding of his attitude towards life at this time.[8] He had already translated about half the first section in Berlin and recorded in his diary how impressed he was with the book's depth and insight. It was much later, at Kokura, that he was asked to give lectures on Clausewitz, and the rest of the translation grew out of these lectures. In fact only the first two sections, 'On the nature of war' and 'On the theory of war', were finished and published in 1901. The rest of the book was translated, or rather summarized, later by students at the Medical Academy in Tokyo from a French version, and Ōgai's translation was republished as the first part of this more complete work in 1903 under the title *Daisen Gakugi.*

The principles of Clausewitz had been taught to the officers of the Japanese army by the German, Major Meckel (1842-1906), who had been trained in the school of Moltke. Meckel taught at the Military Academy in Tokyo from 1885 to 1889. Ōgai's work, however, was the first translation into Japanese, and as such has its own place in the study of military strategy in Japan. That the lessons of Clausewitz had been well learnt was pointed out by the Military Correspondent of *The Times* in 1905 when he entitled one chapter of his account of the Russo-Japanese War 'Clausewitz in Manchuria'.[9]

What is important here, however, is not the influence, direct or otherwise, that Ōgai might have had on Japanese strategy through this translation, but the effect that the work had on him personally. Clausewitz is perhaps most famous for his statement that war is only a continuation of politics by other means, but his book is a complex study of the philosophy of war. One of the central concepts is the principle of 'pure resistance' especially in cases where the opponents are unequally matched. The aim of the weaker side must be to wear out the stronger by a policy of clever defence, contentment with small victories, and playing the time factor to the full. This defensive posture, which Clausewitz argued represented the best and most efficient use of limited forces, should be kept in mind when considering Ōgai's own personal relationships and the way he dealt with them.

The central figure in *Vita Sexualis* (1909) says, talking of his youth:

The fact that I was younger didn't help either. Whatever happened I was always being bullied by my fellow students, so

> I developed the habit of submitting openly but secretly resisting.
> The strategist Clausewitz says that passive resistance is the best
> tactic for weak states. By nature I was unlovable and, what is
> more, easily cowed by events. (V, 113)

As in the case of 'Mōsō' this story treats his early life but is overlaid
with attitudes of the mature man. Passive resistance was certainly the
key note of the years to come.

The Kokura period has often been compared to Ōgai's earlier years
in Germany in the sense that it was a time of preparation for much of
his later work. It was during this time that a decisive shift of interest
away from aesthetics took place which helps to explain the change in
his writings. He began to show interest in ethics, in the motivation for
human actions, especially in the rare atmosphere of such an absolutist
environment as the army, and questions were asked then which were
to become themes in his later historical works.

Ōgai's interest in ethics seems to have been at its height in the latter
part of 1900 when he gave four lectures on related topics. The first,
delivered in July, was entitled 'Futsū kyōiku no gunjin seishin ni
oyobosu eikyō' (The influence of universal education on the martial
spirit). Despite a disclaimer at the outset, this lecture dealt with those
elements in education which were of particular importance if one
wished to produce successful, intelligent soldiers. The argument itself
was rather mundane; intellect must prevail over emotion, and presence
of mind and adaptability must be cultivated. Emotion was so dangerous
that reading at school should be closely controlled lest it developed
into a taste for salacious books.[10] Obedience was of course imperative
in the army and he likened the system to that which the Tokugawa had
developed. He also stressed 'character training' and a de-emphasis on
money matters. The educator, as the prime example to the students,
was burdened with the extremely important task of inculcating such
values.

That traditional values were ideal as a basis of a modern army was
clear to him and the interaction between attitudes in educational
circles and those in operation during compulsory service with the
armed forces he saw as inevitable. One cannot, however, on the basis
of this short lecture, argue a definite shift from earlier liberal attitudes.
Academic freedom he still saw as paramount and it did not necessarily
clash with strict discipline and moral training. His own Confucian
upbringing had always shown itself in his attitude towards education
as a whole. What he was arguing for in this particular lecture was a
more responsible type of soldier who would be able to adapt to every
situation.

What is most noticeably lacking is a discussion of the clash between private conscience and public duty. Whether this form of opposites is a peculiarly Western phenomenon or a common human trait is arguable, but the fact is that Ōgai had to go to Western sources for a rational statement of such a concept. There can be little doubt that he felt such a conflict himself and the need to analyse it. Two other lectures of this period were résumés of two German books, Friedrich Paulsen's *System der Ethik* (1889) and Oswald Külpe's *Einleitung in die Philosophie* (1898). By reading these and other works he was able to gain an insight into the distinction between self and society that was such a marked characteristic of European attitudes, and thus in a sense he could contrast the absolutist and relativist standpoints. In his early days the atmosphere of freedom engendered by the emphasis on the self had come as a revelation. Now, however, it was the divisive effects of such an emphasis that occupied his attention. The change is crucial and represents a common dilemma in the Japanese experience.

The issue of personal conscience versus public duty was raised in a small way in an admonitory talk he gave the medical section in December 1900. A soldier had died of strychnine poisoning but might have been saved if the appeal for a diagnosis had been answered promptly. This was not the first time the medical section had come under criticism and Ōgai suspected that a good deal of selfishness was the root cause of these incidents. Every available man had either pleaded illness or was on duty at the hospital. He was driven to stress that all soldiers, but in particular those in the medical section, had a moral duty over and above the mere fulfilment of regulations; in effect an ethical conscience. The argument stopped short of any deep consideration of the implications of recognizing such a conscience, just as Ōgai himself had felt the need to sublimate such problems during actual warfare.

The many aphorisms that Ōgai wrote at this time are also of interest in this connection.[11] Until recently these aphorisms were considered Ōgai's own work, but the research of Kobori Keiichirō has shown that the majority were translations from a German book of worldly wisdom called *Über den Umgang mit Menschen* (How to Get On in Society) by Adolf Freiherr von Knigge.[12]

This book, which Ōgai read while in Germany and which is mentioned in 'Utakata no ki', is a huge collection of homilies on how best to conduct one's daily affairs. It was read in its day as a book on etiquette, and, although it had first been published in 1788, was still a bestseller of sorts in the 1880s. Ōgai did not attempt a faithful translation however. He felt free to shorten, cut and adapt much of it, and in many places inserted his own observations and Japanese examples, so that it becomes almost unrecognizable in places.

Why he should have made this semi-translation is something of a mystery. It may be that, in the context of his self-appointed role as educator, even worldly homilies were grist to the mill, and did present a picture of European common wisdom. Ōgai, however, not only failed to point out that they were translations, but also concealed his own authorship. They are probably best seen in the context of his own troubled personal relationships, and they represent a kind of discussion with himself. The tone of the majority is passive and their prime object is to point out how to avoid discontent and argument in life.

It was while he was at Kokura that Ōgai married his second wife, Araki Shige, the daughter of a Tokyo Judge Araki Hiroshi. During the years between the day he left Toshiko and arrived in Kokura, he had had a mistress called Kodama Seki, who had been known to the Mori family for some time and who was separated from her husband. The arrangement would seem to have been suggested by Ōgai's mother. During his stay in Kokura he lived a bachelor life, and, judging from the numerous entries in his diary, his maids were a problem. Very set in his ways, he found them either too young, too flirtatious or just downright inefficient.[13] There was for a time a suggestion that Kodama Seki should travel down to Kokura to keep house, but nothing ever came of it.

The marriage with Shige was also arranged by his mother in Tokyo, and the go-between was Okada Kazuichirō who had succeeded Ōgai as the main writer for the *Tōkyō Iji Shinshi* in 1889. Ōgai returned for eight days over the New Year of 1902 to meet his prospective wife, agreed to the marriage and took her back to Kokura. The quick decision after a long bachelor existence suggests that Shige made a strong impression. She herself was divorced, but only twenty-three and, according to all reports, a very attractive woman, in contrast to Ōgai's first wife whose one outstanding gift seems to have been her ability to read classical Chinese with ease. After his return with Shige to Kokura on 8 January Ōgai had only two months before he was recalled from exile, but these two months were some of the happiest he had known or was ever likely to know. A month after he arrived in Kokura he wrote to Kako Tsurudo that everything was going unusually well with his 'objet d'art' (XXXVI, 149). As this phrase might suggest, however, things were to deteriorate rapidly.

Once they returned to Tokyo, Ōgai's mother and Shige soon clashed.

Although Shige had been Ōgai's mother's choice it became clear that they were incompatible. The situation became so acute that a second divorce was seriously considered, but somehow disaster was averted. It is this situation that forms the background to one of Ōgai's most famous stories, 'Hannichi' (Half a day, 1909), in which the tension is vividly portrayed and the conflict of loyalties made painfully clear. This domestic unrest must always be kept in mind when Ōgai's life at this time is considered.

Ōgai's attitude to this problem was complex. On the one side there was the description in 'Hannichi' of one morning in the household when an argument arises over his wife's hate for his mother, and the suggestion is made that her hatred is close to mental illness. The will that Ōgai made on leaving for the Russo-Japanese War specifically deprived his wife of any share of the inheritance, divided the family possessions between his mother and his eldest brother, and in the case of the death of the latter entrusted the proceeds to Junzaburō and Kimiko. Without him there, he reasoned, Shige would never live with the Mori family.

A different attitude is revealed, however, in the valuable record of letters Ōgai wrote to his wife from Manchuria. Shige had taken her first-born, Mari, to her parents while Ōgai was away. Possibly because of censorship problems, these letters tell us nothing of the war, but are mostly concerned with the health of wife and daughter. They reveal a genuine longing for Shige, but show clearly that Ōgai treated his wife as a child in matters concerning Mari's upbringing. This fatherly attitude is understandable, given the twenty years' age difference between the couple, but then so is his wife's reaction. Amid the constant worry that her letters are not reaching him, Ōgai shows a tendency to depreciate her intelligence; at one point he tells her that her attempts at writing poetry are so bad as to be not worth correcting.

'Hannichi', written when matters had reached crisis point, is, however, central to this problem. The entry in Ōgai's diary for 11 February 1909 reads: 'Went to the Palace Sanctuary and attended the banquet. My wife went and stayed the night at Akabune-chō [her parent's home]' (XXXV, 428). Four days later he handed the story to the editor of *Subaru,* Kinoshita Mokutarō. The connection is clear. His mother's diary also has some interesting entries for February that year. '15 February. In the evening went to Koganei's and talked further about what we had discussed the other night. There was a suggestion that Shige was sick and that I should take Otto and go somewhere else, but nothing more . . .'[14]

When 'Hannichi' was published without her prior knowledge, Shige was understandably furious and refused to allow the story to appear in any subsequent collection of her husband's works. There is also evidence that another story entitled 'Hitoyo' (One night) was written, but that Shige found it before it was sent for publication and demanded that it should never see the light of day. This request at least seems to have been complied with. In the December of the same year, however, a story entitled 'Haran' (Troubles), which treated the marriage from the wife's angle, was published in his wife's name. Shige's first work, entitled 'Shashin' (The photograph), had been written a month earlier. She was to write fourteen short stories for *Subaru* and some six others for various magazines. The exact details are a little unclear, but it seems that Ōgai had a hand in at least three of them, in particular 'Haran'. The suggestion that Shige should write her side of the story was doubtless made in order to try and calm the situation. 'Haran' is not a direct reply to 'Hannichi', however, and only treats the Kokura months of their marriage. The wife, very much in love with her husband, suddenly finds that he has been practising a method of birth control without her knowledge. She not only feels that the idea is unnatural and 'Western', but wants children desperately and is angry at being treated like a child. The story is slight, but is well written and reveals a little of the stress at being treated like an 'objet d'art'.

Shige was often described as being outspoken (*shōjiki*) and unusually modern, and she has the reputation in Japan for being a bad wife (*akusai*). This typically Japanese reaction tends to minimize what must have been great provocation. The strong mother and the independent young wife are stock characters in any culture, but the strains must have been magnified out of all proportion in Japan at that time.

It is of considerable interest that Shige was a supporter of the Blue Stocking group of women writers and had some stories published in their magazine *Seitō* which was founded in 1911. Reliable information on her exact relationship to the group is scarce, but in an article written in 1962, Hiratsuka Raichō, one of the main figures in the movement, definitely stated that she had never met Ōgai or his wife, although Shige was a supporter and Ōgai was not unsympathetic.[15]

The Russo-Japanese War
Once back in Tokyo Ōgai set about a new venture with Ueda Bin to produce the journal *Geibun*, but it lasted for only two issues. He then started *Mannensō* which was to carry further translations. The two years between his return from Kokura and his departure for the Russo-

Japanese War, 1903 and 1904, are significant because he was studying the question of racialism and the consequences of the rise of Japan's military and economic power.

Although he was always aware of the problem and knew of the underlying reasons for the Triple Intervention of 1895, Ōgai's concern with European racialism can be dated from the Boxer Rebellion which occurred while he was still at Kokura. The return of Japanese soldiers from Peking in 1901 prompted him to give a lecture entitled 'Hokushin Jihen no ichimen no kansatsu' (Observations on one aspect of the Boxer Rebellion). It showed perceptive understanding. He began by pointing out that the European attitude had elements of a holy war:

> I would now like to look at this drama from one particular aspect: namely that people of different races have raised an army together and have charged forward in unison towards a single goal. If you examine history for a similar phenomenon the Crusades would seem to be the only other example. The Crusades took place from 1096 to 1270, in other words from our Minamoto-Taira period to the Hōjō period. There were seven Crusades in all. Instead of Peking they went to Jerusalem, and they wanted to save not the Allied Legation but the tomb of Jesus Christ and crush not the Boxers but the believers of Islam. But the situation is remarkably similar in that at a given period in history powerful nations banded together to raise an army and then drove forward to a single goal. What is more they too marched shoulder to shoulder into a strange unknown world. (XXXIV, 216–17)

As this was the first time that Japanese en masse had had the chance to come into direct contact with Europeans, Ōgai expected that the experience would influence Japan a great deal. The question was whether such influence would be to Japan's advantage. He chose the conduct of the German soldiers as an example. The Japanese had observed that the Germans were outstanding for their obedience of military orders but acted like depraved animals in other cases. What reason could be found for this?

Ōgai's conclusions went beyond the idea that the Germans fought only according to orders and without any moral sense of their own. Their behaviour he saw as being based partly on racial hatred of White for Yellow and partly on the fact that it was accepted practice in Europe to treat lower class girls as objects for sexual gratification. He also gently hinted that the Japanese were not above a certain amount of hypocrisy in this matter. In contrast to the treatment of lower class women in Europe, Ōgai was at pains to praise the behaviour of European men towards wellborn women. Chivalry was not dead, and in comparison the Japanese idea of marriage was more akin to rape. Ōgai was concerned here to show how human behaviour was the manifestation of varying cultural and religious attitudes and was only understandable within that framework. Judgements by Japanese on the behaviour of the Europeans in China would have to be carefully tempered. Above all he was extremely concerned that the example of the Germans might be copied and extolled by Japan, and moral sense totally repudiated in the conduct of war; a prophetic fear.

It was the emergence of Japan as an international power of some note in this inter-war period, and the ensuing conflict of interests between Japan and Europe, that made Ōgai delve deeper into the psychology behind the European reaction, in an effort to see what fears existed and how best they were to be allayed.

The complex set of prejudices that went to make up the phenomenon known as the Yellow Peril owed its origin, at least in part, to the popularity in Germany in the 1890s of the racial theories of the Frenchman Count Arthur de Gobineau (1816–82), and it was to these ideas that Ōgai turned his attention in a lecture given to the Kokugo Kambun Gakkai (Society for the Study of Japanese and Chinese) in Tokyo on 6 June 1903. The lecture was divided into three parts: a short record of Gobineau's life, a lengthy and fairly detailed account of the main tenets of the theory as expounded in Gobineau's most famous book, *Essai sur l'inégalité des races humaines* (1853–5) and a short section of comment at the end.

It is important to realize at the outset, of course, that Ōgai's sources were German. The biographical record was based on the lyrical introduction to the German translation of Gobineau's *Nouvelles asiatiques,* and the main part of the study was derived from the German translation of the *Essai,* both by Professor Ludwig Schemann of the University of Freiburg. Schemann was the founder of the notorious Gobineau Vereinigung which, inaugurated in 1894, did much to propagate Gobineau's racial theories in a somewhat modified form in the two decades spanning the turn of the century, and which included among its members such worthies as Elizabeth Förster-Nietzsche and H. S. Chamberlain.

The theoretical section of the lecture begins with an explanation of how Gobineau saw the world as being made up of ten civilizations: seven in the Old World – Indian, Egyptian, Assyrian, Greek, Chinese, Roman and Germanic; and three in the New World – Alleghanian, Mexican and Peruvian. Gobineau himself never spent much time or effort on the last three but Ōgai was interested enough to comment:

> The tenth, the Peruvian, refers to the race that founded the famous Inca empire about the time the Spaniards went to America. The Spaniards destroyed them by deceit. The history of the Inca empire is interesting for us Japanese. It was a country of high moral principles destroyed by Spanish cunning. The ruler was called the descendant of the Sun. I was horrified the first time I read of the history of the destruction of that country. (XXV, 509)

Concerning the meaning of the word 'civilization' in this context Gobineau had his own idiosyncratic theory.[16] He rejected the definitions of men such as François Guizot who, in his book *Histoire de la civilisation en Europe,* had claimed that it was closely linked to the founding of political freedom and the promulgation of a constitution. Gobineau posited two important instincts in man, the material and the mental or spiritual; the possibility of civilization developing existed only when both these instincts were sufficiently in evidence. Once this prerequisite had been satisfied another dialectic came into play, that of attraction and repulsion. Civilized countries were essentially dynamic and exerted influence over neighbouring lands, whereas uncivilized nations were the weak, passive partner in the exchange.

According to Gobineau each of his ten civilizations had a common characteristic — each desired that its dynamic influence should continue into the future. But this was a forlorn hope, because in the very act of influencing others the civilization mixed its blood with other races and became in time a different race from the original. This is where we come to Gobineau's central thesis; the reason why all civilizations were destined to decline and perish was that the mixing of blood, itself an inevitable consequence of the original dynamism, leads to degeneration of the original stock.

Gobineau made the arbitrary but common division of three main races — the White, the Yellow and the Black. The Black race was the closest to the animals, having an excellent sense of smell, being spiritually unstable, and having no power to civilize. The Yellow race was not dynamic either, but possessed a greater number of more laudable qualities than did the Black. The ability to civilize others was the exclusive preserve of the White Race. The other two races were enriched by cross breeding but the White race could only be harmed. Gobineau argued, and tried to prove by a long historical study of the seven civilizations of the Old World, that the most remarkable group in the White race was the Aryan, which had been connected in some way or other to all these cultures. It was in fact the only group with the power to civilize others. Where this left the rest of the White race was never really made clear. By a number of extraordinary convolutions Gobineau managed to 'prove' that through blood connections the Aryans had been instrumental in producing every civilization, including that in China.

For Gobineau this conclusion was far from optimistic, as an essential instinct in the civilizing race was the drive to propagate itself and miscegenation was inevitably suicidal. He saw contemporary European civilization as already being in an advanced state of irreversible decline. Fundamentally his was a deeply pessimistic theory. It contains no suggestion that the race could be cleansed, for his aim was to find the cause of the decline of great civilizations. The idea that the Aryan group was still fairly pure and should be cleared of all impurities — a theory that reached its zenith some eighty years later under the Nazis — was a later addition and a twisting of Gobineau's ideas.

At the end of his synopsis Ōgai added a few comments of his own. First of all he criticized the method:

> Firstly it is clear that the concept of race instincts and of the value of a race's blood, which is central to these racist theories, relies heavily on the idea of heredity. Blood, in the words of the later scholar Rudolf Virchow, becomes something akin to a physical movement. Because Gobineau places importance, too much importance, on heredity, he conversely seems to reject the concept of adaptation. To mix with an alien race, at least from the point of view of the White race, is rejected as being detrimental. By emphasizing heredity and underplaying adaptation, the argument tends towards the conservative, and as a result is lacking in any progressive thinking.
>
> It is my opinion that the Count's yearning for the pure races of the past smacks very much of dreaming of a legendary golden era. Of course one cannot definitely state that the results of mixing blood will be progressive — they could also be regressive — but to yearn for the pure blood of the past, to think of the era of pure blood as being a golden era is surely neither logical nor inevitable. (XXV, 529)

He then discussed the biased nature of the whole theory:

> Secondly, the Count's argument is totally self-centred as far as Europe is concerned. It is partial and biased, not that this needs any special comment as it should be obvious to everyone . . . The Count said such things because he was a White man. There are many things said throughout the whole book which could never have been uttered if he had been a member of the Black or the Yellow race. His most important point is that the Aryan race

is the only race with active instincts, the only race with the ability to civilize others . . .

There is a theory that ever since Shang and Chou times the Chinese have mixed with other races. But surely we cannot say, as the Count claims, that the Chinese civilization is Aryan? If the Count had taken into consideration the Japanese civilization he would have probably seen it as being comparable to the 'fake' civilization of the Haiti republic. But as I have said earlier, if he had lived longer he would have been forced to seek proof that the Japanese race had Aryan blood in it. Taguchi Ukichi,[17] I seem to remember, once wrote that the Japanese race was Aryan, but I have my doubts. (XXV, 529–30)

Lastly he referred to the popularity of the idea in Germany. He was optimistic that it was a mere fashion and would soon die a natural death:

Just as there was a period when Hartmann's *Philosophie des Unbewussten* was popular, and then there was a Nietzsche period, so now present-day Europe — no, that is too general — present-day Germany seems to be ruled by the racial instinct theories of Gobineau-Chamberlain. There are many such examples even if we just limit ourselves to the field of literature. German critics say that Naturalism changed to Symbolism, and then Symbolism gave way to *Heimatkunst* which has connections with this *Rassenphilosophie*.

But are the Count's theories worthy of this much favour and popularity? I doubt it very much. On the contrary they contain just enough to excite people's attention momentarily. Firstly the argument seems impressive, although in reality it is merely careless. Secondly it prophesies the collapse of Western civilization; that truly great religion Christianity also enhanced its popularity at first by warning of the imminence of the Last Judgement. Then, last but not least, there is the statement that the only people with the ability and the drive to civilize others now and in the past are the Aryans, and that even after the collapse of the present civilization only a race with the relatively pure blood of the Aryan masses can hope to build the next civilization. This appeals to the self-conceit of the people, or rather the race, and is enough to give rise to numerous repercussions. However, when you reach the stage of listening with pleasure to the theory that only one race has the ability to civilize, perhaps your self-confidence that you are that one race is beginning to wear a little thin. (XXV, 530–1)

So Ōgai ends his account of the theories of Gobineau. It can fairly be said that he had grasped all the essential points: the importance of blood; the division of races into White, Yellow and Black, and the different value placed on the blood of those races; the contradictions thus arising with orthodox monogenesism; and the myth of a pure-blooded Aryan race in the past. Only the deep pessimism of Gobineau's ideas was perhaps de-emphasized, mainly because Ōgai's sources were German and the adaptation of Gobineau's thought was already well under way by the end of the century. One can only marvel at the seriousness of purpose and balance in this fair portrayal of potentially vicious ideas. The only point where Ōgai was unfortunately mistaken was in his prediction of their future importance; and his optimism shows the abiding regard that he still held for Europe and European culture.

It is of some interest to note that, as there was no mention of it in his sources, Ōgai does not seem to have read or heard of the later article by Gobineau entitled 'Ce qui se fait en Asie' first published in a German version in the *Bayreuther Blätter* for May 1881. Here the fear of the Chinese and the concept of the Yellow Peril are brought clearly into the foreground by Gobineau as proof of the correctness of his earlier theories about the impending decline of Western civilization, and it was with this Yellow Peril that Ōgai was primarily concerned.

The connection between Gobineau's essay and the growth of racialism in Europe, in Germany in particular, is not difficult to discern. The process can be traced from Gobineau's friendship with the Wagners, especially Wagner's wife, Cosima, through the founding of the Gobineau Vereinigung by Schemann in 1894, to the racist treatise by a member of that group, the Englishman Houston Stewart Chamberlain, entitled *Grundlagen des Neunzehnten Jahrhunderts* (The Foundations of the Nineteenth Century, 1899) in which anti-Semitism came to the fore and the pessimism of Gobineau was replaced by the hope of a pure Aryan race in the future.[18]

The prophesies of the collapse of Western civilization brought with them fears of a repetition of an invasion like that of the Golden Horde of the thirteenth century which had so very nearly destroyed European culture. The successful and unbelievably rapid modernization of Japan, the possibility of China following suit, and the even more frightening prospect of an alliance of the two were burning issues in 1900. There was a real fear, rooted in Malthus' observations on the principles of population growth, that if industrialization became possible in Asia, the West was threatened with both economic and military disaster.

Fear demanded respect that pride made unthinkable, and the natural recourse was to a form of racial hatred. It was this irrationalism and the dangers it presented that attracted Ōgai's attention.

What made Germany of particular importance in the spread of this fear of the Asian hordes was the paranoia of Kaiser Wilhelm II who, spurred on by the success of the Triple Intervention, took it upon himself to lead the battle against the danger from the East. On the occasion of the departure from Kiel of German troops, who were being sent to Peking as a result of the death of the German Ambassador Ketteler, the Kaiser made his famous 'Hunnenrede' speech in which he ordered them to show no quarter to the treacherous Chinese barbarians. The term Yellow Peril and its German equivalent *Gelbe Gefahr* had come into use during the Sino-Japanese War, but fell into abeyance for a few years, only to reach a high point from 1900 to 1905 when it was continually on the lips of the Kaiser.[19]

The book that Ōgai chose to summarize for a lecture on the Yellow Peril at Waseda University in November 1903 was *Die gelbe Gefahr als Moralproblem* (The Yellow Peril as a Moral Problem, 1902) by Hans-Otto Samson-Himmelstjerna. The author was concerned to show that Europe was in a state of moral and social bankruptcy which had resulted from the loss of Christianity as a viable basis for moral decisions. According to him there was indeed much to fear from the East but the answer was not to be found in confrontation but in a sincere effort to reduce antagonism, together with a drive to re-arm Europe morally. He presented a totally unrealistic picture of a utopian China, but argued that the Japanese, despite appearances, were infantile and not to be feared. He then proposed a number of quite sensible measures to pacify the Chinese. It was an unusual approach to the question, but containing as it did many of the opinions and misconceptions current in Europe at the time, was a good introduction. Ōgai began his lecture:

> You will no doubt feel that the subject of this extracurricular lecture is somewhat removed from both my work and my usual interests. I have, however, always been a student of what the White race thinks and feels of the Yellow race. I have been collecting writings on the subject for about the last ten years. Among them is a book called *Die gelbe Gefahr als Moralproblem*, which was published last year (1902) in Germany and which i would like to summarize for you today . . . As you know, the term Yellow Peril is of recent origin. It arises out of the conflict between the White and the Yellow races and expresses the attitude of the former towards the latter. I believe that we must

study this question in some detail. It is true that we, the Japanese Yellow race, are becoming more and more aligned with the White race, and have even reached the point of fighting other Yellow races as in the recent Boxer Rebellion. It is also true that we are allied with England and are trying to maintain peace in the Far East. But if for a moment we ignore this ally, and also America which for some time has been very sympathetic to Japan, in general the White race treats us and other members of the Yellow race as one and the same thing, and harbours feelings of hate and distrust against us. Like it or not we must wake up to the fact that we are fated to oppose the White race. Once this is realized, to study the Yellow Peril means to reconnoitre the lie of the enemy and is, in the words of one tactician, a part of getting to know the opponent. One can go a step further. Everyone believes that a war between Russia and Japan is almost unavoidable. You do not have to be an intellectual to see that if the war goes against us the members of the White race will rejoice that they have managed to suppress part of the Yellow Peril before it has fully germinated, but if we have the advantage they will try to play down as much as possible the results of our victory using the theory of the Yellow Peril as a last resort. Is it not our urgent duty to study this question?

Recently I gave elsewhere a summary of Count Gobineau's racial theories. Both that lecture and the one today have exactly the same aim in mind. But there were those critics who complained that they did not find these self-conceited theories of the White race in the least bit interesting. Both my study of Gobineau and this study of the Yellow Peril are reconnoitring the lie of the enemy. If you do not listen to me with this in mind I fear that I may be completely misunderstood. (XXV, 539–40)

Ōgai then explained how the Europeans believed that the Japanese and Chinese had an equal hate for the White race, a hate which Samson-Himmelstjerna attributed to the unfortunate history of the propagation of Christianity in both countries. The main fears of Europe concerning the Yellow race were divided into two spheres, economic and military. Concerning the former Ōgai went into some detail, citing and trying to disprove the distorted figures that he found in the book. The usual view had been expressed — that Asia was a captive market, but that it could be easily lost and the tables turned on Europe as a result of cheap labour and the natural industry of the people.

Samson-Himmelstjerna followed this with a comparison between Japan and China designed to show how Japan was not and never would be the real problem. The Chinese were pictured as being superior to the childlike Japanese in every conceivable way.

Ōgai's lecture ended with a few comments of his own:

> When the author talks about the 'peaceful' side of the Yellow Peril he says it seems that a social problem has arisen in the West because they have been mistaken in their moral precepts and so now find they are unable to compete in commerce or industry. If this is in fact the case then I am sorry but the fault lies with them. Then what about the danger of war? The Westerners have taken it upon themselves to create zones for their own benefit in China and have been dishonest in their policies. Recently it would seem that things have not been going so well. They are being chased out of those zones. Matters have become worse — it has even spread to the leased territories! Again, the fault lies with them. As a result, for the White race to be beaten by the Yellow is a morally righteous triumph and should be called the Yellow Fortune rather than the Yellow Peril. Should they not be grateful that we make them reverse their attitudes and make them improve their policy towards China?
>
> Then we have the distinction between the Japanese and the Chinese. In every sphere it seems that the Chinese are praised and the Japanese disparaged. The praise is such a panegyric that it becomes mere idealization, whereas the extreme criticism of Japan becomes mere fault-finding. There is little doubt that they are enamoured of China and hate Japan. This is because Japan is the enemy with whom they are now confronted. But if we look at this in a wider perspective, the Westerners, while having a trial of strength with Japan, are taking a fearful sideways glance at the great shadow of China. They fear the Japanese and so expound the Yellow Peril, but at the same time they refuse to believe that we really are frightening. That the Chinese might become frightening in the future is merely because they are only a shadow at present. I think you will agree with me that the Yellow Peril is a theory based on cowardice. (XXV, 567–8)

The problem, as far as Ōgai was concerned, was that, although he found himself the object of the scorn and hatred of such men as the Kaiser, he had fond memories of his years in Germany and was convinced that Japan still had much to learn from Europe. He knew that no good would come of irrational fears on either side and was particularly worried that hostilities might actually retard rather than hasten Japan's further development. This was exactly the question he had treated in the lecture 'Yōgaku no seisui o ronzu'. There were already many signs that the Japanese felt that the time for sitting at the feet of European learning was perhaps past and that they had little more to learn. In an open letter to the influential magazine *Taiyō* in the first months of 1902 a student called Anesaki Masaharu, later to become a famous figure, wrote from Germany of his experiences there. He was understandably bitter about the 'new barbarianism' that he saw:

> I doubt whether there is a more monarchist state than that of Prussia, the most important power in Germany today. No sooner does the Kaiser make a speech about crushing China and inflicting wounds that will be felt for a thousand years than lo and behold the whole populace suddenly makes common cause with him, discards the veneer of civilization, and performs the barbarian. Every man jack of them now hates the 'Yellow Chinese', and they even go as far as to fling stones and curses at us as we walk along the street.[20]

It was partly as a response to such reports that Ōgai wanted to temper the reaction with a little commonsense and warn of unjustifiable self-confidence.

The problem of the hatred of White for Yellow and Yellow for White was a painful one for Ōgai himself who abhorred the irrational basis to such racism and yet was soon to be involved in the fight against the Russian armies in Asia. This did not, however, prevent him from preparing for the war. In the months that led up to the fighting he was busy studying the matter from a medical point of view. In December 1903 the *Kōshū Iji* carried an article by him on the illnesses encountered by Napolean's army in the 1812 offensive. In January 1904 he wrote a short chronology of Russian military history and in February produced two short articles on the effects of intense cold on the human body and the various methods of combating it.

Information on Ōgai's exact movements during the Russo-Japanese War is plentiful due to the recent discovery of his reports from the front,[21] but they tell us nothing of his emotional reaction. The only source are his letters and the collection of war poems entitled *Uta Nikki* (A Poetic Diary) which was published in 1907. He left Ujina for the front on 21 April 1904 as Chief Medical Officer for the Second Army under General Oku. Landing on the Liaotung peninsula north of Dairen on 8 May, he was with the army until the end of the war and witnessed, albeit at some distance behind the lines, the terrible fighting at Nanshan (25 May), the occupation of Kinchow (26 May), Liaoyang (27-30 August), Shaho (17 October) and eventually Mukden (10 March 1905).

The letters home show an obvious desire to be back in Japan with his new family and talk little of the war. One might expect a more interesting treatment in the poems but they are peculiarly disappointing in this respect. The majority, there are some fifty in all, are either impressionistic pictures of the aftermath of battle, descriptions of sights and sounds with heavy emphasis on nature and the seasons, or rather conventional pieces in praise of the valour of the Japanese warrior. Even when the poems deal with death the tone amounts to something nearer blandness than restraint.

There can be no doubt that Ōgai saw the war as a righteous but unfortunate necessity. One looks for a deeper sensitivity in these poems in vain. There is almost no treatment of the conflict between doctor and witness of piecemeal slaughter, between artist and soldier that would have made this an important collection of lyrics. These vital questions, at the very heart of his predicament, are left alone and repressed. What is one to make of the following poem which has as its subject the carnage at Nanshan:

Blood on their lips

Sandbags piled up ten and twenty high,
Earth packed thickly overhead;
Our shrapnel shells have no effect,
Will never drive them from their trenches.

From slits between the sandbags comes
Machine-gun mixed with rifle fire;
Singly, and in groups, men advance but to fall;
So naturally the leader hesitates.

A rider comes from Hsiao Chin Shan,
They hear the order to attack
Passed down from division and brigade to regiment;
Now Commander, how is their morale?

Afternoon on the twenty-fifth of May,
The soldiers tense and listening hard;
Their faces pale, their eyes are bright
And blood on the bitten lower lip.

What use are plans and tactics now?
In this instant lies the battle's fate.
Soldier! Charge bravely over the corpses
And stand your banner on the summit of Nanshan!

Someone said success costs ten thousand rotten bones.
Though there are tears in the General's eyes
And the Commander may live in wealth and honour,
What of the blood on their lips at Nanshan? (XIX, 135-6)

Compared to the conventionality of this reaction, the next poem in the collection is more personal and convincing in its privacy:

Button

The day they fought at Nanshan
I lost a golden button from my cuff;
It was dear to me.

Bought in a shop with a green light
In a passage off a Berlin street
Twenty years ago.

Friend with the bright epaulettes,
Girl with golden locks, already aged,
Perhaps even dead.

Twenty years of ups and downs
Sharing joys and sorrows,
Now one less.

Soldiers crushed by bullets by the thousand;
Wasted; yet this too was dear to me,
Button on my sleeve. (XIX, 138-9)

The very fact that the expression of such personal feelings is so rare makes this poem stand out. Shutting himself off spiritually from the reality around him, he tried to avoid the painful results of overt treatment of the conflict between artist and soldier as best he could. To do otherwise would have been to invite mental upheaval. The sadness of the necessity of war was expressed in another poem entitled 'Yellow Peril' which he wrote on 19 August 1904:

Yellow Peril in victory, barbarian in defeat;
The White race makes a mockery of criticism.
But who rejoices in the praise
And who laments the slander?

Whether Yellow Peril or barbarian horde,
The nightmare still remains.
Europe drowning in a swollen flood,
A raging Yellow torrent.

Beware the Yellow Peril! Beware the barbarian horde!
Drunk with luxuries the White race
Lies like golden corn threatened by the locust,
And who can stem their ravaging?

White men, have no fear!
We are neither Yellow Peril nor barbarian.
In my tent I dreamed that the guns might cease
But in the long rains the dreams died. (XIX, 161–2)

One man in the war who demanded Ōgai's full sympathy, however, was General Nogi Maresuke. They had first met in Berlin on 18 April 1887 and saw each other quite frequently from then on. Although Ōgai wrote in 1914 that the acquaintance had been nothing above the ordinary, the two men had much mutual respect. The fact that Nogi was among the few people to see Ōgai off to Kokura in 1899 is indicative of the relationship. From about 1902 onwards Nogi would occasionally come to ask Ōgai's advice on matters European, and after the Russo-Japanese War Ōgai translated and explained many of the letters and poems that arrived from all over Europe in tribute to the hero of Port Arthur.

Although Ōgai was not in Nogi's army during the war it was probably for Nogi and his men that he wrote the famous war song, 'Hakoiri musume' (The imprisoned maiden), which referred to Port Arthur as a girl trapped in a box, and which celebrated its fall. He also wrote a poem entitled 'Nogi Shōgun' in sympathy for the loss of both the General's sons during the war. It is thus of no surprise that of all literary men Ōgai should feel the shock of Nogi's death in 1912 most deeply; a circumstance which will be seen to have great significance in the development of his later writing.

When Ōgai returned from the war in 1906 the most interesting literary event was the founding of the Tokiwakai poetry society in the June. The main participants were Yamagata Aritomo, Kako Tsurudo, Ōgai, Inoue Michiyasu, who had known Ōgai since the *Omokage* days, and Sasaki Nobutsuna. Ōgai chose the name of the society naming it after the restaurant where the first meeting was held. The society was formed on the request of Yamagata to Kako Tsurudo, whom he had known and worked with for many years, and it met 185 times, continuing until the death of the elder statesman in 1922.

The aim of the group was to produce 'Meiji' poetry, neither too old-fashioned nor too new but a kind of compromise. In September

1908, two years after the founding, Yamagata sent a letter to the members pointing out that definite rules had not yet been formulated and asking for suggestions. It was in reply to this that Ōgai wrote 'Mongai shoken' (The opinion of an outsider). Although his ideas were not adopted, he opposed the practice of composing poems on a given theme at every meeting, advocated extreme caution in the use of new or foreign words and expressed a hope that they might create a modern style. These rather uncertain suggestions were too advanced for Yamagata who made the society retain its traditional flavour. No doubt this reaction persuaded Ōgai to form his own poetry group in 1908. The Kanchōrō Uta no Kai, as this group was called, included Yosano Hiroshi, Itō Sachio and Sasaki Nobutsuna, and Ishikawa Takuboku who turned up to a few meetings in the May of 1908.

Since Ōgai did not wholly share the aims of the Tokiwakai one is tempted to look elsewhere for an explanation of his continued attendance. There can be little doubt that his association with Yamagata helped him to withstand pressure from his superiors later on, but the extent to which the relationship went beyond the bounds of poetry is unclear. It is not surprising that Yamagata heard of Ōgai's activities through Kako. According to Mori Junzaburō, Ōgai first came to Yamagata's attention through the translation of Clausewitz, but the fact that the General is indirectly referred to in 'Maihime' and wrote the preface to Ōgai's biography of Nishi Amane would suggest an earlier meeting. The relationship between the two men became closer after the founding of the Tokiwakai. In a letter dated 15 January 1909 Kako broached the subject of Yamagata's biography.[22] In a reply dated 18 January Ōgai wrote that although he would dearly like to try, he doubted whether pressure of work would allow such a heavy undertaking. The suggestion was never acted upon.

The favourite view of this relationship is that Ōgai was part of a Yamagata 'think tank' which aided the statesman in his efforts to find a solution to the unrest that became more and more evident in the 1910s.[23] There is little evidence to support this, however, and it must be attributed to a desire to enhance Ōgai's image. The poetry society itself was almost certainly apolitical, and although Ōgai may have been consulted much later about the 'grave court affair' which dealt with the supposed colour blindness of the Imperial Prince's consort, this would appear to be an isolated incident.[24] More importantly perhaps, one can hardly credit that the stiff, single-minded Yamagata, with his deeply felt fears of socialism, and his well known distrust of 'subversive' intellectuals, would have had much time for

Ōgai's attitude towards government repression as expressed in the satire 'Chinmoku no tō'.[25]

The reward for Ōgai's perseverance during the Kokura crisis came in November 1907 when he was promoted to the highest rank for a doctor in the army, that of Surgeon General. He was also made Head of the Bureau of Medical Affairs at the Department of War, thus stepping into Koike's shoes and in the end fulfilling the best hopes of his parents. There was no immediate change in his personal relations within the army, however, and his problems were far from over. Now having direct access to the Minister and Vice-Minister, he was if anything more subject than before to the restraints and responsibilities of his post. He continued to strive somewhat against the odds for an increase in the breadth and freedom of scientific research within the army, and he tried to ensure that the latest scientific findings in Europe were reported in military journals, encouraging the publication of reports and letters from Japanese studying in Europe.[26]

That his troubles were not over can be seen from the clash with his superiors over the banning of the story *Vita Sexualis* in 1909.[27] He also felt forced to offer his resignation on at least three other occasions: February 1911, October 1911 and July 1912. In each case he disagreed strongly with new proposals to break the existing chain of command and make all medical personnel responsible to their company commanders rather than to their superior medical officer. His resignation attempts were not, of course, accepted but could not have made his position within the system any more comfortable.

The real period of creativity began in 1909 with the publication of the new journal *Subaru*, an organ founded by a group of young writers who were dedicated to fighting the influence of the 'Naturalists'. The years from 1909 to 1912 are best studied from the point of view of the works that he produced; three novels and some forty short stories, not to mention plays and innumerable translations.

From 1906 onwards it became clear that writers of the Naturalist group such as Shimazaki Tōson, Tayama Katai and Masamune Hakuchō were rising to a position of prominence. If we remember Ōgai's earlier arguments against the exclusive use of realism to the detriment of beauty, and especially the tendency of the European Naturalists to be obsessed with sexual instincts, his chagrin at seeing a somewhat similar movement establish itself in Japan can be imagined. He might have also felt spurred on to write by the emergence of Natsume Sōseki as a writer of repute. It must not be forgotten, however, that when he did begin to write again his stories owed far more allegiance to the

True than the Beautiful and were in the main semi-autobiographical. His experience of European literature and his early theories had undergone a typically Japanese transformation.

5

A LITERATURE OF IDEAS I

The search for resignation

As will be seen from the foregoing account, the period from 1894 to 1912 was one of much personal suffering and alienation in both his official life and the literary world. Neither were matters helped by the experience of two bloody wars and an extremely delicate situation at home. As a result the lectures, writings and stories produced during this period are concerned, one might almost say obsessed, with this sense of alienation. Possibly because it presents a far less homogeneous aspect than either the period that precedes it or that which follows, any treatment tends to be discursive. It is this period, however, which should prove of most interest to historians of modern Japan, for Ōgai provides a rich and varied commentary on the late Meiji — as yet a relatively uncharted field.

The importance of Ōgai's experience and writings lies in his continual attempt to universalize personal problems, so that through a study of his works one becomes aware of the wider implications behind his own sense of ennui. His ultimate failure, during this period at least, to articulate these problems in an artistic framework of any distinction is another, though related, problem, which has its own important implications in the study of the literature of the time.

The majority of the stories written and published during the years 1909 to 1912 are either autobiographical or semi-autobiographical and they are interesting more as documents shedding light on Ōgai's attitudes than as works of art in themselves. Taken in isolation, many of the stories are slight and unimpressive and the label essay or even tract would not go amiss with some. To say, however, that this merely argues a lack of artistic talent is to miss the point. As the title of this chapter indicates, it is clear that, given his social position, Ōgai felt it necessary to present and argue out his ideas in the form of thinly disguised stories.

Ōgai in 1909, two years after his promotion to Surgeon-General

To begin with the personal aspects. The frustrations of his demotion and the way in which he found himself forever compromising between the demands of his army duties and his literary activities can be well imagined. In his effort to face up to these disappointments with stoicism, to seek a substitute for his earlier optimism, Ōgai turned to a study of philosophy, both Eastern and Western. That he was investigating what the various systems had to offer is clear from some correspondence he had with his family while still at Kokura. His sister Kimiko had written to him complaining of her frustration at having to look after her mother-in-law's youngest children. In a letter dated 29 December 1900, he answered:

> Your letter the other day raised such important questions that I put off answering it. I know it was rude of me but I just kept on delaying it and now there are only two more days to the end of the year. Family problems may be on a smaller scale than affairs of state, but when it comes to matters of reform they have their similarities; long-established customs have such weight and influence . . . I know one is inclined to want to do all one can while not actually causing the older members of the family any displeasure . . . The same applies when you say you have no time for writing. Whatever situation you find yourself in, you should be able to feel at peace with yourself by trying to keep calm and carrying on from day to day. Never reject what is possible. I myself have decided to study day by day with the same aim in mind. You do not have to write a great deal and there is no point in worrying about not reading, as long as you don't give it up altogether. (XXXVI, 84–5)

A letter to his mother soon after elaborated on the matter and revealed that in answering his sister's worries he was also trying to answer his own:

> Thank you for your letter of the 10th. I was interested to hear of the changes to the garden and the morning glory that Kitamura sent. I had a letter from Kimiko the same day. She was complaining that she could get no work done because of family matters. There have been times when I have thought as she does, but I think she may be a little mistaken. Whenever I look at her letter I feel somehow or other that she ought to be persuaded to start studying philosophy. It doesn't matter whether it be Confucianism, Buddhism or Western, but there is no teacher of Western philosophy available so I suggest that you look for someone with a deep knowledge of either Confucianism or Buddhism. Perhaps she could manage to leave the children at Dangozaka and go on Sunday mornings.

> If she turns her attention in this direction even just occasion-
> ally she might find herself thinking why we are here and how
> best we should live our lives. As long as she thinks, it doesn't
> matter whether she learns about Confucianism or Buddhism
> and is sceptical about both. If you call things into question
> you will in time understand; this is what is meant by 'knowing
> the Way'. When you know the Way you can expect all such
> family problems to become trouble-free and a pleasure.
>   Those who excel in the arts are like flowers that bloom in
> profusion. The pine and the oak have no flowers, and yet that
> does not make them inferior. Come what may you must devise
> ways to deal with the position that confronts you. I myself am
> in the process of studying the Way, and so I too am occasionally
> prone to the same doubts as Kimiko, but I never let them get out
> of hand. Doubt is not such a bad thing.
>   Here I am, sitting where I have been put by Koike, the Bureau
> Director. He refuses to recognize me as his superior even where
> intellectual ability is concerned. I do the work I am given to do.
> I do not consider everything I do to be ridiculous or worthless,
> so neither should Kimiko consider it a waste of time to bring up
> children for her mother-in-law. If that is pointless then our whole
> life on this earth is worthless. There are philosophies which see
> life as being totally pointless, but I could not do them justice
> here . . . . (XXXVI, 132–3)

While one might question the propriety of advising one's sister to study
philosophy as a cure for the ills of family duties, it is clear that Ōgai
was deeply concerned to find the answers to his own problems in this
way. One of his closest friends at Kokura was the priest of the
Ankokuji, Tamamizu Shunko,[1] who appears in two of Ōgai's later
stories, 'Dokushin' (A bachelor, 1910) and 'Futari no tomo' (Two
friends, 1915). In return for guidance in the study of Western philosophy, Tamamizu spurred on Ōgai's interest in Buddhism, in particular
the *Yuishikiron,* the doctrine that matter is a form of mind. Neither
did Ōgai neglect to study Confucianism as he had recommended to his
sister. He had been brought up on a diet of Neo-Confucianism of the
orthodox Chu Hsi school in his youth, but now turned instead to the
theories of Wang Yang Ming whose main tenet was that knowledge and
action should be identical. We can see the way his mind was working
and how he was trying to compare the various systems of philosophy
from a letter written to his mother in the autumn of 1901:

> I think that Kimiko finds it impossible to make her peace with
> the world because she has not read any books on ethics or
> religion. One of the books I have bought in Fukuoka is the

Ch'uan Hsi Lu. I have come across it before now but I bought it because it isn't in my library. It is a collection of Wang Yang Ming's sayings compiled by a disciple of his. It really is very interesting. It contains a reiteration of the theory of the unity of knowledge and action. People usually think that concepts such as loyalty or filial piety come first and are then acted out in reality; they think that knowledge comes before action. This is a great mistake. It is like thinking that knowledge about the existence of rice comes first and only then is it eaten. In reality one starts by feeling hungry, rice happens to be around, and so the act of eating arises directly from initial desire to eat. Wang Yang Ming's theory is that loyalty and filial piety do not come in any sequence. He says that: 'The act does not arise from the knowing. It is based on the feeling (the Will) of wanting to act.'

There are points of similarity with the very latest German psychology of men like Wundt; I find it really fascinating. Apart from this there is also a remarkable connection between the Buddhist *Yuishikiron* and Hartmann.

When one ponders over such matters, even men like myself who have no beliefs and who cannot make their peace with the world feel somewhat less distressed by life. There are times when I begin to understand myself. (XXXVI, 133-4)

Ōgai did not stop with Eastern philosophies in his search, but turned as well to the theories of Schopenhauer and Hartmann which he had brought back with him from Germany so many years before. In his youth it had been the aesthetics that had interested him; now it was the philosophy to which he turned. One of the most interesting and yet potentially misleading of his works is the set of reflections entitled 'Mōsō' (1911), where reminiscences of earlier days are coloured and overlaid by his state of mind at the time of composition. Written some ten years after the Kokura period, it can best be seen as a record of the search for an answer to his sense of disillusionment and frustration. The most striking thing about the work is the atmosphere of old age that it evokes; a picture of an old man in his house by the sea remembering the doubts and struggles of a lifetime. In 'Mōsō' Ōgai refers to Hartmann at length. Here he has just described the bouts of depression he experienced occasionally at his lodgings in Berlin:

It was one such night. I felt like reading a book on philosophy and could hardly wait until morning to go out and buy Hartmann's *Philosophie des Unbewussten*.[2] This was the first time that I had dipped into philosophy and I had decided on Hartmann because it was claimed at the time that the nineteenth century had produced two great systems, namely the railway network and Hartmann's thought. Arguments for and against it as 'the first great system' abounded.

It was the 'three stages of illusion' that brought home to me the value of philosophy. In order to prove that happiness was an impossible goal for humanity, Hartmann propounded three stages of illusion. In the first stage humanity hopes to achieve happiness in this world. He listed youth, health, friendship, love and honour and then destroyed each illusion one by one. Love and similar emotions are basically pain. Happiness lies in severing the roots of sexual desire. By sacrificing this happiness humanity contributes slightly to the world's evolution. In the second stage happiness is sought after death. Here one must take as a premise the immortality of the individual. But the individual consciousness is destroyed at death and the central nerve is cut forever. In the third stage happiness is sought in the future world process. This presupposes the development and evolution of the world. But however the world may evolve, the blight of senility is always with us. The nerves become sensitive and so this fact is all the more keenly felt. Pain grows in unison with evolution. Despite a thorough examination of all three stages, the fact remains that happiness is eternally unattainable.

According to Hartmann's metaphysics the world is constructed as well as it could be, but if one were to ask whether it should or should not exist, his answer would be negative. The basis of the world he named the Unconscious. It was no use denying life, however, because the world would continue to exist. Even though present humanity might be utterly destroyed, another human race would arise at another opportunity and the same thing would be repeated. Rather, mankind should affirm life, entrust itself to the world process, accept pain gladly and await the salvation of the world.

I shook my head at such a conclusion. But I was strongly drawn to his destruction of illusions. (VIII, 203–4)

If Hartmann's conclusions were unacceptable, so were the ideas of the pessimist Philipp Mainlaender, who expounded his theory of the will to death in the book *Philosophie der Erlösung* (Philosophy of Redemption, 1876), and those of Elias Metschnikoff with his somewhat naive hope in the power of science to cure all ills.[3] The end result of the search revealed in 'Mōsō' was quite inconclusive, as one can see from the rest of the stories written between 1909 and 1912. Their central theme turns out to be the exploration of the nature and possibility of maintaining an attitude of detachment towards life and its problems. Was the position of a bystander, an onlooker, a dispassionate observer, tenable for a sensitive intellectual? The pessimism of Hartmann and the Buddhist speculations clearly led in the direction of an attitude of resignation; but was this possible? The continual rejection of theories in 'Mōsō' suggests that there were strong doubts.

Many of the stories explore this state of resignation and the central figure is invariably Ōgai's alter ego. In one of the most moving and successful of these works, 'Kompira' (1909), a story which discusses the deep need for superstition even in the modern world, the father whose son has just died from whooping cough stands by the deathbed and tries to comfort his weeping wife:[4]

> While the Professor had thought how very sad it would be if his son died he was shocked at how extraordinarily shallow and unimportant his grief now seemed. It was as if he felt none of the sorrow he had expected. All he felt was that his sense of empty loneliness was somewhat sharper than usual. At the same time the scene in the room struck him with vivid, objective, horrible clarity.
>
> On the *hibachi*, which gave out only a weak heat as they had forgotten to put on more charcoal, lay a metal bowl. Very faint traces of steam rose like intermingling threads from the dirty water that had been boiling. There were a number of medicines for internal use and others for injection lying on a couple of trays. There was also a bottle of Digalen in a cardboard box which had just been opened. His son had not been able to keep the teat of the feeding bottle in his mouth since morning and so there were the remains of the milk in a small tea cup. O-Ei san had soaked a piece of bleached cotton in it and then given it him to suck. A pile of nappies lay on the wooden travelling case. The pale O-Ei san gazing down into the chubby face of his son who looked as though he were sleeping peacefully; the face of his wife red from weeping; and then himself standing there; he saw them all so clearly and with cool indifference as if they were characters on a stage. He felt intensely unhappy to see himself standing there like that as if he were a bystander. (V, 555–6)

In this situation the disgust at his own insensitivity threatens to overcome the desire for detachment. There is a demand for involvement. Ōgai indeed plays the devil's advocate in a number of these stories and this is why they can appear somewhat enigmatic. The most famous statement of his own attitude of detachment was in an article written in 1909 entitled 'Yo ga tachiba' (My position) in which he claims to be unconcerned at what others might think of him and his writings:

> If I were to express this attitude of mine in a single word I think I would call it *resignation*. This applies not only to the arts but

to all walks of life, and when others are convinced I must be suffering I am in fact quite unconcerned. This state of *resignation* may of course mean that I have lost all self-respect, but I have no desire to vindicate myself in that quarter. (XXVI, 393)

A similar negative approach to the question is expressed in 'Asobi' (1910), where the central figure is an official who writes literature in his spare time. He has no position worth mentioning and just accepts his allotted role:

Kimura makes himself comfortable and plods away for ever at his work. But he always looks in the best of spirits. It is a little difficult to explain how he feels at times like this. Whatever he does he is like a child at play. 'Play' can either be interesting or boring, and his office work he sees as being of the latter variety. It is no joke this office work. He is quite aware that he is a small cog in the large machinery of government and that he too is turning; and yet he works as if he were at play – you can see it in his cheerful expression.

When he finishes one job he relaxes with a cigarette. At times like these Kimura's imagination plays tricks with him. Division of labour can also lead to very boring work for the one who picks the short straw, he ponders; but then he has no complaints. This is not to say that he is a fatalist resigned to his destiny. He just wonders what on earth he would ever do if he gave up his work. He tries to imagine himself writing as he does now beneath a lamp, but from morning to night. When he writes he feels like a child who is happy at play. That is not to say he never suffers, mind, but there are obstacles to be overcome in any sport and he is quite aware that art is no joke either. (VII, 243–4)

Here the attitude is one of total dull abnegation of responsibility, a denial of action, an impasse which can lead only to stagnation. The seeds of peace of mind are there but inseparable from boredom. The same theme is taken up in a later satire entitled 'Fushigi na kagami' (The strange mirror, 1911) with a good deal of cynicism. Sitting in his room and listening to his wife doing the accounts, Ōgai suddenly has the strange sensation that his soul has withdrawn from his body and is observing him from the outside:

Seeing that my body was just mumbling when my wife said anything its shadow took an interest. But it had not the slightest feeling of pity. Why? Because they say that my soul treats everything with detachment *(asobi)* and so takes an indiscriminate interest in anything it comes across. Since when has this been common knowledge? I recently described the life of a petty official who led his wretched life with serenity, and in making him confess his attitude of resignation I used the word *asobi.*

No sooner did someone kindly recognize it as my own confession than that whole crowd who love to use an expression
no matter who it comes from as long as it is a *bon mot* pointed
me out to each other crying *asobi, asobi.* Secrets will out and
Heaven speaks through the tongues of men! From then on they
had a marvellous label for my soul.

Now that this detached essence of mind had slipped out of
my body it became interested in everything it saw. Look! He's
mumbling again! Fancy that! How funny! So there was no
reason to expect it to feel sorry when its sloughed-off shell made
incoherent replies and took no heed. It had no sympathy, no
fellow-feeling. This too has long been recognized by the world
at large. Detachment *(asobi)* is an affirmative evaluation, but
lack of sympathy is a negative one; the former is a constructive
assertion, but the latter merely passive. (X, 127–8)

Here we have the two sides of the coin clearly represented. To be
detached is a desirable quality but it brings with it the complications of
inhumanity. The simple man Kimura is safe as long as he is never
subjected to the pressure that the professor in 'Kompira' undergoes.
When the natural instinct is towards uncomplicated sympathy when
faced with human tragedy, the mask of indifference and cool detachment becomes distasteful and untenable. How can the dilemma be
resolved? The question was a very real one for Ōgai who was a rational
intellectual seeking objectivity as an answer to his personal anxieties,
but who was at the same time worried that he was a cold, even sexless,
individual. The question is posed yet again in the short story 'Hyaku
monogatari' (Ghost stories, 1911) where the central character comes
across another of his ilk who actually tends to make fools of others
as a sort of calculated experiment:

I tried thinking very hard about why and how I have been a
bystander all my life . . . Ever since I first played with other
children and later became an adult and entered society with all
its attitudes and prejudices, I have never thrown myself wholeheartedly into the maelstrom or really enjoyed myself, no matter
what emotions boiled up within me. I have stood on this living
stage of life, but I have never played a role that felt like a real
role. I have merely been an extra, and so when I was not on
stage I felt in my element, like a fish in water; for a bystander
feels at home in a world of bystanders. (IX, 143)

Such passages express a real and deeply felt anguish. Twenty years
earlier he had been able to identify himself with a public role and
could feel he was in a position to influence events. Now, out in the
cold, the automatic response was to huddle in on himself and to try

and persuade himself, in recompense, that he did not really need others. A clue to the ideal state that Ōgai was seeking can be found in the portrait of his father in the story 'Casuistica' (Medical records, 1911). Describing himself as a young medical student who is helping his father at the clinic, he writes:

> He always felt as though there was something he wanted to start, something he ought to do, but he never understood what that something might be. Sometimes something would appear like a vision but it would fade away before he could grasp it. Sometimes it took the form of a woman; sometimes a dream of many splendid and glorious things. But then at other times because he had just been reading the *Hekigan* or the *Mumonkan* it would be a Zen-like contemplative meditation. But whatever it was it was always vague. It occurred not only when he was seeing to his patients but whatever he might be doing. He would finish the job in hand, put it aside and think, what next? But he never knew what next.
>
> He did not, however, try very hard to understand what this unfathomable something was. Sometimes he tried seeing it as happiness and at other times he tried to connect it with hope, and yet he never pursued it to the point of claiming that it was necessary for his success or that he would fail if he lost it.
>
> He had, however, felt for some time that this something was missing in his father and at first he thought his father was leading a pointless, empty life: he was old and old people tend to do pointless things. But then he happened to read a book of Kumazawa Banzan's in which it was written that to wash your face and comb your hair every day was as much following the Way as to devote yourself entirely to the state. Reading this, he thought of his father's everyday life and realized that instead of continually arranging things in the present with an eye to the future, his father poured the whole of his soul into ordinary everyday affairs. This attitude of his father, who was content to remain the doctor of a small post-station, appeared to him, albeit vaguely, to be close to that of a man who has attained the Way. From then on he suddenly felt respect for his father. (VIII, 6–7)

It was this kind of resignation, the exhortation to cultivate one's own garden, that Ōgai saw as the answer. Rather than a self-conscious detachment and an artificial refusal to become involved, the ideal was to involve oneself so wholeheartedly in one's job and the very act of living that one had no time to be self-conscious.

The important question that remains is whether Ōgai succeeded in reaching this ideal state. The nature of the stories that have been quoted so far would suggest that he had not, and we need go no further than 'Mōsō' again to substantiate this conclusion. The same problems that are presented to the owner of a restless will were faced by Goethe and a similar answer was proposed:

> Even after such experiences, my mind remains as before, chasing visions of the future and ignoring present realities. What is this phantom that man seeks after, even while he knows his life is already on the downward path?
> Goethe once wrote:
> 'How can a man come to know himself? Never through mere reflection, but possibly through action. Try to do your duty, and in the end you will know your own true worth.
> What is your duty? The demands of the present.'
> To see the demands of the here-and-now as your duty and to carry them out — this is the exact opposite of ignoring present realities. Why do I seem incapable of putting myself in such a position?
> To be able to treat the demands of the present as the whole of your work, you must know that it will suffice, and that I cannot do. I am an eternal malcontent. Somehow I am fated to be misplaced. (VIII, 210)

Ōgai found that it was impossible to relax and accept the demands of mere everyday life as he remembered his father doing. Nor was the calculating and somewhat heartless attitude of the bystander tenable. He was, as he said, the eternal malcontent, applying the principle of passive resistance in the face of disappointment and domestic tragedy, and channelling his frustrated drive into continuous work and study. It was precisely this drive that made him continue where lesser men might well have fallen into uneasy silence.

The new man

If Ōgai was acutely aware of a sense of personal alienation and had considerable difficulty in achieving a modus vivendi, he was also aware that the modernization of Japan in which he had played such a willing part was beginning to set up strains within society that might prove disastrous. Patterns of traditional social behaviour were changing with such rapidity that it must have seemed as though equilibrium might never again be restored, and Ōgai now had to face the consequences of the move towards rationalization that he had so fervently fought for. The conscious relation of personal anxieties to the wider sphere can be seen in a number of stories, the most well-known of which is 'Fushinchū' (Under reconstruction, 1910). The title itself is meant to symbolize the state of Japan and against this background Ōgai wrote a poignant short story of an imagined meeting between a middle-aged Japanese official and a German woman whom he had known in earlier days in Berlin, thus harking back to Elis. The tension of the occasion is masterfully portrayed through a strained conversation between the couple, but what stands out is the moment when she asks him whether he wishes to kiss her. The man replies: 'This is Japan' (VII, 9). The halcyon days of his youth were now far behind and he was more than usually aware of the contrasts as well as the similarities of the Japanese and the European experience.

A central concern of Ōgai's writing during this period is that of values: the vacuum left after the collapse of traditional ones and the nature of those that were taking their place. It is as well to remember that the same problem, if on a smaller scale, was faced by European writers, thus making the possibility of a suitable imported answer even more remote.

One manifestation of the change in values was the concentration on sex in the literature of the time. The rise and popularity of the Naturalists in Japan between the years 1906 and 1912 could well have been another reason for Ōgai's return to active writing, for those very faults that he had criticized in Zola, seventeen years previously in his 'Shōsetsuron', were now appearing in Japanese writers.[5] The main difference between Japanese and European Naturalism can be defined as being one of vision; concern for social realities and social ills was abandoned in favour of personal realities and personal ills. The tendency to concentrate on the more sordid aspects of reality, however, was common to both. Because such Japanese writers as Tayama Katai and Tokuda Shūsei were concerned with self-revelation, they became obsessed with sexual instincts and the stories they wrote were often chronicles of their own depravity, justified in the name of 'sincerity'. Ōgai's criticisms of Zola's attitude towards reality may have mellowed and his allegiance been given to truth rather than beauty, but he still disagreed with the emphasis accorded the sordid. Ōgai took issue with the Naturalists over this specific question, rather than because of their tendency to see personal experience as the sole source of legitimate material. His label as an 'anti-Naturalist' should not blind us to the fact that many of his stories come very close to being *études* themselves.

Writing as Ōgai was for the magazine *Subaru*, much of the criticism of the Naturalists was of a somewhat petulant character, and there are indications that he felt on the defensive:

When I see the stories of contemporary Naturalists it seems that the author's fantasies are invariably dominated by women. Perhaps it is because they are so young. When one is close to fifty as I am sexual desires do not constitute the major part of a man's life. I am not saying this for effect, for what purpose would that serve? (IV, 590)

The three stories which are specifically directed against the Naturalists, 'Sakazuki' (The sake cup), 'Le Parnasse ambulant', and 'Fushigi na kagami', do not contain any serious criticism of their theories, but merely set them up to ridicule. 'Sakazuki' is a short allegory where seven girls drinking from the fountain of inspiration in cups inscribed with the word 'nature' are interrupted by an eighth girl with a strange black cup. After some altercation she too is allowed to drink at the fountain. 'Le Parnasse ambulant' is a piece of whimsy in which he imagines the Naturalists in a funeral procession suddenly being stopped by a Frenchman. The whole procession freezes and then runs back the way it came; Ōgai being more aware than most how far the Japanese movement differed from its European counterpart. In 'Fushigi na kagami' he dreams he is sitting in front of the main figures of the movement who try to intimidate him and force him to read some of his latest work so that they can ridicule him in turn. All these works are very lightweight and one feels that they were merely written as part of *Subaru*'s propaganda.

Not all Ōgai's stories descend to this tactic however. As a doctor he had a professional interest in the problems of sexual behaviour which the Naturalists treated as the mainspring of their lives, and by extension, their art. At this stage he was no longer concerned simply to condemn obscenity, and the real desire to investigate and refute their convictions led him to write the autobiographical *Vita Sexualis* (1909), which traces the development of his own sexual awareness from the age of six to the age of twenty-two when he left for Germany. His concern with the falseness of the Naturalists' claims is mentioned early in the work:

> Meanwhile Naturalism had begun. When he read works of this genre Kanai felt no particular desire to emulate them, but for all that he found them very entertaining. He was amused but at the same time a strange thought occurred to him.
> Whenever he read a Naturalist novel it seemed that whatever the characters in the story were doing it invariably involved the representation of sexual desire, and criticism seemed to accept this as a true reflection of life. While he doubted whether life really was like that, he did sometimes wonder whether he perhaps deviated from the normal human psychological state in that he felt indifferent towards sexual desire; in particular he worried

that he might have been born with that abnormal characteristic called frigidity. Similar imaginings arose when he read Zola's novels. There was for instance the passage in *Germinal,* which describes peasant workers reaching the nadir of misfortune, where one of them goes to spy on a couple making love. His doubts in this case were as to why the author had gone out of his way to write such a scene, not that such happenings were in any way improbable. Of course such things occurred but why had the author written about them? Perhaps the author's own sexual images were abnormal. Perhaps men like novelists or poets did have abnormal sexual desires. There was a connection here with the problem of genius on which Lombroso and others theorized. It was also what Mobius and his followers based their ideas on when they pounced on famous poets and philosophers wholesale, discussing them as if they were mentally ill. The Naturalists who had arisen recently in Japan, however, were quite different: a lot of writers suddenly writing on similar topics and contemporary criticism accepting what they wrote as 'life'. This kind of life seemed to be what psychiatrists might call a life where every single representation had a tinge of sexual desire. Kanai's misgivings became stronger than before. (V, 86–7)

Vita Sexualis is a collection of episodes which chronicle Ōgai's sexual development and, although not without a certain dry humour, it is a serious study underlaid, as Ōgai himself said, by the vague anxiety that he himself might be abnormally passive in sexual matters. It is not too clear here how much this is to be taken as a pose however. Its serious scientific, factual tone marks it off from such works as Katai's *Futon* where the emphasis is more on self-indulgent exposure. It was written as a direct criticism of the Naturalists' attitude toward sex, being a literary counterpart to his earlier article on sexual behaviour, 'Seiyoku zassetsu'.

Most ironical of all, of course, was the subsequent banning of this work by the authorities for corruption of public morals. *Vita Sexualis* came out in *Subaru* on 1 July 1909, but was not banned until the 28th of the month, by which time nearly all the copies had been sold. The ban was therefore more of a warning than a punishment, especially as he was awarded the title of Doctor of Literature a mere five days before the ban took effect. This incident, however, brought back some of the belligerence of former years. Ōgai's diary shows that on 30 July he discussed the story with his old friend Inoue Tetsujirō and sent him a copy in the evening. The entry for 6 August reads: 'The Head of the Police Bureau at the Ministry of Home Affairs came to the Ministry of War to discuss *Vita Sexualis*. As a result I was cautioned by Vice-

Minister Ishimoto Shinroku' (XXXV, 450). Ōgai seemed to have been prepared for something of the sort as he wrote to Kako Tsurudo on 1 August:

> The ban was put into effect nominally on *Subaru* no. 7. I have half been expecting something like this. Ten years ago nude painting was treated in a similar way without any recourse to the rights and wrongs of the matter. They may come to their senses ten years from now. Minister Terauchi too has mentioned the ban in a roundabout way. (XXXVI, 313)

However the pressure was kept up by his superiors. The diary entry for 29 November that year records: 'I was warned by Vice-Minister Ishimoto Shinroku not to sign myself in the newspapers' (XXXV, 464). The banning of *Vita Sexualis* was to result in the bitter story 'Chinmoku no tō' (The tower of silence)[6] a year later in November 1910.

Ōgai ends his account in *Vita Sexualis* with the conviction that sexual desire could and should be kept under control, but there is still no escaping a certain melancholy tone, a tiredness that is a hallmark of all his stories at this time:

> What Kanai had written was not an autobiography in the usual sense of the word; but then he didn't want it to be seen as a novel either. He didn't really mind one way or the other, but he did not want to write anything artistically worthless. He did not believe that only those elements that Nietzsche had called Dionysian were artistic. He also recognized the Apollonian elements. But he had to admit that sexual desire divorced from love lacked passion, and a man of no passion was hardly a fit subject for an autobiography.
>
> He decided he would definitely stop writing.
>
> He thought deeply. Everyone would say when they looked at him now that he had lost his passion because he had aged. But this was not the reason. He had known himself too thoroughly even as a boy. His intellect had withered his passion while it was still germinating. Yet he had quite by chance been led astray by some ridiculous urge and had received that dubbing he did not really need. It was unnecessary. It would have been best to have left it until marriage; and, to go one step further, if there was no point in having it before marriage, perhaps it would have been better not to have got married at all. It really did seem as if he was abnormally indifferent.
>
> He then thought of it in a different light. Of course it had been an unnecessary experience. But it was only on the surface that his intellect had withered his passion. Even beneath the poles which are covered in eternal ice there burns that fierce fire that drives up volcanoes. Michelangelo had quarrelled with his friends in his

youth and had his nose broken by someone's fist. He despaired of love, and yet when he was sixty he met Vittoria Colonna and achieved a love that is rarely won. He himself was not incapable; he was not impotent. People were inclined to let this tiger, sexual desire, range free and then ride it to their own destruction. But he had tamed the tiger and controlled it. There was an Arhant called Bhadra who let a tamed tiger sleep by his side. His young attendant was afraid of the tiger. Bhadra means 'wise man'. The tiger was probably a symbol for sexual desire. It may be tamed but its frightening power never diminishes.

With this new idea in mind Kanai tried re-reading the whole thing slowly from the beginning. When he reached the end it was already late into the night and the rain had stopped without him realizing it. The water dripping from the gutter spout onto a stone below at long intervals sounded like someone striking a Chinese musical stone.

Now he had finished it he wondered whether he could make it public. It would be difficult. There are things which everyone does and yet never mentions. The problem was that he belonged to educational circles which were governed by prudery. In that case could he just casually let his son read it? He would probably neither make him read it nor forbid him to. But you could not forecast the effect it might have on his son. What if his son read it and then turned out like his father? Would that be fortunate or unfortunate? That too was unclear. There was a line of a poem by Dehmel which ran 'Do not obey! Do not obey!' No, he didn't want even his own son to read it. He picked up his brush and wrote VITA SEXUALIS in Latin in large letters on the cover, and tossed it into his bookcase where it landed with a thud. (V, 177–9)

The uncertainty as to whether he had killed his own passion or merely tamed the tiger mirrors the concern with old age and the talk of detached resignation that we have seen in other stories of this period. As an analysis of his own development it comes close to being an *étude* of precisely the type he had earlier deplored, and it reveals the extent to which his ideas about literature had changed and matured since his earliest dependence on the opinions of Gottschall.

The relative success of *Vita Sexualis* contrasts strongly with Ōgai's first attempt at writing a full-scale novel, *Seinen,* which appeared in *Subaru* in instalments from March 1910 to August 1911. The story follows the fortunes of Koizumi Jun'ichi, a young man who has just arrived in Tokyo with aspirations of becoming a novelist, as he encounters a number of women who begin to arouse in him sexual desire. The theme is closely connected to that of *Vita Sexualis,* as Jun'ichi triumphs over his own particular tiger and decides he can become a novelist without indulging his sexual desires. Within the limits defined above, therefore, *Seinen* is an anti-Naturalist novel. The message, however, it too glaringly obvious for this attempt at a *Bildungsroman* to be anything but a failure.

On his arrival in Tokyo, Jun'ichi visits a famous Naturalist writer but is not deeply impressed. A friend called Seto Hayato takes him to a literary society meeting where he hears a talk on Ibsen and where he meets Ōmura Shōnosuke, with whom he is to spend many hours discussing literary and philosophical questions. A performance of the play *John Gabriel Borkman* provides the background for his first meeting with the widow of a famous lawyer, Sakai Kō, who happens to have been a native of the same province as Jun'ichi. Their first brief encounter in the theatre, during which we are treated to a detailed description of the play, is concluded by an invitation for him to visit her to see her late husband's collection of French books. His seduction is chronicled in the form of an extract from his diary which leaves matters suitably vague.

In the meantime Jun'ichi has been getting to know the girl who lives next door to his lodgings, Oyuki, whose attractive naivety arouses his sexual desire. Despite a decision not to see the widow Sakai again he is eventually drawn to her house a second time, somewhat surprised that his lust should have the power to overcome other scruples. This second visit is, however, a failure, as he realizes he is now looking upon her as an enemy to be fought rather than an experience of which he can take full advantage. The widow thus becomes the symbol of unbridled lust and in his rejection of her Jun'ichi finds that his desires can with effort be controlled. The second meeting ends with the widow inviting him to spend a few days with her in Hakone.

A third temptation appears in the form of an attractive geisha, but in spite of her obvious desire to meet him again, he manages to avoid her through inaction. The widow, now in Hakone, is still on his mind however, and so against his better judgement he follows her. He is made fully aware of his mistake when he finds her in the company of another man. At first insanely jealous, he manages to rationalize his position, decides to forget her for good and so leaves Hakone with the conviction that he has at last found the right frame of mind in which he can start creative writing. Lust has been controlled and rational intellect is triumphant.

The failure of this novel to be anything more than a pastiche is due not only to the lack of characterization, plot or structure, but also to

the fact that large sections of it consist of interior monologues or discussions of various problems of the day, which have very little raison
d'être within the novel. But despite its artistic failures, *Seinen* is of
some importance, for the opinions expressed in these discussions help
us to expand an area of Ōgai's personality that proves somewhat elusive.

The main concern behind this portrayal of an insipid lost youth is
the loss of stable values and a pessimism about Japan's ability to pull
out of the relativist morass. Could the 'new man' and the 'new woman'
as portrayed in much of European literature of the time fit into the
Japanese world? Did the social upheaval in Europe mean that answers
had to be sought elsewhere, or might the answer to Japan's problems
lie in that very intellectual turmoil? Ōgai's development from this time
on lies in his gradual realization that Japan's problems were of a
different calibre and would need home-grown solutions. The European
experience might be useful as a reference point but, as he had written
while still in Berlin, 'Civilization is built on historical foundations'.
While science and even art might be imported with reasonable success,
the motivations for people's daily actions, their gut response to their
social environment, was a specifically national phenomenon.

During this period of uncertainty, the two figures in European
culture that Ōgai saw as having the greatest relevance seem to be Ibsen
and Nietzsche. Although his response to Ibsen will be treated in more
detail in connection with those works that Ōgai actually translated,[7]
there is a reference to the playwright in *Seinen* which is of interest:

> At first Ibsen was a little Norwegian, but after he started writing
> social dramas he became a great European. He was reduced in size
> again when he was brought to Japan. Everything we bring to
> Japan becomes diminished. It's the same with Nietzsche and the
> same with Tolstoy. I am reminded of a passage from Nietzsche:
> 'The earth has become small, and on it hops the last man, who
> makes everything small. . . "We have invented happiness," say the
> last men, and they blink.' We Japanese have imported all sorts of
> beliefs and isms which we play around with and blink. As every
> single thing the Japanese get their hands on becomes nothing but
> a little plaything, there is never any call for fear, even if the
> original article was frightening. There is little point in bringing
> Yamaga Sokō, the Forty Seven Rōnin, or the Mito Rōnin back
> from the dead and invoking them against an Ibsen or a Tolstoy
> who have become so diminished. (VI, 313–14)

Ibsen's view of true individualism insists on a striving to break the
bonds of all conventions. But there is another side to his thought:

> If this other side were not there, Ibsen would merely be advo-

cating self-indulgence. But Ibsen is not that kind of man. There is
in his writings a different, transcendent self that is always striving
upwards. This is demonstrated in *Brand* for instance. Why does
Ibsen tear off the outworn shackles of convention and throw
them away? Not to be free to roll in the mire, but free to fly far
and high with strong wings. (VI, 314)

Here Ōgai is clearly referring to the espousal of the Naturalists and
others of 'individualism' as a pretext for self-indulgence. Ōgai himself
knew through his constant contact with Europe and his period of study
there that Western concepts were constantly being warped and
'diminished' in Japan. He understood how this could so easily lead to a
rejection of more worthwhile elements:

> Zola's Claude seeks art. Ibsen's Brand seeks the ideal. He does not
> think twice of sacrificing his wife and children for the sake of
> what he is seeking. He even destroys himself. Some people have
> even made the mistake of interpreting *Brand* as a satire. But in
> point of fact Ibsen is absolutely serious; serious in pointing out
> the way upward. All or nothing – this is Brand's ideal. But in the
> sense that it comes from himself, from his own will, there is a
> limit in what Ibsen seeks. In any case, the path is opened by the
> individual for he himself to tread. Ethics are to be adhered to by
> the individual and so they are made by him. Religion is what the
> individual believes in and so is founded by him. In a word,
> autonomy. I doubt whether even Ibsen can illustrate this openly.
> But in any case he is a seeker, a modern, a new man. (VI, 315–16)

There is in fact a stronger echo here of Nietzsche than of Ibsen, and
it is hardly surprising that this most Western of philosophers is constantly used as a reference point by the youth in *Seinen*; Nietzsche's
ideas had attracted a lot of attention during the Meiji 30s.

Ōgai's first mention of Nietzsche occurs in a letter to Kako Tsurudo
which can reasonably be dated to 31 March 1894. A friend, Irizawa
Tatsukichi, had just brought back some of the latest books on philosophy from Europe and lent them to Ōgai. It is doubtful, however, that
Ōgai read any of Nietzsche's work at this early stage. Internal evidence
suggests that he based his first reactions on Brandes' essay 'Aristo-
kratischer Radicalismus', which appeared in the *Deutsche Rundschau*
for 1890 and later as part of Brandes' book *Menschen und Werke*
(1893).[8] Ōgai's next reference to Nietzsche was after the Sino-Japanese
War in the preface to *Tsukikusa* (December 1896). The context here
suggests that his view was still based on secondary sources, in particular
the last chapter of Volkelt's *Aesthetische Zeitfragen* (1895), which he
was later to summarize,[9] and Ola Hansson's *Der Materialismus in der*

Literatur (1891). Nietzsche is seen mainly as a bulwark of individualism against the pernicious influence on literature of Naturalism, Materialism and Determinism. It is worth noting that Ōgai's interest in primarily the aesthetic side of Nietzsche continued for some time, as he read Julius Zeitler's *Nietzsches Aesthetik* (1900) fairly closely if we can judge from the notes and underlinings in the book.

Ōgai had no responsibility for the first Nietzsche 'boom' in Japan, however, which was started by two young students at Tokyo University, Tobari Chikufū and Takayama Chogyū, who found themselves up against Tsubouchi Shōyō and Hasegawa Tenkei.[10] Tobari, whose first article on the subject was published in May 1900, based his views not on primary sources but on Brandes, and in later essays, on Theobald Ziegler's *Friedrich Nietzsche* (1900). Both Tobari and Takayama, who started writing in January 1901 basing his arguments almost entirely on another work by Ziegler entitled *Die geistigen und sozialien Strömungen des 19ten Jahrhunderts* (Spiritual and Social Trends in the Nineteenth Century, 1899), stressed the individualism and iconoclastic nature of Nietzsche's thought which seemed to be in tune with the spirit of the first decade of twentieth-century Japan. Their opponents, working from English secondary sources, pictured Nietzsche as a monster of depravity who used ultra-individualism as an excuse for every kind of destructive evil. The argument that thus arose repeated the kind of battle between Anglo-Saxon and Germanic viewpoints that had been one of the main causes of the misunderstandings of the *Botsurisō Ronsō*.

Although Ōgai felt he knew enough about Nietzsche to be able to brand Takayama Chogyū's essay '*Biteki seikatsu o ronzu*' (On the aesthetic life) as 'Nietzsche minus nails or fangs' (XXV,270), his interest in the important ethical questions raised by Nietzsche was aroused only after 1907 when he had in his possession the 1906 *Collected Works*. In 'Mōsō' his encounter with the ethics is described as follows:

> To my ears, weary of metaphysical edifices constructed like the harmonies of Dutch church music, came the odd fragmented melodies of certain aphorisms.
>
> I had not been able to accept Schopenhauer's *Quietive*, the effort to break the Will to live and let oneself enter a state of nothingness. But now I became aware and felt myself suddenly whipped out of my soporific state.
>
> It was Nietzsche's philosophy of the overman.
>
> This too, however, was an intoxicating wine rather than a nourishing food.
>
> With keen pleasure I saw the passive altruistic morals of the past treated as if they were the morals of a common herd. I was

interested to see not only the Socialist view of universal brother-
hood described as the morality of a stupid, foolish crowd who
rejected all privilege, but also the way those rampant anarchists
were reviled as dogs barking in the streets of Europe. I could not,
however seriously, accept his rejection of the conventions of
intellect, the argument that the Will to Power lay at the root of
all culture, nor the way he made Cesare Borgia the classic model
for a ruler's morality — a man who never thought twice of using
poison or the dagger for the sake of his family or himself. Moreover, to eyes which had seen the closely argued ethical theory of
Hartmann even the Revaluation of All Values lost some of its
novelty.

Then what of death? The Eternal Recurrence brought no
consolation. I felt sympathy for the man who was unable to write
about Zarathustra's last moments. (VIII,214-15)

One can see here clearly the attraction and the rejection as part of
Nietzsche appealed to the intellectual aristocrat in Ōgai while the idea
of absolute individualism repelled. The intoxication was undoubtedly
caused more by the punch of Nietzsche's German than by his thought.
By this time, Ōgai's reaction was based on a thorough reading of at least
Also sprach Zarathustra, for he was advising Ikuta Chōkō on difficult
passages in the German as the latter was translating it.

The concern with the true nature of this new Western individualism
and the consequences it might have for Japanese society in general and
every Japanese youth runs right through *Seinen*, but apart from portraying the kind of meetings, conversations and worries that most intellectual young men of the time must have experienced, the novel fails to
give us any deep insight into their emotional and spiritual turmoil. The
most outstanding example of this is chapter 20 which is devoted to a
discussion of various differences between Japan and the West.

Although it contributes very little to the novel, it is a very important
passage in the context of Ōgai's own thought. The two young men have
been talking about Maeterlinck's play *L'oiseau bleu,* an example of
symbolist drama well known in Japan at the time:

It seems to me that renunciation comes to the same thing in
both Buddhism and Christianity. But only in the West did thought
develop beyond this. There was no Renaissance in the Orient,
was there? It was the Renaissance which showed us that a
blue bird existed in our own homes as well. Courageous navi-
gators emerged and it became possible to map the world accu-
rately. The heavens were properly understood; science dawned
and the arts blossomed. Machinery became gradually more ela-
borate and the whole world became materialistic, as its detrac-

tors would say. Production and capital absorbed everyone's energy and the transcendental world was left vacant.

Then that eccentric Schopenhauer suddenly opened his eyes and tried to catch a glimpse of the world beyond. Gazing into that world and looking back at this one, the root of all things turned out to be a blind Will. His was a pessimism that found it impossible to affirm life.

Then Nietzsche turned up and proclaimed the reverse. Of course we could not escape the pain of life, but it was cowardice to avoid it by running away. There was a way to grasp the truth of life in the midst of pain. The question 'what?' became the question 'how?'. Somehow we must grasp the truth of this life just as it is. Men like Rousseau have claimed we must return to Nature, but the memory of life stretching from the ancient past to the present is such a powerful reality that it can never be erased.

In Japan we talk of the Confucianism of Ogyū Sorai and the Native Studies of men like Keichū and Mabuchi as if they were a Renaissance, but that was just a return to the past, not a rebirth. So there is no point in spurring on one's soul to a land of beautiful dreams and remembrances of the past, to yearn for the blue flower of the Romantics. Tolstoy was a great man but even he fled the world. In the final analysis we must carry on confronting everyday life in its immediacy. This feeling of constant confrontation is Dionysian. If while doing this, while immersing ourselves in everyday life, we can hang on tightly to our independence of spirit and give way not a step, we are being Apollonian. To try and grasp the truth of life in this way is indeed individualistic. Here in this individualism lies the crossroads between your egoism and altruism. The former is represented by the bad side of Nietzsche — the Will to Power, the idea of self-aggrandizement at the expense of others. If everyone practised it we would reach a state of anarchy. There can be little doubt that if we interpret individualism in this manner it should be rejected.

However, altruistic individualism is a different matter. It is the grasping of the truth of everything in life while still holding on tight to this fortress we call the self, not giving way an inch. Discharge your loyalty to the ruler! But as citizens we are no longer their lackeys as we were in the past when everything was so confused. Discharge your duty to your parents! But as children we are no longer the slaves of the past when children could be killed or sold at will.

Loyalty and filial piety are merely values as we understood them at that time. The whole of everyday life is a matter of values that we are constantly grasping. So is it possible now to discard that which we call our self? Can we sacrifice it? I certainly think we can.

Just as the greatest affirmation of a love is a suicide pact, so the greatest affirmation of loyalty is death in battle. Once the whole truth of all life is grasped, the individual dies. Individualism becomes universalism. This is quite different from a denial of life through asceticism. Well! What do you think? (VI,421-3)

Jun'ichi, fascinated by this exposition, replies:

Didn't I read somewhere recently that some professor or other had been discussing this very problem? He said that individualism was a Western concept and that it could not admit sacrifice of the self. In the East individualism had become familism which had in turn become nationalism. Only then was sacrifice of the self for one's lord or father possible. This kind of theory treats individualism and egoism as one and the same thing and so is quite different from the concept you have mentioned. But isn't it a bit strange that this kind of development from individual to state should only occur in Japan and not in the West?

Of course it's strange! That professor not only treats individualism as being the same as egoism or egocentrism, he even equates it to anarchism. To say that Stone-age men crawled out of their caves one by one and lived alone by themselves like a collection of discrete atoms is to disregard history altogether. If that was the case then the beginning of human life would have been anarchistic, but that has never been the case. A life of anarchy is merely a pipedream of today's anarchists. The idea that man lived like this individually from the very beginning and then artificially constructed societies and states is a little like Rousseau's *Contrat social*, but nobody believes that kind of thing nowadays. The further you look back into the past the more you find that man was bound in a common life. Gradually we escaped these bonds, we won our liberty and became individuals.

Look; we are both interested in literature. Isn't it obvious when you look at the development of literature? Theatre concerned with fact and circumstance became theatre dealing with personality and so developed towards individualism. To try and suppress it now would be like trying to force a child to stay in bed when he is awake and wants to get up. I ask you, is that possible? (VI,423-4)

This passage illustrates how Ōgai was more at home with serious intellectual discussion than with artistic concerns such as structure or characterization. As it appears in a novel, it is dangerous to take it as representative of his own views, but the problems it raises were definitely a major concern with him. It will be seen later how the points raised in this conversation, especially the critique of individualism, foreshadow some of his later work. The immersion of the self in everyday life as an ideal to live by leads on to the concept that the self can be transcended in this very act. From the belief that the ultimate affirmation of life can be in death, it is not far to a work like 'Abe ichizoku' where the question of suicide is treated in detail.

Ōgai's next novel of comparable length was *Gan* (The Wild Goose), the story of Otama, the mistress of a usurer, and her unrequited desire for freedom represented by a young medical student called Okada. The story is told in the first person by a narrator who also takes some small part in the action. In the first three chapters we are given an account of how the narrator meets Okada and a description of the area around Muenzaka in Ueno where the action takes place. Okada has seen Otama, only identified as 'the woman at the window' at this point, and is attracted to her because she represents his ideal of woman as something remote and beautiful. With chapter 4 the story moves to a description of the girl's life up to the moment when she first catches sight of Okada. This part occupies half of the whole novel and it is not until chapter 16 that we again turn to the central plot. We hear of how Otama became the mistress of the usurer, Suezō, and the problems that Suezō has with his neurotic wife once she gets to know of his deception. Otama becomes bored and begins to dream that one of the students in the area might be able to save her from her predicament.

It is at this point that we return to the moment of her first meeting with Okada, described at the beginning of the novel, and from here on the story proceeds to its sad ending. Suezō buys Otama two linnets which are attacked by a snake some days later. Okada happens to be passing by, kills the snake, but then walks off without giving the poor girl time to talk with him further. The result is to transform her vague hope into a violent desire. She arranges that both Suezō and her maid will be away one evening and plans to meet and talk to Okada.

Fate now takes a hand in the form of the narrator who asks Okada to go out for a walk that evening to find something to eat. They pass the house where Otama is waiting, but Okada hurries by and she finds it impossible to call him back. They walk to the pond at Shinobazu, and meet a friend who persuades Okada to throw a stone at a group of wild geese to chase them away. This Okada does, but unwittingly kills one of them. While waiting for nightfall, when they can take the goose home, Okada tells the narrator that he is going to leave for Germany to study medicine the very next day. This is why he refused to react to Otama's presence. As they smuggle the bird home they just catch a glimpse of her standing at the top of the hill at Muenzaka gazing in despair at the youth she cannot reach. The story ends as the narrator is explaining how he came to learn both sides of the affair:

> I have now finished my story. Now I count back, I find that it all happened thirty-five years ago. One half of the story I saw myself through my friendship with Okada, but I learnt the other half when I happened to make friends with Otama after he had left. Just as one can see the two pictures under a stereoscope as a single image, I created this story by combining what I knew before with what I learned later. How did you get to know Otama? How was it that you heard it from her? the reader might well ask. But, as I have said before, the answer to this lies outside the scope of this tale. I would, however, advise the reader to avoid fruitless speculation, as it goes without saying that I lack the qualities that would enable me to become her lover. (VIII,603)

Although *Gan* is a real attempt to write fiction, it fails in the end to satisfy. Admittedly, compared to *Seinen*, more care is taken with the composition, but the structure reveals that Ōgai had not yet solved the problem of how to tell a story. No doubt because of the excessive influence of his study of the novella form, he still tended to see a story as something that had to be introduced and then finished off roundly with a framework. There is, as a result, a fundamental uncertainty of touch in the narration of *Gan*. The ostensible narrator is only active in the first two chapters and then fades quickly into a straightforward authorial voice, thus making the clumsy apologia at the end not only annoying but also unnecessary. It has been suggested elsewhere that Ōgai found the story difficult to end, in view of the fact that it was serialized up to chapter 21 (September 1911 – May 1913), and the last three chapters appeared only when it was published in book form in 1915. This is quite possible, but there is no reliable information on when the later chapters were in fact written. As the killing of the wild goose occurs in chapter 22, one might also expect a different title for the serialized part of the story, but this is not the case.

A more serious objection, however, is the disturbing way in which the reader's sympathies are engaged on behalf of nearly every character at some point in the story. This is particularly noticeable in the section which deals with Suezō and his neurotic wife. The former, whom one might suppose to be judged somewhat harshly, is drawn in a very favourable light, even to the extent that one starts identifying with him. The reader is thus allowed to become involved in this relationship, only to find at the end of the story that it is all just chopped away like so much dead wood and totally forgotten.

There is, too, an inconsistency in the development of Otama from pure, virtuous daughter to scheming mistress. This change, which is too sudden to be really convincing, is mirrored in the change of attitude to the Chinese novels that are referred to during the course of the story. Ōgai had great difficulty in presenting Otama as an idealized, remote figure throughout, and in maintaining the illusion of her essential purity and goodness, an illusion which is central to the whole tale. By a conspicuous lack of any mention of sexual relations between the usurer and his mistress an attempt is made to preserve the original picture of the shy, beautiful daughter which does not square with the theme of awakened youthful passion. Neither does the somewhat naive description of such sexual awareness in terms of pubescent dreaming really stand up to close analysis, for we know, despite the attempts to persuade us otherwise, that she must already be fully aware of what sexual arousal means. There is here a clash between the demands of realism in the portrayal of the girl's feelings and the demands of romanticism in the creation of an illusion of purity.

Yet another area where Ōgai shows a disconcerting lack of care is in the use of symbolism which is at once heavy-handed and suspiciously thin. The relevance of the linnets in their cage needs little comment, but the scene where Okada comes to the rescue of the illusive princess by slowly slicing through the glassy scales of the green snake that is devouring her birds is so laboured as to be almost offensive. The wild goose, too, is an image so loaded with associations in Japanese culture as to be a cliché, and it is far from clear in this story whether it is to be taken as much more than an image of sadness.

For all its faults of structure, however, *Gan* does succeed in creating an effective atmosphere of pathos which is perhaps the main reason it is still read today. Short by normal standards, it is in the tradition of 'Maihime', a romance lightly disguised in modern garb, with all the defects one might expect. One looks for realism and instead one finds idealized characters, such as the usurer with a heart of gold (away from home), the handsome student, and the kept woman who remains essentially pure. In this sense it represents for Ōgai a step back into a precarious lyricism. But if it were not for this lyricism, *Gan* would present a very pessimistic view of human relationships indeed. All communication between individuals in the story fails, and Otama is in a sorry state, striving to escape from the only person who can really help her fulfil her desire to give her father a troublefree old age.

The difficulties that Ōgai experienced with the novel form are no doubt connected to the fact that writing was still a spare time occupation. The prolonged periods of concentration necessary to marry coherence to length were just not available at this time. The fourth of his longer works, 'Kaijin' (Ashes), written at the same time as *Gan* (October 1911 to December 1912), proved too much even for Ōgai and he left it unfinished.

With 'Kaijin' the theme of the young man recurs, but the deadly image of the 'last men' who merely blink becomes intensified into a full-blown pessimism. The novel opens as the hero, a writer called Yamaguchi Setsuzō, is going to attend the funeral of his former patron Tanida, whose house he left some nine years previously. Sitting in the grounds of the temple waiting for the funeral procession to arrive, he is unable to recognize anyone there except Makiyama, an old friend of the family. During the ceremony Makiyama introduces him to Tanida's daughter Otane and her husband. As soon as she sees him, Otane is seized with fear and anger, and we are given to understand through a number of indirect hints that Setsuzō may in fact be the father of her child: as the novel was never finished, we cannot be certain of this. Setsuzō remains calm and indifferent throughout the encounter.

On his way back from the funeral he falls to thinking about the time when he used to live with the Tanidas, and the rest of the novel consists of these reminiscences. Apart from a description of the house, his room and some passages of introspection, the main incident concerns Otane. When she starts going to school she is accosted by a boy called Aibara Mitsutarō. Aibara had the misfortune to be mistaken for a girl at birth and had been brought up accordingly during his early childhood. His strange background gives rise to the belief that he is in some way dangerous, and so when Makiyama hears how he is approaching Otane on her way to school he asks Setsuzō to intervene. More from curiosity about the stories he has heard about Aibara than out of concern for Otane, Setsuzō decides to meet him. Aibara is so impressed by Setsuzō's blunt manner and self-possession that he finds himself agreeing to leave the girl alone. As a result of this incident, Setsuzō is treated with great respect by the Tanida family. The novel breaks off soon after the account of this strange meeting between Aibara and Setsuzō. The latter had decided to become a writer and is just beginning to compose a satire on contemporary Japan.

The most important part of the novel, as we have it, is the portrayal of the central character. On the one hand he is shown as alienated from his fellow man, but on the other hand he seems to be quite self-contained, not needing the company of others. The fact that he is contemptuous of nearly everyone he meets is, of course, necessary compensation for an underlying failure on his part to communicate. Instinctively aware that he is different from other people, he is always losing his friends through bouts of sudden and intense anger. An example of this irrational behaviour akin to mental illness is recounted in chapter 5. Arriving one day at the house of a close friend who is an excellent flute player and has often played for him, he finds that his friend is not in. After waiting for a time, he suddenly has a desire to smash the instrument, takes it outside and calmly crushes it under his foot. Caught in the act by his friend, he appears not to notice and walks away with a blank expression on his face.

Coming to Tokyo, Setsuzō finds that these sudden outbursts of inexplicable frustration no longer come and go in a moment, but 'ashen coloured days' begin to stain the whole of his life. The words 'ashen ' and 'mask' run through the story like a refrain. There is more than a hint of repressed homosexuality in this frustrated individual. This is never really made explicit, but his reaction to the feminine Aibara suggests that the novel might have developed in this direction; and this might well explain why Ōgai felt he could no longer continue with such a delicate subject. The decision to stop writing this novel may have robbed us of one of Ōgai's best works, because the control of situation and character, and the naturalness of dialogue are superior to that in both the novels he had previously written.

When Setsuzō tries to cover up the gap between his own mental life and that of others by wearing a mask of self-composure, he succeeds in fooling not only everyone else but also himself. The false sense of being able to produce great literature without committing himself to anything, and his fundamental inability to understand his own frustration, is most vividly portrayed in the following passage where he is staring out to sea:

> He watched while just this side of the battery where the scaly waves were bathed in sunlight a seagull rose gleaming silver, flew a little way and then suddenly dived again. Close to, that bird was a dirty ashen grey, he thought, but then he suddenly remembered how that ashen grey bird had gleamed for a moment. Everything beautiful or good in this world was a momentary gleam which on a closer look turned out to be ashen grey. To write about the bright side of things was to describe the momentary gleam, and to write about the dark side of things was to describe reality. Writers of the former type did not purposely try to describe things which rarely happened: no, they just saw everyday life as meaningless and valueless and so looked for the momentary gleam. Writers of the latter type recognized the value of this ashen grey everyday existence. There were some who glorified the greyness just as a woman might fall in love with a garment for

its verve or quality. There were some who caressed and portrayed the greyness with a kind of voluptuousness.

He himself was neither blinded by the momentary gleam nor addicted to the ashen grey. He denied all values. He had no preferences. He was impartial and disinterested. If he wrote any-thing it would be more impartial than anyone else's writing. It would have a balance never seen before. People would of course call it cold-hearted literature. (IX,205)

With 'Kaijin' we have returned to the question of detachment and resignation, but the constant churning is beginning to bring an unpleas-ant smell from the depths. In *Vita Sexualis* the question is put in terms of sexual development and Ōgai decides that detachment towards sexual desire is both feasible and desirable. In *Seinin* a similar but rather false result is obtained. In *Gan* deep and painful frustration is covered by a thin romantic film. But with 'Kaijin' the matter finally is put in terms of a denial of all values with overtones of mental illness. Ōgai was beginning to write himself into a corner. The process of intro-spection that had started at Kokura, or even earlier, was proving to be a dead wall. In 'Kaijin' even a mask is intolerable as it merely serves to hide a lack of values, a horrible emptiness. It is hardly surprising that Ōgai should feel compelled to abandon such a pessimistic conclusion.

Although the personal reasons for the search that Ōgai was under-taking in a rather muddled way are clear, it should not be forgotten that behind it all lay the whole atmosphere of ennui that was to afflict nearly every writer in modern Japan.[12] In many the strain of trying to unite and synthesize two divergent cultures led to a despairing death or to an equally dead silence, and it is a measure of Ōgai's strength of character that he rose above the nihilism and never ceased to search for an answer. Setsuzō represents that peculiar state of emptiness which can result from a total lack of moral or intellectual security. In his youth Ōgai had been able to face with enthusiasm the reasonably straightforward task of modernizing Japan in both the scientific and artistic fields. By this time he was suffering the inevitable consequences. As will be seen, the political disturbances did nothing to alleviate this anxiety and Ōgai moved away from the present to seek the answer in the study of history. The somewhat excessive and obsessive examina-tion of personal problems brought with it dangers which had to be avoided if Ōgai was to maintain his balance. At the time it must have seemed as though the choice was one of either blind sublimation or self-destruction.

From beauty to truth

It should be clear from the above account that the majority of these stories are fragmentary, discursive slices of life, closely based on Ōgai's own experience. They range over a wide area, from the collection of reminiscences that go to make the *zuihitsu*-like 'Mōsō' to three allegories, 'Sakazuki', 'Kodama' and 'Le parnasse ambulant', and even one horror story, 'Nezumizaka'. In most, however, the educator threatens to overcome the artist. Life and work become so closely bound that it is almost impossible to discuss one without the other. This is, of course, a severe limitation when one tries to approach the stories entirely on their own merits, and there are not a few where the precarious balance breaks down and scenes become merely the clothing for what is in essence an essay. It has already been explained why this form of writing was chosen, but this cannot excuse the results. There is no intrinsic reason why a private conversation, a voyage of self-discovery, or a discussion of important social phenomena should be presented in such a heavy-handed manner.

The best stories of this period are those where a balance is kept between the intellectual discussions and the 'story' so that the ideas expressed are organic to the scenes described rather than being mere digressions: notably, 'Dokushin', set in Kokura and describing a visit made by two friends who take him to task for not marrying; 'Hannichi', which has already been introduced; 'Masui', a story in which he finds out that his wife has been hypnotized by a doctor and proceeds to discuss the morality of such practices; 'Kompira', where the contradictions between a belief in a rational world and an instinctive urge to accept old-established superstitions are set aginst the poignant background of the death of his one-year old son Fritz; 'Fushinchū' where an aging official who knows the West finds himself utterly trapped within his own mores and cannot bring himself to kiss the foreign woman he had known in his youth; and lastly 'Hanako' where Rodin's admiration of the qualities of a young Japanese dancer's body stands as a hopeful symbol of a beauty in the human form that can transcend racial barriers.[13]

What has happened, however, in the stories that fail? *Seinen*, 'Asobi'. 'Chinmoku no tō', 'Shokudō', 'Kaijin' and 'Ka no yō ni', to name but a few. It is instructive to trace the conflict between reality and fiction back to Ōgai's very earliest pronouncement on literature, 'Shōsetsuron', where he wrote:

> It is of course quite legitimate to use analysis and dissection when constructing a novel. But to treat, as Zola does, the results

of analysis and dissection as a novel is something that no one could regard as appropriate. Ultimately the results of experiment are real facts. We doctors may be satisfied with the search for real facts, but should novelists ever be thus satisfied?[14]

Mere fact was the province of science, not art, and the artist had to 'create beauty by burning most of the dirt that surrounds Nature in the fires of the Idea'. It is worth noting, however, that his warning about the excesses of realism was more a complaint against the total disregard of aesthetic qualities rather than a repudiation of the use of mimetic reality per se. It was a plea for artistry and imagination rather than fiction or invention. A fair practical demonstration of these ideas was given in the first three novellas, where the element of fiction, although by no means absent, was mixed with a high degree of accurate description and autobiographical detail.

When we come to the second creative period not only does the tendency to avoid fiction become more apparent, but the artificial distinction between art and science, the Beautiful and the True, has completely broken down. Commitment to the autonomy of art has been replaced by a desire to present life 'as it is'. The extent of his relaxation of earlier strict ideas on aesthetics can be seen from the following passage written in 1909: 'Recently it has become fashionable to use words like "shackled" and "liberated". But isn't it terribly shackled thinking to claim that one should write a novel on a prescribed subject in a prescribed way?... I submit that one can write a novel about anything one wishes in whatever way one chooses' (IV, 588). Here we have reached the opposite extreme where all preconceived notions of the nature of literature are discarded and the author has carte blanche. It is in this context that it becomes nonsense to label Ōgai as an 'anti-Naturalist'. His stand against this group was confined to their preoccupation with sexual instincts, and in fact his stories are more naturalistic than many of the products of his contemporaries who professed the Naturalist creed. In the sense that Ōgai's stories deal with a realistic portrayal of the writer's own experience and the world around him, he is extremely close to his contemporaries. 'Maihime' can still be legitimately discussed in terms of being an *Ich Erzählung* — a work written in the first person as an artistic ploy, with no necessarily implied connection between narrator and author. But some, at least, of the stories written during this later period come closer to being Japanese *watakushi-shōsetsu*, in that the identity between author and narrator is implied and must be taken into consideration. The imagination is by no means dead, but invention and fiction is either not forthcoming or held in check.

If one may be allowed a little jump ahead, one of the most reveal-ing works in this context is 'Ka no yō ni'.[15] Here Ōgai discusses the theory of fictions as propounded in Vaihinger's book *Die Philosophie des Als Ob* (The Philosophy of As If). Although these ideas are treated mainly in the context of Ōgai's intellectual position vis-à-vis the ques-tion of academic freedom, it is illuminating when they are applied to the study of literature. At one stage in the argument we read: 'The novel is a fiction in the sense that it treats fact as truth, and yet it is made acceptable because from the very beginning it is written in the knowledge that it is not fact but fiction. Within this framework it has a life and a value of its own' (X, 70).

This is as concise a statement of the use of mimetic reality in litera-ture as one might wish. The significance of 'Ka no yō ni' is that des-pite the fact that this is fully understood, the whole concept of 'fictions' and 'as if' is rejected as unworkable. The failure of the theory to pro-vide a satisfactory basis for a modus vivendi seems to bring with it a denial of its usefulness in literature, because the first demand is for intellectual and emotional honesty. It is highly significant that Ōgai's translation for Vaihinger's 'fictions' was *uso*, or lies. Although he under-stood and fought for the autonomy of art, and although he translated much European fiction, when it came to writing himself, 'lies' were somehow unacceptable. Neither did the fact that he knew they were conscious lies seem to help.

There is, as Howard Hibbett has pointed out,[16] something very Confucian about this view of fiction as being unreliable, out of touch with reality, and lacking seriousness. It was as if Ōgai was not suffering from an inability to use his imagination, so much as a reluctance to use it on anything as unworthy as fiction. If this view is correct, then some-thing rather strange had happened to the original aim of men like Shōyō to prove the seriousness of literature, and above all the novel, to their contemporaries. In Ōgai's case the drive to search out his own problems and to teach others was rapidly threatening to overwhelm his artistic judgement.

6

A LITERATURE OF IDEAS II

Plays

Although the principal aim of this section is to investigate Ōgai's own plays, written in the period 1902 to 1910, it must be stressed that this was not his first excursion into the world of drama. The *Botsurisō* debate with Shōyō so overshadows his early criticism that one tends to ignore the work he did towards a modernization of Japanese drama.

In September 1889 he was made one of seventeen committee members of the newly formed Nihon Engei Kyōkai (Japan Entertainments Society), and began in characteristic style to inveigh against the idea put forward by Suematsu Kencho and his Engeki Kairyōkai (Society for Theatre Reform) of building a new theatre. Although the Kairyōkai itself had only lasted from 1886 to 1888 and so was already disbanded, the proposals lingered on. The main theme of Ōgai's two articles, 'Engeki kairyō ronja no henken ni odoroku' (On being shocked at the distorted views of those who are in favour of the Society for Theatre Reform, October 1889), and 'Futatabi geki o ronjite yo no hyōka ni kotau' (A second essay on the theatre in answer to critics of the age, December 1889), was that to erect a brand new European-style theatre while ignoring the content of the plays themselves was putting the cart before the horse. Ōgai's priorities were play (*gikyoku*), performance (*engeki*) and lastly theatre (*gekijō*); modernization had to start with a renovation of the content and style of the plays, and it was perfectly possible to act modern plays in the theatres which already existed. He was totally opposed to the idea that the *kabuki* stage and techniques be abandoned, and astutely pointed out that they were in some ways closer to the theatres of Shakespeare's England than were modern European stages. His was the voice of sanity and gradualism at a time when there was uncritical acceptance of most things Western.

The Nihon Engei Kyōkai itself lasted only until October 1891 and the main highlight was a public meeting in February 1890 at which Ōgai gave a short address entitled 'Engekijō-ri no shijin' (The poet behind the performance), which was printed the same month in *Shigarami-zōshi*. He emphasized the role of the author in modern drama (*shōgeki*) in contrast to his position in traditional Kabuki, a prerequisite to which he was to return later. As the idea of a new type of drama was, of course, only in its infancy at this stage, and it was to be some time before any actual results were seen, Ōgai's articles were primarily concerned with explaining simple, basic truths.

It was during this early period that Ōgai also translated some classics of European drama in conjunction with his younger brother Tokujirō (Miki Takeji) — Calderon's *El Alcalde de Zalamanca* (January-February 1889), Lessing's *Emilia Galotti* (January-June 1889), a fragment from K. T. Körner's *Toni* (November-December 1889) and Lessing's *Philotas* (September 1892-July 1893) — none of which were ever staged. The plays were not really relevant to the state of Japanese drama at the time and their choice would seem to reflect the somewhat erroneous assumption that works representative of the beginnings of German theatre would be equally relevant in Japan. As a result the translations went largely unnoticed in theatrical circles.

Ōgai never lost contact with the development of *shimpa*, the style of acting that was an attempted modernization of *kabuki*, and the later *shingeki* movement at the turn of the century, which was modern theatre in the Western sense. But he produced very little, except for the occasional review, until his first play *Tamakushige Futari Urashima* (1902) which was written at the request of the *shimpa* actor Ii Yōhō (1871-1932) and which was acted at the Ichimura-za in January 1903. There can be little doubt that Ōgai's connections with the theatre in general were kept alive at this period, when he was unusually silent in most other literary fields, by his brother Tokujirō whom he helped to run the journal *Kabuki*. Both this play and his next one, *Nichiren Shōnin Tsujizeppō* (The street Sermon of Nichiren), written in March 1904 and acted in April at the Kabukiza with *kabuki* actors, were traditional in both style and technique, and although they made a few innovations within that field, it was not until 1909 and 1910 that Ōgai tried his hand at the modern drama he had earlier been debating.

Tamakushige Futari Urashima is a two act play based on the Japanese legend of Urashima who returns from a dream world to find he is three hundred years old; on opening a casket he has been given, however, he suddenly ages the full span and dies. Ōgai's adaptation is interesting for a number of reasons. In the first act Urashima wakes up in the sea palace having had a troubled dream. He tells the princess that he dreamt he was back in the world above and was once again fishing in a calm sea when he was overtaken by a storm which threatened to sink the boat. While struggling for his life, he awoke to find himself still in the beautiful dream world beneath the sea. Despite the pleas of the princess that he should stay in this land of eternal peace and idyllic charm, he cannot resist the urge to return to the land of men. He has become weary with the constant peace and luxury and tells her he must carry out some 'enterprise'. The princess belongs to Nature and so can accept that things should take their natural course, but he is a man driven by a desire for change. Eventually, as he is adamant, she weeps for his departure and her tears turn to pearls. These pearls are placed in the jewelled casket which she gives him, telling him not to open it until they meet again.

In contrast to this lyrical scene the second act is more robust and takes place on the shore by his native village. He has returned to find that one of his descendants is making preparations to set sail with a large fleet and subjugate a foreign land for the greater glory of Japan. Urashima is captured on the shore and after a struggle the casket is dropped, the pearls fall out and he becomes a white-haired old man. All is revealed and Urashima is overjoyed that his descendant is to carry out the 'enterprise' that he had been yearning to undertake: 'It is for the forefathers to dream and for their descendants to act out those dreams' (III, 204). He gives the pearls to his descendant to pay for the expedition and decides to retire in seclusion deep in the mountains, content in the knowledge that his dream is to be carried out, for 'that is one form of immortality' (III, 205).

Ōgai tells us a little of the genesis of the play in the article he wrote immediately after its first performance, but gives no clue to the meaning of the play itself:

> I was put in mind of it by a mention of Faust. Ii first asked me about the plot of Faust and then wanted to get one of the company's writers to adapt it as an entr'act. I told him that Faust takes two days to perform and so it was well nigh impossible to choose a part of it for adaptation. He then asked for something instead and so I wrote *Urashima*. One of the reasons that made me decide on *Urashima* was that in this story the youth suddenly becomes an old man, exactly the opposite to Faust who changes from an old man to a youth. Because the witch's potion does not take immediate effect when Faust drinks it, but only afterwards, when he starts to move, he leaves the stage as he is and returns as a young man in the next act. I wrote

my play however so that Urashima would change into an old man in front of the audience, thus using to good effect one of the virtues of Japanese theatre which is skilled in such technique (III, 216-17)

Among the elements which Ōgai could be said to have added to the legend are the comparison of the incompatibility between the princess and Urashima to that between Nature and Man, the drive that Urashima feels towards an 'enterprise', and his gift of the pearls to his warlike descendant at the end. The preparation for a foreign expedition had a precedent in Chikamatsu's *Urashima Nendaiki*, but it is given added weight and emphasis by Ōgai.[1] Frank Motofuji has pointed out the symbolic nature of the play when considered in the light of Ōgai's own experience.[2] He had visited Germany for four idyllic years and yet returned to Japan with a sense of mission that just outweighed the charms of Europe – the situation that lay behind 'Maihime'. Now, in 1902, Japan was well on the way to being a world power and yet Ōgai himself realized that his youthful ideas would take far longer to come to fruition than he had first thought. In the end he would have to be content to make his contribution to the effort in the same way that Urashima made his; by giving the pearls that he had brought back from the dream land to his descendants to strengthen their endeavours. The pessimism of his later work is not yet really evident, for the second Urashima's expedition is seen in a bright light and there is much hope for the future, which reflects the date of composition (1902). There is obviously no one-to-one correspondence between the events in the play and Ōgai's own life but the symbolic connection can hardly be denied.

It is an interesting comment on the state of modern Japanese drama at the time that Ōgai considered it necessary to point out that his play was not on the lines of European opera. The play opens with a kind of chorus by sea-maidens which sets the scene, and he had to explain the difference between this and the traditional Greek chorus. In the intervening years since 1889 not much advance in appreciation of the forms of European drama was evident, as is clear from the following note on the importance of the actual words spoken:

> In the main, Western drama, when compared to our own, places more emphasis on speech. The actors endeavour to let the audience hear the words clearly and to adopt facial expressions which are suitable for those words. For them this matter of expression is what is meant by acting. In some kinds of plays rough action such as killing and fighting, or even the acts of embracing and kissing, amounts to a mere crook of the finger. Apart from that, it is just a matter of two or three characters

coming onto the stage, saying their lines and then walking off. The audience reacts by listening to the words and appreciating their meaning; this is what criticism of the play is based on. The audience sees whether the delivery of the lines and the expression that accompanies them fits the respective characters or not. This is the basis of theatre criticism.

To stage *Urashima* was a very courageous act because up to now there has been nothing like it to speak of. Even though plays by Shakespeare and others have been adapted and staged two or three times, I can hardly believe that the real face of these plays was seen at all. Usually it is the plot which is attractively staged and followed through in these versions, but the plot is not in fact all that important. In the performance of *Urashima* it is worth remembering that when the actors tried hard to enunciate clearly to the audience they were doing something quite unprecedented. Because the audience did not know how to listen to the actors, some of the lines were cut as the actors feared they might be criticized. I think that they succeeded in giving shape to Urashima's dream tale and in making it interesting. Furthermore, to give it shape and let the audience hear the words unconsciously was a step forward in the development of drama, be it ever so makeshift. (III, 214-15)

The importance attached to the spoken word and clear enunciation was doubtless a new departure but the setting and the style — it was written in 7/5 metre — were still very much in the traditional mode. Neither did the play itself go down very well with its audience; at the first performance there was an uproar of laughter when the glass beads symbolizing the pearls the princess had wept rolled about the stage.[3]

Nichiren Shōnin Tsujizeppō, which Ōgai wrote the following year and which was acted at the Kabukiza in April 1904 just before his departure for the front in the Russo-Japanese War, is a slight work of little importance. The action is set in Kamakura where Nichiren is proselytizing and warning the country of the possibilities of a Mongol invasion. Yoshiharu, a retainer of the Hōjō regents, is in love with Tae, the daughter of a devout believer in Nichiren's teachings. The father refuses them permission to marry because Yoshiharu is critical of Nichiren. All this background is skilfully introduced in a short economical exchange between the two lovers, which is interrupted by the arrival of Nichiren himself. The great preacher begins to harangue the crowd, argues vigorously with a Zen priest, and is protected from assault by Yoshiharu. Then there follows a succession of questions and answers which are used to explain Nichiren's convictions. Yoshiharu is won over by his persuasive arguments of the danger to the nation and the threat from the mainland. Tae's father sees him talking with Nichiren, hears of his conversion and allows the marriage to take place.

The main interst of this one act play is not the plot, which is extremely thin, but the realistic way in which Ōgai portrays Nichiren, his forceful street sermonizing, and the freedom with which he adapted the historical details. Later he was to note: 'When I wrote *Nichiren Shōnin Tsujizeppō* I combined the much later proposals for saving the nation with his earlier street sermonizing in Kamakura. On my more recent stories I have totally rejected such methods' (XXVI, 508). The play is best seen as an experiment in writing a *kabuki* act rather than an attempt to introduce any specifically modern elements.

Compared to these two early plays, the four that Ōgai wrote in 1909 and 1910 are far more modern in both diction and conception, reflecting the contacts he had with the *shingeki* movement. The role of his translations of European plays in the context of his own development will be discussed in the following section, but their main influence can be said here to have been felt through their performance as part of the repertoire of the Jiyū Gekijō (Free Theatre). This company, led by Osanai Kaoru and the *kabuki* actor Sadanji, commissioned many of Ōgai's translations, the first performance being of Ibsen's *John Gabriel Borkman* on 27 November 1909. Osanai's Jiyū Gekijō was, together with Tsubouchi's Bungei Kyōkai (Literary Society), the real beginning of *shingeki*, although Osanai was far more interested in modern Western drama and its most famous exponent at the time, Ibsen, than original Japanese work. There can be little doubt that in this sphere too Ōgai made a considerable contribution to the dissemination of Western literature.

Concomitant with the rise of *shingeki* Ōgai's interest in producing some original plays was reawakened and the first of these was the two act *Purumūla* published in January 1909 in *Subaru* but never in fact staged. As he explained in a note to the play, the story emerged during Ōgai's work on the *A'iku-ō jiseki* (Records of King Asoka) which he produced in collaboration with Ōmura Seigai and which was published in the same month as the play.

The first act is set in Sind which is being invaded by Arab forces. Defeat being imminent, the Queen Lala, her sister Sati, and her two daughters Surug and Purumūla make the decision to commit suicide when the news of defeat reaches them; before they can do so, however, the enemy surprises them and they are arrested. The enemy General Kāsim decides he will stay to rule the country and chooses Sati as his queen. He tells how he has been told in a dream that one of the first women he should meet in Sind would be his eventual murderer and the only way he can avoid this is to marry her. Up to this moment Purumūla has said and done nothing, but she suddenly springs to her feet and demands to be crowned herself. Despite her willingness and her beauty Kāsim decides that she and her sister Surug should be sent back to Arabia to enter the harem of his master in Damascus. The act ends as he calls for preparations to be made for their journey.

The second act is set in Dasmascus three years later. Despite the efforts of her sister to keep her happy in the idyllic surroundings, Purumūla broods on her fate. We learn that the Caliph Valid, who had ordered the expedition against Sind, is dead and that his place has been taken by his younger brother Sūlemān. She had already managed to avoid being made Valid's concubine by lying to him that she was raped by Kāsim in Sind and was therefore no longer a virgin. Because of his trust in Kāsim and the counsel of his chief adviser, Valid had refused to take action. Sūlemān enters her apartments and asks her if her story is true. When she repeats the lie he has the corpse of Kāsim brought in on a bier, telling her that he had already taken appropriate measures. Now that the deed is done she admits that the whole story was a fabrication. Sūlemān is furious when he sees he has been duped and condemns both her and her sister to be drawn and quartered the next morning. The play closes as Purumūla is bending over Kāsim's corpse with the words 'The seeds of a lie which I made up on the spur of the moment when pressed by Valid have somehow ripened to a fruit and become my revenge, but in truth the deed was not accomplished with such pure intent' (IV,365).

What Ōgai has done in this case is add to the original story as he found it in his researches a further subtler motive for Purumūla's lies. The basic story of the revenge carried out by a single-minded daughter for the death of her father has been amplified with the second theme of her love for the conqueror Kāsim, which she herself only fully comprehends at the end of the play. In typical Ōgai fashion this slight adaptation is treated with such restraint that it is never made explicit. Ōgai is here beginning to reveal the fascination with strong-minded noble women in a historical context that is a feature of his historical novellas, and which is reflected in the heroines of a number of his drama translations of this period.

In considering the style of this play in contrast to that of the two previous ones, one can do no better than quote Ōgai himself on the subject:

I read these particular histories while I was studying the life of

King Asoka and I thought that the story of the princess Purumūla was a bit out of the ordinary and rather interesting. I felt some Western poet must have used it as the basis for an epic poem or play, but while I did some research I came across nothing. I talked it over with some friends too, thinking I might write it up myself sometime. Then recently they asked me whether, as they were bringing out the journal *Subaru*, I would write up the story I had told them. But I had no time to write a play, what with being dragged to the office and being dog-tired when I got home in the evening. For three or four days during this period, however, I took a short nap immediately after returning home and then got up and composed it hurriedly from one to three in the morning. I'm not trying to explain away a clumsy piece of work by saying I wrote it under pressure like this. I'm just mentioning it so I shall remember it later. When I came to make it into a play I had to try and guess at what the weather was like when the battle was fought in Sind and again in the Arabian capital Damascus, and what kind of trees were blooming and what kind of view there was from the king's palace. I could not avoid a certain incompleteness here as the reference books were not at hand.

I thought a lot about the style but nowadays there is no accepted style for historical plays *(jidaimono)*. In the West it's usual either to write in unrhymed blank verse or in prose but I found it very difficult not having such agreed standards. It was even more difficult because I was writing about the past in a foreign country. If I had tried to write it in a very old style like the adaptation of *Imoseyama* that they tried at Waseda, it would have been too difficult for most people. I had already tried writing in a delicate style somewhat akin to the elegance of *Urashima* and didn't feel like repeating it. Again, when I wrote *Nichiren*, I tried to add the flavour of *kyōgen* vocabulary but that would not do in this case. So I wrote it in a style with a preponderance of seven-five metre as had been used for puppet plays in the past. On finishing it I was not impressed with this either; it gave a far too archaic tone to it all. Anyway, I had neither the time nor the inclination to rewrite it and so left it as it was. I would like it to be seen as another experiment. This is all I have to say. (IV,373-5)

There are two interesting points made here. The style and content are not as modern as one might expect from Ōgai writing in 1909; one can see from the stage directions, which mention the use of *hanamichi* among other traditional elements, that it was written with *kabuki* rather than *shingeki* in mind. Secondly, one sees the extraordinary attention to detail which characterizes Ōgai's meticulous approach to literature and research. His comment on the question of the weather is a symptom of his academic rather than imaginative approach to art in general.

Kamen (Masks) on the other hand is a modern one act play in a contemporary setting using everyday speech. Written in April 1909, it was acted by Ii Yōhō's group of *shimpa* actors at the Shintomi-ya in June of the same year. The action takes place in the waiting room of a doctor Sugimura. A young student called Shiori has been to see the doctor because he is afraid he has contracted tuberculosis. His sister-in-law, Mrs Kanai, comes to talk with the doctor to find out if Shiori is really ill or not and is assured by the doctor that it is bronchitis rather than tuberculosis. Shiori himself then enters to find out the results of the tests. Mrs Kanai leaves but, just before the doctor can reveal the findings to the boy, a gardener is brought in who is critically injured from a fall. Shiori goes into an adjoining room while the doctor does all he can for the gardener in the waiting room. The gardener dies and Shiori returns. We know from his expression that he has seen the report on the doctor's desk and knows that the tests were in fact positive. He works himself up into such a terrible state of fear that the doctor decides to take him into his confidence and reveals that he himself found he was suffering from tuberculosis seventeen years previously. He told no one about it at the time, preferring to keep his own counsel and cure the disease on his own. He himself is not sure whether it was from purely selfish motives. Then, out of the blue, he asks Shiori whether he has ever read Nietzsche.

> *Shiori*: I was stimulated to read him by Professor Kanai's lectures, but only *Beyond Good and Evil*.
> *Doctor*: I see. He often mentions the idea of masks in that book too. He says that what we call the Good is merely having the same attitudes as the common herd of humanity and Evil is when one tries to destroy those attitudes. We should not concern ourselves with Good or Evil. He said he wanted to stand aloof from the common herd, strengthen his resolve and place himself high above them in an aristocratic position of lonely eminence. Such eminent men wear masks and those masks are to be respected. Tell me, do you respect mine? (IV, 502).

Shiori understands that the doctor is enjoining forbearance, self-control and self-reliance and he restates his determination to carry on attending lectures while not breathing a word of his illness. The doctor replies:

> ... as a doctor I must forbid you to attend school and I must order you to move to your brother's house but that would be to prescribe for one of the common herd. I will let you do what you want and strive as best I know to prevent your disease from en-

dangering those around you. We shall cure it. I will do all I can
and stand with you beyond Good and Evil. (IV, 503)

The wife of the dead gardener then enters to thank the doctor for
his help. She is admirably self-controlled throughout and accepts some
condolence money from the doctor with poise. As she leaves the doctor admires her attitude: 'There certainly are times when people of
mere instinct resemble the nobler classes. There can't be many ladies
among the common herd who could carry it off like that' (IV, 505).
The play ends as Shiori and the doctor prepare to go out for lunch and
a Chopin concert.

It is with this play that we find ourselves on more familiar ground
in the sense that the theme is typical of Ōgai's stories of this period.
While the mention of Nietzsche can be explained as an example of his
conscious and often obtrusive didacticism, it does bring into question
the exact connection between the ideas expressed by the doctor and
Ōgai's own attitudes. Given the fact that Ōgai was rather sceptical
about Nietzsche's Overman, *Kamen* can hardly be taken at face value.

What is significant here is the adoption of a mask which was to
appear again as a strong theme in the pessimistic 'Kaijin'. The elitism
is not a natural one built on a foundation of aristocratic birth and
therefore including an element of social responsibility but a kind of
excuse for a 'disengagement from society'. The doctor's claim that the
mask is something to be respected rings somehow hollow and avoids the
more basic reason − it is a refuge in which the man who is afraid of
death can preserve his outward calm. There is more than a suspicion in
this play of ambivalence in the attitude of the author. Although no
preference is actually stated in so many words, the doctor's philosophy
is not above criticism. He lies blatantly to Mrs Kanai about Shiori's
health, he sees his mask as eminently worthy of respect and is willing
to endanger the lives of others for the sake of a fellow 'aristocrat'; he
sees both Shiori and himself as standing 'beyond Good and Evil'. Are
we to identify Ōgai with this attitude? The play is surely more subtle
than this. Ōgai has written as a detached author but his very treatment
of the theme gives away his underlying distrust of such extremes. Even
the doctor worries that the masking might be from purely selfish
motives, and the fact that at the end of the play they go off to a
Chopin concert seems to ring a little false. How much the disease of
tuberculosis symbolizes on the one hand Ōgai's own sense of frustration
caused by mainly personal reasons, and on the other the general malaise
and loss of stable values inherent in the modernizing process is difficult
to gauge, but we have already seen in the study of the stories of this

period how the mask and the attitude of resignation proved to be not a very satisfactory answer.

Kamen stands out at this period as a work of some maturity, showing a sense of detachment and irony. Reminiscent of the Austrian playwright Schnitzler, some of whose works Ōgai was concurrently translating, it is a good one act play which has not received the attention it perhaps deserves. On a more biographical note, it is interesting to record that Ōgai himself had suffered from similar lung trouble when a student and an entry in his diary for 18 July 1907 records a recurrence of the symptoms of pleurisy. Tuberculosis, too, may have been a possible cause of his death in 1922.

Shizuka was the next play that Ōgai wrote. It was published in *Subaru* in November 1909 but not acted until 1921. It is an historical play dealing with the famous feud between the two Minamoto brothers Yoritomo and Yoshitsune, Shizuka being the name of Yoshitsune's mistress. It is also one of the first examples of modern everyday speech being used in conjunction with such a classical theme. The first scene takes place at Yui Bay where Shizuka's son is about to be drowned on the orders of Yoritomo. In a dream-like sequence Adachi orders his men to put a stone into the boat and then puts out to sea by himself. This very short introductory scene ends with a sudden outburst from a 'strange fisherman' who has been silently staring into the distance. The rest of the people on stage are not supposed to see him and his role is purely symbolic. 'Kill!' he shouts, 'If your right hand is stopping you, cut off your left hand and try to add its strength to your right. Take great care of your right hand! Take care of the fingers on that hand. I begrudge neither my left hand nor its fingers. Do not forget! Neither do I begrudge my right hand or its fingers' (V, 576).

The second scene takes place in an inn at Kamakura two months later when Shizuka is preparing to depart for Kyoto. While her maids play *sugoroku* Adachi comes to collect her and there follows a conversation in which their attitude to fate is revealed. Shizuka is described as having an 'attitude of resignation tinged with light irony' and she has decided not to become a nun or to kill herself but to resign herself to her fate and continue living. This Adachi well understands and praises; although a samurai would have to commit suicide, Shizuka need not die as long as she has no strong desire to hang on to her life. Her decision in fact shows her strength. As she leaves for the capital her maids sing a song of farewell and a 'strange girl', fulfilling the same function as the fisherman in the first scene, says in a clear voice: 'See, the footprints still remain. Keep walking until they fade. (Pause) One day the traces will fade away' (V, 587).

Ōgai was clearly interested in the original story because he wished to investigate why Shizuka had not in fact committed suicide on the death of her son. She was fated never to see Yoshitsune again, had lost hope and yet decided to live on. Rather than ascribing it to any motive of selfishness, he preferred to see in this story an example of human fortitude in the face of a cruel fate, symbolized as we have seen by the invisible figures in both scenes. The play itself, rather than the theme, is an interesting experiment in symbolic drama and shows the influence of Maeterlinck in construction and treatment. The use of invisible figures standing for an impersonal fate is also to be seen in Ōgai's translation of the Russian Andreev's *Zhizni Cheloveka* (The Life of Man) which appeared in January 1910. There is in fact little need for the symbolic figures and they prove to be more of an embarrassment than an integral part of the play.

The next play, *Ikutagawa* (The Ikuta River), was commissioned by the Jiyū Gekijō, written in April 1910 and performed at their second programme in the May, together with Ōgai's translation of Wedekind's *Kammersänger* and a play by Chekhov translated by Osanai Kaoru under the title *Inu*. The story was based on a tale from the *Yamato Monogatari* as Ōgai noted in a short postscript to the play. The legend is of a beautiful girl who cannot decide between two men who come to court her. In the end she is forced to commit suicide. Ōgai's play opens with a conversation between mother and daughter which explains the situation. The girl complains that she has headaches caused by the spring weather, but they are only a symptom of the indecision with which she is wracked. She is worried that the man she rejects will kill himself and so stand between her and the man she chooses. The problem appears to be intractable. The two men, Unai and Chinu, come to visit the girl and each brings with him a duck that he has shot over the river. While the girl is out of the room, her mother proposes to the two men that they should hunt a swan which they have seen on the river; the man who manages to shoot it and bring it back will be given her daughter to marry. They both agree to the idea and leave the house.

When her mother tells her of the proposal the girl is upset because she had seen the swan that morning and thought how beautiful it looked. She then looks out of the window and describes the shooting of the swan. Both arrows pierce the bird. Feeling that the matter must be decided that day because of the death of the swan, the girl goes out to take a closer look. The play ends as her mother thinks about what she has just said, feels worried and decides to follow her out.

The girl's suicide is left untold, but we are left in little doubt as to the outcome. In the short space of time between the discovery that both men had managed to shoot the bird and her decision to leave the house, a Buddhist priest comes outside the window and intones a number of chants from the *Yuishikiron*, the doctrine that all phenomena are in essence Mind. The four chants, which propound in turn the ideas that all human suffering lies in man's wayward desires, that the five senses are illusory, that the concrete world is not true reality and that duality is a false doctrine, mirror the gradual formation of a firm decision in the girl's mind.

There can be little doubt that Ōgai has here used an old legend to express his own acute sense of indecision and impotence, using a treatment which has more than a suggestion of Ibsen. Ōgai is at pains to point out that Unai comes from the same province as the girl – who is also known as the 'Maiden of Unai' – but Chinu comes from a different part of Japan. In this case we can see them symbolizing the pull of traditional Japan versus modern Europe which was Ōgai's main concern in this period. If this is so, what does the swan stand for? The girl had been content to leave the problem unresolved until the death of the swan, which brought the impossibility of reconciliation into sharp relief. She was aware of the ultimate conflict but had achieved a kind of modus vivendi by a resigned acceptance of the contradictions. If she came down on any one side it would cause the death of the other. To avoid this she was prepared to hold the balance indefinitely hoping for an eventual solution both natural and gradual. The problem was not to be forced. It is when both men find their arrows in the swan that the confrontation is brought out into the open. The girl is destroyed when a solution is attempted but fails.

Ōgai is here arguing for the necessity of making no choice at all but rather accepting a precarious balance. This is not a cowardly act but a practical decision. For Ōgai the vague ennui was preferable to a direct battle in which the self would be driven to destruction. On an even deeper level this attitude can perhaps be related to the priest's incantations. Duality means inevitable conflict and the only true concept is the oneness of things; if all reality is Mind then opposition becomes meaningless.

The importance of Ōgai's plays therefore lies not only in the pioneering elements, such as the use of modern colloquial language in historical plays and the conscious use of symbolism, but also in their content and themes. It will be seen that he was exploring exactly the same problems in his plays as in his short stories of 1909 to 1912 and the fact that five out of six were concerned with historical or legendary material is a further pointer to later'developments.[4]

Later translations

If much of Ōgai's original work during this period was realistic and concerned with current issues both personal and public, the same cannot be said of his prose translations which show a catholic taste that is at first surprising. The sheer number of stories translated, 69 titles by 51 authors from 8 countries, is a little misleading as they are all short stories or novellas, in some cases only a few pages long, but the range is nevertheless impressive.[5] The same unfortunately cannot be said of the quality of the originals. As all the work was done in Ōgai's spare time little opportunity existed for sustained effort, but that said, it must be admitted that many of the stories are unexceptional and that the majority of the authors have since fallen into obscurity. As in the case of his earlier translations, their choice is at once puzzling and yet an important clue to his attitude towards fiction.

Ōgai was always in the closest touch with European affairs through the medium of German newspapers such as the *Frankfurter Zeitung*, the *Kölnische Zeitung* and the *Berliner Tageblatt* which he received or at least saw regularly. These newspapers, and in particular the last, served as the main source for his column of news and literary events in contemporary Europe, 'Mukudori tsūshin', that ran with hardly a break in *Subaru* from January 1909 to October 1913. Although the majority of the stories translated were taken from the books that he was continually receiving from Germany, at least fourteen and possibly more of these prose translations were taken from the literary supplement to the *Berliner Tageblatt* starting in August 1910 and going right through to December 1913.[6] This random method of selection meant that there was little attempt to choose well-known stories, and the result was that many of the originals fast fell into oblivion in Europe, some never getting past the first printing in the newspaper; hardly indicative of any conscious 'educational' role on Ōgai's part.

The breadth of stories makes it well nigh impossible to present an ordered picture of the whole but there are some salient features which characterize the majority. A large number of the writers represented were worlds apart from French Naturalism: Wied, Eulenberg, Rilke, Vollmöller, H. H. Ewers and Schmidt-bonn to name but a few. Most of the stories show elements which range from gothic horror and grotesque surrealism, to allegory and farce. Ōgai's preference is clear, for even those chosen from such writers as Dostoyevsky, L.Tolstoy and Flaubert — 'Krokodil', 'Otets Sergius' and 'La Légende de Saint Julien L'Hospitalier' respectively — are the least realistic of their writings. The present-day obscurity of many of the authors is by no means unwarranted however, and many of the translations, such as those of Ewers, F. Molnar, J.J. David and Hans Kyser, deserve no more than a passing mention.

The story by Andresen-Wörishöffer, 'El Ramusan Tir', is an excellent example of gothic horror. It concerns a rich man of Bombay who prepares a feast on the thirtieth anniversary of his wedding, a wedding that never in fact took place. Sending all his servants away, he opens up a secret room revealing the two preserved skeletons of his fiancée and her abductor. The gruesome details of his half-crazed conversation with both dead heads is capped when he carries them into the bedroom and gloats over them making love. This particularly nasty story is rivalled by Strobl's 'Aderlassmännnchen' which describes an outbreak of mass hysteria and orgy in a nunnery where the nuns are bled regularly to drain them of physical desire. Another tale of horror is Vollmöller's 'Die Geliebte' where the central theme is the inherent danger of beauty; a strange machine which is never fully described or named exerts a fatal attraction on those who come in contact with it, eventually driving them to destruction on its whirling blades.

On the lighter side there is Samain's 'Xanthis', a fairy tale of a wilful little doll inside a glass case. As a result of her capricious nature she meets an untimely death at the hands of a jealous faun and the story ends with a somewhat meretricious moral about 'la vanité des amours passageres et la mélancholie des fragiles destinées'. Dostoyevsky's 'Krokodil' is altogether of a different standard; a humorous tale of how a man gets swallowed by a prize crocodile, decides that he likes life inside and makes plans to rule Russia from his new-found home.

The main scene in 'Die Geliebte' where the first person hero is desperately trying to crawl away from the mysterious machine is very reminiscent of Edgar Allen Poe and it is no surprise to find him represented by three stories: 'The murders in the Rue Morgue', 'Descent into the maelstrom' and 'The devil in the belfry', the latter being an 'arabesque'. Ōgai's interest in detailed analysis can be also seen in the story by P. Bourget, 'L'expert', which is almost entirely a description of the interrogation of a pathological murderer by a psychiatrist. As a medical man himself it is only to be expected that Ōgai should show interest in the extent to which European writers of the time were exploring themes closely connected to the studies of the subconscious mind being undertaken by men like Freud. What does stand out is the frequency of reference to death. At least twenty stories are concerned with death and suicide directly and, as we have seen, a host of others had elements of the morbid. It is in this context too that his translations from Arthur Schnitzler are of considerable importance; they were 'Andreas Thameyers letzter Brief', 'Der Tod des Junggesellen' and 'Sterben'.

Even at a cursory glance the similarity between Ōgai and Schnitzler is striking. Not only were they born in the same year, 1862, but Schnitzler was a practising doctor in Vienna and had been in the Austrian army, from which he had however been drummed out. The three prose works of his that Ōgai translated stand somewhat apart from the rest of the translations. Despite the fact that they all treat the question of death, there is a restraint which brings to mind Ōgai's own works, and it is partly for this reason that Schnitzler would appear to be one of the most important of the authors represented.

'Andreas Thameyers letzter Brief' is a suicide note which explains in some detail why the writer has decided to die. His wife has given birth to a black child which is proof to most people that she has been unfaithful. Andreas, however, is convinced that she has been faithful and gives a list of supposedly authenticated cases of freak births. In order to exonerate his wife and prove to the world that she has been faithful he decides to commit suicide, believing that when he is dead everyone will realize their mistake and reinstate his wife. The irony running throughout is that the death will have the opposite effect. Knowing this the reader is constantly torn between pity for the well-meaning Andreas and contempt for his crass stupidity. It is an effective use of what Martin Swales in his recent study of Schnitzler calls 'the ambiguous narrator',[7] in that the reader is kept in the dark as to the author's own attitude. It could be argued that the juggling with the reader's sensibilities entailed by this is too obtrusive and artistically damaging, but the use of the first person narrator, with whom the reader usually tends to identify, set against the pedantic and rhetorical style, calculated to alienate the reader, is very typical of Schnitzler's careful method. The deliberate craftsmanship is a far cry from many of the stories that Ōgai was to write in this period.

'Sterben', a much longer *novelle,* is a study of physical decay. A girl first swears to die with her ailing young man but at the moment of his death she finds life too precious and leaves him alone crying out for her in fear and loneliness. This moving portrayal of the intensity of love in conflict with the desire for life was to be widely read in Japan where love suicides were such a popular theme. The sense of the absurd and the uncertainty of anything except death is also strong in the short 'Der Tod des Junggesellen'. A dying bachelor summons three friends to his death bed. Knowing that they will arrive too late he leaves them a note in which he confesses to having had an affair with each of their wives. The story then traces by a form of internal mono-logue the reactions of the three men.

Schnitzler had no illusions about the degenerate society he was portraying, and the concern with the effects of the loss of traditional values must have been of great interest to Ōgai. The sympathy that Ōgai had for Schnitzler's approach, however, is not obvious in his prose at this point. The influence of the grotesque and unnatural aspects of many of the other translations can in fact be more easily seen. There are, for instance, those works which appear as somewhat freakish exceptions to Ōgai's more usual semi-autobiographical style such as the allegorical 'Sakazuki' and the strange 'Le Parnasse ambulant'. The influence of Peter Altenberg and O. I. Dymoff can be seen here. To go one stage further, the later 'Okitsu Yagoemon no isho', though hardly derivative, was clearly not original in the sense that it took the form of a suicide note. Three of the translations take this form and some four others are connected with explanation of a death. Moreover, Ōgai's translation of Kröger's 'Socrates Tod' which deals with the question of euthanasia, and comes out in favour of a doctor agreeing to give a suffering friend a fatal dose of medicine, antedates 'Takasebune' by some eight years.[8] To say this, however, is not to claim any direct or definite influence — the points are merely of interest.

It will be seen that in the same way that *Sokkyō Shijin* tells us much of Ōgai in his younger days the vast range of this later group of translations reveals a side of Ōgai that would otherwise be relatively hidden. The anti-Naturalism of his early years has here given way to a flood of examples which illustrate the possibilities open to a writer who does not subscribe to Naturalist theories. They give us a very different picture of Ōgai's literary tastes, belying to some extent the impression of obsessive self-criticism that one might receive from a reading of his own stories at this juncture.

The importance of these translations is not simply that they allow a fuller appreciation of the man however, for there is good reason to suppose that they had a far greater effect on the development of Japanese prose fiction than any of his earlier polemical articles. They were produced over a long period from 1908 to 1915 and appeared in a number of prominent journals; but four collections were published in book form and it is to these that we must look when seeking an evaluation of their influence. The collections were *Ōgonhai* (January 1910), *Gendai Shōhin* (October 1910), *Jūnin Jūwa* (May 1913) and *Shokoku Monogatari* (January 1915). It is generally accepted that the last named was the most important. Not only did it consist of thirty-four stories as against an average of ten in the others but it appeared at a time when Japanese literature was ready for a change. Both the study by Ishikawa Jun and that by Kobori Keiichirō emphasize the 'revolutionary' nature of the book.[9] The collection became what Satō Haruo later called a 'textbook' for the new generation of young Taishō-period writers in that it finally broke the spell of Naturalism.

Since the end of the Russo-Japanese war in 1906 Japanese writing had been predominantly realist and very much concerned with the confessional aspect of a writer's 'sincerity'. This is not to say that nothing else was written, but men like Kōda Rohan and in particular Izumi Kyōka, whose stories are in some ways similar to these later translations by Ōgai, consciously disassociated themselves not only from the realism of their contemporaries, but also from Western literature. The impact of *Shokoku Monogatari* was that the stories came from Europe which was thought of as the birthplace of modern realism. By his examples Ōgai managed to illustrate that this narrow view of European literature was false and thus provided an added justification for young writers such as Akutagawa and Tanizaki to break away from the main stream, a process which in Tanizaki's case had already started with *Shisei* in 1910. Anti-Naturalism was given additional support in the form of a European precedent.

The marked difference between these translations and Ōgai's own works at this period suggests very strongly that, while finding himself drawn closer and closer to fact rather than fiction and personal rather than impersonal themes, he had by no means lost interest in the role of the Imagination. They were a kind of vicarious creativity — like most translating — and satisfied an urge for a type of literature quite different from either his work up to 1912 or the historical novellas produced thereafter.

A comparison of the subject matter and the style of the poems translated in *Omokage* with those translated at this later stage shows a similar change to that in the prose works. In the volume of poetry about the Russo-Japanese War, *Uta Nikki* (1907), Ōgai also included nine German war poems by Lenau, Platen, Freiligrath, Bleibtreu, Mörike and others. These were in the classical language and are of only minor interest. It is when we come to the collection entitled *Sara no Ki* (The Sal Tree, 1915) that Ōgai again surprises with his ability and willingness to keep up with the latest trends in European literary taste.

Sara no Ki included some of his own poetry in the modern style, a hundred *tanka*, and a selection of translations, the most important of which were nine by Richard Dehmel (1863-1920) and eleven by Klabund (Alfred Henschke) (1890-1928).

Although Ōgai had done very little in the way of translation since *Omokage*, he had kept in close touch with modern developments in Japanese poetry in all three fields of *haiku, tanka* and *shintaishi*. The exact relationship between Ōgai and the *haiku* poet Masaoka Shiki (1867-1902) is a little unclear but it would seem that they first met as early as 1893 or 1894. During the short period between this first meeting and the Sino-Japanese War Ōgai might have attended the *haiku* sessions at Shiki's house and there he may also have met Sōseki for the first time. This would explain why Shiki called on Ōgai in Manchuria on 10 May 1895. Their friendship carried on after the war and Ōgai had great respect for Shiki's talents as a poet, asking him for help with the journal *Mezamashigusa* in 1896.[10]

Ōgai's interest in modern *tanka* and his friendship with Yosano Hiroshi (1873-1935) and his wife was mainly the result of the founding in 1908 of the poetry society, the Kanchōrō Uta no Kai. It was also through Yosano that Ōgai met Ishikawa Takuboku (1886-1912) on 2 May 1908. Ōgai helped this forthright young man in a number of ways. He managed to get one of his stories accepted for publication in the June and found him work as a compiler for *Subaru* for a time.[11]

In the sphere of modern poetry it is Ōgai's friendship with Ueda Bin which is of most interest. There is again no definite record but they seem to have met after Ōgai's return from Kokura to Tokyo in 1902, starting the joint venture of *Geibun* and then *Mannensō*. The epoch-making translations of European poetry that Ueda brought out in 1905 in the collection *Kaichōon* (Sound of the Tide) were dedicated to Ōgai who was then in Manchuria. Ōgai was also one of the organizers of parties on Ueda's departure and return from Europe, and it was through a joint recommendation from these two that Nagai Kafū was offered a post at Keiō University in April 1910.

The three most important publications of translated poetry before the real birth of the modern native tradition — Hagiwara Sakutarō's *Tsuki ni Hoeru* (Baying at the Moon) of 1917 — were *Kaichōon* (1905), Kafū's *Sangoshū* (Corals, 1913) and Ōgai's *Sara no Ki* (1915). Both the previous collections were written for the most part in the classical style and used traditional 7/5 metres in various combinations with only the occasional excursion into new metres such as the 8/6

-syllable lines that Ōgai had tried in *Omokage*. *Sara no Ki* was remarkable for the attempt to use the modern idiom throughout. It was also the first collection to include a large number of modern German lyrics, for both Ueda and Kafū had touched but lightly on German poetry.

Richard Dehmel was already an established poet in Germany and a few of his poems had been translated into the vernacular by Katayama Kōson. Klabund, however, had never before been translated into Japanese, or possibly into any other language. The poems were taken from the first volume of poetry he published, at the age of twenty-four, *Morgenrot! Klabund! die Tage dammern* (1913). As Ōgai wrote in his preface, the choice would have surprised the majority of Germans who had hardly heard of the new writer Klabund. It was not, of course, to be the last time that a European author was translated into Japanese before any other language.

Many of Dehmel's poems were translated into a free style:

Stillleben	*Seibutsu*
Im Frühling, wenns zu nebeln anfängt —	Haru ni naru. Kasume hajimeru.
auf dem Dorfteich —	Mura no numa de
eines Abends: raake:	Aru ban, koro
erster Frosch.	Hatsugaeru.
Raake-racka-paake: zweiter.	Koro koro, wa suru kaeru.
Und so weiter, bis der ganze Chor	Sate oi oi to kazu ga fue
Raake-paake-racker-quacker-Pack macht.	Koro koro koro koro koro to naku
Über ihnen	Ue ni wa
dampft der Sonnenglanz —	Hi ga keburu
gaukelt still ein Azurfalter drin —	Yurameku aoi chō hitotsu.
herrlich — — [12]	Medeta ya. (XIX,359)

Although Ōgai never wrote anything about these particular translations, it would seem that behind the apparent free rendering there is a relation of line length to the original. Lines 1, 6, 7 and 10 all have three extra syllables; lines 2, 4, 5 and 11 have two extra syllables, and lines 3, 8 and 9 have the same number of syllables as the German. The three 9-syllable lines are all rendered as 5/7 in the Japanese. However, if the poem is related to the original in shape, there is a noticeable change in tone.[13] The sharp contrast of the German between the butterfly and the harsh sounds of the frogs is softened out of all recognition by the onomatopoeic 'koro koro'.

A totally different effect is achieved in a wry poem by Klabund:

Die englische Fräuleins
Die englische Fräuleins gehen in langer Kette durch die Stadt,
Zwei und zwei, in ihren schwarzen Mänteln wie Morcheln, die
man aus dem Boden gerissen hat.
Aber in Sommer tragen sie violette
Schärpen um den Leib. Sie schlafen allein im Bette

Manche ist so schön
Man möchte einmal mit ihr schlafen gehn,
Aber sie sind so klein und klein in ihren schwarzen Kapuzen,
Ich glaube, wenn man sie lieben will, braucht man ein ganzes
Dutzend.[14]

Igirisu no jō-san tachi
Igirisu no jō-san tachi ga nagai gyōretsu o shite machi o tōru.
Futari zutsu narande, hikkonuita amigasa koke no yo ni
Kuroi gaitō o kite tōru. Mottomo natsu ni naru to
Sono ue ni murasaki no obi o shimete iru.
Yoru wa hitori zutsu toko ni neru no da.
Naka ni wa ichido issho ni netai yō na
Utsukushii no ga majitte iru. Da ga mina hidoku chiisai.
Kuroi zukin o kabutta sugata ga hidoku chiisai.
Ichi dasu gurai issho ni kawaigaranakute wa dame rashii.
(XIX, 372)

The German poem is held together by the judicious use of rhyme.
Owing to a lack of this device in Japanese Ōgai produced what amounts
to a prose poem with no line to line correspondance with the original.
The conversational style flows well, however, and transmits the meaning and the tone of the German with considerable fidelity. What is in
danger of breaking down here is the form itself. It is indicative of the
problem that the traditional 7/5 combination still sounded more poetic
as in the following translation of another of Klabund's poems:

Still Schleicht der Strom	*Kawa wa shizuka ni nagareyuku*
Still schleicht der Strom	Kawa wa shizuka ni nagareyuku,
In gleicher Schnelle,	Onaji hayasa ni,
Keine Welle	Namigashira no
Krönt weiss die Flut.	Shiroki mo miezu.
Steil ragt die schwarze	Nozokeba kuroku
Gurgelnde Tiefe.	Uzumaki fuchi no kewashisa yo.
Da ist mir, als riefe	Ko wa ika ni. Izuku yuka
Mich eine Stimme.	Ware o yobu.

Ich wende das Auge   Kaerimite ware
Und erbleiche   Iro o ushinau.
Denn meine Leiche ₁₅   Tadaeru wa
Tragen die Wasser...   Waga mukuro yue. (XIX, 380-1)

Here the language is poised between classical and modern and its undoubted success testifies to Ōgai's versatility.

However, the temptation to credit *Sara no Ki* with great influence
must be resisted. It cannot be ranked with either *Kaichōon* or *Sangoshū*
in this respect, but it was nevertheless a step forward in the introduction of modern rather than romantic poetry and foreshadowed the
later interest in the work of German poets such as Rilke.

Ōgai's translations of European drama show considerable differences
from the prose works. Not only are there many more works of importance and less emphasis on any particular genre, but there are signs that
Ōgai felt certain plays to be of particular significance. The majority
were one act plays because of the same lack of time which made him
translate short stories rather than novels. In January 1908, moreover,
Ōgai's brother Takeji died which meant that Ōgai himself took over
much of the work for the journal *Kabuki* they had founded together.
Many of the plays were dictated to Ōgai's amanuensis Suzuki Shumpo,
a process which resulted in a good readable style but inevitably the
occasional mistake. This would explain the almost total concentration
on one act plays during 1909.

As in the case of the prose translations it is impossible to make a
significant generalization about the plays. Like the three plays which
he translated on his return to Japan, Calderon's *El Alcalde de Zalamanca* and Lessing's *Emilia Galotti* and *Philotas*, the aim in many cases
was to introduce some representative European drama. If one includes
the articles and lectures he gave, the scope in this later period is all-
embracing: to name but a few, a lecture on Maeterlinck's *Monna Vanna*
in June 1903, notes on Sudermann's work in March 1904, a sizeable
study of the life and works of Hauptmann in book form in November
1906, and over a hundred synopses in the period from 1909 to 1913.
But the playwrights to whom he seems to have a more personal reaction
and whose works he read with his own troubles in mind are Rilke,
Schnitzler, Ibsen and Goethe.

The first mention of Rilke's name was in 'Mukudori tsūshin' in
August 1909 and two months later he translated the play *Das tägliche
Leben* (Everyday Life). The play itself is of no special merit and would
deserve merely a passing mention if it were not for the fact that Ōgai

published it with the record of a conversation entitled 'Gendai shisō' in which he discussed certain facets of the play. This is sufficiently rare an occurrence to warrant a second look.'

The play concerns an artist, Georg, and a young model, Mascha, whose love for him is unrequited. She is totally selfless in her dedication to his welfare and yet he is blind to her attentions. The important part of the first act is a conversation between Georg and his sister Sophie. A friend of Georg's is coming to the flat and Georg wonders whether Sophie would perhaps prefer not to meet him as she has recently turned down his offer of marriage. She does not mind in the least, but is annoyed that there is no accepted behaviour for a couple who have decided *not* to get married. 'For that very reason it should be possible to establish a relationship which has no predetermined rules, a relationship outside all conventions[16]', she argues. The conversation then turns to their ailing mother and the way in which Sophie is sacrificing herself to look after her:

> *Sophie*: To establish a relationship outside all conventions —
> (softer) I left my mother long ago, Georg, but I have found
> someone, someone who is in need and who complains, someone
> whom I serve and for whom I am everything. In the evenings
> I pull the curtains in her room bringing her darkness and late
> in the morning I bring her light by opening up the shutters. My
> hands bring her food and medicine and she falls asleep lulled
> by my quiet voice reading aloud... You remind me that this
> someone is my mother...[17]

In the second act we find that Georg has met a girl at a party that evening. There has been an immediate rapport between the two and the whole evening has been spent in total and absorbing rapture. When however she comes to see Georg in the morning she declines his passionate appeal for her hand. The affair that night was a timeless moment, an affair 'outside all conventions', which cannot be repeated. The intensity of the affair belonged to another world and Georg's happiness lies with someone else. The woman in question is of course Mascha and the play ends with a love scene between her and Georg.

The moral of this rather juvenile play is that the real relationship the artist must seek is 'outside all conventions' but at the same time within the context of normal everyday life, and hence the title. In his commentary Ōgai was specifically concerned with the point about conventions:

> There is one thing that occurs in one of the episodes; the rela-
> tionship between the sister of the artist who is the central fig-
> ure and her mother. The indications are that the sister's efforts

on behalf of her mother are those of an admirably filial daughter. She has not married and sacrifices herself to take care of
her. What is her own attitude? Read the conversation that she
has with her brother carefully. The idea of filial piety as it was
taught to us is utterly destroyed; she is in no way looking after
her mother merely because she is her mother.

Now try to imagine a modern Japanese girl in this situation.
Assume that she too looks after her mother. Having been educated at high school she can understand English and reads the work
of modern writers. Will she think differently from the artist's
sister in the play or will she have the same ideas? Just consider
this one question, think about it in depth, and you will see
what a grave educational and ethical problem it presents. (V, 512)

So what is Ōgai's own reaction to Sophie's unusual statement?

The following train of thought will inevitably suggest itself.
Perhaps concepts such as filial piety, compassion and righteousness, were originally as they are presented in these modern
writings. Even though they may not have been exactly the same,
there must have been similarities to a certain extent. Perhaps
these concepts have become set through the years into forms
that we now call filial piety, compassion and righteousness, just
as ancient religious ideas set into the laws of the Church. This
line of thought suggests itself because some of today's writers
seem to be men of great devotion, as if they have their own
religion; Rilke is one of them.

Now, while we seem to have a clue to an answer in one direction, the problem becomes greater in another. It may be that
basic concepts are born and change in this way, but there can be
no doubt that the destruction of settled moral concepts is a
matter of great import, just as the destruction of the Church
would be important as far as religion is concerned. So there will
be those who ask, why translate a work that is so obviously dangerous as *Das tägliche Leben*. I suppose it is dangerous from their
point of view, but if we cannot make a thing public because it is
considered dangerous we will be unable to translate any works
that express modern ideas, and that includes Tolstoy, Ibsen,
Maeterlinck and Hofmannsthal. You would have to reject the
whole of modern literature and enforce a kind of literary seclusion policy. Could this ever be put into effect? What do you
think? This too is a vital question, don't you agree? It's when
you start thinking on these lines that problem begets problem and
there's no end to it. (V, 513-14)

The latter half of this discussion is clearly a reference to the banning
of his own *Vita Sexualis* in the June of that year and this was a subject

to which he was to return. The first part mirrors the concern with the collapse of traditional values that we have seen in his own works of this period. The suggestion is that the casting off of outworn conventions could be a liberating experience, revealing and releasing the deeper human feelings that had gradually been obscured by time. This view of things allowed Ōgai to rationalize any sympathies he felt for the new iconoclasts and was a far more hopeful line of thought than that which he was to explore in 'Ka no yō ni'.[18]

Schnitzler was represented by three one act plays, *Der tapfere Cassian, Weihnachtseinkäufe,* and *Die Frau mit dem Dolche,* and the three act play *Liebelei.* There is evidence to suggest that Ōgai thought very highly of Schnitzler's plays and took a deeper interest than might at first be apparent. There are records of him expressing admiration to a number of his friends, and between 1900 and 1912 he amassed twenty-two of Schnitzler's books. He may also have corresponded with him on the subject of translation rights.[19]

Schnitzler's plays focussed on the decadent Viennese society of his day and explored the psychology of a class whose main interest was in ephemeral sexual exploits. Why should Ōgai have shown particular interest in this portrayal? Part of the reason could well have been that the emphasis on sexual desire was common to much of the literature being produced in Japan at this time. Vienna at the turn of the century was, of course, poles apart from Meiji Japan, but Schnitzler's writings were essentially an investigation into the process of moral and social degeneration. As Martin Swales has pointed out,[20] the revaluation of traditional certainties has two results: a great sense of liberation and energy because of the overthrow of hardened conventions and yet a concomitant sense of loneliness. With no traditional values to rely on man becomes a threatened being. In Viennese life this led to a search for an intensity of experience that could obliterate this threatened self, and the interest in sexual exploits can be seen as a manifestation of this. The sexual experience itself is after all a microcosm of the whole world of complications which arise when life is seen as a series of intense quanta with no sense of continuity.

In a reverse sense this view could be applied to Meiji Japan where the experience was one of regeneration rather than degeneration. The demand for the revaluation of traditionally accepted values was the same and so in a sense were the results. This might go some way to explaining the excessive interest in sexuality that characterized the Japanese Naturalists and the fact that it was this element in European Naturalism that they emphasized.

If Rilke showed Ōgai one answer Schnitzler showed the opposite side of the coin. On the one hand we have true reality emerging from the destruction of old values and on the other we have a picture of the serious dangers that a society which discarded those values was prone to.

Ōgai's reaction to Ibsen was similar. Ibsen in fact provides the best illustration of the extent to which the earlier Ōgai had matured in his attitude towards literature. Initially he was as uncompromising in his attitude towards Ibsen as towards Zola, as late as 1896 still calling him 'that Scandinavian bigot' (XXIII, 295). By 1900, however, the situation had changed somewhat and in this later period we find that Ōgai translated three plays, appending copious explanations to two of them. Apart from a fragment of *Brand* which was printed in 1903, the first Ibsen play was *John Gabriel Borkman,* translated for the opening of the Jiyū Gekijō and performed on 27 November 1909 with Ichikawa Sadanji in the title role. To this was added a translation of the German introduction by Paul Schlenther which gave a résumé of the play and pointed out its main themes. The second play was *Ghosts* (December 1911) and the third *A Doll's House* (November 1913), which he prefaced with a lengthy explanation.

The way in which Ōgai was now reading European literature with a constant eye on his own doubts can be seen from the revealing introduction to Chiba Kikkō's translation of *The Master Builder:*

Chiba: What do you think of Halvard Solness?

Ōgai: Well, I don't have much sympathy for him. He's just a miserable man deceived by his own imagination and ignorant of the limits of his own energy.

Chiba: So you don't think he is a suitable type for a dramatic hero?

Ōgai: No, on the contrary, I find him very appealing in many ways.

Chiba: Isn't that a little contradictory?

Ōgai: Yes, I suppose it is. But in spite of the fact that I see him as a poor man of limited energy, the things a man like that does and says can be deeply moving, can't they?

Chiba: Of course.

Ōgai: That's how it is with me. (Pause) In fact I'm probably a bit of a Solness myself.

Chiba: How's that?

Ōgai: It's an old story now of course, but I too put a wreath on the weather vane of Lysanger tower in my own way. (Pause) In my dreams as a young man.

Chiba: I see.

Ogai: Now I am the father of a number of children and feel somewhat hemmed in. It feels as though the frightening young men of the new age are outside the door sharpening their swords of revenge. Then the door suddenly opens and in comes a charming Hilde Wangel.

Chiba: Who was this 'Hilde'?

Ogai: Don't you know? My 'Hilde' was *Subaru.*

Chiba: Of course! I like that! (Laughs)

Ogai: Do you see how I am a little like Solness? This Hilde-like 'Subaru' stood under the banner of a new age and came to me reawakening all my faded memories. (Pause) I too studied quietly and rebuilt my house. A tower was built and there was scaffolding, but I never dreamt of climbing it. I did have yearnings to reach the top of course, but never decided actually to go up myself. This is what my Hilde-like *Subaru* came to tempt me with.

Chiba: But surely you're not worried that you might fall off!

Ogai: If that's what you think then you're another of Hilde's group! You too would doubtless wave your white scarf as you saw me being foolhardy. I expect there was still some hair on Solness's pate when he broke it falling off the tower. I might manage to get through unscathed before I go grey and balding, but in any case it would be dangerous for me to climb the tower. Actually it looks as though I too have a Dr Herdal worrying about my nerves.

Chiba: Really?

Ogai: You see, I hear there are those who really wonder what on earth I'm doing. (Pause) But if there had been just one or two people who imagined they heard a song and harps in the air when they saw me climb, don't you think I would have at least had a go? (V, 363-6)

Here we are allowed a rare glimpse of Ōgai talking specifically about his own sense of ennui without the trappings of a story. 'Hemmed in' is probably the best way of describing how he felt during these years of transition.

Then we have Ibsen the portrayer of modern individuals, in particular Nora in *A Doll's House*, who claims that her duty to herself is at least as important as her duty to family and who leaves her husband to prove the point. 'Nora kaidai', the appendix to the translation, traces the development of Ibsen into a fully-fledged realist, explains the circumstances surrounding the feminist movement and praises the accuracy of Nora's predicament. This hopeful portrait of the 'new woman' is all the more striking when we compare it to John

Gabriel Borkman who flouts convention to the same degree but who comes to grief and dies of a broken heart. Just as Ōgai himself was trying to get to grips with the 'new man' in such works as *Seinen* and 'Kaijin', he chose many translations in which European authors were dealing with the modern emancipated female counterpart: Ella Rentheim in *John Gabriel Borkman*, Sophie in *Das tägliche Leben*, Anna Mahr in *Einsame Menschen*, and Nora. One might be forgiven for seeing a suggestion of Nora in his wife Shige, given the number of times she stayed away from home. But was such dangerous behaviour in fact natural morality reborn as Rilke was trying to suggest? Ōgai's answer would almost certainly be negative, as he was to show more and more interest in his historical work in women who were paragons of the traditional womanly virtues. Their strength was equal to if not greater than their modern free-thinking counterparts. Ōgai had himself been an iconoclast in his youth, but now it was the apparent wholesale destruction of the deep social structure that loomed large. He was never to feel at home with the social consequences of the modernization.

It would be impossible to leave Ōgai's translations at this point without a mention of his famous translation of Goethe's *Faust*. Begun in July 1911 on a request from the Committee of Arts of which he was a member, he finished the whole work in a matter of six months. It was eventually published in two parts, in January and March 1913, and was followed in the November by two studies: *Faust Kō*, which was a shortened version of Kuno Fischer's *Goethes Faust* (1901), and *Goethe Den*, a similar adaptation of Albert Bielschowsky's *Goethe: Sein Leben und seine Werke* (1904).

Ōgai had of course studied *Faust* in Germany, and the entry in the 'Doitsu nikki' for 27 December 1885 reads: 'Went to the Auerbachskeller with Inoue in the evening. We chatted about the possibility of translating Goethe's *Faust* into Chinese poetic form and in the end he pressed the job on me. I accepted for a joke' (XXXV, 122). This suggestion was never, of course, acted upon. It would have presumably been an attempt to transmit both rhyme and rhythm by using Chinese tones, as was in fact tried with two poems in *Omokage*, a truly stupendous task. When Ōgai finally set his hand to a translation it was in colloquial Japanese, so colloquial indeed as to be highly unusual, and although Ōgai himself would have been the first to admit the keen loss of rhyme, he managed to transmit the raciness of the opening lines in a way that many Japanese feel has never been surpassed:

Habe nun, ach! Philosophie,	Hate sate, ore wa tetsugaku mo
Juristerei und Medizin,	Hōgaku mo igaku mo
Und leider auch Theologie	Arazu mo gana no shingaku mo
Durchaus studiert, mit heissem	Nesshin ni benkyō shite, soko
Bemühn.	no soko made kenkyū shita.
Da steh' ich nun, ich armer Tor,	Sō shite koko ni kō shite iru.
Und bin so klug als wie zuvor![21]	Ki no doku no , baka no ore da na.

Ōgai's position as one of the greatest translators of modern Japan is undisputed but it raises one large question mark. Does it mean that his was a life of vicarious creativity, of living off the West as the sole source of intellectual stimulus? There can be little doubt that, at this stage, as Masao Miyoshi argues in his chapter on Ōgai,[22] he instinctively found himself putting Japanese problems in a Western frame of reference, and the confession in 'Fushigi na kagami' of excessive borrowing would suggest that Ōgai was very well aware of this distressing tendency. He still had another ten years to live however and it was then that he tried to remedy the situation by immersing himself in the study of Japanese history.

The question of academic freedom

In the June of 1910 Kōtoku Shūsui was arrested for an alleged plot to assassinate the Emperor Meiji and the witch hunt against anarchists and socialists reached a new peak. Some of Ōgai's work during this period dealt more or less directly with this problem of harsh government repression, 'Fasces' (September 1910), 'Chinmoku no tō' (The tower of silence, November 1910) and 'Shokudō' (The restaurant, December 1910) in particular. These works are so overtly didactic that they are best recognized as essays rather than stories.

Ōgai's central concern was to clear up the muddled thinking that grouped anarchists, Socialists, Naturalists and any other people with new ideas into one dangerous mass. In *Seinen* he had been concerned with the facile equation of individualism with anarchism, and he was worried lest literature be dragged into politics, not surprising for a man who had had one work of his own banned and had translated such notoriously dangerous works as *A Doll's House* and *Ghosts*.

'Fasces' takes the form of a dialogue in two parts, one between an official and a reporter and the other between the official and a writer. The official's view is that criteria for the banning of books must be based on 'contemporary general opinion in Japan'. The extreme vagueness of this proposal is attacked by the writer who makes various suggestions of his own, such as 'artists should judge artists' and that a distinction should be drawn between out and out pornographers and conscientious pioneers. Ōgai had of course been strongly in favour of banning pornography from the very beginning and, as one might expect, the matter is left more or less unresolved. The dialogue ends, however, with a strong plea for restraint; a demon rushes in and shouts at the official:

> The state gives you authority; it gives you power. For what purpose think you? 'I am the law maker and so I judge according to my own opinions! History be damned! World Culture be damned! Anyone else's judgement which differs from mine is mistaken!' you claim. Talk of the infallibility of the Pope! 'Godiamoci il Papato, che Dio ce l'ha dato.' Do you really think that the literary world in Japan will knuckle under because of that? Power is given so that justice may be done. Respect learning and the arts! (VII, 319)

'Chinmoku no tō' takes the form of a satire on contemporary Japan. The scene opens with a sombre description of the land of the Parsi where government repression has reached the stage of banning nearly everything in sight. There is a lengthy treatment of the process by which Naturalism became equated with anarchy:

> Then they started looking for Naturalism and Socialism in everything that appeared in print. Men of letters and artists were looked at askance in case they might be Naturalists or Socialists.
> The world of the arts became a world of suspicion.
> Then some of the Parsi discovered the phrase 'dangerous Western books'. Dangerous Western books introduced Naturalism, they introduced Socialism! To translate was to retail the dangerous goods themselves, and to write original work was to copy the Westerners and thus produce dangerous goods, imitation imports!
> Ideas that were destructive of peace and social order, ideas that corrupted the public morals were transmitted through dangerous Western books! (VIII, 387-8)

After a long list of the extraordinary number of books and authors from the West who have been banned, Ōgai turns to a serious discussion of the problem:

> From the Parsi point of view any art in the world today which is of the slightest value and not absolutely trite is considered a danger. This is only to be expected.
> Values recognized by art entail the destruction of convention. Any work which loiters within the bounds of convention is bound to be mediocre. All art when seen through the eyes of convention appears dangerous.
> Art penetrates through surface considerations to the impulses

which lurk beneath. Just as in painting one paints in colours that will not change, and in music one seeks chromatic variation, so in the literary arts one tries to create an impression through words. It is quite natural that literature should penetrate the impulsive side of life, and when it does so, the impulse of sexual desire must needs be revealed.

Because this is the very nature of art there are many artists, especially those men we call geniuses, who find it impossible to lead an ordered life in this real world. Men like Goethe, who was the Minister for Home Affairs in his state albeit a small one, and in more modern times Disraeli, who was a member of a cabinet and carried out Imperialist policies, are exceptions; the majority have radical views and are unrestrained in their actions. But even though people like George Sand and Eugène Sue associated with Leroux and advocated Communism and even though Freiligrath, Herwegh and Gutzkow joined with Marx in writing articles for a Socialist magazine, literary historians do not see this as detracting from their work.

It is the same thing with learning. Learning too advances by destroying conventions. If ever it is suppressed by the tastes of any country in any age it will die. (VII, 391-2)

Ōgai ends on a note of warning which is very reminiscent of his attitude during the 'Bōkan kikan' debate seventeen years previously:

It is only to be expected that both art and learning should appear dangerous from the conventional Parsi point of view. Why? Because in every country and in every age behind the men who tread new paths there are always a herd of reactionaries spying in every corner. Persecution arises at the slightest opportunity. Only the pretext changes depending on the country and the age. 'Dangerous Western books' is merely a pretext. (VII, 392)

One must be careful not to read into 'Chinmoku no tō' any sympathy for anarchism in general or Kōtoku Shūsui in particular. He feared the destructive elements but was also worried about the results of a backlash, so that what the problem needed was more light, rather than a hasty, panic-stricken reaction of blanket repression. In his view the best interests of the country would be served by further study of Socialism and allied ideologies; as a doctor he well knew the dangers of eradicating the symptoms without fully understanding the underlying causes of a disease. It was with this aim in mind that he agreed to help one of the lawyers for the defence of Kōtoku, Hiraide Shū, find out more about the intellectual background to the alleged plot. 'Shoku-dō', the main section of which is devoted to an outline of the history of anarchism and nihilism and a few short biographies of figures such as

Stirner, Bakunin and Kropotkin, was the result of some of this study. According to Yosano Hiroshi Ōgai talked to Hiraide, who was a long-standing friend and sponsor for *Subaru*, for four nights on the subject. Ōgai's own diary mentions a number of meetings with Hiraide about this time but never refers once to the Kōtoku affair by name, presumably feeling that he had caused enough trouble with his superiors.

The other side of Ōgai's scepticism was expressed in the story 'Fuji-dana' (The wisteria trellis, May 1912) where he discussed the necessity of controls of one sort or another if life in the social context was to be at all possible. The wisteria trellis of the title, being modern, made of iron and rather artificial looking, is used as a symbol of the unnatural results of modernization, in a somewhat similar vein to the hotel under reconstruction in 'Fushinchū'.

> He considered the question of social order. Freedom and libera-tion were just other names for the intention of modern man to destroy the existing social order. The new morality they called it. But social order is the outward expression of morality, not morality itself. In the bonds of this outward form we call order there exist very old established matters which must be changed. Looked at from the point of view of morality itself this outer order is nothing, but this is not to say that it does not have considerable value in itself. Only when it exists can society con-tinue to resist the various adverse powers of destruction. Those who see order as useless suppression and who believe that har-mony in life can be created through limitless freedom are perhaps too contemptuous of the strength of human desires. They are perhaps too optimistic.
>
> If social order was destroyed and authority annihilated would this not bring about on the contrary the opposite of a harmonious life? Man is neither angel nor beast. 'Le malheur veut que qui veut faire l'ange fait la bête.' They try to destroy social order and pro-pound a new morality, but can one found morality without either duty or self-control? And even if you do just manage to maintain a balance between conflicting desires, is this the sole object in life? Are there not demands which transcend this in life? Is mere ins-tinctual passivity the ultimate ideal? They are apt to cry out for a return to Nature, but are instinctual desires which one stores up and then tries to release really Nature? Wouldn't that sort of Nature be like this wisteria trellis? (X, 104-5)

The problem of censorship as it was fast developing was that it might permanently damage the spirit of enquiry into all facets of human exist-ence that was an index to a country's culture. His fears were well-founded. It is possible that, as Tayama Katai was to write later, Naturalism might have developed along more European lines if the Kōtoku affair had not happened, although Ishikawa Takuboku, in his incisive essay 'Jidai heisoku no genjō' (The times are at a standstill, August 1910), was already bemoaning its irrelevance and sounding its death knell. What is certain is that the question involved was far broader than merely literature and politics. What was at stake was the right of an author to say anything of importance about the society in which he lived. As Ōgai said in a lecture entitled 'Konton' (Confusion, January 1909), the fact that one was living in a period of confusion did not necessarily mean that the whole of society was about to collapse about one's ears. He knew very well that repressive measures could breed a darkness where any kind of meaningful culture would find it difficult to glimmer.

Government obscurantism was of course not confined to the sphere of literature, and in academic circles the heaviest pressure was brought to bear on those misguided souls who wished to study Japanese history and pre-history. In the story 'Ka no yō ni' (As if, January 1912), Ōgai took up this question along with the more general problem of the growth of scientific scepticism and the resultant undermining of traditional beliefs.

The original impetus for the composition of 'Ka no yō ni' is still a little unclear. In a letter to his son-in-law Yamada Tamaki dated December 1918 Ōgai wrote: 'As I have already explained, the work is based on a concept of Vaihinger's, but you may think that the whole thing is just a hodge-potch of ideas. Deep down, I suppose, it stems from my state of mind as regards a superior of mine. I wrote it believing it to have some justification thereby' (XXXVI,530).

The question is, who is this superior? The chief candidate until quite recently was Yamagata Aritomo. Behind 'Ka no yō ni' must surely have been the question of the correct interpretation of the mid-fourteenth-century Northern-Southern court dispute which was a subject of heated debate and controversy throughout 1911.[23] Ōgai was also a member of the Committee for School Textbooks where matters such as this were considered vital. The drastic measures taken by the Katsura cabinet to secure the legitimacy of the Southern court and the consequences such action had for the future of scholarly historical research in Japan were almost certainly in the back of Ōgai's mind. What is more there are two entries in his diary concerning the affair. The one for 23 February 1911 reads: 'Kako Tsurudo came to tell me he had gone with Ichimura Sanjirō and Inoue Michiyasu to the Kokin'an and advised support for the Southern court theory' (XXXV,516).[24]

On the 27 February 'Kako Tsurudo came this evening and told me of the activities of those who supported the Southern court theory.' There is, however, no indication that Ōgai ever talked directly to Yamagata about the affair or did anything except remain informed by Kako of what was transpiring.

The second and more recent candidate is General Nogi, first suggested by the scholar Hirakawa Sukehiro.[25] Nogi was Chancellor of the Peers School, which is mentioned in 'Ka no yō ni', and he was having some trouble at the time with the members of the Shirakaba literary group most of whom were students at the school. We know from a diary entry for 24 April 1912 that Nogi asked Ōgai to pay some attention to what the Shirakaba group were saying. There is no proof in this case either, but if the story was written for Nogi rather than Yamagata it would make the transition to 'Okitsu Yagoemon no Isho' all the clearer.

'Ka no yō ni' is essentially a wide ranging discussion on the possibility of serious historical research in Japan. The subject is taken up in the form of a letter sent by the central figure, Hidemaro, from Germany to his father in Japan. Hidemaro explains that one of the reasons that Germany is so powerful and stable is that it is based on a sure foundation – Protestant theology. The central scholar who acts in some ways as a government theologian is Adolf Harnack, although there appears to be no state intervention as far as his theological studies are concerned. Harnack's view is that a strong religion is necessary because it still has much influence over the masses who have 'faith'. In Russia where the church is left to stagnate and the people just treated like fools we see the rise of anarchism. Theology itself is useless for the uneducated majority but it does have its uses where intellectuals are concerned, because it is virtually the only way of controlling dissidents. The argument goes as follows:

> Properly speaking intellectuals do not have what the churchmen call faith. Even if you were to try and order such people, people with education but no faith, just to worship God and the Gospels they would find it impossible. As they have no faith they come to doubt the necessity of religion at all. Such people are dangerous thinkers. There are some of them, however, who pretend to have faith although they actually have none and who pretend to see the necessity for religion although they do not. There are in fact a great many people like this.

> Now once we have something like the German Protestant theology where the history of both doctrine and church has been fully studied, intellectuals can if they wish examine this doctrine

that has been cleansed by specialists and cleared from all impurities. On examining it they come to understand that religion is a necessity although they themselves might not believe in it. This is the way one gets healthy thinkers. (X,51-2)

If Harnack seems to have found a way to accommodate radical thinkers by allowing them to study a rationally and carefully researched body of doctrine, we are told neither how this doctrine happens to be in tune with the aims of the state nor how the mysterious process by which one may become convinced as to the necessity of religion through a study of 'pure' theology takes place. The main question, however, is the possibility of such religious study being carried out in Japanese intellectual circles. What was the situation as regards religion in Japan? Hidemaro's father thinks as follows:

His own family had always had their own family temple but at the Restoration his father had broken off relations and left funerals and festivals in the hands of a Shinto priest. Thereafter they had had no connections with Buddhism at all; he recognized nothing now but the spirits of his ancestors. There was indeed a shrine in the grounds of the mansion itself where they were worshipped and the rites duly performed. But did he himself believe that the spirits of his ancestors existed? Whenever he performed the rites he remembered the passage in the Analects about how one should consider one's ancestors present when worshipping them, but all that really meant was that one must carry out the ceremonies as if one's ancestors existed. As far as he himself was concerned, he did not really believe that they did in fact exist. Perhaps he never even bothered pretending. (X, 52)

Facing up to his own scepticism he then had to tackle the question of whether education destroyed faith:

With a modern education you could hardly regard myth and history as being one and the same thing. Once educated, however shallow a man's studies might be, he would inevitably be obliged to wonder sometimes how the world had come into being and how it had developed, and how Man had undergone the same process. You could not just treat myth as if it were reality in such speculations. But once you drew a clear distinction between myth and history the existence of one's ancestors and other spirits came into doubt. Were there not terrible dangers in such a prospect?

What did the ordinary mass of people think about this problem? Didn't they just accept as inevitable the fact that the existence of spirits which their ancestors believed in was now denied? In that case didn't they also see it as perfectly natural that festivals and the like had become mere empty forms, or that their

children were being taught myths as if they were history? Surely
everyone just accepted the fact that while they themselves
thought of myth and history as being clearly defined their children were taught a mixture of the two on purpose. Surely everyone was just vaguely carrying on with customs in a laissez-faire
sort of way while not actually believing in spirits in the slightest
and they were quite indifferent as to how long these customs,
which were formed in the past when spirits were believed in and
remained today when that belief no longer held, should be maintained in their present form or destroyed at some stage. They
carried on pretending to believe in things they did not believe.
They had no qualms about their hypocrisy and never even considered what effect such teaching might have on the minds of
their children. (X, 53-4)

It would appear that for some strange reason the father did not quite
grasp that unhindered study of myth on the one hand and history on
the other was not possible in Japan. A properly researched Shinto theology might possibly help to avoid the growth of dangerous thinkers,
but the first vital step of recognizing the clear distinction between myth
and history invited untold dangers itself. Once that step was taken the
whole edifice might crumble.

Here we see another side of Ōgai's concern that the spirit of rational
enquiry was not taking root in Japan as fast as he had hoped. Even if
Japanese science was beginning to show signs of producing results, the
spirit was not filtering down through society. Now the government was
actively stopping it in literary and intellectual circles. By 1911 the
amalgam of myth and history taught to children in schools was firmly
established as the norm. Despite the welcome given in academic circles
to Minobe's liberal views on the Constitution which he first propounded
in July 1911, the process was to continue and harden. Only eight years
later a professor at Tokyo University, Morito Tatsuo, was to be houn-
ded out of his post and imprisoned for two months for publishing a
scholarly article on Kropotkin.

The second part of 'Ka no yō ni' discusses the kind of pragmatism
that allows the worried intellectual to accept the necessity of religion
while remaining sceptical. Ōgai bases this on an explanation of the
ideas contained in Hans Vaihinger's *Die Philosophie des Als Ob* (The
Philosophy of As If, 1911).[26] Vaihinger took as his starting point
Kant's epistemology and his theory that man can never know the
'thing in itself' because of built-in perceptual limitations. His central
concept was that of *fictions*, which Ōgai translated as *uso*, which
perform a similar function to hypotheses but differ in one important

respect — the user knows and recognizes them to be false but necessary. Hypotheses are constructed with the aim of verification, but fictions are found to be essential despite their falseness; for instance concepts such as God and immortality. The connection here with Harnack and his pragmatic approach is clear.

The argument is that all forms of human knowledge are based on a tacit understanding that man is dealing with conscious fictions. Concepts such as point and line in mathematics, atoms in chemistry, and liberty in the ethical sphere are more than hypotheses; they are assumptions without which these various disciplines could not exist. If everything that man can know is based on a fiction, this levels the ground between myth and history. If the intellectual can be persuaded of this truth, he can study history in one compartment and myth in another and remain fully convinced of the necessity of the latter for the maintenance of a healthy society. In this case there will be no need for oppressive state intervention in the scholar's work.

This rather shaky proposal is introduced by Ōgai only to be rejected. He knew very well that the only way to stop the constant progress of sceptical thought was 'to destroy all the universities, everything, and plunge the world into darkness!' (X, 76). The reason that *as if* is rejected is that he himself was no Vaihinger, and although he appreciated that both the spiritual and material had to be cultivated, he did not see why or how a science such as medicine should be reduced to a fiction. The problem with the failure of *as if* to provide a solution, however, is that the alternatives are either to stop thinking altogether or to come to a head-on clash. It would be no exaggeration to say that 'Ka no yō ni' represents a crisis point in a long period of tension and ennui which began during the Kokura days. Ōgai was instinctively worried that the growth of anarchist and Socialist concepts might destroy the social order, and yet he was passionately committed to the independence of the intellectual and felt that the modern spirit of rational investigation could not be stifled without doing irreparable damage to the cultural life of the nation. He himself had felt the heavy hand of censorship and saw with frightful clarity how this road could so easily lead into darkness. The nihilist despair evidenced in 'Kaijin' is not so surprising when we see the failure of such attempts at compromise as evidenced in 'Ka no yō ni'.

It is against this background that the death of Emperor Meiji, the suicide of General Nogi, and Ōgai's interest in the study of history should be viewed and appreciated. Whether he actually saw himself as destined for a direct assault on the obscurantist measures of the gov-

ernment or not, there can be no doubt that he saw himself as an un-
believer who yet recognized that something vital might be lost if
certain myths were openly repudiated. What is more he was faced in
late 1912 with a vivid example of the depth and continuing power of
myth, Nogi's suicide. The death of such an esteemed friend would have
been a shock in any case, but, in Nogi, Ōgai was faced with a man who
in this supposedly modern day and age had followed his Emperor into
death for what was essentially a myth. Ōgai's subsequent concentration
on historical subjects can be in large part attributed to this one event,
although as we have seen other factors were leading him in the same
direction.

Was Ōgai running away from reality when he turned to history? This
is partly true in the sense that, with 'Kaijin', he was clearly beginning to
exhaust the present as a source of literary inspiration. Recognizing that
he was no master in the portrayal of the present, Ōgai's move towards
history was motivated as much by artistic as by intellectual considerations. In view of the fact that much of his historical work after 1912
treated social questions with a directness that would not have otherwise
been possible, he was in part following the time-honoured practice —
more often seen in China than Japan — of carrying out social
commentary in a historical context, infinitely preferable to staying
silent or having everything he wrote banned.

PART III

1912 – 1922

7

THE STUDY OF HISTORY

The samurai spirit

The Emperor Meiji died on 30 August 1912, and a fortnight later on the evening of 13 September, as the funeral procession left the palace, General Nogi and his wife committed suicide together in their Akasaka mansion. This revival of a traditional sign of loyalty, *junshi*, where the servant followed his master into death, was a shock to the whole nation; the variety of response to the event showed the extent to which the country was in a schizophrenic state of mind. Except for the well-known example of the Kyoto University lecturer Tanimoto Tomeru who came under great pressure for his critical views, the public response was on the whole laudatory. Private attitudes however were rather different. The younger generation, as one can tell from the diaries of Shiga Naoya and Mushanokōji Saneatsu, considered the act not merely anachronistic but almost totally pointless; such ideals had no place in a world striving for a deeper understanding of the West.[1]

For older men, Nogi's suicide symbolized with terrible finality the struggle which they themselves had been waging between the security of tradition and the pull of modernity. We know from a famous passage in *Kokoro* that Sōseki reacted as many of his generation must have done: he was in sympathy with Nogi and could accept that the act had been carried out with total sincerity, but there was also an uncomfortable sense of disbelief that the traditions of the past had proved so strong. For Ōgai, who was that much closer to Nogi, the death was little short of traumatic.

It may be argued with hindsight that Nogi's act was a decisive element in the process by which the increasing tide of individualism was stemmed and the tradition of loyalty to feudal lord became fully transferred to the Emperor. For men in the Tokugawa period to commit suicide for their Emperor would have been anathema. There can be little doubt that Ōgai recognized the important implications of such an

Ōgai in 1916, the year of his voluntary retirement from the army

event and his subsequent historical novellas and biographies, widely considered to be his best work, stem from this date. Here was proof, if proof were needed, that the roots of Meiji Japan were to be found in the Tokugawa period, and that was where Ōgai went for his material in an investigation of the spiritual background of his age.

The comments in Ōgai's diary for the day of the suicide are in the the usual cryptic style: 'Sept. 13: Was in attendance at the hearse on the way to Aoyama. We left the Palace at 8 pm and reached Aoyama at 11. Returned from Aoyama at 2 the next morning. On the way back someone told me that Nogi Maresuke and his wife had died. I found it difficult to believe. (*Yo hanshin hangi su*).' The diary continues: 'Sept. 15: . . . In the afternoon I stood by Nogi's coffin . . . Sept. 18: Went to funeral of Nogi Maresuke at Aoyama cemetery. Wrote 'Okitsu Yagoemon' and sent it to *Chūō Kōron*' (XXXV, 568-9). Clearly, the immediate impetus for the writing of 'Okitsu Yagoemon no isho' (The last testament of Okitsu Yagoemon) was Nogi's death, and although some attempt has been made to see it as a public refutation of criticism of the act of *junshi*, it is best seen as a work concerned less with public protestations than with a very private, personal matter. Nogi's suicide note, suppressed by the authorities until September 16 is important for an understanding of 'Okitsu'. It begins:

> For my suicide by which I now follow in the footsteps of my Emperor, I crave indulgence. I realize the enormity of my offence and yet ever since I lost the standard at the battle in the tenth year of Meiji I have set my heart on finding an opportunity to die. That opportunity never came.
>
> While I have in the past basked in the warmth of the Imperial favour and received so many kindnesses, I am now failing in my old age and can no longer be of any use. I pray for forgiveness but my resolution here is final.[2]

The hero of Ōgai's story dies in very similar circumstances and the beginning echoes the words of Nogi:

> My ritual suicide today will come as a great shock and there will be those who claim that I, Yagoemon, am either senile or deranged. But this is very far from the truth. Ever since my retirement I have been engaged in building a hut of the simplest kind here at the western foot of Mt Funaoka. The rest of my family moved from the castle town of Yatsushiro in Higo after the demise of my former master Lord Shōkōji and they are now living in the same province of Higo, but at Kumamoto. They will, as a result, be extremely shaken when they set eyes on this testament, but I request that someone should send it to them at the first

opportunity. I have for some years now lived the life of a Buddhist priest, but compose this last testament because at heart I am a warrior and thus deeply concerned about my posthumous reputation. (XXXVIII, 497)

Okitsu then proceeds to explain the reason for his suicide. Some thirty years previously he had been commissioned by his master Hosokawa Tadaoki (Lord Shōkōji) to travel to Nagasaki and buy some rare wood for incense burning. A man had also been sent down from Sendai to buy a similar article and so the price was gradually forced up. Okitsu's companion thought it would be foolishness to throw away a vast sum of money on a mere piece of wood, but Okitsu maintained that his orders were to buy the rarest wood he could find and he must at all costs obey his master to the letter. They came to blows and Okitsu killed his companion in self-defence. He bought the wood, returned to his master and requested permission to commit suicide. The request was turned down on the ground that he had been perfectly correct to obey his master to the letter. 'If we looked at everything with an eye to its utility there would be nothing left to value in the world' (XXXVIII, 499). Okitsu's testament then goes on to explain how he had already made up his mind to die but had to wait for the right occasion. Eventually after the Hosokawa's fortunes seem to be firmly established:

> I now no longer had anything on my mind and yet I felt it would be a pity for me to die of old age. I waited for today, the thirteenth anniversary of the death of Lord Shōkōji, from whom I have received so many favours and whom I yearn to follow, despite having left it so long. I know very well that to follow one's master into death is officially prohibited, but I do not expect to incur censure. I did kill my companion and should have committed suicide many years ago in my youth.
>
> I have no real friends, but as I have recently been on intimate terms with the priest Seigan at the Daitokuji, I earnestly request that those who live nearby should show him this letter before sending it to my home province.
>
> I have been writing this note by the light of a candle which has just gone out. But there is no need to light another. There is sufficient reflection from the snow at the window to enable me to cut across my wrinkled stomach. (XXXVIII, 499-500)

It was while Ōgai was living at Kokura in Kyushu, ten years before, interesting himself in local history, that he first collected material for this story, and so it was now ready to hand. Close research into his sources by, among others, the scholar Ogata Tsutomu has established that Ōgai's main addition to this material was the dialogue between

Okitsu and his companion and Hosokawa's remark on the importance of spiritual values.[3] More importantly perhaps one of the main elements in the story is the way that Okitsu commits a technical offence by dying at a time when *junshi* was prohibited. In actual fact Ōgai was later to realize that the decree banning *junshi* was passed in 1663, *after* Okitsu's death. In the revised version of the work he felt obliged to change both the reason for the testament and the ending accordingly.

Even in the first version however Ōgai's attitude to *junshi* is rather unclear. There is a question, for instance, of whether a suicide postponed for so long can really be justified. For Ōgai the problems raised by Nogi's death were not simply a matter of condoning or explaining away the act, but were of a wider nature. The significance of the act lay, as we have already mentioned, in the fact that a friend and a man of great integrity had died for a myth. To Ōgai the sceptic, concerned in 'Ka no yō ni' with a proper delineation of history versus myth, it was a disconcerting example of the extreme power of ideas based on spiritual rather than rational or scientific foundations, of Japanese tradition in the face of Western thought. It is not difficult to imagine how deeply he must have been shaken.

While Ōgai's decision to turn to Tokugawa history and examine the well springs of this tradition that was proving to be so strong did have elements of a retreat into the past, it was also an investigation into the very roots of his own culture. *Junshi* was not a remote historical phenomenon but a vital present force. Was it a vestige of a dying past, an anachronism, or an admirable part of Japanese spirituality? The study of history for Ōgai was the best way in which he could clarify for himself and others the psychological make-up of his contemporaries. It would seem as though he needed to preserve a certain temporal and emotional distance between himself and the object of study, for we have seen the confusion into which he was apt to lapse when treating contemporary themes in a contemporary setting. The convoluted introspection of the works from 1909 to 1912 had merely led to the impasse of 'Kaijin'. The state of depression and emptiness was engendered by a contemplation of the loss of stable values Ōgai knew to be self-defeating. It proved more fruitful to examine a period when human actions and decisions had been based on secure indigenous values in an effort to redefine the nature of his own culture. With his deep understanding of the West and his consciousness of the huge debt that he and Japan as a whole owed in that direction, there was little fear that he would lose his balance or ever dream of anything as foolish as facile nationalism. But one side of the equation that made up modern

Japan remained unstudied and this balance had to be restored. Neither must it be forgotten that the Japanese past was not so remote for Ōgai as it might seem to us today; it was for him, as it was for Basil Hall Chamberlain, distinctly within living memory.[4]

The next work, 'Abe ichizoku' (The Abe family), which was finished on 29 November 1912 and appeared in *Chūō Kōron* in the January of 1913, grew out of the material on which he had based 'Okitsu Yagoemon no isho'. The story concerns the spate of suicides that followed the death in 1641 of Hosokawa Tadatoshi, the son of Yagoemon's master Lord Shōkōji. One retainer, Abe Yaichiemon, is refused permission to die. In spite of this he is driven to commit *junshi* by public opprobrium and yet this very act of disobedience leads the whole family to its tragic destruction. The story starts with impressive solemnity:

> It was in the spring of the eighteenth year of Kan'ei that Hosokawa Tadatoshi, holder of the junior fourth rank lower grade, a captain in the Imperial Guard of the Left and Lord of Etchū, was preparing to turn his back on his province of Higo where the cherries were the first to blossom and, surrounded by the glittering retinue befitting a daimyo worth five hundred and forty thousand *koku,* start his progress towards Edo in the wake of spring as it wended its way north. Suddenly he fell ill and, as the medicine prescribed by his physician proved ineffective and the illness grew worse as the days went by, an express messenger left for Edo to inform them of his delayed departure.
>
> The Tokugawa Shogun, Iemitsu of the third generation renowned as a wise ruler, was concerned about the condition of Tadatoshi who had rendered him great service by capturing the rebel commander Amakusa Shirō Tokisada at the time of the Shimabara Rebellion, and on the twentieth day of the third month he had instructions drawn up in the names of Matsudaira Lord of Izu, Abe Lord of Bungo and Abe Lord of Tsushima for a man skilled in acupuncture to go down from Kyoto. On the twenty-second he sent the samurai Soga Matazaemon as his messenger with another order similarly signed by the three Elders. It was an exceptional courtesy for the Shogun's house to afford such treatment to a daimyo. Three years previously after the suppression of the Shimabara uprising in the spring of the fifteenth year of Kan'ei the Shogun had presented him with extra land for his Edo mansion, given him a crane hunted with the hawk, and had gone out of his way to be unusually solicitous; and so it was only to be expected that when he now heard of his serious illness he should show concern for his health as far as precedent might permit. (XI, 311)

As a result of the death of Tadatoshi a number of retainers commit suicide, but permission has to be obtained before this expression of loyalty can be countenanced. Whether this permission is granted or not depends very much on the individual and his relationship to his lord. Ōgai is at pains to point out too that many men doubtless kill themselves not so much from a sincere personal wish but because it is more or less expected of them. The lord who grants permission must also go through much torment:

> They were all samurai whom Tadatoshi trusted implicitly and so he longed to leave these men behind to protect his son Mitsuhisa. He was also keenly aware that it was cruel to let these men die with him. But while it hurt him to do so, he gave permission to each of them for he had no other choice. He knew that these men who had served him personally did not begrudge their lives and he knew too that they considered it no hardship to commit *junshi,* but on the other hand what if he were to forbid them to die and they were to carry on living? Every family would doubtless treat them as men who had failed to die when they were expected to; they would be ostracized as ingrates and cowards. If that were all, they might perhaps endure it and wait until the time came for them to offer their lives to Mitsuhisa. But if it should be said that their former lord had employed them unaware of their ingratitude and cowardice — that they would not be able to bear. How they would resent it! Seen in this light he had no alternative but to give his permission and this he did in an agony of mind worse even than his physical pain.
>
> When the number of retainers to whom he had given permission reached eighteen, Tadatoshi, who had survived over fifty long years of peace and war and thus had a deep understanding of human nature and the ways of the world, even in the midst of his pain thought seriously about his own death and that of the eighteen warriors.
>
> That which has life must needs perish. Besides the old tree as it withers thrives the young sapling. From the point of view of the young warriors who surrounded his son Mitsuhisa the older men in his service were better out of the way. They were even a nuisance. He wanted them to live on and serve Mitsuhisa with the same devotion they had given him, but there were already many prepared and waiting eagerly to devote themselves to his son. Those men who served himself must have earned the resentment of others while working in their respective posts throughout the years. At least they must have become the butt of envy. In that case it was hardly very prudent to try and compel them to stay alive. Perhaps he had been compassionate in allowing them to

commit *junshi*. He felt he could get a measure of consolation from these thoughts. (XI, 321–2)

Abe Yaichiemon is refused permission to die merely because Tadatoshi had a vague dislike of his manner and of the maddening way in which he always seemed to do the right thing without being asked. It is because of this stubborn refusal of Tadatoshi's that the whole Abe family is brought to ruin. At first Yaichiemon decided to accept his lord's refusal with fortitude but very soon he becomes ostracized and public opinion brands him as a coward. In the full knowledge that he has been driven into a corner, he calls together the members of his family, warns them of the ignominy they must expect, and commits *seppuku* in front of his children.

As a result of Abe having died without permission, his son is barred from the succession and the stipend split into portions and divided among the younger brothers. At the first anniversary of Tadatoshi's death there is a ceremony at his grave during which all the families of men who had committed suicide are allowed to burn incense. When it comes to the Abes' turn the eldest son Gombei cuts off his topknot and renounces his life as a warrior. Mitsuhisa is greatly offended, has Gombei incarcerated and later beheaded like a common criminal. This brings such shame on the family that they decide they can no longer show their faces among their colleagues and shut themselves inside their mansion. Mitsuhisa hears of their defiance and preparations are made for battle.

The attack places many people in a dilemma, such as their friend and neighbour Tsukamoto Matashichirō who reveals his sympathy by sending his wife to visit them on the eve of the battle, but who feels he must show his loyalty to his lord and fight on the actual day. 'Sympathy was sympathy, but duty was duty.' The battle, described in graphic detail, ends with the destruction of the Abe family and much credit for those who acquitted themselves with distinction.

Less than a year later both 'Okitsu Yagoemon no isho' and 'Abe ichizoku' were re-published, together with a third story entitled 'Sahashi Jingorō', with considerable revisions. In the case of 'Okitsu Yagoemon' a totally new work results. The two opening paragraphs are replaced by a long and detailed history of Yagoemon's grandfather, father and elder brother; the name of his companion is given as Yokota Seibei; the story is closely tied to 'Abe ichizoku' by a mention of the suicides that took place on the death of Tadatoshi and we are given to understand that these deaths played their part in persuading Yagoemon to follow suit later on; more importantly he is in fact given permission to die by

Mitsuhisa and the date of his death is corrected from 1647 to 1658; lastly, the suicide note itself is followed by a long genealogy which traces the Okitsu family down to the 1890s.[5]

The fact that Yagoemon receives permission to die changes the whole emphasis of the first version and, together with the removal of the opening lines, serves to divorce the work from its first immediate inspiration − Nogi's death. It comes much closer to 'Abe ichizoku' in a critical appraisal of *junshi* and shows very clearly the way Ōgai was developing.

The revisions to 'Abe ichizoku' were not so drastic and most changes are confined to one section of the story where Ōgai inserted a long list of the eighteen men who committed suicide together with a record of their ancestors. The effect of these revisions, in particular in the case of 'Okitsu Yagoemon', is rather unfortunate and makes the original version preferable. This sacrifice of intensity for factual emendation is of the utmost importance when one comes to consider the nature of Ōgai's historical novellas, and is symptomatic of oscillation between fact and fiction that runs throughout his literary output.

In the third story, 'Sahashi Jingorō', first published in *Chūō Kōron* in April 1913, Ōgai goes farther back in Japanese history to the period just before and after 1600 when Ieyasu was consolidating his hold on Japan; a time when the total subservience of servant to lord was not yet an established ethic. At an audience granted to some Korean envoys in 1607 Ieyasu thinks he recognizes one of the interpreters as a former retainer of his, Sahashi Jingorō.[6] However as nothing can be proved and the Koreans cannot corroborate this theory they exchange gifts and then return home.

The scene then changes to the time some thirty years earlier when Sahashi Jingorō had become a page to Ieyasu's eldest son. He is bright and intelligent with a talent for music as well as the martial arts. One day Jingorō manages to shoot down a heron at an almost impossible range thereby winning a bet made by a fellow servant Hachiya. The next day Hachiya is found dead but with no visible wound and Jingorō has disappeared. Nothing more is heard of him until his brother appears and explains how Jingorō had demanded a precious dagger from Hachiya as payment for the bet. Hachiya had refused and a fight had ensued during which Jingorō struck Hachiya, took the dagger and ran off to the hills.

Hearing this explanation Ieyasu decides to pardon Jingorō if he will do him the important service of killing a retainer of his enemy Takeda Katsuyori. The actual death of this retainer, Amari Shirosaburō, is portrayed in a dreamlike sequence where Jingorō is never actually alluded to by name. A noisy gathering has just taken place at the castle of Oyama. As everyone leaves Amari asks a youth who has only recently joined the band to stay behind:

> 'What a noisy crowd they are! Now we can view the moon. Play your flute again,' and so saying Amari lay down with his head in the youth's lap. The young man played. He was always being asked to play and so kept his flute by him. It gradually became darker. The long wick of the candle that was almost burnt out was white at the top and bright red at the lower end. The wax hung down like icicles piling round the base. The clear sharp moon shone its pale light into the whole room making the candle light look dark and muddied by comparison. The chirping of the crickets nearby mingled with the sound of the flute. Amari felt his eyelids getting heavier.
>
> Suddenly the flute stopped. 'Don't you feel at all cold?' said the youth putting down the flute and feeling with his left hand over Amari's left breast as he lay face upwards. It was just where the crest was dyed into the pale blue kimono. Amari, on the border of sleep, thought he was rearranging his dress which was loose around his neck, but then something as cold as ice sunk deep into his breast at the point where just a moment before he had felt the palm of a hand. Something strange and warm flooded back up into his throat. He lost consciousness. (XI, 515–16)

Jingorō takes Amari's topknot back to Ieyasu and is granted an audience. He is forgiven his earlier misdemeanour but no mention is made of Amari. It becomes apparent that Ieyasu has decided not to show Jingorō any further favours. Despite the fact that he serves his lord well and faithfully he receives no word of praise. When at last he overhears Ieyasu criticizing the way he despatched Amari he decides he can no longer serve him and so leaves immediately, disappearing without trace. The story ends on a wry note:

> Did Jingorō who left Hamamatsu in the eleventh year of Tenshō (1583) in fact return from Korea in the twelfth year of Keichō (1607) under the name Interpreter Kyo? Or was it just a mistake of Ieyasu's. No one can tell for certain. Even when the Sahashi family were questioned they insisted they had not the slightest knowledge of the affair. But it turned out later that they had enormous stocks of high quality ginseng, the roots of which were grown into human shape, and there were those who wondered how it had been come by. (XI, 518)

The research of Ogata Tsutomu has revealed that Ōgai's source for this story was the *Tsūkō Ichiran* which had been republished in, three volumes in February 1913.[7] The original story mentions only that Ieyasu thinks he recognizes Jingorō among the members of a Korean embassy 'near the end of the Keichō era'. All the records mention only two interpreters and so Ōgai has invented a third, Kyo, whom he suggests is Jingorō. Compared to his sources Ōgai goes out of his way to portray Jingorō in a good light, inventing the heron episode to give a plausible basis for the fight with Hachiya, writing the death scene in a lyrical style, and making Ieyasu seem an unattractive and even vindictive man. When Jingorō leaves his lord it is seen as a reasonable act.

What Ōgai has done here is to study the same kind of clash between master and servant as we have seen in 'Abe ichizoku', but in an age before convention had frozen and when Jingorō still found it psychologically possible to assert his own individuality. The tragic impasse that faces the Abe family is therefore very much a result of the age in which they live.

In 'Ka no yō ni' an attempt was made to 'act is if duty existed' and to see the old traditional myths as 'fictions' which, while being recognizable untruths, were necessary for man's peace of mind. With 'Okitsu Yagoemon' Ōgai went a stage further. Nogi's suicide had impressed on him the palpable fact that the old traditions were still very real; if Nogi had been induced to die, how much more binding must these ideas have been to the warriors of Tokugawa Japan. For these men the idea of duty and self-sacrifice was never a fiction to be accepted but a binding ethic which governed every act. Okitsu is a convincing example of that 'altruistic individualism' that he had hinted at in *Seinen*, an example of the essential worthiness of self-sacrifice. After writing this work the problems posed by the samurai's fierce pride and his fierce loyalty must have appealed to Ōgai as a fruitful field for study.

'Abe ichizoku' is a portrayal of the inevitable tragedy when the individual clashes with authority in a society where servant must obey master. The act of *junshi* is studied from the angle of both lord and servant in a more dispassionate light than a suicide note could allow. From the point of view of Tadatoshi it was less a question of expecting the action as a right, than a matter of public pressure and social mores; and from the point of view of the men who died, their own personal initiative was inextricably linked to this social pressure. *Junshi* is revealed as a complex phenomenon only partly understood by the society in which it was the accepted code of practice. The movement from an initial sympathetic reaction to Nogi's death to a more detached analysis of the reasons and causes of such an act can in part explain Ōgai's decision to revise 'Okitsu Yagoemon' to the extent he did. The *junshi* in this second version is a condoned act, carried out not in a lonely mountain hut but surrounded by a crowd of onlookers and with the full-hearted consent of his lord.

The events culminating in Okitsu Yagoemon's decision to die lead to a very different conclusion in a society in flux, such as when Jingorō is serving Ieyasu. Ōgai shrewdly observes that there is much more in common between pre-Tokugawa times and the present, and portrays Jingorō as a rational man who feels little compulsion to commit suicide when spurned by his lord. The man who stands up and asserts himself in pre-Tokugawa times manages somehow to survive even though he lives in voluntary exile, but his counterpart in a later age is destroyed when he challenges absolute authority as we see in the case of 'Abe ichizoku'. Ōgai clearly recognized the elements of tragedy in this latter story. Tragedy is only really possible in a world of absolutes, both external and internal. The pointless slaughter of the Abe family is a consequence of the clash between two unyielding forces, loyalty to family and self on the one hand and the ethic of loyalty to lord on the other, an endemic problem in Tokugawa Japan.

Although Ōgai first called the collection of these three stories *Itsujihen* (Miscellanies) the editor asked him to change it to *Iji*,[8] a word which combines the idea of 'steadfastness' with that of 'obstinacy' and 'stubbornness' and which is a concept that is closely linked to the nature of the samurai spirit. The title was appropriate for each story explores the interaction of an individual will with the rigid framework in which it is sometimes compelled to exist.

The next story after 'Sahashi Jingorō' was 'Gojiingahara no kata-kiuchi' (The revenge at Gojiingahara) which was published in the journal *Hototogisu* in October 1913. After his treatment of *junshi* Ōgai was drawn to another social phenomenon which had particular significance in Tokugawa Japan, that of organized vendetta. Revenge was at once a very strong tradition and a potentially disruptive practice, but by a stroke of administrative genius the Tokugawa authorities preferred not to ban the practice but to give it official sanction, hedging it about with rules and regulations. It thus operated as a controlled and useful safety valve.

Ōgai chose to illustrate the process of vendetta with an account of the revenge of a Yamamoto Sanemon who was killed in 1833, and which was especially noteworthy for the presence of his daughter who took part in the final act of retribution. The story opens with a dramatic murder scene; Yamamoto Sanemon is cut down while guarding his master's treasure house in the grounds of his Edo mansion. Some detective work reveals that the murderer was one Kamezō, a twenty year old retainer of a neighbouring family. Just before his death Sanemon asks his son Uhei to revenge him, and at his burial his daughter Riyo asks for and receives his dagger. At this point Ōgai inserts one of the very few passages of interpolation:

> When the parent of a samurai is murdered revenge must be taken. How much more so in the case of Sanemon's family where the revenge had been the old man's dying wish. As a result the whole family gathered to confer on this matter many times and in the end a formal petition for revenge was made about the middle of the first month of the next year, 1834. (XIV, 409)

Sanemon's younger brother Kurōemon arrives in Edo to help Uhei but their departure is delayed by an outbreak of fires which devastate the area. Riyo expresses a wish to go on the journey with her uncle. He refuses but promises that they will send for her before they kill the culprit. Official permission being granted Kurōemon and Uhei leave Edo in the company of a retainer called Bunkichi who has offered his services because he knows and can recognize Kamezō. All three set out in the knowledge that the task of tracking down Kamezō is almost impossible.

The second part of the account traces their travels through Japan, down to the Kii peninsula, through Shikoku and Kyushu and back to Osaka. They meet a number of excellent clues but many false trails, and by the time they reach Osaka all three have suffered badly from disease and deprivation. It is here that an important turning point is reached. While they are recuperating Uhei becomes more and more sullen and eventually confesses that he finds the search a waste of time. He rebels against the fatalism of Kurōemon's approach and walks out. It turns out that we shall hear no more of him; he has left for good. Ōgai draws a strong contrast between Uhei in his 'modern' self-willed approach and that of Bunkichi who decides to stay with Kurōemon to the bitter end. It was this unusual story of the son abandoning the tiresome process of revenge which clearly drew Ōgai's attention.

Eventually Kurōemon and Bunkichi receive news that Kamezō has been seen back in Edo. They return, find him, keep him bound until the daughter Riyo has been summoned, and then let him free to be struck down by Riyo using her father's dagger. The story ends with a detailed description of the aftermath, the examination of the body and the formal regulations concerning the registering of the deed accomplished.

According to Ogata Tsutomu and others, Ōgai's account follows closely, both in details and in the sequence of events, his original source, the *Yamamoto Fukushūki*.[9] He merely added a few details about the fires in Edo before their departure and effected a slight change of emphasis with regard to Uhei and his sister. Ōgai stresses Uhei's scepticism, which leads him to think of revenge in the cold light of reason and decide that he is wasting his time, and it provides a nice point of contrast with the more 'traditional' approach of his sister Riyo. However, Ōgai is at great pains here to avoid any subjective reactions to the material he is using and so makes no overt comment on the desirability of either attitude. It needs to be said too that although Ōgai sticks very closely to his materials the result is not a dry narrative but a vivid, fast moving story. The dramatic presentation of events reveals the presence of a conscious craftsman, but whether the credit should go to Ōgai or the writer of the *Yamamoto Fukushūki,* is another, more delicate, question.

Deliberate and careful dramatization is even more pronounced in 'Ōshio Heihachirō' (January 1914). In this study of the uprising in Osaka in the second month of 1837, Ōgai treated yet another aspect of a warrior's *iji*; the explosive results when sincerely concerned intellectuals find there is no way for them to express their dissatisfaction with the incompetence of the authorities and generally disastrous economic policies. If all the stories mentioned so far had a certain relevance to contemporary life, in that a similar phenomenon of individual versus absolute authority was beginning to emerge before Ōgai's very eyes, 'Ōshio Heihachirō' has by far the closest connection. The Kōtoku affair had shown that there were no channels into which violent unrest or dissention could be safely led. But more to the point, the second decade of the Taishō era was a period of economic uncertainty and rice riots were not uncommon and were to get worse. This account of a Tokugawa uprising therefore had relevance far beyond the confines of the year 1837.

The story is divided into thirteen scenes, each of which concentrates on one aspect of the action so that the reader is given a composite picture of the uprising built up from a number of carefully selected angles. The opening is a model of skilful scene setting and economy of expression:

> 1. *The Office of the Commissioner for the Western Sector*
> At about four o'clock on the morning of the nineteenth day of the second month of the eighth year of Tempō there was a knocking at the gate of the office of the Commissioner for the western sector of Osaka. The office was situated to the west of the main gate of Osaka castle on the north side of Uchihonmachi-dōri just before it crosses the Honmachi bridge. Due to the famine

that had been going on for four years now they were kept constantly busy even during the night what with all the destitute
thieves and the people collapsing in the streets. The day before,
which had been a day for official business, the Commissioner Hori
Toshikata Lord of Iga had returned in a somewhat flustered state
from a conference with the officers of the eastern sector who
were on duty that month. He had immediately called for Yoshida
Katsuemon, a member of the mounted guard for the western
sector, and had had a long private discussion. As a result, the tour
of inspection that Hori was to hold between the two offices on
the nineteenth, today, as part of the ceremony for his taking up
the post, was cancelled. The order was given by one of Hori's
elders Nakaizumi Senshi that all guards at the office were to be
especially vigilant throughout the night, so that when there came
a knocking at the gate the guard on duty rushed out immediately
to demand the name and business of the man outside. (XV, 3)

Here we are given a full, compact account of the situation the night
before the uprising, with a mention of the famine, the worried state of
the Commissioner, the alerting of the guards, and the cancellation of an
important ceremony. The passage begins with a dramatic moment, the
time sequence then jumps abruptly back to a point in the past and then
advances again until it reaches the original moment of departure, so
encapsulating all the necessary information. It is this subtle use of time
that distinguishes the story from straightforward narrative and makes
for dramatic reading.

The knocking at the gate brings a letter for Hori from a Yoshimi
Kuroemon, informing him of the planned insurrection but consisting
mainly of excuses for the writer's own complicity. Hori finds himself
unable to take any firm decision on the matter and reveals an incompetence that is to mark the behaviour of the officials throughout the
conflict.

The second scene takes place at the office of the eastern sector
where the Commissioner Atobe proves to be just as procrastinating as
his counterpart. On Hori's recommendation he orders the arrest of two
of the conspirators, but the matter is badly handled and one man, Seta,
escapes to warn Ōshio that the plans have been leaked. We move next
to Ōshio's house and a detailed description of the preparations that
have been made and the men who make up his band. Two of the
members of Ōshio's household are then introduced and it is through
their conversation that the reader is first made fully aware of the
reasons behind the uprising. The concept of the unity of idea and
action which is central to the philosophy of Wang Yang Ming means

that there comes a point when the true sage must cleanse the rotten state by force. Ōshio in his idealistic fervour cannot see that the act will merely be a futile gesture by a few hundred men. Idealism will end in the pointless destruction of much of the city of Osaka and nothing will be achieved.

As the warning has been given there is nothing else Ōshio can do but order the plans to be set in motion, and the narrative at this point is interrupted by a long passage of interior monologue in which Ōshio himself contemplates on how and why matters have reached this stage. Through this self-examination we learn of the terrible famines, the disaster and distress among the people, the hoarding by the merchants and the uselessness of official measures. Things had become so bad that Ōshio felt he was betraying his beliefs and teachings by remaining inactive. Should he sit and do nothing, lecture the rich and the officials, or take their money and rice by force and distribute it to the poor? The latter seemed to be the only choice if he was to maintain his own integrity. The feeling is more one of being an agent of a mysterious process rather than a positive instigator: 'You could almost say that things had now come to such a pass by a natural process. I have not urged on the conspiracy myself; it has dragged me along with it. How on earth will it all end, he thought' (XV, 25).

Once the uprising gets under way we are given a series of scenes which reveal the haphazard nature of the rebel plans and the gross incompetence of the authorities when actually faced with the crisis. The man who proves to be their salvation is Sakamoto Gennosuke who virtually takes charge of the defensive operations. It soon becomes clear, however, that the rebels will not succeed in their main aim which is to rouse the ordinary populace to follow them. Riot, plunder and destruction by fire seem to be the only outcome. Ōshio realizes the end is near:

> Heihachirō had a bench set up at the southern end of the Namba bridge, told Shirai, Hashimoto and the other young men in his group to sit down beside him, and eat some of the rice balls he had brought with him. They could hear the rumble of the guns and watched the flames burning fiercely. He felt that sense of unutterable loneliness which up to now he had managed to resist. (XV, 31–2)

The manoeuvring and fighting continues, described from one side and then the other, until defeat is imminent. Ōshio disbands his followers and leaves the city. Travelling south to Yoshino, Ōshio and his son eventually shave their heads and return in disguise to the city. Run to earth a month later he kills his son and then dies in a grand gesture, setting fire to his room and committing suicide. The last chapter records the final decisions made at Edo together with details of rewards and punishments.

Ōgai's interest in the uprising as a historical and social phenomenon, and his sympathetic treatment of Ōshio in his misguided efforts, was carried over in a long appendix which was published in a different journal, *Mita Bungaku,* in the same month. In it he wrote:

> I have been interested in studying the affair of Ōshio Heihachirō ever since I borrowed a manuscript from Suzuki Motojirō. . .
>
> As the manuscript was mainly composed of hearsay I tried to extract the historical facts, but the haul was very meagre. In as much as the record was full of holes my imagination was spurred on.
>
> Then I read Kōda Shigetomo's *Ōshio Heihachirō* which makes use of the most sources and which gives the most detail of all the books that have actually been published on the subject. I also read the article of the same title by the same author which appeared in the journal *Shinshōsetsu.* Then, referring to an old map of Osaka and the official history of Osaka castle, I tried co-ordinating the given facts into a pattern both temporally and spatially.
>
> I was thus occupied with Ōshio Heihachirō the man for a fair length of time. . .
>
> Then I took the liberty of writing a piece called 'Ōshio Heihachirō' which appeared in the *Chūō Kōron.* Heihachirō's uprising occurred on the nineteenth day of the second month of the eighth year of Tempō. I wrote about the events that happened on that one day adding some of my own conjectures to the historical facts. (XV, 59–60)

The appendix then continues with details of the verifiable events, a chronology of the main events in Ōshio's own life, a discussion of the reasons for the uprising, and a list of those who died. Discussing the reasons, he went into the famine conditions in detail and wrote of the man:

> If Heihachirō had been an individualist and had felt that he should let matters take their own course because differences between high and low, rich and poor, were part of some natural order, the riots would not have occurred.
>
> If it had been possible to work out a system of relief based on the state or the local authorities while maintaining social order he might well have worked out a kind of social policy. Although it was not possible for men like Heihachirō to advise the Bakufu, if he had been given some room to act in Osaka, which had developed a certain degree of autonomy stretching back to the

days before it had fallen into the hands of the Tokugawas, the riots would not have occurred.

Because both these channels were blocked, Heihachirō tried to fulfil his desires by destroying the social order. His philosophy was that of unawakened Socialism. . .

Heihachirō was a philosopher. But his philosophy of intuition gave birth neither to promising social policies nor the spectre of Socialism. (XV, 72–3)

By comparing Ōgai's version with the accounts by Kōda Shigetomo, Koizumi Kōichirō has shown that Ōgai changed the emphasis in a number of ways.[10] He was strongly critical of the authorities and their impotence in the face of crisis. The cowardliness of both commissioners is constantly alluded to and brought into relief at the very end of the story. This has in turn an effect on the treatment of Ōshio himself, a figure in whom he had been interested for some time. Ōshio is portrayed not so much as the instigator of an insurrection, a fomenter of revolution driven by hate for the rich and officialdom, but rather as a man who feels himself to be the instrument of fate driven to rebel more by historical accident than design. The effect of Ōgai's deep sympathy for Ōshio's predicament is to switch the major blame onto the system; the kind of absolutism which blocks any kind of unorthodoxy from finding satisfactory expression and which is bound to produce violent reactions. To blame the system rather than the rebel for the destruction of half the city of Osaka is an unusual approach but quite in tune with the Ōgai we have seen in 'Chinmoku no tō'. 'Ōshio Heihachirō' is in this sense a pungent comment on the times in which Ōgai himself was living.[11]

With 'Sakai jiken' (Incident at Sakai) published in February 1914, Ōgai turned to an incident which had taken place in his own lifetime, an incident which illustrated a vital turning point in the attitudes of common people towards their country. The action takes place in the early months of 1868 when the country is in turmoil, the Tokugawa Shogun has been defeated at a number of battles and the area around Osaka is for a time left with no civil government. Order in the closed port of Sakai has been entrusted to men of the Tosa clan. On 28 February a detachment of French troops are turned back at the entrance to Sakai because they do not hold the requisite passes. French marines then land in the harbour and during an altercation with the Tosa troops thirteen of the foreigners are shot and the rest retire in confusion. Although the French seem to have started shooting first, tempers were in fact roused by the absence of an interpreter and the subsequent misinterpretation of threatening actions.

As a result of the incident the French Consul Roches demands reparation and the execution of a number of Tosa men. An enquiry is set up and twenty-nine men, out of seventy, admit to having shot at the French. Twenty of these are to die and so lots are drawn. The condemned men, who are not samurai but ordinary enlisted soldiers, resent the implication that they have taken part in a criminal act: they merely obeyed orders and shot at the enemy. If they are to die for their country they demand to be allowed to die by *seppuku,* a request which is eventually granted. There are two crucial points here: firstly the men are aware that their lord is asking them to die for Japan, the Emperor's land (*kōkoku*), so that we are witnessing the moment when the allegiance of the common people moves imperceptibly from feudal lord to Emperor — and it is this shift which will enable General Nogi to die with his Emperor over forty years later; secondly common soldiers demand and receive rites due to a samurai, and such treatment immediately ensures they will be heroes. By an interesting twist of fate the style of their deaths will create capital out of defeat.

We now have the build-up for the splendid procession and the public exhibition of mass suicide in front of many dignitaries and the French Consul. Whether calculated or not, the grand display of courageous self-sacrifice has the effect of striking fear into the hearts of the French. The death of one of the men, Minoura, is described in detail:

> 'Listen to me, Frenchmen,' he said. 'I die not for you but for Imperial Japan! Mark well how a Japanese dies!' He loosened his dress, gripped his short sword with the point held downwards and thrust it deep into the left side of his stomach. Cutting down three inches he dragged it across to the right and then up again three inches. The blade had pierced deep and the wound opened wide. He threw away the sword, plunged his right hand into the wound, gripped his guts and pulled them out. He glared at the French. Baba drew his sword and brought it down on his neck but the cut was shallow.
>
> 'Baba! What are you doing!' he screamed. 'For God's sake keep calm!'
>
> The second blow snapped his neck with a crack. He screamed again, louder this time. They heard him several hundred yards away.
>
> 'Still alive! Again!'
>
> The French Consul who had been watching it all from the start was showing signs of shock and fear. Already ill at ease on his seat he jumped up in alarm at this sudden scream.
>
> Baba managed to sever the head completely at the third attempt. (XV, 191–2)

As a result of being subjected to such a shocking sight the French Consul hurries out after only eleven men have died. The proceedings are halted while explanations are sought. The Consul eventually asks for clemency for the remaining men which is in turn granted. There is here another twist of irony, for the pardon is agony for those who have seen their companions die. Their tragedy is further compounded by their miserable end. Reprieved, they lose their special status as samurai and return to Tosa to be banished to some remote area. They are again men who have broken some law. In this story, which was based very closely on a record of the incident entitled *Senshū: Sakai Rekkyo Shimatsu*, Ōgai stresses again the feeling of men at the mercy of events, caught up in a historical process they cannot comprehend. His unerring eye has picked out another of those moments in history where various forces combine and pivot to effect far-reaching changes.

With the possible exception of one other work, 'Kuriyama Daizen', which is written on similar lines to the works described above, 'Sakai jiken' marks the end of a certain genre of writing peculiar to Ōgai. The stories written after this date and before he settled into fully fledged biography, works like 'Sanshō Dayū' and 'Takasebune' that will be discussed in the next section, are quite compatible with the usual designation 'historical fiction'. They are set in a recognizable period in the past and are realistic in that the norms of historical and geographical reality are not violated; but their characters, their dialogue, actions and inner thoughts are by and large treated with a great deal of freedom. In a word, they conform to our normal expectations of fiction. The later biographies can be safely treated as being primarily historical in intent, although, as will be seen, Ōgai's idiosyncratic habit of shifting himself as author in and out of his work does give some pause for thought. The real problem occurs with the works from 'Okitsu Yagoemon' to 'Sakai jiken'. These works cause many difficulties of literary interpretation because, even at a cursory glance, they raise fundamental questions as to the distinction between literature and history which are not easily solved. They stick so closely to the historical 'facts' as Ōgai found them in his sources — characters, speech, thought and actions included — that one really hesitates to use the word fiction at all. We are up against the same problem that Defoe's *Journal of the Plague Year* and, to take a more modern example, Truman Capote's *In Cold Blood* presents critics of the novel.

There can be little doubt that part of the problem is the inadequacy of present terminology. All these works are known in Japanese as *rekishi shōsetsu* (historical stories) a phrase which is so widely appli-

cable as to be almost useless. A term which can encompass 'Okitsu
Yagoemon', Bulwer Lytton's *Rienzi* and Manzoni's *I Promessi sposi*
in the same breath is not too nice a critical tool. Much of the muddled
thinking about these works of Ōgai's would be dispelled if they were
recognized from the outset to be 'historical reconstructions' designed
to keep as close as possible to the historical facts while giving a vivid
representation of a moment of particular significance. Ōgai himself
knew very well the problems to which they would give rise, and he
discussed the nature of these works in an essay entitled 'Rekishi sono
mama to rekishi-banare' (History as it is and history altered) in
December 1974:

> There is discussion even among my acquaintances as to whether
> or not my recent works which treat historical figures are *shōsetsu*.
> This is, however, very difficult to judge at a time when there are
> few scholars either dedicated to normative aesthetics or prepared
> to define the nature of a *shōsetsu*. I myself realize that in what I
> have written up to now there is a great disparity in the degree to
> which I have dealt objectively with my material. . .
>
> . . .the kind of works that I have mentioned above are different
> from anyone else's *shōsetsu*. This is because it is usual to adopt
> and reject facts freely and to have an ordered plot, neither of
> which can be found in my works. When I wrote the play *Nichiren
> Shōnin Tsujizeppō* I combined the much later proposals for saving
> the nation with his earlier street sermonizing in Kamakura. In my
> more recent works I have totally rejected such methods.
>
> Why is this? The motives are simple. Firstly I felt like investi-
> gating historical materials and I set much store by the 'nature' I
> found there. I disliked changing it for no good reason. Secondly
> I noticed how modern writers were writing about their own lives
> quite candidly: if it was all right to portray the present as it is, it
> could also be done with relation to the past, I thought. . .
>
> There are some of my friends who say that whereas other
> writers treat matters with 'feeling' I treat matters with 'intellect'.
> But this is something common to all my work and is not limited
> to those stories in which I treat historical figures. In the main my
> work is Apollonian rather than Dionysian. I have never tried to
> write a Dionysian work. If there is anything at all that I have
> striven for it would be to bring an objectivity to my writing.
> (XXVI, 508–9)

The strong desire not to meddle with historical fact was a healthy
attitude for a man of medicine and science, but not one usually associated with a writer. It also, of course, contrasts with his earlier view of
literature as expressed in 'Shōsetsuron' of 1889. The central theme is
clear; these reconstructions were written in an effort to bring alive a

series of events, to capture and illustrate a number of important incidents. In this case he may be said to have succeeded well, but they do lie right on the borderline between literature and history. Novels and stories are often separated from biography and history along the dividing line between fact and fiction, but such criteria would place these works by Ōgai on the historical axis, whereas the aesthetic experience of actually reading them suggests the contrary. In any case, recent advances in the theory of literature have shown that the concept of fictionality is quite unacceptable as the major determinant of literature. Neither can mere factuality be the measure of history. Hayden White in his recent book *Metahistory* presents a convincing case for the historian as artist and for historiography as an essentially poetic act subject to the same laws that govern literary narratives. He defines history as follows: 'a verbal structure in the form of a narrative prose discourse that purports to be a model, or icon, of past structures and processes in the interests of explaining them'.[12] Such a definition would easily accommodate a work like 'Abe ichizoku' and brings us no closer to distinguishing it from what, for want of a better word, we shall call history proper. Common sense, however, demands that some kind of distinction be made. Is there no clear line between these two kinds of narratives? Can we not perhaps define the nature of these stories with a little more clarity?

Ōgai's statement about bringing 'objectivity' to his writing does not really help us here for two reasons. Firstly the idea of historian as purely objective narrator is a myth; he is continually faced with subjective decisions in relation to his material and must distort reality to a certain extent in favour of clarifying his theme. Secondly there is no evidence to suggest that Ōgai was an objective recorder in any case, despite his claims to the contrary. It should be patently clear from the foregoing description that he is palpably present at every turn. One must also take into consideration the open bias of the sources that he chose to use. The *Abe Sajidan,* where he obtained most of his material for 'Abe ichizoku', was written primarily as an apologia for the Abe family and is openly prejudiced, as is the *Yamamoto Fukushūki,* written to commemorate the revenge. By their very nature all his sources bent historical fact to suit their themes. The account of the incident at Sakai reads very differently from the pen of Lord Redesdale; and Nakayama Gishu, a close friend of Yokomitsu Riichi, once recalled that 'Sakai jiken' had struck him as being 'as dry as dust'. He was moved to write an account of his own entitled 'Tosa hei no yūkan na hanashi' (1965) where the Tosa men were shown to be in the wrong.[13] We have also seen how Ōgai felt free to change the emphasis in a number of crucial ways. Ōoka Shōhei in his recent book on *rekishi shōsetsu*[14] has pointed out that Tsukamoto Matashichirō in 'Abe ichizoku' sends his wife to see the condemned family as part of 'sympathy', while himself loosening the fence between the two mansions as part of his 'duty'; this may be in reality a subtle ruse to put the Abe family off their guard. Ōgai thus shows Matashichirō in a good light. Similarly Bunkichi, the servant who joins the revenge party in 'Gojiingahara no katakiuchi', may well have been motivated not by an altruistic ideal but by the simple fact that he was out of a job and might secure himself a bright future if the revenge succeeded. Again a degree of partiality on Ōgai's part is inevitable.

If objectivity is no real guide then what of stylistic features? Can one argue that there are certain linguistic features of literary narratives which distinguish them from non-literary narratives? Perhaps the most impressive attempt to date to define the realm of literature on purely textual grounds is Käte Hamburger's *The Logic of Literature.*[15] Hamburger argues that fictive narrative statement is characterized by certain stylistic phenomena which clearly distinguish it from what she calls reality-statement, that is non-literary narrative. The most important of these features are the use of verbs of hoping and thinking with reference to the third person, and the technique of *erlebte Rede* (narrated monologue) with all its attendant signs, including the use of deictic adverbs of time and place with what appears morphologically to be verbs in the past tense, the best known example being the sentence 'tomorrow was Sunday' which Hamburger says can only occur in a literary narrative.

It has since become clear that these features that she claims are indicative of literary narrative are not definitive but merely commonly used. In other words there is nothing to stop the writer of a scholarly work of history using such techniques when he feels they will lend a vividness to the text. Hamburger's claim that the past tense of the verb loses its pastness in relation to real time and becomes instead a special narrative tense when used in a literary milieu is an important observation, but it does not really help us to decide in the initial stages whether we are reading a work of literature or not. The loss of pastness occurs when the reader becomes aware of the nature of the narrative he is reading. It cannot act as an initial marker. In this respect Hamburger's argument tends to be tautological.

In passing it may be of interest to mention that although her insight into the workings of narrative tense still stand, such features as *erlebte*

Rede can be better explained by the theory of a double text, that is the existence in all narratives of a narrator's text and a character's text which can often overlap in the same phrase and even in the same word, thus producing sentences like 'tomorrow was Sunday'.

It would seem, therefore, that there is no way of distinguishing between a real statement and a literary one by purely textual means. The account of the death of the samurai in 'Sakai jiken', for example, *could* appear in either kind of narrative. The fact that it uses dialogue, a notoriously unsafe form of historical truth, is no proof in itself that we are dealing with a literary text. Our distinction, if it is to be drawn, must come from some other source.

A recent article on this very subject by Mas'ud Zavarzadeh helps to shed light on this problem.[16] After a discussion of the traditional distinction of literature as fiction and history as fact, he introduces the term 'non-fictional novel', which he claims to be a distinct genre demanding its own critical approach. The fictional novel is usually self-contained and although the author draws on the real world for his material he transforms it so that the 'truth' of the finished work of art is generated from within; characters do not have a life outside the aesthetic boundary. The biography or history, on the other hand, as factual narration, refers outwards to the external world; their 'truth' depends very much on the world outside the confines of the work itself and the characters do have an independent existence beyond the verbal matrix. The newly proposed genre of 'non-fictional novel' operates between these two extremes and is a more complex phenomenon. Instead of referring only inwards or only outwards it operates on both levels at the same time and includes both aesthetic and factual 'truth'. What this means is that the nature of the work itself demands that we discard the idea of a novel as a purely aesthetic phenomenon existing on an entirely different plane to reality, and that we accept it as an open system. Here, in this concept evolved to explain certain developments in modern American literature, can be found the answer to the problem posed by the works of Ōgai now under consideration.

The key that allows us to determine what kind of narrative we are dealing with is the attitude of the author towards the facts. Fictive narratives of the kind we are most conversant with use facts to support and illustrate a particular interpretation of reality held by the author; the facts thus become subordinate to the fictional world created by the writer. History records the facts in order to understand them and give them a shape and pattern; the facts are thus all-important, for it is only through them that the historian can impose order on his world. The non-fictional novelist approaches facts in a similar way to the historian, but he does not believe in the existence of an order or essential truth within fact. Fact thus becomes an end in itself and the author refuses to foist upon reality a pattern he cannot apprehend. The aim is to describe reality as it is found and as a consequence the random nature and apparent meaninglessness of the world is brought into relief.

If this analysis is correct and Ōgai's novellas from 'Okitsu Yagoemon' to 'Sakai jiken' are of this type, then we would expect his approach to be equivocal and lacking somewhat in direction. What do they reveal about Ōgai's view of history? Is it static, dynamic, or possibly a Confucian conception of the past as the root and the touchstone of the present? It is instructive to use as a framework here Nietzsche's early classification of historical attitudes as put forward in the second *Untimely Meditation* entitled 'On the use and disadvantage of history for life'. Ōgai almost certainly read this particular essay[17] and in 'Rekishi sono mama to rekishi-banare' wrote of his attitudes to composition in Nietzschean terms.

Nietzsche, whose main concern was to define modes of historical consciousness in relation to their value for present and future life, outlined three basic kinds of history: Monumental, Antiquarian and Critical.[18] Monumental history, as the study of great men of the past, is creative when the great achievements of these men are stressed but destructive when, as is often the case, the past is romanticized and any possible future progress is lost sight of. Antiquarianism can be a matter of finding and rejoicing in one's own roots but can easily degenerate into a blind reverence for all that is old, a belief that the present is nothing but a consequence of its past, and a distrust of all change. Critical history, whereby the historian examines the past in as objective a manner as possible, lays all myths bare and is an excellent antidote to the depressive effects of the two previous attitudes, but can lead to a state of mind where nothing of worth is left either in history or the present. By measuring Ōgai's attitude in relation to these basic types it should be possible to analyse the nature of his view of the past and the reason he studied history.

A close reading of the works between 'Okitsu Yagoemon' and 'Sakai jiken' reveals that none of Ōgai's figures is heroic on the grand scale. Men are stubborn and willing to die when the occasion demands, showing admirable qualities of strength of character, but ultimately they are always at the mercy of the larger historical situation which they cannot hope to understand, let alone control. In this sense Ōgai's view of history is highly pessimistic; a literature of futile gestures. Men are not quite reducible to social formulae but every one of them is hemmed in and almost fated to act along predestined grooves. The voice of cold reason is always represented and one is left with the sneaking feeling that men like Yokota in 'Okitsu Yagoemon', Uhei in 'Gojiingahara no katakiuchi' and Utsugi in 'Ōshio Heihachirō' are right in their condemnation of the gesture which is to be carried out at all costs. From this angle the system and the counter gesture are both seen as absurdities, quite the opposite of a romantic, Monumentalist conception.

What of the Antiquarian approach? Certainly the revised version of 'Okitsu Yagoemon' is a definite step towards mere love of detail, scholarship for its own sake. But there is no blind reverence for the past in these works and the themes of such works as 'Abe ichizoku' and 'Ōshio Heihachirō' have clear and intentional relevance to the present. What we have in fact is reconstruction in the Critical mode, the laying open and critical analysis of myth, with exactly the attendant dangers that Nietzsche had foretold. The original attempt prefigured in 'Ka no yō ni' to divide myth from history and subject the latter to reasoned criticism had been accomplished only to lay bare a great emptiness. Reality in history turned out to be just as cruel and meaningless as reality in the present and the impasse reached was somewhat similar to that reached during the writing of 'Kaijin' two or three years earlier. If Ōgai was trying to use the past in the service of the present it seemed that there was an ironic confirmation of his own alienation. Whether it was Ōgai's preconceived ideas of history that made him study in detail a series of failures is difficult to decide, but one has the spectacle at this stage of a man who in his youth was convinced that he was playing an important role in a great historical movement but who now begins to be soberly aware that man is captive to an unknown and inscrutable fate. In a sense Ōgai himself was a being of futile gestures.

A further problem posed by this work is the vexed one of originality, although it must be recognized that a charge of unoriginality is almost meaningless in a non-Western literary environment, indeed in a pre-modern Western one. It is not possible after reading these vivid pieces to accuse Ōgai of a lack of imagination, but anyone who takes not only his characters, background, plot and even theme from historical reality as he finds it in his sources lays himself open to certain doubts. How much is creative and how much is merely reworking of a high quality? The least one can say is that Ōgai possessed a very sharp eye for the dramatic incident which his chosen form demanded, but as in the case of 'Gojiingahara no katakiuchi' there is a strong temptation to give the chief praise for the dramatic presentation to the writer of the original *Yamamoto Fukushūki*. A comparison of the text of the source with Ōgai's work reveals that much of Ōgai is almost pure rewriting into modern Japanese. In a sense this is inevitable given Ōgai's approach to his work and the way he restricted himself so tightly; if one is not going to invent history, then history itself, or the sources that represent that history as we find it, must be ultimately responsible for whether a certain incident or chain of events has historical or dramatic significance or not.

This approach to given fact could on occasions be turned to good use. Rewriting is even more starkly revealed in a non-historical work entitled 'Hatori Chihiro' that Ōgai wrote in July 1912, which is in essence a condensed and slightly altered version of a very long letter sent to him by a student of the same name, Hatori. Hearing that the student had died, Ōgai published his version of the letter, rewritten from *sōrōbun* into modern Japanese, as an act of commemoration. This extraordinary document in which a young man pours out his frustration at failure to his idol, Ōgai, is indeed reality in the raw and a moving experience. Here we have Ōgai grasping at drama in the very midst of life, preferring to *recognize* the significant element rather than invent it. The approach is surprisingly effective and very, very modern.

The concept of a non-fictional novel or novella which has simultaneous significance as an aesthetic object and as a statement about reality is not only of use in the confined area of these few works by Ōgai; it is also of help when approaching other works of modern Japanese literature, in particular the autobiographical *watakushi-shōsetsu*.[19] It has been the custom to condemn the ease with which many modern Japanese writers can slide from the aesthetic to the real world within a work of art. Criticized for ignorance of the true principles of art and for an inability to transform fully life into art, the *watakushi-shōsetsu* authors have come under attack for being artistic deviants who have wrought untold harm on modern Japanese letters. This characterization is both unfair and incorrect. There existed a mutual contract between author and public that reality was to play a large part in the appreciation of these works and the appeal of authenticity and sincerity of experience was paramount. There can be no doubt that the existence of such a contract led to some extreme cases where authors found themselves forced to play certain stereotyped roles in real life in order to be able to write at all, but the whole genre cannot merely be dismissed on grounds of distortion. Rather than condemning Shimazaki Tōson for muddling fiction and reality with such consummate ease in the novel *Shinsei*, this ability should be accepted and even prized as a feature of the genre. The difference between *watakushi-shōsetsu* and autobiography is exactly the same as that between the non-fictional novel and history. Indeed it would seem that the writers of such work shared with Ōgai a distinctive attitude towards literature and reality; fact, description for its own sake, and a distinct lack of interest in fictionality are hallmarks of much of modern Japanese writing. Rather than continually criticizing the Japanese of this period for their inability to write a proper Western novel, it would seem preferable to treat the literature on its own merits. To assume that Japanese writers even wanted to write such novels betrays at best a rather parochial attitude and at worst a species of cultural arrogance.

But to return to Ōgai. Although the marriage of artist and historian was admirably managed in most of these works it proved to be of short duration, ending indeed to all intents and purposes with 'Sakai jiken'. The unusual form of presentation that Ōgai chose was only amenable to the representation of particular moments of historical interest — moments where the historical process became crystallized and could be reconstructed in mid-flight. It was useless for the description of the process itself which is the more usual concern of the historian. As a result, when Ōgai's interest proved to be caught more and more by history and in particular certain historical figures this form had to be abandoned. The breakdown of this form into stories where the inventive impulse was given more rein on the one hand and into biographies where the drive towards the academic study of history was satisfied on the other was in this sense inevitable.

'Sakai jiken' thus presents an end and a beginning. There was little point in creating a repetition of what he had written if it were to prove merely the mirror of a desert. His interests turned from events to people, and his attitude from the ironic to the romantic. A strongly personal element was introduced into his work as he gave up trying to destroy myth and instead create it in the form of an idealized past: his own idealized concept of humanity in a historical framework.

Lyrical tales

The change in attitude that is revealed by the difference between 'Sakai jiken' and the next story, 'Yasui fujin' (Yasui's wife) was commented on by Ōgai in the essay 'Rekishi sono mama to rekishi-banare': 'Reluctant as I was to change the "nature" in history I somehow found myself fettered by history. I was groaning in pain under these bonds and so finally decided to cast them off' (XXIX, 509). 'Yasui Fujin' testifies not only to a much closer identification between author and subject but also to a significant shift in interest from event to personality, which brings with it a lyricism that has been absent since *Gan*. It is also of note that six out of eight of these tales have women as their central characters.

'Yasui Fujin' is a short account of the life of a Confucian scholar called Yasui Chūhei and his unusual wife Sayo. As a boy Chūhei is ugly, one-eyed and pock-marked like his father. As he grows up however he proves to be clever, and after studying in Osaka and Edo with the tenacity and discipline of a dedicated young scholar he returns to his home province to help his father teach. The father begins looking around for a wife, but he knows the problems he had himself on account of his ugliness and considers the task a difficult one. They eventually decide on a bright intelligent girl called Kawazoe Toyo who, however, refuses the proposal. The younger sister Sayo overhears this and tells her mother that she wishes to marry Chūhei instead. After some initial problems both sides agree and the strange match is made; the beautiful young sixteen-year-old girl becomes the wife of ugly Chūhei who is in his thirtieth year.

The rest of the story describes their very ordinary and uneventful life until Sayo dies at the age of fifty-one. She proves to be an ideal wife, constantly willing to sacrifice herself for her husband and looking after him as he studies, teaches and becomes a famous scholar. Ōgai was particularly impressed by her selfless devotion and the idyllic but spartan life the couple seemed to have lived. The story ends with Chūhei's death at the age of seventy-eight and is followed by an appendix which consists of a chronology and details of the remains of the Yasui family to be found in the Tokyo area.

Although Ōgai could check most of the facts in the story to be historically correct, gone is the sharp reality of 'Sakai jiken' and we are left with a fairy tale; an ugly man winning a beautiful bride who turns out to be the ideal wife. The conscious creation of a legend — that of the traditional loyalty and devotion of Japanese womanhood — is in stark contrast to the comparatively ruthless objectivity of the works that have gone before, and we are back, in a sense, with literature as the realm of the Beautiful.

'Sanshō Dayū' is a welcome return to the narrative technique used so successfully in 'Ōshio Heihachirō' which lends to Ōgai's best work a remarkable immediacy. The story was based on a tale in a collection of *sekkyō-bushi*[20] that had interested him for some time. Out of the bare bones he created a moving story of the separation of a mother from her children, and the self-sacrifice of the daughter so that the son might again find their mother. The story opens as the mother, two children and a maid set out on a journey from the north of Japan to see their exiled father in Kyushu. They do not realize that they are travelling through dangerous country where kidnapping is common. The local inhabitants are not allowed to take in travellers and so the group is forced to spend the night huddled out in the open.

From this point the narrative moves forward in a series of fourteen vignettes. Before the unfortunate family realizes what is happening they are deceived by a ship's captain and are kidnapped; the mother being sent to Sado, the children being carried off to the south, while the maid drowns. After some difficulty the captain manages to sell the children to a cruel task master in Tango called Sanshō Dayū. Befriended by one of the master's more humane sons, Jirō, but kept under constant watch and threatened with branding by the other son, Saburō, the little brother and sister are in the depths of despair. There is a vivid branding scene which turns out to be a dream, but the forehead of a statue of Jizō that the boy, Zushio, always carries with him is found to bear the scar of a brand.

When spring comes his sister, Anju, manages to get permission to go with her brother into the mountains to cut wood and while they are alone she persuades him to escape and look for their parents, promising to wait for his return.

> The two children hurried down the mountain. They walked much faster than before as if the girl's enthusiasm had somehow been transmitted by suggestion to her brother. They came to where the spring bubbled up. Anju got out a wooden bowl that was part of the lunch box she had brought and scooped up some of the clear water. 'Here's some *sake* to celebrate your departure,' she said taking a sip and handing it to her brother. He drank it off. 'Goodbye Anju,' he said. 'I'll get to Nakayama without being caught, you'll see.'
>
> Zushio ran the ten paces to the bottom of the slope, skirted the pond and came out on the main road. He hurried away upstream along the river Ōkumo.
>
> Anju stood by the spring watching him as his receding figure was now hidden now visible among the lines of pine trees. Although the sun was nearly at its height she did not bother to climb the mountain again. Luckily it seemed as though no one was cutting wood in this part of the hills that day, so there was nobody to scold her for standing on the path waiting for the time to pass.

Later when out looking for the children Sanshō Dayū's men picked up a little straw sandal by the edge of the pond at the bottom of the slope. It was Anju's. (XV, 680-1)

Zushio manages to escape detection with the help of nearby monks and eventually makes his way to Kyoto where he meets the Regent, Fujiwara Morozane, who has had a vision that the statue of Jizō the boy is carrying will cure his daughter's illness. Befriended by the Minister, Zushio is made Lord of Tango, returns to the area to punish Sanshō Dayū and erects a shrine by the pond in memory of his sister. This accomplished, he sets out to find his mother. The story ends with a moving scene where mother and son are reunited. He finds her sitting in the middle of a pile of millet, quite blind, and employed to keep birds off the grain. He finds her singing a song about him and his sister:

He stood transfixed and listened to the words with rapture. He had to clench his teeth to stop himself from crying out like an animal as his heart seemed to churn over. Suddenly he rushed in through the fence as if his bonds had been broken.

Scattering the millet with his feet he fell on his face in front of the old woman. With his right hand he raised the statue of Jizō to his forehead.

The old woman realised that something rather larger than a sparrow had just scattered the grain. She stopped her incessant chanting and stared unseeing in front of her. Then, like two dried shells steeped in water, her eyes became moist, and she opened them.

'Zushio!' she cried, and they embraced tightly. (XV, 687)

This small masterpiece was followed by a tale set in T'ang China entitled 'Gyogenki' (August 1915), an imaginative reconstruction of the life of the T'ang poetess Yu Hsuan Chi. The story, a typical example of Ōgai's narrative technique, begins with a bald statement: 'Yu Hsuan Chi was put into prison for murder', and then unfolds from a point much further back in the past, ending roughly where it begins. Destined to be a great poetess from her youth, Yu comes to the notice of another poet, Wen, who guides her in the art. Wen himself, a much older man, is a reluctant bureaucrat who is highly regarded for his poetry but is bitterly contemptuous of sycophancy. At the age of eighteen, famed for her beauty and her poems, Yu is sold by her parents to a man called Li, who also happens to be a friend of Wen. She succeeds in repelling Li's advances until he tires of her and decides to send her home. Yu however refuses to return in disgrace and so Li is given no option but to give her into the care of a Taoist temple.

It is while Yu is at the temple that she is initiated into various sexual practices and receives sexual awareness. The immediate result of this however is to draw her into a lesbian relationship with a fellow acolyte, Ts'ai P'in. When this latter runs off with a carpenter, Yu begins to take an interest in men, eventually falling desperately in love with a man called Ch'en. When this becomes widely known, her many suitors retire into the background. The tragic end of the relationship comes when she suspects Ch'en of having an affair with her maid. Partly out of jealousy and partly out of pique she strangles the maid one night and buries her in the garden. The body is found later, Yu is arrested and condemned to death. Wen, now an old man, cannot help her for he is living in a far-off province, but he is the most affected by her death.

Although Ōgai gave a long list of references at the end of the tale, subsequent research has revealed that he only used two books for background material, both collections of poetry, by Yu and Wen respectively, the first one of which he had been given by Sasaki Nobutsuna as early as 1904. He invented the episode with Li, the lesbian attraction to Ts'ai P'in, and indeed the whole theme of Yu's discovery of her own sexuality.[21] The plot of a famous T'ang poetess who is eventually condemned for murdering her maid is interesting enough in itself, so why did Ōgai add a kind of female *Vita Sexualis* touch?

The scholar Ogata Tsutomu has argued very cogently that this part of the story was suggested to Ōgai by the affairs of Hiratsuka Haruko (Raichō), one of the central figures of the feminist movement that founded the journal *Seitō* (Blue Stocking) in 1911 and whom we have already had occasion to mention in relation to Ōgai's wife Shige. Hiratsuka's private life had certain similarities to Yu's and many of the details were not exactly secrets in the literary world at the time. If this supposition is correct, it would be a revealing clue as to the nature of 'Gyogenki'. Historical detail is in this case used merely as clothing for a theme that could be set in any age; nothing could be further from a work like 'Ōshio Heihachirō' where the theme is history itself. 'Gyogenki' is thus a precursor of the later tales of Akutagawa and Kikuchi Kan.

The theme of woman's love and devotion that we have seen treated in both 'Yasui fujin' and 'Sanshō Dayū' forms the basis of another tale entitled 'Jiisan bāsan' (The old couple, September 1915), which is the story of a wife who waits thirty-seven long years until her husband returns from exile. This very short work also ends where it begins, starting with a description of the couple's reunion, retracing the story of the man's exile and concluding with the reunion again. In a similar continuation of themes, 'Saigo no ikku' (The last word), which was published in October 1915, is the portrait of a little girl who feels an innate drive to sacrifice herself for her father, just as Anju dies to help her brother in 'Sanshō Dayū'.

The basic material for 'Saigo no ikku' was a story from a collection entitled *Ichiwa Ichigen* compiled by a well-known collector of tales called Ōta Nampo (1749-1823), and Ōgai treats it with the freedom that we have come to expect in this particular group of works.[22] In 1738 an Osaka shipowner called Katsuraya Tarōbei is convicted of misappropriating part of a cargo of rice assumed lost in a shipwreck. When the family hears the sentence is to be death, the mother despairs, but the resourceful daughter Ichi decides to try and save her father. Early in the morning on the day after the news has broken she creeps out of the house with her brother and younger sister and takes a petition to the Commissioner on duty. Impressed by her unusually cool and fearless attitude the officials eventually decide to accept her petition for consideration.

Suspecting that the mother has put the children up to this escapade, the Commissioner holds an enquiry, but it turns out that it is all the genuine work of the daughter Ichi. Even a threat to the children that they will be killed in their father's stead is to no avail.

> 'Right. There's one more thing. If this exchange is granted you will all be killed immediately. You won't be able to see your father. Do you understand?'
>
> 'Yes,' she replied in the same cool tone as before. A moment later she added, as if it had just occurred to her, 'For the authorities would never make a mistake.' . . .
>
> Watching the children as they left the courtroom, Sasa turned to Ōta and Inagaki. 'The future looks grim, doesn't it,' he said. It was not the touching figure of the filial daughter nor the sight of the foolish children who had been egged on by others that he was thinking about, but those last words of Ichi's, cool as ice, sharp as a blade, which echoed in his mind. A Tokugawa official of the *Genbun* era would not of course know the Western word 'martyrium', nor was the Japanese translation *kenshin* to be found in dictionaries of the time, and so it was only natural that he did not recognize that there is a process of the human spirit, common to all, of the kind revealed in the daughter of Tarōbei the criminal. The spearhead of resistance which is latent in the act of self-sacrifice was deeply felt not only by Sasa who had actually talked with Ichi, but by all the officials present in the room. (XVI, 174-5)

That these 'last words' are the crux of the story is clear from the title, and research has shown that this section of the story is Ōgai's major addition.[23] Moreover the comment on 'the spearhead of resistance which is latent in the act of self-sacrifice' is of very great importance with reference to every one of Ōgai's historical works. Although the attitude of the author in the works after 'Sakai jiken' is extremely different from that in the earlier works, this phrase reveals that the paradox of self-sacrifice as a manifestation of individual will is a basic theme of all the stories from 'Okitsu Yagoemon' onwards. Whether subjected to critical appraisal or seen idealistically, the theme of all these works inevitably draws us back to the central passage of *Seinen* where Ōgai started to talk of the concept of 'altruistic individualism'.

Ōgai wrote two more stories in which he allowed himself free rein, 'Kanzan Jittoku' and 'Takasebune', before he took another turn and the shift from event to character came to its logical conclusion in biography. 'Kanzan Jittoku', which he said he wrote for his children, is an amusing account of a visit of a government official in China named Lu Ch'iu Yin to see the famous pair of living deities Han Shan and Shih Te who were serving in the monastery of Kuo Ch'ing. It brings out the pomposity of the official in lively contrast to the mad behaviour of the monks, but is a slight little work. 'Takasebune' on the other hand is a moving tale that deals with the problem of euthanasia. The scene is set on one of the boats that used to take criminals down from Kyoto to Osaka prior to exile to some distant island. The criminal, Kisuke, explains to a constable how his brother had fallen ill and, in order to bring his pain to an end, had tried to commit suicide by cutting his throat. Kisuke had returned home to find his brother still alive and, as an act of love, had pulled out the blade causing his brother to expire. Found standing by the bedside staring at his brother with the bloody weapon in his hand, he was arrested. The story ends as the boat glides smoothly on down the river with the contented Kisuke contrasted to the rather worried constable who cannot help wondering whether the man might have been in the right. The tale is given especial poignance when one remembers that Ōgai's younger brother, Tokujirō, died from a haemorrhage of the throat in 1908.

Biography as a form of self-expression

The move away from the unrestricted use of material back to the relatively severe historical perspective of a work like 'Sakai jiken' can be dated from 'Suginohara Shina', written in January 1916, but it was of course by no means as sudden as this might suggest. One most unusual story entitled 'Tsuge Shirōzaemon', composed in March 1915 between 'Sanshō Dayū' and 'Gyogenki', is quite different from these tales and already incorporates many of the elements of the later biographies. 'Tsuge Shirōzaemon' is a work in two parts; an account of the life and character of the man of the title who assassinated Yokoi Shōnan in 1869, followed by an explanation of the genesis of the text with further notes. As one learns from this latter account, Ōgai had known Shirōzaemon's son, Masataka, for some time. Masataka had been a university friend of Ōgai's younger brother Tokujirō. One day in October 1913 Masataka visited Ōgai and had a long discussion about his father; the first part of the work purports to be a record of this conversation.

The work that immediately suggests itself here is 'Hatori Chihiro', as there are similar motives at work in both these stories; but it will be seen that 'Tsuge Shirōzaemon' is more complex and operates on a number of different levels. The main thread is the account of Shirō-zaemon, which quickly takes on the aspect and atmosphere of a reconstruction like 'Abe ichizoku'. This is prefaced and interwoven with a commentary on the historical and social processes at work in the late Bakumatsu–early Meiji period, with particular emphasis on the split between those who knew they had to open the country and those who blindly believed the barbarian had to be expelled. It soon becomes clear that much of this short but acute treatment of the various psychological factors at work during this crucial period of Japanese history is the work of Ōgai and probably has very little relationship to Masataka's actual conversation. It is possible, therefore, to study the work on this level and discuss Ōgai's view of the Restoration.[24] Such a study tends to confirm the view that when Ōgai viewed history in the cold light of reason he found himself an unwilling determinist.

The first part of this work is presented through a fully personalized Masataka so that when we reach the point where his father dies the emphasis is changed to allow the son to speak directly about himself to the reader. He explains how social pressure on him and his family, as descendants of a criminal, has led to failure after failure. He is obsessed by a desire to clear his father's name by putting the whole matter into its correct historical perspective, for only then will Shirōzaemon's act be seen to be lacking any intrinsically evil intent. While this is ostensibly an apologia for those men who were convinced that their duty lay in expelling rather than welcoming the barbarian, an implicit underlying motive for Masataka's wish to clear his father's name must also be that it will also be an apologia for himself. This theme of a son's love-hate relationship with his father merges with an exposition of the historical perspective, chiefly provided by Ōgai, to form a first part of some complexity.

A totally new element is added in the second half of the work where Ōgai's sympathy for the son Masataka is clearly delineated, thus shifting the emphasis once again. 'Tsuge Shirōzaemon' is thus an intricate merging of many cross currents which are extremely difficult to define. The overall effect of the different viewpoints and the change from reconstruction to explanation and thence to a mere appendix of notes is unsettling to say the least. There is also a willing abandonment of some of the artist's most effective tools. The work begins with a sentence full of possibilities: 'Tsuge Shirōzaemon was my father.' If the reader knows of Tsuge as an historical figure and, having not read the second part of the work, believes that the author is Ōgai and Ōgai alone, then this sentence can be seen as an interesting literary device. But Ōgai is very careful to shatter the illusion immediately, the next sentence reading '(It will be revealed who "I" is later).' This has the suspicious hallmark of a mere second thought and has the effect of not only breaking the initial impact, but also immediately transferring the interest away from the story which follows and onto the storyteller. This constant habit of referring back to the narrator, usually Ōgai himself, is common to most of the works that will now be discussed. At the worst this creates the impression of an author irritatingly aware of himself, but at its best it can create an unusually intimate dialogue between writer and reader.

The work where the final change becomes apparent and Ōgai the historian reasserts himself is 'Suginohara Shina', written between 'Takasebune' and his most famous work of later years, *Shibue Chūsai*. Although it might be argued that the idealization of traditional woman and the overt sympathy for his characters carries through from the lyrical stories that precede it, the form of the work marks a definite break.

Just as has been the case with 'Tsuge Shirōzaemon' there is perennial discussion among Japanese critics as to whether 'Suginohara Shina' is a *shōsetsu* or not. The first and lasting impression of this work, however, is of a lecture in which the author is speaking personally to the audience. Not only is the motive for its composition primarily historical, but Ōgai indulges throughout in a direct conversation with the reader. It begins with an explanation in the first person of how the work came to be written. Ōgai happened to read a historically incorrect account, a popular misconception, concerning a concubine by the name of Takao. She was supposed to have lived with the daimyo Date Tsunamune, who had succeeded his father as head of the family in 1658 but then had to endure some fifty years of house arrest in Shinagawa. The real concubine's name was Suginohara Shina. Rather than recapitulate the exhaustive research of Ōtsuki Fumihiko on this subject, Ōgai is content to point out that the story he has read is erroneous.

After this factual opening Ōgai begins to expand on his sympathy for both the daimyo who was forced to live such an unnatural existence for so long, and the concubine who proved so loyal a companion and yet managed to live under the same roof as Tsunamune's wife. We are introduced to the main outline of Tsunamune's arrest and the kind of life he led under house arrest, and it becomes clear that Ōgai was particularly interested in how the daimyo had consoled himself in his political impotence by immersing himself in the arts:

> I felt like writing about Tsunamune who was a mere onlooker during the disturbances at Date. My interest was aroused by his mental attitude as a man forced to remain a purely objective bystander, utterly powerless to act in such external matters. I wanted to lay bare both the elegant and gentle Hatsuko and the intelligent Shina who seemed to have such a strong personality. I wanted to reconstruct the tensions underlying the serenity of this triangular relationship. But I eventually abandoned this plan, hindered as I was by a lack of imagination and my constant habit of sticking to historical facts. (XVI, 220)

Whether 'Suginohara Shina' remains a short speculative excursion because Ōgai did not have the historical sources to hand, or just because he felt that there was little sense in repeating what the scholar Ōtsuki had already done in detail, is difficult to decide. What is more important is that, given the material, the emphasis is now not upon events but upon human relationships, and it is in this sense that this work is a direct forerunner of *Shibue Chūsai* which was begun some months previously but started serialisation in January 1916. Although the outstanding feature of the historical works written after this date is the constant attempt to present biography in as objective a manner as possible, it remains a fact that their value as literature is heavily dependent upon the degree to which the author identified with his subject and managed to impart life into what would otherwise be a straightforward piece of historical research.

Shibue Chūsai is an account of the life of a Tokugawa Confucian (1805–58), a retainer of the Tsugaru daimyos who were based at Hirosaki in present day Aomori-ken and whose main interests were medicine and literature. Consisting of 119 'chapters' designed for newspaper serialization, the work can conveniently be divided into five sections: introduction (1–9); account of Chūsai's life, his teachers and his companions (10–53); a discussion of his habits, hobbies and philosophical beliefs (54–65); the story of his family, and in particular his wife, with emphasis on the problems brought by the Meiji Restoration and the gradual loss of status (66–106); and lastly an account of the two children who were still alive in 1916 (107–119). It will be seen at a glance that the structure is unusual and covers much more than just the biography of one man.

It is Ōgai's introduction to this work that gives it the particular vitality that marks it off from other similar biographies, setting a tone of intimacy between writer, reader and subject that governs the whole. Beginning with a commentary on a poem of resignation written by Chūsai in his thirty-seventh year, a poem which is close in feeling to a number of Ōgai's own compositions written during this period, it develops into a skilfully constructed description of an intellectual hunt. The reader is taken bodily through the process by which Ōgai came to learn of Chūsai and set about searching for the facts of his life. As part of his research for the historical stories already treated, Ōgai had collected copies of the lists of feudal officials compiled by the Shogunate and known as *Bukan*. Finding that many of them had Chūsai's seal on them, Ōgai embarked on a series of enquiries which revealed that Chūsai was not only a physician but also had a great interest in books and was a proponent of the tradition of rigorous textual criticism (*kōshōgaku*), which Ōgai considered one of the most important achievements of Tokugawa intellectuals. It is as if Ōgai has found a man of almost identical interests as his own:

> Then I thought as follows. Chūsai was both a physician and a government official. He read books of a philosophical nature such as the Confucian classics and the Taoist texts, but he also read history and books of an artistic nature such as collections of poetry. In fact we were very similar. The only difference was one of time in that our paths had never crossed. But no, wait. There was one important difference. Chūsai had reached a position where he was actually established as a researcher into both philosophy and the arts, whereas I had not been able to escape the confines of an inconsistent dilettantism. Looking at Chūsai I could not help feeling ashamed.
>
> Chūsai had walked a similar path to mine, but I had not the measure of his healthy stride. He was far better equipped than I was. He was a man I had to hold in awe.
>
> But strangely enough he had not always marched down the main highway; he had from time to time frequented the byways too. He had not only hunted out Sung versions of the classics but he had also played around with old *Bukan* and maps of Edo. If we had been contemporaries our sleeves might well have brushed

over the mud-boards of some back street. Thus there grows an intimacy and affection between us. (XVI, 268–9)

As in the case of 'Tsuge Shirōzaemon' there was another more immediate connection. The search for information had led to a meeting between Ōgai and Shibue's son, Tamotsu, on whose notes, documents and general knowledge the major part of the work was based.

After a treatment of a number of Chūsai's contemporaries, especially those who had great influence on him such as Ichino Meian and Kariya Ekisai in textual research, Isawa Ranken and Ikeda Keisui in medicine and Tani Bunchō, Nagashima Gorōsaku and Ishizuka Jūbei in the artistic field, we are taken in more or less chronological progression to the point where Chūsai marries his fourth wife, Io. There is then his audience with the Shogun in 1849, the problem of his rather wayward son Yasuyoshi, and then Chūsai's sudden death from cholera in 1858. Here, at chapter 65, after a short discussion of the theory behind *kōshōgaku*, his attitude to the Emperor and the question of the possible threat of foreign invasion, we leave the central figure and move on to his family.

While continuing to see the history in terms of Chūsai himself by the simple expedient of numbering the years from his death, Ōgai gives us a picture of the family throughout the troubled years of the Restoration. Io manages to keep everyone together except Yasuyoshi who shows no sign of repenting. There are great problems of readjustment when that part of the clan resident in Edo is called back to Hirosaki in the first year of Meiji. Eventually as the new era progresses we have the irony of seeing Yasuyoshi succeed as a local bureaucrat in the new government while the more serious son, Shigeyuki (later Tamotsu), finds great difficulty in pursuing his study of English.

Apart from the valuable annalistic record of a family from 1805 to 1916, *Shibue Chūsai* contains much information about other figures connected with the Shibues, and about a number of important cultural questions of the day, in particular the advances in the study of medicine. But none of this can account for the great reputation of this work which is often cited as being Ōgai's masterpiece. The reasons must be sought elsewhere.

The first point is that at this stage, in great contrast to the biographies that were to follow, Ōgai is not yet the totally dispassionate historical researcher he would like to be, and for this we must be thankful. *Shibue Chūsai* is sufficiently close to the spirit of the 'lyrical tales' to partake of their idealism, for Ōgai's sympathy for his characters is open and unequivocal. It is ironic that it is precisely this element of personal involvement that gives life and breath to *Shibue Chūsai* which he tried rigorously to exclude from the rest of his work. The interest that Ōgai must have felt in the figures and relationships he was delineating was suppressed in future works as part of a conscious objectivity.

The result of this strong bond between author and subject is that certain subtle yet discernible liberties are taken with the sources as his disposal. Research has revealed how the tone is so changed as to make Chūsai and his wife Io appear more modern, in that their reactions to certain realities and events are phrased so that the feudal aspect is dimmed and they appear in a stronger, more individualistic light.[25] This is true especially in the case of Io who is portrayed as an extremely unusual woman of great strength. Father, mother and the two sons are perfectly natural historical creatures yet tinged with idealism. As has been argued above, this does not invalidate the work as history, but it gives certain extra qualities which make it reasonable to discuss *Shibue Chūsai* in terms of its literary significance. It is seen in Japan to have almost the aspect of a novel, a family chronicle, by virtue of the strength of the central characters and the activity of the author within the work itself. Taking into consideration the aspect of Ōgai's dialogue with the reader over the very process of research, which is not peculiar to this work alone, a further dimension is added.

This approach to the biography is in agreement with the more fluid concept of the nature of historical fact and fiction that characterizes the 'non-fictional' novel mentioned earlier. But the chief drawback of the work would seem to be the slack format due to the pressing demands of serialization. Many of the interesting anecdotes are crowded into certain sections leaving others a little dry, and information discovered in the process of composition had to be inserted wherever possible. It has been argued that this binds the work tighter together[26] but, if this is indeed the case, it was quite involuntary.

A more interesting approach to *Shibue Chūsai* is that it was not so much a disguised novel as, in a sense, disguised autobiography. By studying the life of a man in the past who could almost have been himself, he could maintain the distance and perspective between author and subject that seems to have been a major necessity for him. Not finding it possible to study either himself or his family with the objectivity he demanded – as Tōson was to do in *Yoakemae* some years later – he threw all his energies into recreating the story of a family who had had similar problems to his own during the Restoration, and the life of a man who had managed to work to the full within a framework and set of restrictions far greater than any Ōgai had to battle with. It was thus a reflection upon his own life. He found in the not too distant past a man who had known his own limitations and controlled the eternal malcontent within him, immersing himself in the 'demands of the present'. This was the prime motive for his idealization of the characters he found.

It is important not to forget, however, that to a certain extent this great appeal of *Shibue Chūsai* is unintentional. As will be seen from the rest of his biographies his aim was to write unadulterated history, to put down on paper the results of historical research in as objective a manner as possible. In the next long work, *Isawa Ranken,* Ōgai was careful to suppress the expression of any sympathy or value judgement as he purposely moved out of the realm of imaginative literature and into the sphere of plain academic research.

One short work written as an outcome of his study of Chūsai was 'Juami no tegami' (May–June 1916), which is an interesting experiment in the presentation of the results of research but little more. It is based on a long letter from Nagashima Gorōsaku, otherwise known as Juami, to a Kuwabara Hitsudō, a letter which was mentioned in the twenty-second chapter of *Shibue Chūsai,* and Ōgai takes the reader through from start to finish using it as an introduction to the host of figures mentioned therein. This commentary, which yields much of interest to the historian in this particular field, continues for nine chapters. The next twenty-two chapters deal with the life of Juami, centring on the question of the relation of his family to that of the Mitō daimyos and revealing Ōgai's meticulous approach to research. Although there are moments when one becomes infected by Ōgai's enthusiasm for his study and his delight in visiting and discovering the relics of the past, the work never comes alive and any vitality that Juami might have to offer is buried in the factual detail.

With the monumental *Isawa Ranken* which took well over a year to serialize Ōgai concentrated all his energies on the biography of Shibue Chūsai's teacher. In this work Ōgai succeeded in detaching himself from his material while at the same time preserving the presence of the author within the work; fully integrated into the main flow of the narrative is a dialogue between Ōgai and the reader about the sources used and the process of research, but the facts are allowed to speak for themselves. Chapters 1 to 194 treat Ranken, with frequent lengthy excursions into his travels and his relationships with many famous men of the time, in particular Rai Sanyō, Kan Chazan, Ikeda Keisui and Hōjō Katei. The second half, from chapter 195 to 368, treats the history of his son, Shinken, his grandson Hakuken and his great grandson Tōken who died in 1875. In construction it seems very similar to *Shibue Chūsai*, but it is three times the length, much looser in composition and lacks the memorable characters that make *Shibue Chūsai* something more than mere history. The effect is of a huge canvas rather than a family portrait. The canvas depicts a whole complex of human relationships and is a mine of historical information, most of it accurate, about a certain section of society in Tokugawa Japan. This said, however, it is extremely doubtful that anyone who had no particular interest in the period would ever read it for pleasure; it is by no stretch of the imagination anything more than unashamed scholarship. During the serialization and also after the conclusion of *Isawa Ranken* in September 1917 Ōgai wrote one more long work entitled *Hōjō Katei*, in which he succeeded in confining himself to one man and avoided the excessive spread that had made *Isawa Ranken* so unaccountably long, and four short sets of biographical notes. 'Tokō Tahei' (January 1917), the shortest, is a description and careful dating of two episodes in the life of a retainer of the Hosokawa family. 'Saiki Kōi' (September–October 1917) is another very typical blend of past fact and present research in which Ōgai sketched the life and habits of a Tokugawa patron of the arts and theatre-goer. Having first come across the name in a *ninjōbon* of Tamenaga Shunsui, he then found that Saiki had a close connection with the house that he bought for his father's retirement and where he had lived ever since – the Kanchōrō. 'Kojima Hōso' (October 1917) treats the life of a man of letters who was mentioned in *Shibue Chūsai*, but reveals an irritating self-consciousness about the problem of boring the reader. Probably the most interesting of these works is 'Suzuki Tōkichirō' (September 1917) which represents a return to many of the elements we have seen in 'Tsuge Shirōzaemon'.

The prime motive of this work is ostensibly to help a living relative of the subject correct a false and injurious public impression of an ancestor. This piece of research is highly unusual, however, in that the question revolves around whether or not Suzuki was an *eta*. This theory, which must have been a terrible blight on his descendants, was given currency by the account of Suzuki Tōkichirō in a story (*kōdan*) written by a teller of battle stories called Matsubayashi Hakuen (1812–55). Approached by one of Suzuki's descendants with a written refutation of the story, Ōgai decided that the matter needed further research and so set about examining all available sources both written and verbal in an attempt to get to the truth. There is no doubt that a truer picture of the man emerges, but it is a lifeless work. It soon emerges that Ōgai cannot find any definite proof that Suzuki was not an *eta* any more than he can prove he was; the corollary of this is that Ōgai is far more interested in the practical problems posed by the research than the man behind his studies, and this is where the work differs so markedly from 'Tsuge Shirōzaemon'. More than any other work that Ōgai ever wrote this demonstrates the disturbing consequences of depersonalized writing and strengthens the hand of those who argue that Ōgai's study of history ended in a sterile world of unemotional reportage.[27]

Ōgai himself was very much aware of how little his work was either read or appreciated at the time. The reaction was so strong that he received a number of abusive letters accusing him of having no thought for the reader and totally lacking commonsense. In the face of such complaints he was characteristically passive and said defensively: 'I do not like theorizing as to whether I serve any useful purpose by writing these historical biographies or not. I just write them because I want to' (XXVI, 547). However he was also aware of the danger of producing work that was neither good literature nor good history; as he phrased it in *Tokō Tahei*:

> . . . In this case that would leave just five years until the fall of Haranoshiro in Kanei 15, and during this period Musashi probably had audience with Tadatoshi and at that time picked out Tahei. At least this is what I am proposing. If this were a novel I would just date it thus and not bother about the above explanation.
>
> I have here revealed the process of thought that I employed when writing my *rekishi shōsetsu*.
>
> A historian might well criticize my self-indulgence at this point, but a novelist would probably laugh at me for being hidebound. There is a Western proverb – to sleep between two beds [*sic*]. I often look back at myself and feel it applies to me. (XVIII, 6–7)

Of his actual aims there is little doubt. He wished, as he wrote at the end of *Isawa Ranken*, to construct as objective and factual a picture as possible of his subject and leave all questions of character and any value judgements to the reader. Criticism and choice was reserved for the sources only. In the advertisement for the three biographies, *Shibue Chūsai, Isawa Ranken* and *Hōjō Katei*, he wrote:

> Mori's aim has been to study the records of the *kōshōgaku* scholars in Japan from the Bunka-Bunsei era to the Tempō era. . . The author can guarantee that these three books are written from letters and documents of the time and that there is not one loose phrase. (XXXVIII, 316)[28]

What this amounts to is a rejection of all that literary artists usually hold dear – the ability to control and guide their readers in the attempt to create a wholly believable fiction. It was in effect a repudiation of any attempt to produce imaginative literature, the very thing that he had studied with relish abroad and done more than most of his contemporaries to revive in Japan.

What then, as historical research, do these works offer apart from a valuable mine of information? It would seem that despite Ōgai's depth of understanding of the West and Western literature, they reveal very strong influence from Chinese annalistic writing. Apart from the fact that many passages are quotations in *kambun* which is inevitable in view of the subject being Tokugawa intellectuals, the style and construction is a throwback to those Chinese histories that he read as a youth. This means that to the average Western taste they appear somewhat flat, lacking not width but depth. The effect of the style, however, which is a model of clarity, is of short sentences piled up in logical progression to produce unusual drive and chronological momentum.

Within this framework Ōgai's special gift is that of a conscientiously 'scientific' approach to his sources. He claimed that one of the reasons he began writing the biographies was that he was dissatisfied with those he had read. To him they lacked the careful appraisal of sources that he saw as the basis of good history, an opinion which is evident in his admiration for the Tokugawa *kōshōgaku* scholars. History, however, is not so much a scientific as a rational act, and one can see here that rational spirit of enquiry that he had fought for in his youth. There is good reason to believe that his approach to the practical problems of the study of history were somewhat in advance of many of the so-called professional historians in Japan at the time.

As one must assume that Ōgai understood exactly what he was rejecting, the question of why he turned away from a life-long interest is crucial, not only to an understanding of the man but also the period in which he lived. With the advantage of the perspective of his past life and activities the question can be seen to be a basic one in the study of Ōgai. He fought within himself a constant battle to justify to himself the significance of fiction in the modern world, a significance which a writer like Sōseki had grasped almost intuitively. The story of Ōgai's literary experience is one of continual strain between artist and intellectual; the uncomfortable feeling that fiction might well be incompatible with his own sense of intellectual honesty. *As if* had failed and so in the end had the attempt to idealize the past. This is not to say that he despised fiction. To say that would be to fly in the face of much of his work as author and as translator, which was after all his main claim to fame during his lifetime. Despite a good appreciation of the nature of fiction, however, he revealed the extent to which he was very much part of his age; problems of life came to predominate over questions of art and amid the strains that were necessarily part of the modern Japanese experience reality was writ so large that fiction paled into insignificance. One is left with the picture of the ideal Confucian mentality; literature should in the last analysis be in the service of a wider cultural organism and the duty of the intellectual was the cultivation of that delicate plant. History to such a man takes the place of religion and provides a solid foundation for the present; one begins to see why he felt such a strong attraction to his spiritual forebears. The attitude towards history has moved from the critical, through the romantic and finally to the antiquarian.

In a letter written to Yamada Tamaki on 5 June 1919 Ōgai discussed the improbability of Japan yet rivalling the West in the scientific or medical field but expressed the hope that great work might be done in an area such as the study of Chinese thought, where the Japanese had a head start. He ended the letter on a rather sombre note: 'I did say above that I thought there was a possibility of becoming a great writer. But on second thoughts this too might well be impossible; there are too many restraints in Japanese society to allow a writer to develop his full potential' (XXXVI, 540). As a man deeply concerned about the damaging effects on the healthy growth of the nation's culture of undue social restraint Ōgai was for ever in a cleft stick. His careful and painstaking research into the lives of men such as Shibue Chūsai and Isawa Ranken was an expression of this concern. A certain amount of reassurance could be gained from the very act of reaching back and ratifying the past.

8

THE LAST YEARS

Apart from the occasional offer of his resignation over administrative matters, Ōgai's official life from 1907 to 1916 when he occupied the highest post of his profession, was generally uneventful. Most of his energy was absorbed in creative writing and historical research where he clearly found himself much at ease. It is difficult to assess with any certainty when he finally decided to retire, but the first real sign of weariness comes in a Chinese poem written on 18 July 1915 and sent to Kako Tsurudo on the 30th. It is full of a sense of ending and a hint that he had never really managed to come to terms with his frustration:

> As a boy I was the wonder of the world;
> Why when the road was long did I weary at the halfway mark?
> Three years abroad measuring the snow like a disciple of Ch'eng I,
> Then twice in battle I managed to avoid a soldier's death.
>
> To speak one's mind when drunk invites another's anger,
> And my feeble efforts are met with others' ridicule.
> Above all my love of office weakens with the advancing years,
> Glancing back to that promise made on leaving home.
>   (XIX, 601–2)

On 16 September 1915 a report of his impending retirement was carried in the magazine *Fujin Tsūshin* and he was besieged by reporters to whom he strenuously denied the rumour. It is clear, however, that it was only a matter of time and on 22 November he formally applied to the Vice-Minister Ōshima. On 20 March 1916 he wrote to Kako reporting that the date had been fixed for 13 April. Eight days later on 28 March his mother, who had been ailing for some time, died at the age of seventy-one. It was in many ways appropriate that she should leave him as he himself left an institution to which he had given the major part of his life and which he had joined partly for her sake. One might be tempted to mark an end to Ōgai's life at this point were it not for the energy with which he continued his historical research.

On Ōgai's retirement from the army the question arose as to what post he might then be appointed to. As early as 6 December 1915 Ōgai wrote a letter to his former superior Ishiguro Tadanori which makes it clear that a suggestion of a possible seat in the House of Peers had been made, and we know from the letters of Kako Tsurudo, which have only recently seen the light of day,[1] that his lifelong friend also tried his best to exert his influence with Yamagata and others to obtain such a favour. For a time indeed the proposal seemed almost certain to take effect, and although there is no reliable information on Ōgai's attitude it is difficult to believe that he would have been strongly averse to such recognition of his work. A mention of his possible election appeared in the newspapers for 8 May 1916 and even as late as 23 April 1917 Kako was still convinced. For some reason we shall never know however, the plan fell through and in December 1917 Ōgai was appointed Director of the Imperial Museum and Library, a post he was to hold until his death five years later.

1917 had thus been a year of much uncertainty; a year when for the first time in his adult life he did not have to commute to his office or attend to official duties. This simple fact must in itself have increased his sense of uselessness, expressed in concrete and vivid terms in a poem he wrote that February beginning:

> Loosening the braids of office is a prosaic matter;
> Hanging up my cap to make way for wiser men.
> Indecisive and useless like the carving of rotten wood
> I have grown old avoiding merely further degradation. (XIX, 607)

In the September of this same year he wrote what must be considered his final statement on his life and his hopes, a farewell to the literary world; it is worth translating in full:

NAKAJIKIRI (A temporary statement)

Old age draws ever nearer. It is a common desire for man to review the shadows of his past when the light of future hopes grows dim. With old age comes a world of retrospection.

I studied medicine and worked as a doctor, but as a doctor I never became involved in social problems. Recently I wrote the following lines:

> Indecisive and useless like the carving of rotten wood
> I have grown old avoiding merely further degradation.

Publically it is as a man of letters that I have been more or less recognized. Feeling that, as far as lyric poetry was concerned, the *waka* form was too insubstantial to encompass modern thoughts and Chinese poetry in the end too prone to archaisms and hardly the way to build up a national literature, I allied myself to the Shinseisha and Araragi groups and dreamt of the resurgence of Japanese poetry.

As far as prose works were concerned, I tried my hand at a large number of short stories as practice for greater things but failed when I was confronted with a novel. Similarly in drama I only managed a few one act plays as a starter and it all came to naught when I saw those mountainous three act plays in the distance. In the field of philosophy I was confused as a doctor by the lack of unity in the natural sciences and looked to Hartmann's philosophy of the unconscious as a temporary foothold. Possibly I was drawn in the direction of Schopenhauerian ideas because I still had faint reminiscences of the theories of *li* and *ch'i* of the Sung Confucianism I had been taught in my youth. I never got as far as expressing my own opinions as a philosopher. As far as history was concerned my own experiences and encounters led me in the end to write historical biographies for people, despite the fact that it was an area in which I had not originally expected to be involved. Perhaps that same impetus from the natural sciences that made the writer Zola pursue the lineage of the Rougon-Macquart made my work take the shape of dreary genealogies.

However I never set out with the intention of being a writer or an artist, neither did I see myself as a philosopher or a historian. When I happened to be in the countryside I just cultivated the land and when I found myself by the bank of a river I went fishing. In short, I was always known as a dilettante.

When doing the year's accounts one makes out a temporary statement. These few lines are such a temporary statement of my life but may turn out to be the final account. As far as my official life is concerned that is exactly what it is.

So much for the past. Now what of the present?

I am idle. I live like a man of leisure but man cannot live a mere vegetable existence. As long as man is alive he must needs use his brain. This is why even men of leisure have the occasional game of *go* or cards.

The question remains however — what plaything do I give my childish thoughts? Let us investigate this trifle. I read books; Chinese classics because Western books are difficult to come by at the moment and those one does get from time to time talk of nothing but the war in Europe. This is on the receptive side. On the side of productivity the habits of a lifetime as a writer remain only in the sphere of lyric poetry and history – a *vita minima*.

I compose both Chinese and Japanese poetry. The former are published from time to time by a friend of mine, but the latter are only seen by a private group of friends. Why now compose Chinese poetry which I previously rejected as archaic ' and Japanese poetry which I rejected as being too insubstantial to encompass modern thoughts? For no other reason than that there is still no new form on which one can depend. So much for lyric poetry.

I write descriptive prose such as biographies of past figures for newspapers and also inscriptions as required. Why do my thoughts tend towards the genealogical form of biography? I am still not too sure about it myself, but in any case the influence of the natural sciences that I have already mentioned would not seem to constitute the whole motive. Chao I criticized Wei Shuo[2] and said that 'he compiled genealogies instead of writing about men', but I suspect that different motives lie behind my writing of biographies and the Chinese study of history. I write the inscriptions in Chinese because there is as yet no other accepted style. So much for history. This is how I keep myself employed.

Recently many people have come and asked me for my opinions on matters literary, artistic and social, and there have also been requests for stories. I find this all very distressing. By explaining about the past and the present in clear terms I am trying to stem the demand at source. Ku Yen Wu[3] once hung a tablet up in his room and refused to engage in any further poetic correspondence. This 'temporary statement' is the equivalent of Ku's tablet. (XXVI, 543–5)

While Ōgai was working in his second post he was concentrating on the biographies *Isawa Ranken* and *Hōjō Katei*, publishing a study of Imperial Postumous Names (*Teishikō*) in March 1921, and working on an unfinished study of era names (*Gengōkō*). These last five years of Ōgai's life were much enlivened, however, by his continual concern with the questions presented by the rise of Socialism and the possible repercussions of war and revolution in the West on Japan.

The disclaimer in 'Nakajikiri' that he had never become involved in social questions is for the most part true, especially if, as was probably the case, he was thinking of the example of Virchow. However it is not difficult to trace throughout his life a deep concern with social problems such as poverty, bad living and working conditions and, of course, the repression of freedom of speech; many of his early writings show at least signs of a Virchow-like annoyance with illiberal government measures. A long and detailed critique of Yano Fumio's book

Shinshakai (1902), written in February 1903, reveals an extensive knowledge of both utopian and Socialist literature, and finally there is the outburst of criticism against government obscurantism in 'Chinmoku no tō' and other works. 1919 and 1920 were, however, years of extreme social unrest in Japan as elsewhere, and the threat to the stability of the established order awakened a new interest in the whole ideology of Socialism and Communism.

By 1917 all the signs were that when the war in Europe was over Japan would be wide open to the dangers of the tide of Socialism. 1918 was a year of rapid inflation and widespread rice riots coupled with an extraordinary increase in the number of workers' strikes for better pay and conditions. With the end of the war in the November, the destruction of the German empire must have brought fear to the hearts of many of Japan's rulers. On 13 November Ōgai wrote to Kako:

> The only countries left with a monarch now seem to be Japan and England. I would think that in these circumstances the rise of parliamentary government is inevitable and universal suffrage probably unavoidable. Of course this movement will be greatly assisted by the efforts of the American president to spread democracy throughout the world now that the war has been won. In such a situation the question of our interests at the Peace Conference is a minor matter. For better or worse we really are coming up against a time of crisis. I can well imagine how men like Yamagata must be worried.
>
> With the political situation as it is at present every move made will have repercussions on the fate of the Imperial system. We intellectuals should, like Tung Fang Shuo,[4] keep an eye from the sidelines on how the politicians display their abilities. (XXXVI, 514)

The period when Ōgai really concentrated on this question, however, was a little later, from December 1919 to March 1920, when there was almost daily correspondence between himself and Kako. Much of what Ōgai writes is merely factual, giving Kako information on the development of Socialist and Communist thought with very few comments of his own. There are however one or two clues. On 24 December 1919 he wrote:

> I would like to talk to you in detail about the social policies I have in mind and will pay you a visit in the near future. I suppose you could call my idea one of 'Collectivism adapted to the polity' (Collectivism being the opposite of Communism) or perhaps 'State Socialism' (because the state would control production). However this is quite different from what is now being proposed —

success through union strikes and mass coercive action. I am still in the process of working it out. (XXXVI, 559)

Ōgai was extremely concerned that a real solution for the problem in Japan should be found, in contrast to what he called the mere 'palliative' measures put forward during the Peace Conference (letter for 8 January 1920), and he was worried that no one would treat the matter seriously until 'a certain amount of blood is spilt' (6 January). He was in favour of keeping the Imperial system (10 January), but wanted the government to concentrate on the fairer distribution of wealth rather than merely a further increase in the gross national wealth (28 April). He found Yosano Akiko's suggestion that 'the capitalists should voluntarily give up their class status just as the samurai did fifty years ago, and in the future industry should be left to the workers to run themselves' totally unrealistic, because 'it seems she is not aware that the workers just do not have the ability to run it themselves' (3 January). As a further bolster to his idea that the state should control production he drew an example from Chinese history:

> I found that the P'ien Chun Shu of the *Shih Chi* was most interesting. P'ien Chun was a State Monopoly. Salt and iron were put under government control and those who had formerly dealt in salt and iron (capitalists) were made government officials. This was condemned as merely 'selling official posts' but as a measure of expediency it is quite reasonable. No one yet seems to have published a study of Han Wu Ti's social policies... (13 February)

There was one further matter in which Ōgai took great interest; the hounding of professor Morito Tatsuo in 1920. About this he wrote:

> The Morito Tatsuo affair was in the newspapers today. They say that Morito was at fault for publishing a study of the thought of the Russian noble Kropotkin.
>
> Ever since he went on an observation tour of Siberia Kropotkin has propounded the theory that it is the nature of animals to help each other. He is a respected scholar whose ideas rival those of Darwin with his theory of the survival of the fittest. He was chased out of Russia and now lives in London. He has joined up with anarchist and Communist sympathizers. He said for instance:
>
> 'Let us suppose a country has a certain amount of rice and a certain number of inhabitants. Everyone should be allowed to obtain and eat that rice. As long as they work hard they should be allowed to eat. There should be no question of payment (Communism). The fact that we now have to pay is the fault of the present system and so this system must be destroyed (Anarchism).'
>
> I do not know whether Morito agreed or disagreed with this.

If he agreed then I suppose he was at fault. But the theory of *mutual aid* at least in part is worth some consideration. (12 January)

Obviously none of this can be considered of great importance, but it is of interest in the limited context of Ōgai's last years. The existence of this correspondence between Ōgai and Kako has naturally given rise to speculation as to the possible connection between Ōgai and Yamagata. There seems to be no real evidence, however, that Kako was acting as a go-between, although he might well have asked Ōgai's help indirectly so that he himself would be in a position to respond to any questions that Yamagata might put to him. The idea put forward by some critics that Ōgai and Yamagata were planning a *coup* on the lines of 'Collectivism adapted to the policy' must be dismissed as a piece of nonsense. There is reason to suppose, however, that Ōgai was consulted by the statesman on the question of the colour blindness of the Prince's consort a year later, for this was a specific question in which the knowledge of a medical man would have been required.[5] In a letter to Kako dated 13 October 1920 Ōgai wrote: 'I just gave my card in at the Yamagata mansion soon after he arrived in the capital. There were two men loitering outside the gate, and they looked at me suspiciously. I don't know whether they were police or detectives, but in any case they were a nuisance' (XXXVI, 586), and there are two mentions of the affair in Ōgai's diary for 12 and 15 February 1921. Such evidence, however, is extremely flimsy and merely gives rise to speculation that can never really be satisfied. It would indeed be safer to assume that such connections as did exist between the two men were mainly limited to the poetic sphere and only occasionally involved political matters. As has been stressed before, Ōgai was hardly the man to have much sympathy for Yamagata's draconian measures however much he might have understood his initial concern.

Ōgai's death when it did come on 9 July 1922 came as little surprise to those who knew him well and as even less of a surprise to himself. He had been in bad health for some time and had had prolonged periods off work in December 1918 and January and February 1920. It was during the latter illness that Koganei Yoshikiyo warned him that he was probably suffering from atrophy of the kidney, a disease from which his father had died and for which there was no cure. Ōgai knew very well what this meant and drove himself to continue with his work in the effort to forget. On 26 May 1922 just before leaving for Nara and the customary opening of the Shōsōin at which he was usually present, he wrote the following lengthy letter, in the margin of which Kako later wrote, 'The letter where he rejected medicine'.

In ancient China there were oracles who knew by looking at you exactly when and why you would die. When a man found this out it would obsess his mind and he would be unable to think of anything else. A doctor's diagnosis is somewhat similar. Say for instance that stomach cancer is diagnosed. No matter how wise or intelligent the patient he will never be able to rid his thoughts of this cancer from that moment on. It's no use the doctor just keeping silent about it because when something like cancer breaks out you will know about it anyway — you don't need a doctor to tell you how ill you are. It is precisely because millions of people do not know what is going on inside them or what the future holds for them that they can live out their lives from day to day quite unconcernedly. But when something does break out inside them the most nonchalant person will become worried; he will talk to people; he will go to the doctor; he will experience an emotional collapse due to this pathological process, and this sounds his death knell.

But there are elements of this process which doctors understand and there are some about which they are ignorant. If you know of your illness as well as if you had been told about it to your face by a famous doctor, and if you also know how it will develop in the future, then the same phenomenon will occur as when you have been seen by an oracle. Is this a desirable thing to happen?

If I knew in advance that I would fall from the tram tomorrow, hit my head and die, I would be frantically worrying about what to do about my half finished works and who to entrust my children's welfare to and how to do it. But if you think about it dispassionately there would be absolutely no point in doing so. I would be no different from dying without the foreknowledge.

I have something wrong with my left lung. I contracted pleurisy in my graduation year and ever since then it has hurt a little whenever I have felt cold. Sometimes it has turned into bronchitis and I would bring up phlegm, and recently it has turned into a cough which almost feels like asthma. I have also got something wrong with my kidneys. I know very well that if I showed myself to a doctor he would say that both my lungs and my kidneys are far from healthy. Rather than just knowing that something is wrong, one would then know exactly what was wrong and how far advanced it was. And if the doctor was well known you would be all the more convinced. I know enough about myself to know whether this would improve or aggravate my mental state. I think much of life and death and am not exactly unexperienced in such matters. I once decided to commit suicide. However if I knew how bad my insides were and knew the rate of progress of the disease, I would not be able to carry on just as if I did not know. In other words I know that my mental state would deteriorate. And even if I did know, are there any precautions I can take? I have nothing to do with women, wine, smoking or parties any more so the only thing left is to retire from work. But this would affect the research that I am now doing ('Studies into Japanese and foreign era names') — my longest work yet. Whether I should stop writing and breathe for another year, or carry on my work and so shorten my life by one year is a debatable question. I am doubtful whether I could in fact lengthen my life if I abandoned the will to write. I have therefore decided not to see any doctor, no matter how famous he may be. (XXXVI, 631-2)

Unfortunately he was not to be granted even the year that he wished. In Nara from 20 May to 8 June, he returned to his office at the Imperial Museum and for some two weeks struggled to work every morning, fighting the process of premature ageing and pain that his illness brought in its wake. Kojima Masajirō, writing of Ōgai's last years, mentioned a harrowing story he had heard from a friend:

> One morning he was going up the slope to the library hall of residence when he saw not ten paces in front of him an old man slowly crawling up the hill. He was dragging his right foot forward and then his left in like fashion. It was a perfect illustration of the phrase 'his last gasp'. Suddenly as he was passing the old man he looked round and was shocked to find that it was Ōgai.[6]

Kojima also wrote the following description of Ōgai's last days at the office:

> His complexion gradually worsened. You could see the veins standing out on his temples like withered ferns. That day sitting at his usual desk in the office he suddenly said very quietly: 'I'm not long for this world.'
>
> I gasped, powerless to say anything.
>
> 'It's atrophy of the kidney. A fatal disease. There's no cure,' he said and pointed to his veins.
>
> 'When this happens it's the end.' He smiled and there were wrinkles at the corner of his eyes.
>
> 'No use calling for a doctor. He couldn't do anything,' he said. Whenever the subject of illness had come up he had always claimed that medicine could never cure an illness. That could only be done by one's own vital force. What was more, medicines had side effects. He claimed he had never taken any.
>
> 'If you catch cold go to bed and it will cure itself. There's no need for aspirin or anything like that.'

That was all very well for something like a cold, I said, but what about a more serious illness?

'If it's a case for surgery of course that's different. But for an internal illness, serious or mild, just rest and it'll get better. When I was about twenty I had a chest ailment and when I was thirty I caught cholera and both times I got better without medicines merely by resting,' he said.

'In that case shouldn't you stay home now and rest?' I asked.

'It wouldn't help. This is a fatal illness.'

Sufferers of atrophy of the kidneys have a frequent desire to pass water. When at last they do get to sleep they sleep soundly till morning. Ōgai however would not give in and when he woke up in the middle of the night would say: 'It's a good thing I've woken up. I can get up and carry on with my *Gengōkō*.' It was gruesome.

'As the illness proceeds,' he said, 'my legs will swell. Then it's the end.'

He would always talk in the same way, in the same tone. I say the same but the ravages of illness were on his face. Perhaps because of that he seemed a little cold at times.[7]

In the end Ōgai had to give in and on 15 June he took to his bed. He was still refusing to take any medicines or even to see a doctor, but eventually on 19 June he gave in to his wife's entreaties and agreed to send a sample of urine to Kako to be tested. With it he sent a note: 'Herewith a urine sample for the period from 10 pm 18 June (when I took the medicine) to 5 am 19th. My urine is my wife's tears. Excuse the jest! This is the first time I have shown my body fluid to anyone. I have no doubt that it is full of malignancy' (XXXVI, 633). From this time on he gradually weakened, by 29 June was unable to write in his diary and died peacefully at 7 o'clock on the morning of 9 July.

It was Ōgai's eldest son Otto who first intimated that there had in fact been another cause of death. In a radio interview in 1954 he gave an account of a talk he had had with Nukada Susumu, a relative of Kako Tsurudo's who treated Ōgai during the last two weeks. Nukada told Otto:

Ōgai never had a physical check up with any doctor except me. In his urine I found clear signs of fairly advanced atrophy of the kidney. But what really shocked me was his phlegm. Under the microscope it was chock full of tuberculosis bacilli — it was just like examining a culture. 'Now you know,' he said and asked me not to divulge it as the children were still young. So from the two diseases the kidney one was chosen to go down on the medical report and only Kako, Koganei Yoshikiyo and I knew the real truth. Your mother of course was told the usual story but I understand that Ōgai had been in the habit of spitting up his phlegm into tissue paper and then burning it himself in a corner of the garden for some time, so she probably guessed.[8]

This suggestion that Ōgai had been suffering from tuberculosis for some considerable time has since been corroborated by observations of a number of his children. It would seem that he could even have contracted the disease as early as 1889 from his first wife Toshiko, for we know for certain that she died from tuberculosis in 1900. If this were true it would cast interesting light on the play *Kamen* and indeed the whole of his life. At least one medical scholar, Kawamura Keiichi, has taken this fact as the basis for a study which traces the passage and effect of the disease throughout his life. If Ōgai knew that he had contracted the disease and that it would take so long to cure as to be hardly worth his while, it would indeed be an interesting commentary on his early frenetic activity, his later pessimism and his truly vast output. It would suggest a man hounding himself and constantly aware that he was living on borrowed time; a man who had sacrificed full ten years of his life from a sense of mission.[9]

Three days before his death, on 6 July 1922, Ōgai had Kako draw up his final will. It stands as a fitting epitaph to his troubled life:

> Here in the face of death I trouble Kako Tsurudo, my lifelong friend from whom no secrets have been held, that he might write my will. Death is a momentous event that brings all things to an end. I am convinced that the authorities despite their powers are impotent in the face of death. I wish to die Mori Rintarō of Iwami. I have had connections with both the Department of the Imperial Household and the army, but at the very moment of death I repudiate all outward signs of this connection. I wish to die Mori Rintarō. All I want written on my grave are the words: 'The Grave of Mori Rintarō'; not a single word more. I request that it may be written in the hand of Nakamura Fusetsu. I demand that any further honours from the Department of the Imperial Household or the army must be refused. The various necessary formalities I leave to my one and only friend. No one else must be allowed to interfere in what remains. (XXXVIII, 112)

As Ōgai's legal will had been made long before and revised when he left for the Russo-Japanese War in 1904, this last testament was not a legal document so much as a public message. As such it is couched in surprisingly strong language and suggests that his self-discipline had been achieved at great cost. Particularly striking is the almost fanatic obsession with the question of his own identity. At the moment of death it was not the fate of his wife, his children or his friends, but his own name that was paramount. Such a passionate concern to identify oneself to one's own satisfaction is indicative of a deep insecurity. There is, too, something sadly moving in the last desperate attempt to define oneself in terms of such intangibles as a name and a birthplace, mere trappings of the soul. Ōgai, who never once returned to Tsuwano and who never once evinced any desire to do so, was driven in the end to rely on the simple fact of his birth as the only meaningful proof of his existence.[10]

As a young man Ōgai had been belligerently self-assured and intensely aware that he was playing a major part in a major historical experiment. Reacting naturally to the stimulus and challenge offered, he found little difficulty in identifying himself with his family, his country and his mission; a mission which proved to be exhilarating and self-fulfilling. A sense of belonging was particularly easy to sustain in Germany where the stimulus was strong and well-nigh continuous. There was little time to worry about the whys and wherefores.

When, however, the pressure was taken off and a combination of professional disappointment and personal unhappiness conspired to set him back, he turned inwards and to his dismay was faced with a blank. What had it all been for? As always one is drawn to quote from 'Mōsō' with its penetrating self analysis. Talking of the possibility of dying abroad, Ōgai wrote:

> At such times, the first thing I thought of was how grieved my parents waiting at home would be. Then I remembered the others who were close to me; in particular my curly haired young brother who had been so affectionate. He had only just started to walk when I was leaving, but the letters were full of how he was always asking when brother was coming home. How sad he would be if they told him that brother was never coming back. And then, I was studying abroad and it would be such a waste if I died without completing my studies. Viewed in the abstract like this, one had a sense of mere callous obligation; but when I looked at what each person meant to me in concrete terms, I experienced of course the same pain of longing, the same reaction of sympathy as I did towards my family.
>
> So thoughts of all one's multifarious social ties crowd in and come to rest on the individual self. The self is a collection of threads drawn together from all directions, and death is its unravelling.
>
> Ever since childhood I have enjoyed reading novels, so having learned other languages I now read foreign novels too, whenever I have the time. Without exception the extinction of this self is seen as the greatest, deepest agony of all. But to me the mere fact that I will cease to be does not seem painful. If I died by the

sword there would be the momentary sensation of physical pain, and if I died of disease or drugs, I would feel the pain of suffocation or convulsion depending on the symptoms of that illness or the nature of that medicine; but there is no pain in the extinction of the self. . .

But this is not to say that I am indifferent to the loss of this self. How mortifying to have this thing called the self disappear for ever, without having known or even tried to consider what kind of thing it was while it still existed. Such a pity! Sad to live one's whole life 'living a drunkard and dying a dreamer'. But in the midst of this remorse and this regret there lies an acute emptiness of the spirit, an indescribable loneliness, which turns to anguish, turns to pain. (VIII, 201–3)

This is not only evidence of an ability to face reality but is, in retrospect, a passage of most brutal irony. The self was a mere collection of threads, of social connections and relationships, and its demise was a quiet painless unravelling. The agony read about in Western novels was remote and unreal. But then on second thoughts, not to know this self did breed a sense of waste, of time ill spent. Ten or more years later, when death approaches, the overriding concern is the definition of the self, the frantic search for a sense of belonging. Death far from being an untying of the knots is full of painful spiritual suffering.

Where did this insecurity stem from? Every man needs a number of reference points in his life, a collection of habits, relationships and corner stones within which he can orientate himself and create a sense of belonging. Most people when faced with the frightening sense of uncertainty in life seek out for themselves a context and a role in which they create security. This usually takes one of three forms, a solid cultural heritage, personal ties, and work. The first of these was hardly available to men like Ōgai, because it was precisely this milieu that was in a state of flux; he himself was actually engaged in creating a new foundation and so it is not surprising that the present should appear to be constantly shifting and giving way. His interest in history was an expression of an underlying desire to form a reliable cultural bedrock, however vicarious it might be. The strong nostalgia for the Germany of his youth was another undercurrent which ran counter to this. To most Japanese Ōgai appeared very Western in his habits and there is no doubt that he often felt himself a man apart, not only because of his deep understanding and appreciation of Western ways of thinking, but also for the simple reason of his intellectual stature.

The next refuge, that of personal relationships, was, as we have seen, hardly conducive to solace. By nature somewhat insular and by education a firm believer in emotional restraint, love did not come easily and his emotions were always letting him down. His encounters with women were a series of mistakes, and the fact that he had been entrusted with the future of the family fortunes always seemed to clash with other personal wishes. The enormous power wielded by his mother in the background was a constant source of tension, which came near to destroying his second marriage, and which strung him between two 'families', both his own. Denied satisfaction either as a Japanese or a social entity, he could only turn to work. His official post was not so much a constant block to his creativity as a writer, as a vitally necessary part of his being, without which he would have felt lost.

The identification of self with occupation was a valid form of belonging only as long as it provided spiritual security. When his role became less important and events turned against him, there must have been a bitter sense of humiliation, which had to be given some outlet. The object was no longer fulfilling his allotted role, but was in work itself. Such was Ōgai's drive that one job, especially a job which had let him down, was not good enough; he had to be army doctor, administrator, critic, translator, writer and a lot else besides. Only in a man with extraordinary energy and intellectual powers could such a wide range of activities lead not to dilution of the results but to an astounding multiplicity of achievements. It was at this point, however, that his efforts rebounded again. Sōseki, who psychologically was probably the greater sufferer, could at least identify himself as a writer. The very range of Ōgai's interests meant that he felt unable to identify himself with any one role. This is why in 'Nakajikiri' he analysed his position in terms of a dilettante and why in his will he was still concerned with the question of self-definition. The imagery of masks and the acting of roles occurs regularly in his writing, and a representative passage can again be found in 'Mōsō':

> What had I been doing all my life? I had been engrossed in my studies almost as if something were whipping me on. I believed that this was shaping me so that I would be capable of certain tasks, and it is possible that this aim was to some extent fulfilled. But I felt that all I was really doing was emerging on a stage to act out some part like an actor. There had to be something behind this role I was performing, something else, but because of the constant whipping it never had time to reveal itself. Studying as a child, studying as a student, studying as an official, studying abroad; it was all just an act. However much I longed to wash this painted face of mine, come off the stage for a moment, and think about myself in peace; however much I hoped to catch a glimpse

of the face of that something behind, I just continued performing role after role, the director's whip at my back.

That this role was life itself was unthinkable. Surely what lay behind was real life. Yet while my constant hope was to see this something awaken, it remained dormant. At such times I often experienced intense homesickness as the movement of a water weed carried far away by the action of the waves somehow still echoes to its roots; such homesickness did not feel like an act performed. But this impression no sooner lifted its head than it immediately withdrew again. (VIII, 200-1)

The drive for endless work, the production in his spare time of everything for which he is now remembered, and the dependence that he placed on constant activity is a direct consequence of his loneliness. Incapable of putting a stop to the constant performing of different roles and reaching some kind of haven, he no sooner resigned his job in the army than he was looking for another. The sublimation of anxiety in pure activity explains his stubborn, almost bloody minded, refusal to see a doctor when he knew he was dying, and his struggle to carry on working to the bitter end. As he wrote to Kako Tsurudo, if he stopped working he would die in any case. We are left in the end with a very sad spectacle indeed; a man who on his death bed can think of little else but defining and identifying himself both to himself and for posterity, but who can only produce his name and couple it with Iwami, the name of a province already defunct and representative of little more than nostalgia.

In the cultural sphere he was for ever conscious of the responsibilities of the intellectual. Before the Restoration the Confucian scholar had been able to reconcile the different areas of 'science' and art as two elements stemming from an essentially common source. With the advent of modernization, not only were old values discarded and the foundations of mental and spiritual stability loosened, but science began to look like a totally alien product. Thus it was that in the beginning Ōgai found it so necessary to attempt to draw an unnaturally rigid distinction between the Good, the True and the Beautiful, in the form of morality, science and art. This broke down in the face of practical problems and the deep need to construct a unified cultural basis once again. It was not possible in his lifetime and some would say it has not yet been achieved; but the attempt had to be made.

In the sense that Ōgai's experience was one of the conflict between public and private, science and art, and Western learning and Japanese tradition, his life represents in microcosm the whole process of the modernization in Japan. Although it is doubtful whether his art will ever be considered of the highest, his seriousness, dedication and self-sacrifice to the cultural welfare of his country has earned him the position of prominence he holds in the spiritual history of modern Japan.

APPENDIX OF ŌGAI'S TRANSLATIONS

This appendix consists of those poems, stories and plays that Ōgai translated into Japanese. Full details of the actual books and sources used can be found in the notes appended to the relevant volume of the latest *Ōgai Zenshū* (Iwanami Shoten, 1971–5).

I POETRY

Title	Title of original	Author
OMOKAGE (Aug. 1889)		
Ineyokashi [Metre: extended *imayō*,[1] rhyme attempted. Tr. by Ochiai from Heine's trans. of *Childe Harold's Pilgrimage*]	'Good night'	G. G. Byron (1788–1824)
Gekkō [Metre: attempt to use Chinese tone patterns to correspond to German stress. Tr. by Ōgai]	'Das Mondlicht'	N. Lenau (1802–50)
Mignon no uta [Metre: 10/10, based on original. Tr. by Ōgai from *Wilhelm Meisters Lehrjahre*]	'Mignon'	J. W. Goethe (1749–1832)
Shikyō [Metre: 2 7-character and 4 5-character line *ku-shih*. Tr. by Ōgai]	'Heimweh'	K. Woermann (1844–1933)
Fue no ne [Metre: extended *imayō*, rhyme attempted. Tr. by Ochiai]	from *Der Trompeter von Säkkingen*	J. V. Scheffel (1826–86)
Ama otome [Metre: extended *imayō*. Tr. by Ōgai]	'Du schönes Fischermädchen'	H. Heine (1797–1856)
Hana sōbi [Metre: *imayō*. Tr. by Inoue]	from 'Die Rose im Staub'	K. Gerok (1815–90)
Wakarekane [Metre: *tanka*. Tr. by Inoue]	from 'Abschied'	A. J. Kerner (1786–1862)

Title	Title of original	Author
Kikai ga shima [Metre: 190 7-character line *ku-shih*. Tr. by Ichimura]	from *Heike Monogatari*	
Waga hoshi [Metre: extended *imayō*. Tr. by Koganei from *Meister Martin der Küfner und seine Gesellen*]	'Wo bist du hin'	E. T. A. Hoffmann (1776–1822)
Ashi no kyoku [Metre: 8/7, based on original. Tr. by Ōgai]	from 'Schilflieder'	N. Lenau
Aru toki [Metre: 8/6, based on original. Tr. by Ōgai]	'Einst'	E. Ferrand (1813–42)
Ophelia no uta [Metre: extended *imayō*, rhyme attempted. Tr. by Ōgai from English with ref. to Schlegel's German]	from *Hamlet*	W. Shakespeare (1564–1616)
Manfred hitofushi [Metre: 10/10, based on original. Tr. by Ōgai from Heine's trans.]	from *Manfred*	G. G. Byron
Manfred [Metre: attempt to use Chinese tone patterns to correspond to German/English stress. Tr. by Ōgai]	from *Manfred*	G. G. Byron
Yabai [Metre: extended *imayō*. Tr. by Ōgai from *Collected Poems* vol. 18]	from 'Kan mei man ch'eng san shou'	Kao Ch'ing-ch'iu (1336–74)
Betsuri [Metre: 24 5-character line *ku-shih*. Tr. by Ōgai]	from *Der Trompeter von Säkkingen*	J. V. Scheffel
Seikyūshi[2] [Metre: free variation of 5 and 7 syllables. Tr. by Ōgai]	'Ch'ing-ch'iu tzu'	Kao Ch'ing-ch'iu
Tōkyōkō[2] [Metre: 174 7-character line *ku-shih*. Tr. by Ōgai. Originally published in *Tōyō Gakugei Zasshi* (Jan. 1885)]	from 'Die Geschichte von der abgehauenen Hand'	W. Hauff (1802–27)

UTA NIKKI (Sept. 1907)

Totari	'Die letzten Zehn vom vierten Regiment'	J. Mosen (1803–67)
Sanki	'Die Drei'	N. Lenau
Komori uta	'Wiegenlied einer polnischen Mutter'	A. Platen (1796–1835)

Title	*Title of original*	*Author*
Rappa	'Die Trompete von Gravelotte'	F. Freiligrath (1810–76)
Kirisuto no ki	'Der Deutsche Weihnachtsbaum'	K. Bleibtreu (1859–1928)
Koshu	'Der Tambour'	E. Mörike (1804–75)
Mizuumi	'Am Ammersee'	E. Ziel (1841–1921)
Kinko	'Mit Trommeln und Pfeifen'	D. Liliencron (1844–1909)
Hitoyo no yado	'Rast auf dem Marsche'	A. Strodtmann (1829–79)

SARA NO KI (Sept. 1915)

Umi no kane	'Die Glocke im Meer'	R. Dehmel (1863–1920)
Oyogite	'Der Schwimmer'	R. Dehmel
Ue kara no koe	'Stimme von oben'	R. Dehmel
Shūkyō	'Religionsunterricht'	R. Dehmel
Seibutsu	'Stilleben'	R. Dehmel
Tōkei	'Der Hahnenkampf'	R. Dehmel
Kusari	'Die Kette'	R. Dehmel
Natsu no sakari	'Hochsommerlied'	R. Dehmel
Yoru no inori	'Nachtgebet'	R. Dehmel
Tsuki no de	'Mondaufgang'	C. Morgenstern (1871–1914)
Maekōjō	'Prolog'	Klabund (1890–1928) (A. Henschke)
Ore wa kita	'Ich kam'	Klabund
Igirisu no jō-san tachi	'Die englischen Fräuleins'	Klabund
Izumi	'Ein Brunnen'	Klabund
Netsu	'Fieber'	Klabund
Monogatari	'Ballade'	Klabund
Mata	'Wieder'	Klabund
Kami no hedo	'Es hat ein Gott'	Klabund
Kawa wa shizuka ni nagareyuku	'Still schleicht der Strom'	Klabund
Garasu no ōmado no uchi ni	'Hinter dem grossen Spiegelfenster'	Klabund
Himei o motte batsu ni kau	'Epitaph als Epilog'	Klabund
Washi no su	*Unidentified*	B. Björnson (1832–1910)
Orpheus	'Orpheus' (libretto)	C. W. Gluck (1714–87)
Atenejin no uta	'Gesang von Athener'	K. Schottelius (?–?)

Title	Title of original	Author

OTHER POEMS

Title	Title of original	Author
Nobara (Nov. 1890)	'Heidenröslein'	J. W. Goethe
Jukai (Aug. 1902)	'Die junge Nonne'	J. N. Craigher (?-?)
Bunshin (Aug. 1902)	'Still ist die Nacht'	H. Heine
Hikari no yoi (Sept. 1907)	'Glanzrausch'	P. Scheerbart (1863–1915)
Dangensha no uta (?)	'Lied des Harfners'	J. W. Goethe
Messina no hanayome (?)	from 'Die Braut von Messina'	F. Schiller (1759–1805)
Numa yori sora e (Jan. 1916)	'Aus dem Dreck in den Himmel'	G. Falke (1853–1916)
Jōdan (Jan. 1916)	'Scherz'	G. Falke
Yatte miro (Jan. 1916)	'Probatum est'	G. Falke
Kodomo no shi (Jan. 1916)	'Kinderreim'	G. Falke
Futansei (Jan. 1916)	'Was will ich mehr'	G. Falke

II PROSE

Title	Title of original[3]	Author	Nationality
Rokuyō no tan (Feb. 1889)	'Kadour et Katel'	A. Daudet (1840–97)	French
Tama o idaite tsumi ari (Mar.–July 1889)	'Das Fräulein von Scudery'	E. T. A. Hoffmann (1776–1822)	German
Sensō (Mar. 1889)	'Le Cabecilla'	A. Daudet	French
Shin Urashima (May–Aug. 1889)	'Rip van Winkle'	W. Irving (1783–1859)	American
Kōzui (Oct. 1889– Mar. 1890)	'High Water Mark'	B. Harte (1836–1902)	American
Suisu kan (Nov. 1889)	'Lyutsern'	L. Tolstoy (1828–1910)	Russian
Futayo (Jan.–Feb. 1890)	'Zwei Nächte'	F. W. Hackländer (1816–77)	German
Baka na otoko (Jan. 1890)	'Durak'	I. Turgenev (1818–83)	Russian
Jishin (Mar. 1890)	'Das Erdbeben in Chili'	B. H. W. Kleist (1777–1811)	German
Aku innen (Apr.–July 1890)	'Die Verlobung in St. Domingo'	B. H. W. Kleist (1777–1811)	German
Umoregi (Apr. 1890)	'Die Geschichte eines Genies'	O. Schubin (1854–1934) (L. Kirschner)	Austrian
Rōma (Kaiser) (June 1890)	'Prizraki-fantaziya'	I. Turgenev	Russian
Ukiyo no nami (Aug.–Nov. 1890)	'Die Flut des Lebens'	A. Stern (1835–1907)	German
Ōjushō (Mar. 1891)	'Fünfter Windstoss' in *Geschichten einer Wetterfahne*	F. W. Hackländer	German
Zange-ki (Mar.–May 1891, Apr.–Sept. 1892)	*Confessions*	J. J. Rousseau (1712–78)	Swiss
Mikuzu (June 1891)	'Un teneur de livres'	A. Daudet	French
Jojōfu (Aug. 1891)	'Charlotte Corday'	K. Frenzel (1827–1914)	German
Nukeuri (Oct. 1892)	'Taman'	M. Y. Lermontov (1814–41)	Russian
Sokkyō Shijin (Nov. 1892–Feb. 1901)	*Improvisatoren*	H. C. Andersen (1805–75)	Danish
Hageatama (Jan. 1897)	'Ein Carnevalsfest auf Ischia'	A. Kopisch (1799–1853)	German
Yamabiko (June–Nov. 1902)	'Die Geschichte einer Liebe'	H. Hippel (?–?)	German

Title	Title of original[3]	Author	Nationality
Shukumei ronja (Feb. 1907)	'Fatalist'	M. Y. Lermontov	Russian
Sokuratēsu no shi (Jan. 1908)	'Sokrates Tod'	T. Kröger (1844–1918)	German
Andoreasu Tāmaieru ga isho (Jan. 1908)	'Andreas Thameyers letzter Brief'	A. Schnitzler (1862–1931)	Austrian
Chichi (Feb. 1908)	'Der Vater'	W. Schaefer (1868–1952)	German
Itsu ka kimi wa kaerimasu? (Apr. 1908)	'Der treue Johnie'	A. Croissant-Rust (1860–1943)	German
Ōgonhai (May–June 1908)	'Sara Malcolm'	J. Wassermann (1873–1934)	German
Bokushi (Oct. 1908)	'Prästen'	S. Lagerlöf (1858–1940)	Swedish
Wakare (Nov. 1908)	'Ein Abschied'	A. Holz (1863–1929); J. Schlaf (1862–1941)	German
Kao (Jan. 1909)	'Das Gesicht'	R. Dehmel (1863–1920)	German
Gogo jūichiji (Jan. 1910)	'Den yderste Termin'	G. Wied (1858–1914)	Danish
Shiro (Jan. 1910)	'Weisses Glück'	R. M. Rilke (1875–1926)	Austrian
Tsuri (Jan. 1910)	'See-Ufer: Zwölf'	P. Altenberg (1859–1919)	Austrian
Inu (Jan. 1910)	'Kusaka'	L. N. Andreev (1871–1919)	Russian
Karasu (Mar. 1910)	'Raben'	W. Schmidt-Bonn (1876–1952)	German
Shitsū (Mar. 1910)	'Ben Tovit'	L. N. Andreev (1871–1919)	Russian
Sei Jurian (May–July 1910)	'La légende de Saint Julien l'Hospitalier'	G. Flaubert (1821–80)	French
Zainin (May 1910)	*Original unidentified* German title: 'Ein Verbrechen'	M. P. Artsybashev (1878–1927)	Russian
Uzushio (Aug. 1910)	'Descent into the maelstrom'	E. A. Poe (1809–49)	American
Shi (Sept. 1910)	'Podpraporshchik Gololobov'	M. P. Artsybashev	Russian
Warai (Sept. 1910)	'Smekh'	M. P. Artsybashev	Russian
Ni dokuro (Jan. 1911)	'El Ramusen Tir'	H. Andresen-Wörishöffer (?–?)	German
Eri (Jan. 1911)	*Original unidentified* German title: 'Berlin und meine Kragen'	O. I. Dymov (1878–1959) (Perelman)	Russian

Title	Title of original[3]	Author	Nationality
Ippiki no inu ga nihiki ni naru hanashi (Jan. 1911)	'Monsieur Bonichon mène perdre son chien'	M. Berger (1885–?)	French
Tō no ue no niwatori (June 1911)	'Der Turmhahn'	H. Eulenberg (1876–1949)	German
Sekai manyū (June 1911)	'Die Weltreise des kleinen Tyrnauer'	J. J. David (1859–1906)	Austrian
Kusanchisu (July 1911)	'Xanthis'	A. Samain (1858–1900)	French
Bara (July 1911)	'Roser'	G. Wied	Danish
Itabasami (July 1911)	'Tsenzor'	E. N. Chirikov (1864–1932)	Russian
Miren (Jan.–Mar. 1912)	'Sterben'	A. Schnitzler	Austrian
Karafuto datsugoku ki (Jan. 1912)	'Sokolinets'	V. G. Korolenko (1853–1921)	Russian
Onna no kettō (Jan. 1912)	'Ein Frauenzweikampf'	H. Eulenberg	German
Ore no tomurai (Jan. 1912)	'Mein Begräbnis'	H. H. Ewers (1871–1943)	German
Fuyu no ō (Jan. 1912)	'Erling'	H. Land (1861–?) (Landsberger)	German
Rōsōchō (Jan. 1912)	'Der alte Wachtmeister'	D. Liliencron (1844–1909)	German
Kisha kaji (Jan. 1912)	Unidentified	H. Kyser (1882–1940)	German
Saijitsu (Jan. 1912)	'Das Familienfest'	R. M. Rilke	Austrian
Kakeochi (Jan. 1912)	'Die Flucht'	R. M. Rilke	Austrian
Chichi to imōto (Apr. 1912)	'Der Amerikawillm'	W. Schaefer	German
Fukasetsu (May 1912)	'L'inexplicable'	H. Régnier (1864–1936)	French
Wani (May 1912)	'Krokodil'	F. Dostoyevsky (1821–81)	Russian
Shōtai (June–Aug. 1912)	'Die Geliebte'	K. G. Vollmöller (1878–1948)	German
Gorotsuki no shōten (Aug. 1912)	'Altató Mese'	F. Molnár (1878–1952)	Hungarian
Jūsanji (Oct. 1912)	'The devil in the belfry'	E. A. Poe	American
Inaka (Oct. 1912)	'Provinciale'	M. Prévost (1862–1941)	French
Rōjin (Jan. 1913)	'Greise'	R. M. Rilke	Austrian
Seigan (Jan. 1913)	'Die Petition'	H. H. Ewers	German
Hitorimono no shi (Jan. 1913)	'Der Tod des Junggesellen'	A. Schnitzler	Austrian
Batei (Jan.–July 1913)	'Arkhip'	A. N. Tolstoy (1882–1945)	Russian

Title	Title of original[3]	Author	Nationality
Fukushū (Jan.–Apr. 1913)	'La courte vie de Balthazar Aldramin'	H. Régnier	French
Saru (Mar. 1913)	*Original unidentified* German title: 'Affenpsyche'	J. Claretie (1840–1913) (A. Arnaud)	French
Saishū no gogo (May 1913)	'Az utolsó Delután'	F. Molnár	Hungarian
Rōdō (May 1913)	'Arbeit'	K. Schönherr (1867–1943)	Austrian
Byōin yokochō no satsujinhan (June 1913)	'The murders in the Rue Morgue'	E. A. Poe	American
Tsuji basha (June 1913)	'A Kocsi'	F. Molnár	Hungarian
Frorus to zoku to (July 1913)	*Original unidentified* German title: 'Florus und der Räuber'	M. A. Kuzmin (1875–1936)	Russian
Sentsamani (Aug. 1913)	*Skazki ob Italy* (chapter 23)	M. Gorky (1868–1936)	Russian
Shiraku (Aug.–Oct. 1913)	'Das Aderlassmännchen'	K. H. Strobl (1877–1946)	German
Pāteru Serujiusu (Sept. 1913)	'Otets Sergius'	L. Tolstoy	Russian
Hashi no shita (Oct. 1913)	*Original unidentified* German title: 'Unter der Brücke'	F. Boutet (1874–?)	French
Sei Nikorausu no yo (Nov.–Dec. 1913)	'La Saint-Nicholas du batelier'	A. L. C. Lemonnier (1844–1913)	Belgian
Bōkasen (Dec. 1913)	'Das grosse Vergnügen'	G. Hirschfeld (1873–1942)	German
Ama (Jan. 1914)	'Kyddet'	G. Wied	Danish
Butō (Mar. 1914)	From 'Pierre Nozière, livre deuxième, notes écrites par P. N. en marge de son gros *Plutarque*'	A. France (1844–1924)	French
Gōkō (Apr. 1914)	*Original unidentified* German title: 'Die Glorie'	M. Lengyel (1880–1957)	Hungarian
Kaeru (July 1914)	'La granouio de Narbouno'	F. Mistral (1830–1914)	French
Chichi no ada (Aug. 1914)	*Original unidentified* German title: 'Fürstin Monguschko'	A. Madelung (1872–1949)	Danish
Kanteinin (Jan. 1915)	'L'expert'	P. Bourget (1852–1935)	French

III PLAYS

Title [Performance]	Title of original	Author	Nationality
Shirabe wa Takashi Gitarura no Hitofushi (Jan.–Feb. 1889) [Not performed]	El alcalde de Zalamanca	Calderón de la Barca (1600–81)	Spanish
Ori Bara (Oct. 1889–June 1892) [Not performed]	Emilia Galotti	G. E. Lessing (1729–81)	German
Denki Tōnii (Nov.–Dec. 1889) [Not performed]	Toni	K. T. Körner (1791–1813)	German
Toriko (Sept. 1892– July 1893) [Not performed]	Philotas	G. E. Lessing	German
Bokushi (June–Sept. 1903) [Not performed]	Brand	H. Ibsen (1828–1906)	Norwegian
Waga Kimi (Oct. 1907) [Not performed]	Mein Fürst	W. von Scholz (1874–1969)	German
Tanken o Mochitaru Onna (Nov. 1907) [Not performed]	Die Frau mit dem Dolche	A. Schnitzler (1862–1931)	Austrian
Shuppatsu mae Hanjikan (Jan. 1908) [Yūrakuza, Apr. 1910]	Der Kammersänger	F. Wedekind (1864–1918)	German
Okusoko (Jan. 1908) [Yūrakuza, Apr. 1910]	Die tiefe Natur	H. Bahr (1863–1934)	Austrian
Hanataba (Sept. 1908) [Not performed]	Margot	H. Sudermann (1857–1928)	German
Mosa (Nov. 1908) [Yūrakuza, Apr. 1912]	Der tapfere Cassian	A. Schnitzler	Austrian
Chijin to Shi to (Dec. 1908) [Yūrakuza, Apr. 1911]	Der Tor und der Tod	H. von Hofmannsthal (1874–1929)	Austrian
Yaso Kōtansai no Kaiire (Jan. 1909) [Not performed]	Weihnachtseinkäufe	A. Schnitzler	Austrian
Sōbōmu (Jan.–Mar. 1909) [Yūrakuza, June 1911]	Elga	G. Hauptmann (1862–1946)	German
Nenne Hatago (Apr. 1909) [Yūrakuza, Feb. 1913]	Da Baby skulde paa Hotel	G. Wied (1858–1914)	Danish
Kiseki (Apr. 1909) [Yūrakuza, June 1911]	Le miracle de St. Antoine	M. Maeterlinck (1862–1949)	Belgian

Title [Performance]	Title of original	Author	Nationality
Saiki (June–Aug. 1909) [Rōyaru kan, Mar. 1917]	*Fordringsägare*	A. Strindberg (1849–1912)	Swedish
Jon Gaburieru Borukuman (July–Sept. 1909) [Yūrakuza, Nov. 1909]	*John Gabriel Borkman*	H. Ibsen	Norwegian
Sarome (Sept. 1909) [Not performed]	*Salome*	O. Wilde (1854–1900)	Irish
Kajō Sahan (Oct. 1909) [Yūrakuza, Oct. 1912]	*Das tägliche Leben*	R. M. Rilke (1875–1926)	Austrian
Shūsekimu (Nov.–Dec. 1909) [Not performed]	*Il sogno d'untramonto autumno*	G. D'Annunzio (1863–1938)	Italian
Maketaru Hito (Jan. 1910) [Teikoku Gekijō, Nov. 1913]	*Der Besiegte*	W. von Scholz	German
Hito no Isshō (Jan.–May 1910) [Marunouchi Hoken Kyōkai, Sept. 1916]	*Zhizni Cheloveka*	L. N. Andreev (1871–1919)	Russian
Hikōki (June–Sept. 1910) [Yūrakuza, July 1912]	*Myrrha*	E. Stucken (1865–1936)	German
Uma Dorobō (Oct.–Dec. 1910) [Yūrakuza, Nov. 1910]	*The Shewing-up of Blanco Posnet*	G. B. Shaw (1856–1950)	Irish
Hitori Butai (Jan. 1911) [Not performed]	*Den Starkare*	A. Strindberg	Swedish
Pariasu (Jan. 1911) [Yūrakuza, June 1914]	*Paria*	A. Strindberg	Swedish
Jinryoku Ijō (Jan.–May 1911) [Not performed]	*Over Evne I*	B. Björnson (1832–1910)	Norwegian
Sabishiki Hitobito (Feb.–Apr. 1911) [Teikoku Gekijō, Oct. 1911]	*Einsame Menschen*	G. Hauptmann	German
Chimata no Ko (May–Oct. 1911) [Yūrakuza, Oct. 1912]	*Mutter Landstrasse*	W. Schmidt-Bonn (1876–1952)	German
Yūrei (Dec. 1911) [Yūrakuza, Jan. 1912]	*Gengangere*	H. Ibsen	Norwegian
Tebukuro (Dec. 1911– Mar. 1912) [Not performed]	*En Hanske*	B. Björnson	Norwegian
Sōin (Jan.–Sept. 1912) [Not performed]	*Le Cloître*	E. Verhaeren (1855–1916)	Belgian

Title *[Performance]*	*Title of original*	*Author*	*Nationality*
Jiogenesu no Yūwaku (Apr. 1912) [Yūrakuza, May 1912]	*Die Versuchung des* *Diogenes*	W. Schmidt-Bonn	German
Ren'ai Zammaï (Apr.–Sept. 1912) [Yūrakuza, Mar. 1914]	*Liebelei*	A. Schnitzler	Austrian
Gyottsu (Oct. 1912– Mar. 1913) [Not performed]	*Götz von Berlichingen*	J. W. Goethe (1749–1832)	German
Yoru no Futaba (Jan. 1913) [Not performed]	*Original unidentified* German title: *Zwei* *nächtliche Szenen*	F. Steenhof (1865–?) (Harold Gote)	Swedish
Fausuto I (Jan. 1913) [Teikoku Gekijō, Mar. 1913]	*Faust I*	J. W. Goethe	German
Fausuto II (Mar. 1913) [Not performed]	*Faust II*	J. W. Goethe	German
Makubesu (July 1913) [Teikoku Gekijō, Sept. 1913]	*Macbeth*	W. Shakespeare (1564–1616)	English
Nora (Nov. 1913) [Ōsaka Chikamatsu za, Nov. 1913]	*Et Dukkehjem*	H. Ibsen	Norwegian
Inazuma (Jan.–May 1914) [Teikoku Gekijō, June 1916]	*Storm dräder*	A. Strindberg	Swedish
Nazo (May 1914) [Not performed]	*Ödipus und die Sphinx*	H. von Hofmannsthal	Austrian
Wasurete kita Shiruku Hatto (July 1914) [Not performed]	*The Lost Silk Hat*	Lord Dunsany (1878–1957) (E. Plunkett)	English
Byakui no Fujin (Jan. 1916) [Not performed]	*Die weisse Fürstin*	R. M. Rilke	Austrian
Perikan (Sept. 1916) [Not performed]	*Pelikanen*	A. Strindberg	Swedish

NOTES TO THE TEXT

CHAPTER 1. A SENSE OF MISSION

1 The *koku* was a measurement of rice yield (about 5 bushels) used to compute the size of fiefs in pre-Meiji times.

2 Koganei Kimiko, *Mori Ōgai no Keizoku* (Ōokayama Shoten, 1943), pp. 21–2.

3 Ōgai was later to refer to this aspect of his father's character in the story 'Casuistica' (1911).

4 Ōgai's great aunt had married into the Yonehara family and Ōgai's younger brother Junzaburō was later to marry Tsunae's daughter.

5 Mori Junzaburō, *Ōgai: Mori Rintarō* (Morikita Shoten, 1942), p. 3.

6 Suzuki Mitsuru, 'Ōgai yōshōji no kyōiku', *Hikaku Bungaku Kenkyū* 13 (Nov. 1967), 87–92.

7 For details on his reading at this time, see Kanda Takao, 'Wakaki Ōgai to kanshibun', *Hikaku Bungaku Kenkyū* 13 (Nov. 1967), 1–29.

8 This letter is reproduced in Hasegawa Izumi, *Ōgai: 'Vita Sexualis' kō* (Meiji Shoin, 1968), pp. 230–1.

9 Rintarō was Ōgai's given name. In accordance with general usage he has been referred to throughout this book as Mori Ōgai, this being his *nom de plume*. The provenance of this name, which means 'beyond the seagulls', has been the subject of two recent articles in the journal *Ōgai*. See Okada Masahiro, 'Ōgai to iu gō ni tsuite', *Ōgai* 14 (Jan. 1974) and Nakai Yoshiyuki, 'Ōgai to iu gō ni tsuite', *Ōgai* 15 (Nov. 1974). It appears that the particular character combination comes from a poem by Tu Fu, and that the 'seagulls' refer indirectly to the Yoshiwara pleasure quarters, not far from where Ōgai was living.

10 Quoted in Kobori Keiichirō, *Wakaki Hi no Mori Ōgai* (Tōkyō Daigaku Shuppankai, 1969), pp. 5–6.

11 This letter was first made public in July 1956 in the journal *Bungei*. Miyake Hiizu was head of the medical department at the university at the time.

12 This work, entitled 'Isei zensho kōhon' (A compendium of medical administration in manuscript), was based on the comprehensive two-volumed *Das preussische Militär-Medicinal-Wesen in systematischer Darstellung* by C. J. Prager (Berlin, 1875). Kobori, *Wakaki Hi no Mori Ōgai*, p. 13.

13 For a lengthy explanation of this somewhat difficult poem, see Kanda Takao, 'Wakaki Ōgai to kanshibun'.

14 For a translation of excerpts from the diary with special reference to the Leipzig/Dresden period, see Karen Brazell, 'Mori Ōgai in Germany', *Monumenta Nipponica* 26 (Summer 1971).

15 This and the following quotation are in Brazell's translation.

16 This translation appeared in the *Tōyō Gakugei Zasshi* for January 1885; Ōgai evidently sent the manuscript back to Japan after Inoue had seen it. Kobori, *Wakaki Hi no Mori Ōgai*, p. 29.

17 A full list of the *novellen* read during this period can be found in Kobori, *Ibid.* pp. 34–44.

18 This paper was published in the *Archiv für Hygiene* under the title 'Über die Kost der niponischen Soldaten'. A summary appeared in the *Rikugun Gun'i Gakkai Zasshi* for January 1886.

19 'Ethnographisch-hygienische Studie über die Wohnhäuser der Nipponer'. Ōgai had hoped to have it published in the *Archiv für Hygiene* but it eventually appeared in the *Verhandlungen der Berliner anthropologischen Gesellschaft* for May 1888.

20 'Über die diuretische Wirkung des Biers' and 'Über die Giftigkeit und Entgiftung der Samen von Agrostemma Githago', both published in the *Archiv für Hygiene*. Ōgai also left two further pieces of unfinished research, on the humidity of walls and the poisonous effect of analin vapour, which were handed on to someone else on his departure for Berlin.

21 Here he would have found a Western ally in the shape of Kaempfer who was greatly in favour of Japan continuing its policy of seclusion. D. Keene, *The Japanese Discovery of Europe* (London: Routledge and Kegan Paul, 1952), p. 98.

22 Published in the *Zeitschrift für Hygiene* in 1888 as 'Über pathogene Bacterien im Canalwasser'.

23 For a full discussion of this affair see pp. 47-55

24 The two books were A. Schwegler's *Geschichte der Philosophie im Umriss* (A History of Philosophy in Outline) (Stut.: Conrad, 1887) and a German version of a book by the Swede J. J. Borelius, *Blicke auf den gegenwärtigen Standpunkt der Philosophie in Deutschland und Frankreich* (Glimpses of the Present Standpoint of Philosophy in Germany and France) (tr. Emil Jonas, 1886).

25 For details of these notes, see Kobori, *Wakaki Hi no Mori Ōgai*, pp. 320–71.

26 The best introductory guide to Ōgai's non-literary activities during this period is Isogai Hideo, 'Mori Ōgai no hihyō undō: sono ichi; iji hyōron ni tsuite', *Hiroshima Daigaku Bungakubu Kiyō* 20 (Jan. 1962).

27 'Hi Nihonshoku ron wa masa sono konkyo o ushinawan to su' (The argument against Japanese food will soon lose its foundation), privately published in December 1888.

28 The most important article was 'Shiku Kaisei wa hatashite eiseijō no mondai ni arazaru ka' (Isn't the renovation problem basically a question of hygiene?) (Jan. 1889).

29 Ōgai was given a column in the influential *Tōkyō Iji Shinshi* from January 1889. Finding, however, that a journal of his own was more to his liking, he founded *Eisei Shinshi* in March 1889 and *Iji Shinron* in December 1889, after having been ousted from the pages of the *Tōkyō Iji Shinshi*. These two journals were combined into the *Eisei Ryōbyōshi*, which ran from September 1890 to October 1894.

30 Maruyama Hiroshi, 'Ōgai to igaku', *Mori Ōgai Hikkei*, ed. Inagaki Tatsurō (Gakutōsha, 1969), p. 32.

31 See for instance the article 'Nihon igaku no mirai o toku' (XXVIII, 169–70).

32 For details of these two debates, see Hayashi Fumihiko, 'Nihon tōkeigakushi kō', *Mori Ōgai*, 'Nihon Bungaku Kenkyū Shiryō Sōsho' series (Yūseidō, 1970) and Isogai Hideo, 'Daiikkai Nihon Igakkai ronsō', *Hiroshima Daigaku: Kokugo Kyōiku Kenkyū* 8 (1963).

CHAPTER 2. FIRST STEPS TOWARDS A NEW LITERATURE

1 D. Keene, *Modern Japanese Literature: an anthology* (Tokyo: Tuttle, 1957), p. 13.

2 *Ibid.* p. 57.

3 For a more detailed discussion of Shōyō's *Shōsetsu Shinzui* see M. G. Ryan, *Japan's First Modern Novel* (New York: Columbia U.P., 1967), pp. 55–73.

4 Quoted in Seki Ryōichi, '*Omokage* Kaidai', *Shōyō: Ōgai* (Yūseidō, 1971), p. 328.

5 This is a slightly adapted version from the translation of Manyōshū poems published by the Nippon Gakujutsu Shinkōkai (rev. ed. New York: Columbia U.P., 1969), p. 106.

6 For a full list and details of these translations see Appendix.

7 Kobori Keiichirō, '*Omokage* no shigaku', *Hikaku Bungaku Kenkyū* 25 (Mar. 1974), pp. 46–50.

8 Prose translation: 'When I saw you for the first time I was struck dumb; then all my thoughts dissolved into a crescendo. So I stand here, poor trumpeter that I am, playing on the lawn. I cannot tell you my desires, but only blow my love to you.'

9 Prose translation: 'Do you know that land where the lemons blossom, the golden oranges glow in their dark foliage; where a soft breeze comes from the blue sky, the myrtle stands hushed and the laurel stands high? Do you know it? There, there is where I wish to go with you, my love!'

10 Prose translation: 'The sun takes its leave in the distance and the weary day falls asleep. Here the willows hang low to the pond, so quiet and so deep.'

11 This phrase is used in the context of poetic language by David Hawkes, 'Chinese poetry and the English reader', *The Legacy of China,* ed. R. Dawson (London: Oxford U.P., 1964).

12 Kobori, '*Omokage* no shigaku', pp. 54–68.

13 Ningetsu refers to the young critic Ishibashi Ningetsu (1865–1926).

14 '*Omokage* ni tsukite', which was included in *Tsukikusa* (1896), but was in fact merely a reworking of the last section of a much earlier essay entitled 'Meiji nijūninen hihyōka no shigan' (April 1890).

15 For a full list and details of these translations see Appendix.

16 Toku: Tokujirō, the second son of the Mori family.

17 Text from Miyoshi Yukio, *Mori Ōgai* (Yūseidō, 1966), p. 323.

18 As the article was written for Mori Otto, the uncle is Tokujirō. The house at Ueno was the one in which Ōgai was living with Toshiko, his first wife, in the grounds of her father's mansion.

19 Text from Miyoshi, *Mori Ōgai,* p. 324.

20 Details on Takeshima Tsutomu from Hasegawa Izumi, *Zoku: Ōgai 'Vita Sexualis' Kō* (Meiji Shoin, 1971), pp. 160–220.

21 For the relevant quotations from Ishiguro's diary, see Hasegawa Izumi, *Zoku: Ōgai 'Vita Sexualis' Kō,* pp. 235–6, and from Koganei Yoshikiyo's diary see Hasegawa Izumi, 'Erisu "jiken no Doitsu fujin" ', *Ōgai* 15 (Nov. 1974).

22 Shibukawa Gyō, *Mori Ōgai* (Chikuma Shobō, 1964), pp. 91 ff.

23 First seriously suggested by Hirano Ken, 'Maihime (Ōgai) ron', *Kindai Bungaku* (Dec. 1952).

24 This refers to an English translation of 'Maihime' by F. W. Eastlake, entitled *My Lady of the Dance* (Tokyo, 1894 (rep. 1907)).

25 For more information on Harada and Ōgai, see Haga Tōru, 'Mori Ōgai to dōjidai bijutsu', *Bungaku* 40 + 41 (Nov. 1972, Jan., Mar. 1973).

26 Translation by Karen Brazell.

27 Mori Junzaburō, *Ōgai: Mori Rintarō,* p. 32.

28 Ōgai's later diaries were written, or possibly rewritten, with half a mind to his public image; thus the frustrating lack of comment on the reasons for his separation here. Another instance of his reluctance to see personal and private views, his own or anyone else's, appear in print was his strongly held belief that Higuchi Ichiyō's diary should be carefully doctored before publication. In a letter to Kōda Rohan dated 22 Sept. 1908 he confessed his fear that Ichiyō's name might be sullied if no cuts were made, and he took no further part in the subsequent publication of what is now recognized to be a diary of great and lasting literary worth. See Wada Yoshie (ed.), *Higuchi Ichiyō Shū* (Kadokawa Shoten, 1970), p. 432.

29 Translation by Karen Brazell.

30 Quoted in Naruse Masakatsu, *Ōgai: Sōseki* (Sanseidō, 1964), pp. 120–1.

31 Yamamoto Masahide, 'Ōgai to genbunitchi', *Ōgai* 9 (June 1971).

32 For a treatment of Ōgai's literary theories see the following chapter.

CHAPTER 3. THEORY FOR A NEW LITERATURE

1 Dichteritis: a German word play meaning poetry fever.

2 Text from Miyoshi, *Mori Ōgai*, pp. 181–2. It is interesting that this manifesto had considerable impact on young writers at the time. Tokuda Shūsei knew the beginning of it off by heart. Yoshida Seiichi, *Kindai Bungei Hyōronshi* (Shibundō, 1975), pp. 269–70.

3 G. J. Becker (ed.), *Documents of Modern Literary Realism* (Princeton: Princeton U.P., 1963), pp. 207–8.

4 A full survey of the reception of Zola in Germany can be found in W. H. Root, *German Criticism of Zola: 1875–1893* (New York: Columbia U.P., 1931).

5 *Ibid.* p. 3.

6 Kobori, *Wakaki Hi no Mori Ōgai*, pp. 377–89.

7 Root, *German Criticism of Zola*, p. 3.

8 For a list of these books see Maeda Ai, *Kindai Dokusha no Seiritsu* (Yūseidō, 1973), pp. 73–89 (chapter entitled 'Ōgai no chūgoku shōsetsu shumi', first published in *Kokubungaku: Gengo to Bungei* 38 (Jan. 1965)). Ōgai read, or perhaps reread, the salacious *Chin P'ing Mei* after his return from Germany, as one passage has a note referring to Gottschall written in the margin. He might well have been thinking of *Nana* in this connection.

9 Kobori, *Wakaki Hi no Mori Ōgai*, pp. 389–408.

10 Maeda, *Kindai Dokusha no Seiritsu*, pp. 83–4.

11 Two other essays of this period, 'Gendai shoka no shōsetsuron o yomu' (On reading contemporary essays on the novel, Nov. 1889), and 'Meiji nijūninen hihyōka no shigan' (Critics' attitudes towards poetry in the year 1889, Jan. 1890), contain similar denouncements of didacticism. At this point Ōgai utterly repudiated both the *kanzen chōaku* type of literature, and the *tendenzroman*, which might almost be considered the German equivalent. While the True might have some place alongside the Beautiful, the Good had, theoretically, no place at all.

12 For more details on 'Shōsetsu sōron' see Ryan, *Japan's First Modern Novel*, pp. 151–8.

13 This and the next quotation are from 'Shōyō shi to Uyū sensei to'.

14 Entitled 'Toyama Masakazu shi no garon o bakusu' and 'Toyama Masakazu shi o saihyō shite shoka no bakusetsu ni bōkyū su'.

15 Kanda Takao, 'Mori Ōgai to E. v. Hartmann', *Hikaku Bungaku Hikaku Bunka* (July 1961) (also to be found in Hasegawa Izumi (ed.), *Mori Ōgai,* 'Gendai no Esupuri' series). A translation of the passage in question can be found on pp. 129-30.

16 In an article entitled *'Shimbi Kōryō* no hihyō ni tsuite' (Sept. 1899), and in the preface to the collection of articles entitled *Tsukikusa*.

17 *Gendai Bungakuron Taikei* (Kawade Shobō, 1954) I, pp. 114–15.

18 In the article entitled 'Emile Zola ga botsurisō'.

19 This novel has been translated into English by M. Howitt, *The Improvisatore* (London: Ward, 1845).

20 Entitled 'Mumeishi no ron ni kotauru *Shigarami-zōshi* no sho'.

21 *Masamune Hakuchō Zenshū* VI, 112.

22 E. Hartmann, *Philosophy of the Unconscious,* tr. W. C. Coupland (London: Trubner, 1931), p. 13.

CHAPTER 4. TWO WARS

1 Donald Keene, *Landscapes and Portraits* (Tokyo: Kōdansha, 1971), p. 265.

2 For an account of the discovery of Rubner's book see Kobori Keiichirō, '*Eisei Shimpen* no genten ni tsuite', *Ōgai Zenshū Geppō* 31 (July 1974). Most of the articles were carried in *Eisei Shinshi* and *Eisei Ryōbyōshi.* In the latter they were all placed in a special appendix entitled 'Eisei shinron', which was designed to be collected by the reader in book form. They were forced to discontinue this practice in Feb. 1894 because it contravened the postal regulations.

3 Ōgai had only two books by Freud in his library: *Über den Traum* (Wies: Bergm. 1901) and *Drei Abhandlungen zur Sexualtheorie* (2 Aufl. Wien: Deuticke, 1910).

4 In the article 'Senji Ryōshōdan' (XXXIII, 723–6).

5 *Taifun* (1909): a play by Menyhert Lengyel (1880–1957) which dealt with a young Japanese in Europe and revealed the predominant racialist attitudes of Europeans. It was, for some reason, very popular in Japan. See Hirakawa Sukehiro, *Wakon Yōsai no Keifu* (Kawade Shobō Shinsha, 1972), pp. 249–78.

6 It was in one of these articles that Ōgai singled out Higuchi Ichiyō's story 'Takekurabe' (Growing up) for special praise (XXIII, 484–9).

7 This point is made by T. R. H. Havens in his book *Nishi Amane* (Princeton: Princeton U.P., 1970).

8 The importance of Ōgai's study of Clausewitz was first pointed out by the scholar Inagaki Tatsurō in 1939. See 'Ōgai to "junkōtei" ', *Mori Ōgai*, ed. Hasegawa Izumi, 'Gendai no Esupuri' series.

9 *The War in the Far East* (London: Murray, 1905), chapter 45.

10 Ironical in view of Ōgai's own self-professed reading habits as a youth.

11 These were published in a variety of journals and magazines under various titles such as 'Chie-bukuro' and 'Shintōgo'. See *Ōgai Zenshū* XXV.

12 Kobori Keiichirō, 'Mori Ōgai no shosei tetsugaku: "Chie-bukuro" "Shintōgo" no genten ni tsuite', *Hikaku Bungaku Kenkyū* 20 (Nov. 1971).

13 The prolific writer Matsumoto Seichō uses this period of Ōgai's life as background in his modern detective story *Ōgai no Hi*.

14 Quoted in Miyoshi Yukio, *Mori Ōgai*, p. 327.

15 Hiratsuka Raichō, 'Ōgai sensei ni tsuite', *Bungei Sampo* 15 (Oct. 1962).

16 Information here from M. D. Biddiss, *Father of Racist Ideology: the social and political thought of Count Gobineau* (London: Weidenfeld & Nicolson, 1970).

17 Taguchi Ukichi (1855–1905), economist and historian. Ōgai wrote a short article in memory of him in 1911 entitled 'Teiken sensei'.

18 H. S. Chamberlain (1855–1922) married Wagner's daughter Eva and became a naturalized German citizen in 1916. It comes as a shock to find that he was a younger brother of Basil Hall Chamberlain, known to all students of Meiji Japan as a sympathetic and intelligent observer.

19 H. Gollwitzer, *Die Gelbe Gefahr* (Göttingen: Vandenhoeck & Ruprecht, 1962), pp. 43–6.

20 Quoted in Hirakawa Sukehiro, *Wakon Yōsai no Keifu*, p. 142.

21 Discovered in late 1974, these reports can be found in volume XXXIV of the new *Ōgai Zenshū*.

22 *Ōgai* 2, 19.
23 A view first proposed by Karaki Junzō.
24 For further information on the poetry society see Furukawa Kiyohiko, 'Mori Ōgai to Tokiwakai', *Mori Ōgai,* 'Nihon Bungaku Kenkyū Shiryō Sōsho' series.
25 This work is discussed in detail on pp. 186-8. For a portrait of Yamagata in this light see R. F. Hackett, *Yamagata Aritomo in the Rise of Modern Japan* (Cambridge, Mass.: Harvard U.P., 1971).
26 This period is considered in detail in Shigematsu Yasuo, 'Gun'ikan Mori Ōgai shōkō', *Kokugo to Kokubungaku* 49 (Apr. 1972).
27 Treated in detail on pp. 138-9.

CHAPTER 5. A LITERATURE OF IDEAS I

1 A short biography of Tamamizu can be found in Matsubara Jun'ichi, 'Ōgai to tōyō shisō', *Kokugo to Kokubungaku* 40 (Jan. 1963).
2 This has been proved to be one of the fictional elements in this work. See above, p. 76.
3 Mainlaender: real name Philipp Batz (1841–76). His theory reappears in Masamune Hakuchō's story 'Meimō' and in Akutagawa Ryūnosuke's 'Aru kyūyū e okuru shuki'. Kobori Keiichirō believes that Ōgai only knew of Mainlaender's ideas through a reading of one of Metschnikoff's books. *Mori Ōgai no Sekai* (Kōdansha, 1971), pp. 269–87.
4 This story too is essentially autobiographical. Ōgai's own son Fritz died of whooping cough on 5 February 1908 when only one year old.
5 For a good short summary of Japanese Naturalism see W. E. Sibley, 'Naturalism in Japanese literature', *Harvard Journal of Asiatic Studies* 28 (1968).
6 For a treatment see below, pp. 186-8.
7 See below, pp. 182-4.
8 Information for this section from Kobori Keiichirō, 'Ōgai no Nietzsche zō', *Nietzsche to Sono Shūhen,* ed. E. Hikami (Asahi Shuppansha, 1972).
9 See above, p. 86.
10 This and following information from Sugita Hiroko, 'Nietzsche kaishaku no shiryōteki kenkyū', *Kokugo to Kokubungaku* 43 (May 1966).
11 M. Miyoshi, *Accomplices of Silence* (Berkeley: California U.P., 1974), p. 53.
12 Natsume Sōseki, in particular in his later works, reveals this ennui to an unusual extent, compounded as it was with the misery of illness.

13 For a treatment of the facts behind this story see Keene, *Landscapes and Portraits*, pp. 250-8.
14 See above, p. 67.
15 Treated in detail on pp. 189-93.
16 H. Hibbett, 'Tradition and trauma in the contemporary Japanese novel', *Daedelus*, 95 (Autumn 1966).

CHAPTER 6. A LITERATURE OF IDEAS II

1 Okazaki Yoshie, *Ōgai to Teinen* (Hōbunkan, 1969), p. 130.
2 F. Motofuji, 'Mori Ōgai: three plays and the problem of identity', *Modern Drama* (Feb. 1967). The plays treated are *Urashima*, *Kamen* and *Ikutagawa*.
3 Kusunoki Masao, 'Ōgai no gikyoku', *Mori Ōgai Kenkyū*, ed. Yoshida Seiichi (Chikuma Shobō, 1960), p. 142.
4 One play has not been treated here: *Soga Kyōdai* (1914). It is not an original play but a modern adaptation of the earlier *Youchi Soga Karibe no Akebono* by Kawatake Mokuami.
5 For a list of all Ōgai's translations and their original titles see Appendix.
6 For details see R. J. Bowring, 'Honyaku no gendai ni tsuite', *Ōgai Zenshū Geppō* 27 (Iwanami Shoten, Jan. 1974).
7 M. Swales, *Arthur Schnitzler* (London: Oxford U.P., 1971), pp. 93-7.
8 For a discussion of 'Okitsu Yagoemon no isho' and 'Takasebune' see part III, chapter 7.
9 Ishikawa Jun, 'Shokoku Monogatari', *Mori Ōgai* (Mikasa Shobō, 1941) and Kobori Keiichirō, 'Honyaku ga kizuita sekai', *Mori Ōgai no Sekai*.
10 Ishikawa Yoshio, 'Ōgai to Shiki', *Kaishaku* 17 (Dec. 1971).
11 Hasegawa Izumi, 'Ōgai to Takuboku', *Zoku: Mori Ōgai Ronkō, Zōhoban* (Meiji Shoin, 1971).
12 Prose translation: 'In spring when mist begins to rise on the village pond one evening – raake – the first frog. Raake-racka-paake, a second, and so on until the whole chorus sounds raake-paake-racker-quacker-Pack. Above them the sunlight dies, an azure butterfly hovering there; how beautiful.'
13 The influence of *haiku* in Ōgai's version is unmistakable, but then the same might well be said of the German original.
14 Prose translation: 'The English girls walk in a long line through the town, two by two, in their black coats which look like mushrooms pulled out of the ground. But in summer they wear violet sashes. They sleep alone . . . some of them are so attractive one wouldn't mind sleeping with them. But they are so small, so very small in their black capes, I think you'd need at least a dozen of them.'

15 Prose translation: 'Peacefully the river steals at an even pace; not a wave shows white on the stream. Steeply shelve the black roaring deeps; it seems as if a voice is calling me. I turn my eyes and pale; for my corpse rides on the waters.'

16 R. M. Rilke, *Sämtliche Werke* (Wiesbaden: Insel, 1961) IV, 889. The whole question of Ōgai and Rilke is treated in a little more detail in Koizumi Kōichirō, 'Ōgai to Rilke', *Kokubungaku: Gengo to Bungei,* 6 (Sept. 1964).

17 Rilke, *Sämtliche Werke,* IV, 891.

18 For a discussion of 'Ka no yō ni' see below, pp. 189-93.

19 Seita Fumitake, 'Ōgai to Schnitzler', *Hikaku Bungaku* 12 (1969), notes that 'Leutenant Gustl' seems to have been one of Ōgai's favourite stories. However, none of Ōgai's letters is to be found in Schnitzler's papers, as the author can testify.

20 Swales, *Arthur Schnitzler,* pp. 1–26.

21 Prose translation: 'Oh! I have studied philosophy, law, medicine and, I'm sorry to say, even theology with thoroughness and much application. But here I am, an old fool and no cleverer than before.'

22 Miyoshi, *Accomplices of Silence,* p. 53.

23 For details of this dispute see H. P. Varley, *Imperial Restoration in Medieval Japan* (New York: Columbia U.P., 1971), pp. 156–83.

24 For the interpretation of these elliptic passages see Kobori Keiichirō, 'Meijijin: Ōgai no kōshitsukan', *Chūō Kōron: Rekishi to Jimbutsu* 30 (Feb. 1974), p. 107.

25 Hirakawa Sukehiro, 'Nogi shōgun to Mori Ōgai', *Chūō Kōron: Rekishi to Jimbutsu,* 30 (Feb. 1974).

26 Note the speed with which Ōgai received such books from Germany and the short time it took him to expound what seemed to be an impressive theory.

CHAPTER 7. THE STUDY OF HISTORY

1 For a study of the reactions to Nogi's death see Ikimatsu Keizō, 'Nogi shōgun no junshi', *Kokubungaku: Kaishaku to Kanshō* 34 (Jan. 1969).

2 *Ibid.*

3 Ogata Tsutomu, 'Ōgai: Rekishi shōsetsu no shiryō to hōhō – "Okitsu Yagoemon no isho", "Abe ichizoku"', *Mori Ōgai,* 'Nihon Bungaku Kenkyū Shiryō Sōsho' series, p. 240.

4 B. H. Chamberlain, *Things Japanese* (London: Kegan Paul, Trench, Trubner, 1939), p. 1

5 Exhaustive details of the revisions and sources used by Ōgai for both 'Okitsu Yagoemon no isho' and 'Abe ichizoku' can be found in Ogata 'Ōgai: Rekishi shōsetsu no shiryō to hōhō'.

6 It would seem that the correct historical reading of this name was Sabase. Ogata Tsutomu, ' "Sahashi Jingorō" no tenkyo to hōhō', *Bungaku* 32 (Oct. 1964).

7 *Ibid.*

8 The diary entry for 9 April 1913 reads: 'Uetake Kishirō [the printer] came to see me and asked me to change the title from *Itsujihen* to *Iji*' (XXXV, 591).

9 Ogata Tsutomu, 'Ōgai: "Gojiingahara no katakiuchi" no ichi kōsatsu', *Kokugo to Kokubungaku* 42 (June 1965).

10 Koizumi Kōichirō, ' "Ōshio Heihachirō" ron — tenkyo to hōhō', *Kokubungaku: Gengo to Bungei* 21 (Jan. 1969).

11 For a study of Ōshio as a rebel leader of great drive but politically naive see Tetsuo Najita, 'Ōshio Heihachirō', *Personality in Japanese History*, ed. A. M. Craig and D. H. Shively (Berkeley: California U.P., 1970).

12 H. White, *Metahistory* (Baltimore: John Hopkins U.P., 1973), p. 2.

13 Ooka Shōhei, *Rekishi Shōsetsu no Mondai* (Bungei Shunjū, 1974), p. 21.

14 *Ibid.* pp. 17–19.

15 K. Hamburger, *The Logic of Literature*, tr. M. J. Rose (Bloomington: Indiana U.P., 1973).

16 M. Zavarzadeh, 'A typology of prose narrative', *Journal of Literary Semantics*, 3 (1974).

17 This volume is, strangely enough, missing from Ōgai's library, but in any case he also had in his possession the complete works of Nietzsche.

18 This account is based largely on the discussion of Nietzsche's view of history in White, *Metahistory*.

19 It would be useful to try and distinguish between the two terms *shishōsetsu* and *watakushi-shōsetsu*, reserving the former for the Japanese translation of the German *Ich Roman* and the latter for the indigenous variety.

20 Buddhist homilies and morally instructive stories, mostly of oral origin.

21 For details see Ogata Tsutomu, ' "Gyogenki" to "atarashii onna" tachi', *Kokugo Kokubun* 32 (Dec. 1963).

22 A comparison with the source can be found in Hasegawa Izumi, 'Saigo no Ikku', *Zōho: Mori Ōgai Ronkō* (Meiji Shoin, 1970).

23 *Ibid.*

24 See the chapter entitled 'Sonnō jōi to kaikoku washin' in Hirakawa Sukehiro, *Wakon yōsai no keifu*.

25 Koizumi Kōichirō, 'Shibue Chūsai', ron', *Kokubungaku: Gengo to Bungei* 8 (July 1966).

26 Shibukawa Gyō, *'Shibue Chūsai'*, *Mori Ōgai Hikkei*, ed. Inagaki Tatsurō, p. 180.

27 The most famous example of this criticism is Katsumoto Seiichirō, 'Sekaikan geijutsu no kussetsu', *Mori Ōgai*, 'Nihon Bungaku Kenkyū Shiryō Sōsho' series.

28 These works in fact presented Ōgai with very different problems. Most of the research for *Shibue Chūsai* was already done by Tamotsu and was rewritten by Ōgai. *Isawa Ranken* involved more work on his part, but with *Hōjō Katei* he was faced with a pile of letters that he had to date and order purely on internal evidence. It is the most impressive piece of work from a research point of view.

CHAPTER 8. THE LAST YEARS

1 'Kako shokan', *Ōgai* 2 (Mar. 1966).

2 Chao I (1727–1814), a Ch'ing period historian interested in textual criticism of the classics and histories. Wei Shuo (506–572), man of letters in the state of Ch'i.

3 Ku Yen Wu (1613–1682), Ch'ing confucian scholar, known as the father of the school of textual criticism *(kōshōgaku)* that men such as Shibue Chūsai followed in Japan.

4 Tung Fang Shuo (*c.* BC 154–93), a favourite courtier of the Han Emperor Wu Ti.

5 For Yamagata's part in this affair see Hackett, *Yamagata Aritomo in the Rise of Modern Japan*, pp. 333–41.

6 Quoted in Hirakawa Sukehiro, *Wakon Yōsai no Keifu*, p. 413.

7 *Ibid.* pp. 412–13.

8 Quoted in Hasegawa, *Zoku: Ōgai 'Vita Sexualis' Kō*, p. 24.

9 *Ibid.* p. 28.

10 For this last section I am indebted to a reading of Yamazaki Masakazu's *Ōgai: Tatakau Kachō* (Kawade Shobō Shinsha, 1972).

APPENDIX

1 For an explanation of these terms see above, p. 38.

2 Both these poems were added when the collection was reprinted in *Minawashū* in 1892.

3 These titles are listed in the language in which the work was originally written, but it should be borne in mind that Ōgai always translated from the German.

BIBLIOGRAPHY

The bibliography on the life and works of Ōgai is immense and growing every year. As a full listing would be neither practical nor desirable, the arrangement is as follows:

Works in Japanese Those books and articles to which I have specifically referred in the text and the notes.

Works in European languages As above but with a few extra articles added for the sake of comprehensiveness.

Translations A list of translations of Ōgai's works into English, arranged under title of original in alphabetical order. Where two or more translations of the same work are available I have listed the one that I consider the best. For a full list of translations into a variety of European languages see *Modern Japanese Literature in Western Translations, a Bibliography* (Tokyo: International House of Japan Library, 1972).

For the student who wishes to delve further into any particular aspect, the most convenient bibliography with which to start is the one in *Mori Ōgai Hikkei*, ed. Inagaki Tatsurō (Gakutōsha, 1969). A more comprehensive bibliography for the years up to 1964 can be found in *Ōgai: Sōseki*, ed. Naruse Masakatsu *et al.* (Sanseidō, 1965), but this is almost too detailed and rather difficult to use owing to its purely chronological format. Much of the best research has been carried out in recent years and the bibliography covering April 1971 to March 1973 in *Kokubungaku: Kaishaku to Kyōyō no Kenkyū* 18 (Aug. 1973) is useful. The short introduction to post-war Ōgai studies by Miyoshi Yukio in the special issue of the above journal *Kokubungaku* for December 1973, entitled 'Gendai Bungaku Kenkyū Hikkei' is also highly recommended. This special issue is an indispensable reference tool for every student of modern Japanese literature and has recently been reissued in book form.

Complete collections of Ōgai's works are as follows:

Ōgai Zenshū, ed. Kako Tsurudo *et al.* 1st ed. (Ōgai Zenshū Kankōkai, 1923-7), 18 vols; 2nd rev. ed. (1929-31), 17 vols.

Ōgai Zenshū, ed. Kinoshita Mokutarō *et al.* 1st ed. (Iwanami Shoten, 1936-9), 35 vols; 2nd ed. (1951-5), 53 vols; 3rd ed. (1971-5), 38 vols.

(The second and third editions respectively were greatly revised and expanded.)

Of these, by far the most complete and easiest to use is the latest edition, which is also the first to arrange the stories, critical articles, medical articles, diaries and letters in more or less chronological order. Care must be taken with some of the earlier critical articles however. The texts of these in vols. 22 and 23 are mostly the revised *Tsukikusa* versions; for the original texts it is necessary to turn to the reference appendix in vol. 38. Initially the student is advised to turn to a different collection, namely *Mori Ōgai Zenshū*, ed. Yoshida Seiichi *et al.* (Chikuma Shobō, 1959-62, repr. 1971), 8 vols. This is invaluable for the copious notes appended to each story.

WORKS IN JAPANESE

Bowring, R. J., 'Honyaku no gendai ni tsuite', *Ōgai Zenshū Geppō* 27 (Iwanami Shoten, 1974).

Furukawa Kiyohiko, 'Mori Ōgai to Tokiwakai', *Mori Ōgai*, 'Nihon Bungaku Kenkyū Shiryō Sōsho' series (Yūseidō, 1970).

Gendai Bungakuron Taikei (Kawade Shobō, 1954).

Haga Tōru, 'Mori Ōgai to dōjidai bijutsu', *Bungaku* 40 + 41 (Nov. 1972, Jan., Mar. 1973).

Hasegawa Izumi, *Ōgai 'Vita Sexualis' Kō* (Meiji Shoin, 1968).

– *Zōho: Mori Ōgai Ronkō* (Meiji Shoin, 1970).

– *Zoku: Mori Ōgai Ronkō, Zōhoban* (Meiji Shoin, 1971).

– *Zoku: Ōgai 'Vita Sexualis' Kō* (Meiji Shoin, 1971).

– 'Erisu "jiken no Doitsu fujin"', *Ōgai* 15 (Nov. 1974).

– (ed.), *Mori Ōgai*, 'Gendai no Esupuri' series (Shibundō, 1968).

Hayashi Fumihiko, 'Nihon tōkeigakushi kō', *Mori Ogai*, 'Nihon Bungaku Kenkyū Shiryō Sōsho' series (Yūseidō, 1970).

Hirakawa Sukehiro, *Wakon Yōsai no Keifu* (Kawade Shobō Shinsha, 1972).

– 'Nogi Shōgun to Mori Ōgai', *Chūō Kōron: Rekishi to Jimbutsu* 30 (Feb. 1974).

Hirano Ken, '"Maihime" (Ōgai) ron', *Kindai Bungaku* (Dec. 1952).

Hiratsuka Raichō, 'Ōgai sensei ni tsuite', *Bungei Sampo* 15 (Oct. 1962).

Ikimatsu Keizō, *Mori Ōgai* (Tōkyō Daigaku Shuppankai, 1958).

– 'Nogi Shōgun no junshi', *Kokubungaku: Kaishaku to Kanshō* 34 (Jan. 1969).

Inagaki Tatsurō, 'Ōgai to "junkōtei"', *Mori Ōgai*, ed. Hasegawa Izumi.

– (ed.), *Mori Ōgai Hikkei* (Gakutōsha, 1969).

Ishikawa Jun, *Mori Ōgai* (Mikasa Shobō, 1941).

Ishikawa Yoshio, 'Ōgai to Shiki', *Kaishaku* 17 (Dec. 1971).

Isogai Hideo, 'Mori Ōgai no hihyō undō: sono ichi; iji hyōron ni tsuite', *Hiroshima Daigaku bungakubu kiyō* 20 (Jan. 1962).

– 'Daiikkai Nihon Igakkai ronsō', *Hiroshima Daigaku: Kokugo Kyōiku Kenkyū* 8 (1963).

Kanda Takao, 'Mori Ōgai to E. v. Hartmann', *Hikaku Bungaku Hikaku Bunka* (July, 1961). (Also in Hasegawa Izumi (ed.), *Mori Ōgai*.)

– 'Wakaki Ōgai to kanshibun', *Hikaku Bungaku Kenkyū* 13 (Nov. 1967).

Katsumoto Seiichirō, 'Sekaikan geijutsu no kussetsu', *Mori Ōgai*, 'Nihon Bungaku Kenkyū Shiryō Sōsho' series.

Kobori Keiichirō, *Wakaki Hi no Mori Ōgai* (Tōkyō Daigaku Shuppankai, 1969).

– *Mori Ōgai no Sekai* (Kōdansha, 1971).

– 'Mori Ōgai no shosei tetsugaku: "Chie-bukuro" "Shintōgo" no genten ni tsuite', *Hikaku Bungaku Kenkyū* 20 (Nov. 1971).

– 'Ōgai no Nietzsche zō', *Nietzsche to sono Shūhen*, ed. E. Hikami (Asahi Shuppansha, 1972).

- 'Meijijin: Ōgai no kōshitsukan', *Chūō Kōron: Rekishi to Jimbutsu* 30 (Feb. 1974).
- '*Omokage* no shigaku', *Hikaku Bungaku Kenkyū* 25 (Mar. 1974).
- '*Eisei Shimpen* no genten ni tsuite', *Ōgai Zenshū Geppō* 31 (Iwanami Shoten, 1974).

Koganei Kimiko, *Mori Ōgai no Keizoku* (Ōokayama Shoten, 1943).

Koizumi Kōichirō, 'Ōgai to Rilke', *Kokubungaku: Gengo to Bungei* 6 (Sept. 1964).
- '*Shibue Chūsai* ron', *Kokubungaku: Gengo to Bungei* 8 (July 1966).
- '"Ōshio Heihachirō" ron – tenkyo to hōhō', *Kokubungaku: Gengo to Bungei* 11 (Jan. 1969).

Kusunoki Masao, 'Ōgai no gikyoku', *Mori Ōgai Kenkyū,* ed. Yoshida Seiichi (Chikuma Shobō, 1960).

Maeda Ai, *Kindai Dokusha no Seiritsu* (Yūseidō, 1973).

Maruyama Hiroshi, 'Ōgai to igaku', *Mori Ōgai Hikkei,* ed. Inagaki Tatsurō (Gakutōsha, 1969).

Masamune Hakuchō, *Masamune Hakuchō Zenshū* (Shinchōsha, 1966).

Matsubara Jun'ichi, 'Ōgai to tōyō shisō', *Kokugo to Kokubungaku* 40 (Jan. 1963).

Miyoshi Yukio, *Mori Ōgai* (Yūseidō, 1966).

Mori Junzaburō, *Ōgai: Mori Rintarō* (Morikita Shoten, 1942).

Mori Ōgai, *Ōgai Zenshū* (Iwanami Shoten, 1971-5).

Mori Ōgai Kinenkai, *Ōgai* (Oct. 1965–).

Nakai Yoshiyuki, 'Ōgai to iu gō ni tsuite', *Ōgai* 15 (Nov. 1974).

Naruse Masakatsu, *Ōgai: Sōseki* (Sanseidō, 1964).

Nihon Bungaku Kenkyū Shiryō Sōsho Kankōkai (ed.), *Mori Ōgai* (Yūseidō, 1970).

Ogata Tsutomu, 'Ōgai: Rekishi shōsetsu no shiryō to hōhō – "Okitsu Yagoemon no isho", "Abe ichizoku" ', *Tōkyō Kyōiku Daigaku Bungakubu Kiyō* 7 (Mar. 1962). (Also in *Mori Ōgai,* 'Nihon Bungaku Kenkyū Shiryō Sōsho' series.)
- ' "Gyogenki" to "atarashii onna" tachi', *Kokugo Kokubun* 32 (Dec. 1963).
- ' "Sahashi Jingorō" no tenkyo to hōhō', *Bungaku* 32 (Oct. 1964).
- 'Ōgai: "Gojiingahara no katakiuchi" no ichi kōsatsu', *Kokugo to Kokubungaku* 42 (June, 1965).

Okada Masahiro, 'Ōgai to iu gō ni tsuite', *Ōgai* 14 (Jan. 1974).

Okazaki Yoshie, *Ōgai to Teinen* (Hōbunkan, 1969).

Ōoka Shōhei, *Rekishi Shōsetsu no Mondai* (Bungei Shunjū, 1974).

Seita Fumitake, 'Ōgai to Schnitzler – gikyoku *Kamen* o chūshin toshite', *Hikaku Bungaku* 12 (1969).

Seki Ryōichi, *Shōyō: Ōgai* (Yūseidō, 1971).

Shibukawa Gyō, *Mori Ōgai* (Chikuma Shobō, 1964).
- '*Shibue Chūsai*', *Mori Ōgai Hikkei,* ed. Inagaki Tatsurō.

Shigematsu Yasuo, 'Gun'ikan Mori Ōgai shōkō', *Kokugo to Kokubungaku* 49 (Apr. 1972).

Sugita Hiroko, 'Nietzsche kaishaku no shiryōteki kenkyū', *Kokugo to Kokubungaku* 43 (May 1966).

Suzuki Mitsuru, 'Ōgai yōshōji no kyōiku', *Hikaku Bungaku Kenkyū* 13 (Nov. 1967).

Wada Yoshie (ed.), *Higuchi Ichiyō Shū* (Kadokawa Shoten, 1970).

Yamamoto Masahide, 'Ōgai to genbunitchi', *Ōgai* 9 (June 1971).

Yamazaki Masakazu, *Ōgai: Tatakau Kachō* (Kawade Shobō Shinsha, 1972).

Yoshida Seiichi, *Kindai Bungei Hyōronshi* (Shibundō, 1975).

– (ed.), *Mori Ōgai Kenkyū* (Chikuma Shobō, 1960).

WORKS IN EUROPEAN LANGUAGES

Andersen, H. C., *The Improvisatore*, tr. M. Howitt (London: Ward, 1845).

Becker, G. J. (ed.), *Documents of Modern Literary Realism* (Princeton: Princeton U.P., 1963).

Biddiss, M. D., *Father of Racist Ideology: the social and political thought of Count Gobineau* (London: Weidenfeld & Nicolson, 1970).

Borelius, J. J., *Blicke auf den gegenwärtigen Standpunkt der Philosophie in Deutschland and Frankreich*, tr. Emil Jonas (1886).

Bowring, R. J., 'Mori Ōgai: a re-appraisal', *Journal of the Association of Teachers of Japanese* 10 (Sept. 1975).

Brazell, K., 'Mori Ōgai in Germany: a translation of "Fumizukai" and excerpts from *Doitsu Nikki*', *Monumenta Nipponica* 26 (Summer 1971).

Chamberlain, B. H., *Things Japanese* (London: Kegan Paul, Trench, Trubner, 1939).

Dower, J. W., 'Mori Ōgai: Meiji Japan's eminent bystander', *Papers on Japan* 2 (Harvard East Asian Research Center, Aug. 1963).

Freud, S., *Über den Traum* (Wien: Bergm., 1901).

– *Drei Abhandlungen zur Sexualtheorie* (2 Aufl. Wien: Deuticke, 1910).

Gollwitzer, H., *Die Gelbe Gefahr: Geschichte eines Schlagworts* (Göttingen: Vandenhoeck & Ruprecht, 1962).

Gottschall, R. von, *Literarische Todtenklänge und Lebensfragen* (2 Aufl. Berlin: Allgem. Verein für Deutsch. Lit., 1885).

– *Poetik* (Brels: Trewendt, 1873).

Hackett, R. F., *Yamagata Aritomo in the Rise of Modern Japan* (Cambridge, Mass.: Harvard U.P., 1971).

Hamburger, K., *The Logic of Literature*, tr. M. J. Rose (Bloomington: Indiana U.P., 1973).

Hartmann, Karl Eduard von, *Philosophy of the Unconscious*, tr. W. C. Coupland (London: Trubner, 1931).

– *Aesthetik*. Vols. 3 and 4 of *Ausgewählte Werke* (Leip.: Friedrich, 1889).

Hasegawa, I., 'Mori Ōgai', *Japan Quarterly* 12 (April 1965).

Havens, T. R. H., *Nishi Amane* (Princeton: Princeton U.P., 1970).

Hawkes, D., 'Chinese poetry and the English reader', *The Legacy of China*, ed. R. Dawson (London: Oxford U.P., 1964).

Heyse, P. & Kurz, H., *Deutscher Novellenschatz* (Munich: Oldenbourg, 1871).

– & Laistner, L., *Neuer Deutscher Novellenschatz* (Munich: Oldenbourg, 1884-7).

Hibbett, H., 'Tradition and trauma in the contemporary Japanese novel', *Daedelus* 95 (Autumn 1966).

Hopper, H. M., 'Mori Ōgai's response to suppression of intellectual freedom 1909-12', *Monumenta Nipponica* 29 (Winter 1974).

Johnson, E. W., 'The historical fiction and biography of Mori Ōgai', *Journal of the Association of Teachers of Japanese* 8 (Nov. 1972).

Keene, D., *Modern Japanese Literature: an anthology* (Tokyo: Tuttle, 1957).

– *The Japanese Discovery of Europe* (London: Routledge and Kegan Paul, 1952).

– *Landscapes and Portraits* (Tokyo: Kōdansha, 1971).

Manyōshū, tr. Nippon Gakujutsu Shinkōkai (Tokyo: 1940; rev. ed. New York: Columbia U.P., 1956).

Military Correspondent of *The Times, The War in the Far East* (London: Murray, 1905).

Miyoshi, M., *Accomplices of Silence* (Berkeley: California U.P., 1974).

Morita, J., *'Shigarami-zōshi', Monumenta Nipponica* 24 (Spring 1969).

Motofuji, F., 'Mori Ōgai: three plays and the problem of identity', *Modern Drama* (Feb. 1967).

Najita, T., 'Ōshio Heihachirō', *Personality in Japanese History*, ed. A. M. Craig & D. H. Shively (Berkeley: California U.P., 1970).

Rilke, R. M., *Sämtliche Werke* (Wiesbaden: Insel, 1961).

Rimer, J. T., *Mori Ōgai* (Boston: Twayne, 1975).

Root, W. H., *German Criticism of Zola: 1875-1893* (New York: Columbia U.P., 1931).

Ryan, M. G., *Japan's First Modern Novel: Ukigumo* (New York: Columbia U.P., 1967).

Sibley, W. F., 'Naturalism in Japanese literature', *Harvard Journal of Asiatic Studies* 28 (1968).

Swales, M., *Arthur Schnitzler: a critical study* (London: Oxford U.P., 1971).

Swann, T. E., 'The problem of "Utakata no ki" ', *Monumenta Nipponica* 29 (Autumn 1974).

Schwegler, A., *Geschichte der Philosophie im Umriss* (Stut.: Conrad, 1887).

Vaihinger, H., *Philosophie des Als Ob* (Berlin: Reuter & Reichard, 1911).

Varley, H. P., *Imperial Restoration in Medieval Japan* (New York: Columbia U.P., 1971).

White, H., *Metahistory* (Baltimore: John Hopkins U.P., 1973).

Zavarzadeh, M., 'A Typology of prose narrative', *Journal of Literary Semantics* 3 (1974).

TRANSLATIONS

Abbreviations

I.S.	*The Incident at Sakai and other stories*, volume 1 of *The Historical Literature of Mori Ōgai*, ed. D. Dilworth and J. T. Rimer (Honolulu: University Press of Hawaii, 1977).
M.N.	*Monumenta Nipponica* (Tokyo: Sophia University).
Paulownia	*Paulownia, Seven Stories from Contemporary Japanese Writers* (New York: Duffield, 1918).
S.K.	*Saiki Kōi and other stories*, volume 2 of *The Historical Literature of Mori Ōgai*, ed. D. Dilworth and J. T. Rimer (Honolulu: University Press of Hawaii, 1977).

Abe Ichizoku	Dilworth, D., 'The Abe Family', *I.S.*
Doitsu nikki (extracts)	Brazell, K., 'Mori Ōgai in Germany', *M.N.* 26 (Spring 1971).
Fumizukai	Brazell, K., 'The courier', *M.N.* 26 (Spring 1971).
Fushinchū	Morris, I., 'Under reconstruction', *Modern Japanese Stories: an anthology* (Tokyo: Tuttle, 1962).

Gan	Ochiai, K. and Goldstein, S., *The Wild Geese* (Tokyo: Tuttle, 1959).
Gojiingahara no katakiuchi	Dilworth, D., 'The vendetta at Gojiingahara', *I.S.*
Gyogenki	Dilworth, D., 'Gyogenki', *I.S.*
Hanako	Taketomo, T., 'Hanako', *Paulownia.*
Hannichi	Murray, D., 'Half a day', *M.N.* 28 (Autumn 1973).
Hebi	Dower, J. W., 'Snake', *M.N.* 26 (Spring 1971).
Jiisan Bāsan	Dilworth, D. and Rimer, J. T., 'The old man and the old woman', *I.S.*
Ka no yō ni	Sinclair, G. M. and Suita, K., 'As if', *Tokyo People: Three Stories from the Japanese* (Tokyo: Keibunkan, 1925).
Kanzan Jittoku	Dilworth, D. and Rimer, J. T., 'Kanzan Jittoku', *I.S.*
Kuriyama Daizen	Rimer, J. T., 'Kuriyama Daizen', *S.K.*
Maihime	Bowring, R. J., 'The dancing girl', *M.N.* 30 (Summer 1975).
Mōsō	Dower, J. W., 'Delusion', *M.N.* 25 (Autumn 1970).
Okitsu Yagoemon no isho (first version)	Bowring, R. J., 'The last testament of Okitsu Yagoemon', *I.S.*
Okitsu Yagoemon no isho (second version)	Wilson, W. R., 'The last testament of Okitsu Yagoemon', *I.S.*
Sahashi Jingorō	Rimer, J. T., 'Sahashi Jingorō', *S.K.*
Saigo no Ikku	Dilworth, D. and Rimer, J. T., 'The last phrase', *I.S.*
Saiki Kōi	Wilson, W. R., 'Saiki Kōi', *S.K.*
Sakai Jiken	Dilworth, D., 'The incident at Sakai', *I.S.*
Sakazuki	Dower, J. W., 'Cups', *M.N.* 26 (Spring 1971).
Sanbashi	Taketomo, T., 'The pier', *Paulownia.*
Sanshō Dayū	Rimer, J. T., 'Sanshō the steward', *I.S.*
Suginohara Shina	Dilworth, D., 'Suginohara Shina', *S.K.*
Takasebune	Skrzypczak, E. R., 'The boat on the River Takase', *I.S.*
Tokō Tahei	Rimer, J. T., 'Tokō Tahei', *S.K.*
Tsuge Shirōzaemon	Skrzypczak, E. R., 'Tsuge Shirōzaemon', *S.K.*
Tsuina	Dower, J. W., 'Exorcising demons', *M.N.* 26 (Spring 1971).
Utakata no ki	Bowring, R. J., 'Utakata no ki', *M.N.* 29 (Autumn 1974).
Vita Sexualis	Ninomiya, K. and Goldstein, S., *Vita Sexualis* (Tokyo: Tuttle, 1972).
Yasui Fujin	Dilworth, D. and Rimer, J. T., 'Yasui Fujin', *S.K.*

INDEX

UNITEDVERSITY OF CAMBRIDGE
ORIENTAL PUBLICATIONS PUBLISHED FOR THE
FACULTY OF ORIENTAL STUDIES

1 *Averroes' Commentary on Plato's Republic,* edited and translated by E. I. J. Rosenthal.
2 *FitzGerald's 'Salaman and Absal',* edited by A. J. Arberry.
3 *Ihara Saikaku: The Japanese Family Storehouse,* translated and edited by G. W. Sargent.
4 *The Avestan Hymn to Mithra,* edited and translated by Ilya Gershevitch.
5 *The Fusūl al-Madanī of al-Fārābī,* edited and translated by D. M. Dunlop (out of print).
6 *Dun Karm, Poet of Malta,* texts chosen and translated by A. J. Arberry; introduction, notes and glossary by P. Grech.
7 *The Political Writings of Ogyū Sorai,* by J. R. McEwan.
8 *Financial Administration under the T'ang Dynasty,* by D. C. Twitchett.
9 *Neolithic Cattle-Keepers of South India: A Study of the Deccan Ashmounds,* by F. R. Allchin.
10 *The Japanese Enlightenment: A Study of the Writings of Fukuzawa Yukichi,* by Carmen Blacker.
11 *Records of Han Administration.* Vol. I *Historical Assessment,* by M. Loewe.
12 *Records of Han Administration.* Vol. II *Documents,* by M. Loewe.
13 *The Language of Indrajit of Orchā: A Study of Early Braj Bhāsā Prose,* by R. S. McGregor.
14 *Japan's First General Election, 1890,* by R. H. P. Mason.
15 *A Collection of Tales from Uji: A Study and Translation of 'Uji Shūi Monogatari',* by D. E. Mills.
16 *Studia Semitica.* Vol. I *Jewish Themes,* by E. I. J. Rosenthal.
17 *Studia Semitica.* Vol. II *Islamic Themes,* by E. I. J. Rosenthal.
18 *A Nestorian Collection of Christological Texts.* Vol. I *Syriac Text,* by Luise Abramowski and Alan E. Goodman.
19 *A Nestorian Collection of Christological Texts.* Vol. II *Introduction, Translation Indexes,* by Luise Abramowski and Alan E. Goodman.
20 *The Syriac Version of the Pseudo-Nonnos Mythological Scholia,* by Sebastian Brock.
21 *Water Rights and Irrigation Practices in Lahj,* by A. M. A. Maktari.
22 *The Commentary of Rabbi David Kimhi on Psalms cxx-ci,* edited and translated by Joshua Baker and Ernest W. Nicholson.
23 *Jalāl al-dīn al-Suyūtī.* Vol. 1 *Biography and Background,* by E. M. Sartain.
24 *Jalāl al-dīn al-Suyūtī.* Vol. 2 *"Al-Tahadduth bini'mat allāh",* Arabic text, by E. M. Sartain.
25 *Origen and the Jews: Studies in Jewish–Christian Relations in Third-Century Palestine,* by N. R. M. de Lange.
26 *The Vīsaladevarāsa: A Restoration of the Text,* by John D. Smith.
27 *Shabbethai Sofar and His Prayer-book,* by Stefan C. Reif.
28 *Mori Ōgai and the Modernization of Japanese Culture,* by Richard John Bowring

CAMBRIDGE ORIENTAL SERIES

1 *Modern Arabic Poetry: An Anthology,* by A. J. Arberry.
2 *Essays and Studies presented to Stanley Arthur Cook,* edited by D. Winton Thomas (out of print).
3 *Khotanese Buddhist Texts,* by H. W. Bailey (out of print).
4 *The Battles of Coxinga,* by Donald Keene.
6 *Studies in Caucasian History,* by V. Minorsky.

(This series was first published by Taylor's Foreign Press and then by Vallentine, Mitchell & Co. There was no number 5.)

Date Due